Maggots
in my sweet potatoes

Maggots
in my sweet potatoes

women doing time

PHOTOGRAPHS AND TEXT BY

SUSAN MADDEN LANKFORD

HUMAN EXPOSURES PUBLISHING, LLC   SAN DIEGO, CALIFORNIA

Front Matter Photographs
Front Cover: San Diego Men's Detention Facility
Page 2: San Diego Men's Detention Facility; *Page 8 and 9:* Fencing
Page 14: San Diego Men's Detention Facility
Photo 130 & 231: Polly Doll, photograph by Polly Lankford Smith
Back Cover: San Diego Men's Detention Facility

EDITORIAL STAFF
Susan Madden Lankford, Kelly Birch, Barbara Ellis

ART BOARD
Susan Madden Lankford, Polly Lankford Smith, Barbara Jackson

LAYOUT DESIGN
Susan Madden Lankford, Barbara Jackson, Polly Lankford Smith

GRAPHIC DESIGN
Polly Lankford Smith

PHOTOGRAPHY
Susan Madden Lankford

PRODUCTION
Polly Lankford Smith, Richard Leonhardt

COPYEDITOR
Kelly Birch

Library of Congress Control Number: 2007930595

07 08 09 10 / 5 4 3 2 1 0

HUMANE EXPOSURES PUBLISHING, LLC.
Maggots in my Sweet Potatoes: Women Doing Time
by Susan Madden Lankford — 1st ed.
Includes Index.

ISBN-13 978-0-9792366-1-7 (cloth)
ISBN-13 978-0-9792366-0-0 (paper)

Printed in China.

The Polly Doll

Little girls have been known to play with their dolls; talking, cuddling, encouraging them, as though the doll were the child and the child were the mother. Watching a child heal herself at a time of crisis or chaos by retreating and finding her doll, she will clutch and mend the doll in ways the child intuitively knows she herself should be nurtured.

The child is confident she can take care of the doll and any trauma that should befall the doll. This confidence is enough, in some cases, to soothe the child and prevent despair so deep that the child's learning might otherwise be impaired and her emotional growth halted.

Polly doll finds herself in places where there is no child to love or care for her.

Every child is born innocent.

I'm hungry, alone, and in danger. She feels distress and also feels unable to regulate herself. So dependent, her only response is to cry out, hoping that a responsive adult will come to protect and feed her.[1]

Experience can change the mature brain—but experience during the critical periods of early childhood organizes brain systems.[2]

The human brain mediates all human behavior—aggression, violence, fear, ideology—indeed, all human emotional, cognitive and social functioning.[3]

Bruce Perry, M.D., Ph.D.

CONTENTS

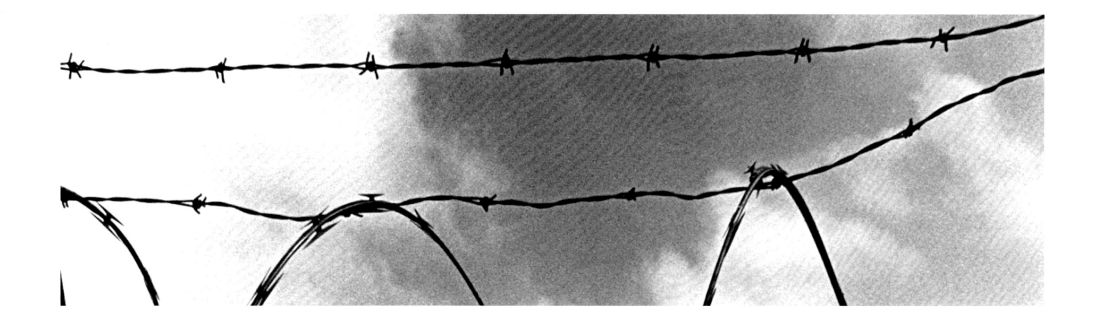

Author's Note

All of the individuals you are about to meet in the pages of this book consented to be photographed and quoted for publication, and they generously shared their personal experiences with me. I am grateful for their willingness to do so, and I have relied on their kind cooperation in bringing this book into existence and putting it in print. However, the reader should be aware that I have used fictional first and last names for the women and men who have been incarcerated in place of their real names throughout the book. Fictional names have also been used in describing the individuals involved in a murder trial, including the decedent and witnesses. For that reason, any similarity between the fictional names in this book and the names of real persons is strictly coincidental.

FOREWORD

While a great many books describe in lurid detail life in American prisons, very few have been written about what goes on in the more than 3,000 jails in the United States. There's a big difference between prisons and jails. The former are the penitentiaries, state and federal institutions where inmates spend years of their lives walled off from society. Jails are the gateways to our national criminal justice system. Run in most states by county and municipal governments, they house about one-third of the people incarcerated in the United States, mainly those sentenced to less than one year and those awaiting trial. The latter are presumed innocent, of course, and are confined because they've been denied bail or cannot raise bail. But they suffer no less than convicted inmates from the overcrowding, inadequate medical care, and lack of recreational facilities that characterize many (if not most) American jails.

Susan Lankford, a professional photographer, took her camera and a tape recorder into a more or less typical jail, this one for women in San Diego County, California. She visited it not once or twice, like the reporters who spend a day or even a night in lock-up in order to tell the public about the grizzly noise of clanging cell doors, but many times over a period of two years. She started on a quest for understanding by photographing and getting to know the street people who congregate in the shadows and fringes of downtown San Diego, where they can be ignored during the day and forgotten at night.

A lot of them wind up in jail. Their crimes, for the most part, are possession of drugs, prostitution, and petty theft. For these minor offenses, they serve a little time, then are let out onto the streets, are soon arrested again and jailed, released, and on and on, until eventually an overdose or mortal illness removes them permanently from the streets. Except for the few who take hold of themselves or are imprisoned for a serious crime, that is the pattern of their lives. Lankford asked why. How did it get started? And are these jailbirds really dangerous, are they potentially violent—should they be confined for the protection of society? Her conversations with the street people rid her of the illusion that they were simply innocent victims of failed opportunities and social injustice. There was a difference between the denizens of the streets and the truly homeless. As one of the latter put it, "Street people want to live on the streets; nobody dumped us here. The homeless ain't got no choice."

Since jail was as much a part of their lives as hanging around in parks and alleys, she had to get inside somehow, if she were to find answers to her questions. A visitor's tour, which probably could be arranged, would not be enough. She had to talk with the inmates, get to know them, and if at all possible breach the wall of mistrust that separated her world from theirs. The custodians, however, did not welcome public scrutiny of their domain. It wasn't so much that they had something to hide (in San Diego the jails are comparatively well run). But unless you worked there day in and day out, unless you had to keep often unruly and bored inmates in order, unless you had experience in differentiating justifiable from fabricated complaints, unless you had to handle the crazies, the addicts suffering through detoxification, and the suicidal, you could not understand the jail environment. Out of self-preservation, as well as inclination perhaps, the custodians tend to be insensitive to the humanity of their charges.

One important exception was the assistant sheriff responsible for all San Diego County's detention services. About to retire after 32 years in law enforcement, Ben McLaughlin knew that the justice system was not working. Society was putting more and more people in jail and prison without the facilities to house them, without services they need, and without properly trained personnel to look after them. Overcrowding was exacerbated by the lengthy sentences imposed on recidivists convicted of a long list of serious or violent offenses under California's "Three Strikes" law. People convicted of misdemeanors, except drunk driving and domestic violence, were no longer sent to jail in San Diego—there simply was no room for them. Thus the jails are populated by people with substantial social and psychological problems. Very few come out better for the experience, and most are decidedly worse.

Had Lankford applied to anyone but McLaughlin for permission to photograph and interview the inmates, her request would probably have been refused (later events bore this out). Even he hesitated; apparently her pictures of the street people helped convince him. They were not sensationalistic, but penetrating portraits. In fact, he remembered some of the people from when he had been a cop on the beat. His main reason for consenting, however, was her avowed purpose of telling the story of the jail experience. "Well, I would just dearly love to see the public somehow understand . . . what jails are really about," he said. "What does it mean in our society?" It was true that she intended to tell the story—after all, she was a photographic journalist. But at that point, learning about jail, not telling about it, was her overriding motive. The difference had a profound effect on the way she has gathered her material and presented it in this book.

She allowed herself to become involved. Her interviews were conversations, not the usual questions and replies in the stilted interrogations that barely distinguish journalists from prosecutors. She encouraged people to talk, just talk, ramble on, until the lies turned to half-truths, then to confessions. Despite warnings from guards and psychologists and McLaughlin himself, she sometimes let the inmates manipulate her and take advantage of her generosity. She was not fooled. Her encounters with the street people had taught her about their wheedling, their cunning, their utter self-absorption. But she recognized the underlying desperation.

In time, Lankford got to know many of these distraught women well, better in some instances than the guards or the psychologists. She talked often with an accused murderess, an embezzler, burglars, thieves, addicts, prostitutes, and a variety of other transgressors of the law. With their permission, she recorded what they said and photographed them. She also interviewed and photographed guards, psychiatrists, psychologists, social workers, and others on the custodial side.

Lankford tells their stories with poignant photographs, excerpts from their conversations, and a unique narrative in which she traces her discovery of answers to her questions: the tragedy of broken lives, the futility of our criminal justice system, a society gone awry.

—Edward Pearlstien
Writer and Editor of History and Economics

PREFACE

MAGGOTS IN MY SWEET POTATOES: Women Doing Time is a remarkable piece of work. As photojournalism, it beautifully and engagingly presents important information that is itself ugly and uncomfortable. It implicitly raises questions about the role of childhood experiences in shaping the people we become. And, through the excerpts of inmate interviews that accompany the photographs taken at Las Colinas Detention Facility, it provides insight into what the answers might be.

We keep prisons, as we do asylums and chronic disease hospitals, safely out of our awareness by their distant geographical location—they house our failures—and we do this at enormous expense. Their location and our denial prevent us from learning from those failures. What is the function of a prison? How much do we use prisons to protect ourselves from knowing about the really frightening things—and at whose expense?

The women who consented to appear in these photographs and interviews have provided us an unusual opportunity to think about the way we treat children. Their frank comments repeatedly refer, usually without rancor, to abusive and sexually exploitative childhoods, to parental abandonment and neglect, to the abdication of responsibility by the most significant adults in their lives. One cannot avoid thinking of Harry Harlow's famous experiments demonstrating the effect of maternal deprivation in infant monkeys. If you were given an infant with the instruction to turn her into a prison inmate in twenty years, how would you go about it?

These women often mention drug use as having followed their earlier childhood experiences, almost as though it were an attempt to treat what went before. Is it a coincidence that the most common street drug, methamphetamine, is closely related to the first antidepressant medication introduced into America in 1932?

One cannot help noting that many prisoners who led violent lives on the street often function almost normally in the Big House. Is this slang term for prison an insight into the similarity of a well-regulated prison to a well-run house, to the much-needed stable home of which these people were deprived? In both, one has one's own place to sleep, dependable mealtimes, performance expectations, and enforced rules of behavior. One of the women memorably says that prison has been the safest part of her life: "I dread going out there, being cold, and getting rained on. I mean, that's a sad thing, to say I'd rather be in here."

We need prisons; without question, even the warehousing of human beings has its place. However, if prisons are our only response to the problems they house and hide, they are an enormous failure. MAGGOTS IN MY SWEET POTATOES is the first of a series from HUMAN EXPOSURES that show us what we need to see about how all of our lives become the threads of the social fabric. Don't look away.

—Vincent J. Felitti, M.D.
Kaiser Permanente Medical Care Program
Clinical Professor of Medicine, University of California

DEDICATION AND ACKOWLEDGEMENTS

DEDICATION

To the women and staff who made contributions to this collection. They trusted me and it was that trust and their willingness to share their lives with me that encouraged me and made this book possible.

ACKNOWLEDGEMENTS

Grateful appreciation is extended to San Diego County Sheriff's Department, Bill Kolender, Sheriff; and Ben McLaughlin, Former Assistant Sheriff, without whom this project would not have been possible.

Particular appreciation is extended to Las Colinas Detention Facility: Jim Bull, Ph.D; [Ellen Conner], Pregnant Inmate Program (PIP); Lieutenant Jenene Milakovich; Deputy V.L. Price; Deputy Kristin Harper; Deputy J. Bilyeu; Deputy Mentes; and Counselors Dar Inman and Sally Quigley.

I am forever grateful to Vincent J. Felitti, M.D., co-founder of the Adverse Childhood Experiences Study (ACE) for his encouragement and professional contributions. Bruce D. Perry, M.D., Ph.D., Senior Fellow, The ChildTrauma Academy, offered endless support and education on the effects of trauma and attachment-related conditions. Additional thanks go to Edward W. Pearlstien for his generous comments in the Foreword and for his feedback in the development of this work. I also wish to thank Stephanie S. Covington, Ph.D., L.C.S.W., co-director of the Center for Gender & Justice.

I wish to extend sincere appreciation to Alex Landon, Attorney-at-Law, who answered multitudes of questions regarding criminal trial conduct and strategies throughout the course of this project. His invaluable contributions highlight the importance of a strong and fair criminal justice system.

Special thanks to [Kath Anderson], and [Cindy Mulloy], former inmates, who encouraged me to look deeper into the maximum-security division of jail and shared during their rehabilitative process outside the confines of incarceration.

I would also like to extend my gratitude to Barbara Jackson, my close friend and assistant; Polly Lankford Smith, my daughter and graphic designer; Rob Lankford, my husband and advocate; Rick Leonhardt, assistant graphic artist; Jim House for hours of editorial advice; Scott Brandt, Ph.D.; Maryam Razavi Newman, Ph.D.; Diane Campbell, M.D.; Paul Fink, M.D.; Bessel A. van der Kolk, M.D.; T George Harris, founding editor of Spirituality & Health; Ramon Eduardo Ruiz, author; Robert Paxton, M.D., County Mental Health; Christine Forester; Todd Siler, Ph.D.; and Anna Luise Kirkengen, M.D., Ph.D.

Finally, I wish to thank Barbara Ellis, Scribes Editorial & Literary Agency, and Kelly Birch for their editorial services.

PART ONE

INTRO TO LAS COLINAS DETENTION FACILITY

I've always been interested in incarceration and confinement. As a child, I hiked to a deserted dairy barn a mile away from my home. It was a handsome old structure filled with smells from the empty haylofts and painted concrete floors where the dairy cows had once been confined. Light traveled through the high loft windows and fell on the stalls leaving strong smoky trails of fine dust. In the Midwest, there was warmth inside this barn in spite of the brutal cold winds outside. The fragrances invited visions of complacent black and white cows tied up and fastened to sterile suction equipment tended to by hired hands. This experience lay dormant for several decades, an unfinished chapter of time.

Years later, I rented the old Seaport Village Jail, an old mission-style facility. Images of the light falling on the milking stalls popped into my mind when I set foot through the empty cellblocks where light streamed in from the second-story windows onto the bars and cots. Scratched out graffiti and plumbing fixtures brought about the harsh reality of a bleak human existence – confinement.

While photographing the inside of the barren jail, I saw a homeless man come in. He said, "What you doing in an old, nasty place like this? You realize homeless break in and sleep here at night? It's not safe. You wanna know about jail, come outside and let me tell you about it. I been there." He introduced me to the homeless street life. I took a detour. No longer could I photograph the places without the people in them. I had to fill the image with society's reality and not my imagination.

3/21/95   Meeting, Grill at the Horton Grand
          Tom Keohane - Public Relations for the San Diego County Sheriff's Department
          Karen Shaw - A member of the San Diego Grand Jury

Tom Keohane: You ask about a homeless guy. He ain't going nowhere. We got homeless mental cases in jails. We're running a nut house. On the street they're doing devious deeds, get put in my place and they can't afford bail. They ain't going nowhere. Write a book about this. The public needs it—but don't put any diarrhea in your writing.

Read *The Hot House*. I used to be inside jails all day and I never saw any of the professors who write stats about jails come inside. Keep it simple and put down the dialogue. There's millions locked up and 70 percent have no father in the home.

Karen Shaw arrives. She says, "What's interesting inside the jail is to watch the big prisoners and the little female sheriffs with their little hairdos." She tells me, "You need to talk to the Sheriff. He's a great guy. Name drop and you'll get his attention."

It's clear that I need to approach the Sheriff with a formal letter requesting permission to conduct interviews inside the jail. The following week, I attend a local breakfast to support the Sheriff. I introduce myself in the line. He smiles, shakes my hand. I tell him my interest and he smiles and waves at the next in line. I nudge a little and hand him the letter I had prepared. He took the letter and put it in his breast pocket, then moved on along the line of contributors.

A couple of days later I get a call from Assistant Sheriff Ben McLaughlin. He says he has read my request to enter the jail to photograph and interview inmates and staff. He tells me, "We really don't do that type of thing." I mention that I conducted a project on the homeless in downtown San Diego and discovered most of them were in and out of jail several times. Knowing nothing about jail, I tell him, I'm curious to see the inside and to learn how people live on the streets, go to confinement in jail, and return to the streets.

He suggests that I bring a few of my photographs to his office. But I'm pretty certain from the tone in his voice this is just a courtesy invitation.

1. *Street Person, 1991*

2

3

4

5

6

We're putting people in jail in unprecedented numbers. There's no end to it. There are not enough jails and prisons.

Assistant Sheriff Ben McLaughlin

3/31/95 Sheriff's Headquarters, Ben McLaughlin's office

I enter the San Diego Sheriff's Department Headquarters, hand over my ID and go with a deputy to the assistant sheriff's offices on the third floor. A receptionist takes me to Ben McLaughlin's office. Ben asks to see my photographs of the homeless. I set the mounted black-and-white images against chair backs. He laughs freely, "This is great. I know these people. I remember Papa Smurf and Mama." Eventually, we talk about the number of homeless who go to jail repeatedly and are released to the streets again and again. Ben tells me that the county has cut back on funding to California's mental health programs. As a result, the jail is overcrowded, with an increase in people arrested on drug-related charges.

2. Papa Smurf; 3. Caroline; 4. Collin;
5. Mama; 6. "God" Tommy; 7. Papa Smurf;
8. Name unknown

I tell Ben that I want to prepare a book of images for the public to view. He becomes interested and says he supports anything that will educate the public. Then he's interrupted by his secretary and excuses himself to deal with an emergency on the phone. Moments later, he hangs up the receiver and explains, "I just heard that we had a booking clerk at Las Colinas who was murdered by her husband, a retired deputy sheriff. Apparently he beat her to death with a baseball bat in front of their 13-year-old son."

I can tell Ben is distressed over the news. He says jails house a little of everything, plus many of the deputies have problems too.

"I remember reading that one can tell the health of a nation by the condition of its jails. I don't know how much you can reveal with photography, but I think it should be revealed." Ben agrees to let me enter the jails and begin my project. But he wants everyone that I interview and photograph to sign a waiver, and he wants to receive a copy of each document. He explains to me that such a project hasn't been done before, but he feels strongly that the public should know more about jail. "I've been in this business 32 years and don't feel like I've accomplished anything. It's more than a place to confine criminals. It's a big business. We're putting people in jail in unprecedented numbers. There's no end to it. There are not enough jails and prisons."

He tells me we need to tour some of the jails.

San Diego County has seven jails. We set up a time to tour the first one. Ben tells me he will probably conduct the tours so he can see firsthand how I handle myself inside the environment.

The first jail we tour is Downtown Central, a men's facility—the oldest jail in the county. Ben introduces me to sergeants as we enter. We head up a dark, tight staircase and he tells me about how he and his partner used to move inmates into the Holding Tanks and some of the wild scenes that took place. I drop my tape machine and the cassette clicks down the stairs, leaving a trail of tape pulled from the spindle. "Better have that working the next time," he tells me. I fidget and pull out another small tape player; it's clear I'm nervous trying to grasp his rapid description of jail order and chaos. Men yell and shout, rush the bars as we pass the large Holding Tanks. I realize Ben has eyes in the back of his head as I follow him. He's aware of everyone in the jail and he's aware of me.

Later, we have lunch and Ben begins to educate me on the business of jailing people. He describes jail as a holding tank for felons waiting to go to prison, as well as

a destination for persons serving sentences of one year of less. Prisoners returning on appeal are also housed in the jail. "It's a hodgepodge of criminal sophistication." Prisons house those convicted of felonies serving terms of a year or more once they've been convicted and leave the jail.

"People want to think that jail only handles the petty thefts. Oh no, no, no. What most people don't realize is that for every rotten, dirty inmate in state prison, we had them first and we trained them how to live in the jail and custody environment. That's what we do, and most people don't have a clue that that's what we have to put up with day in and day out on a local level.

"As assistant sheriff, I run seven county jails, over 5,000 inmates on any given day." He explains that a major problem in the dynamics of housing people behind bars and steel doors is in the design of the system. "We don't have a correctional curriculum for correctional officers. Our criminal justice program focuses on law enforcement —street cops. For cops to be good on the street they have to learn the culture, and with daily exposure they become subject to battlefield syndrome—not conducive to dealing with felons who are institutionalized."

Ben says, "We have gotten out of control. There's no room in the jails. Misdemeanors no longer go to prison. Drunk driving, spousal abuse, under the influence of a drug or narcotic are the only misdemeanors sent to jail. All low-risk felons are going to be cut out of prison and returned to the jails. They're talking about dumping 2,000 inmates from prison on me. I gotta let 2,000 somebody elses out to make the room. When I talk to the Deputy Sheriff's Association, I tell them if you can buy stock in this business, buy because you're going to make a lot of money."

By this point, we have gone up and down corridors, in and out of the Safety Cells (formerly called "rubber rooms"), in and out of maximum- and minimum-security units, through the kitchen, laundry, counseling, and classrooms.

I tell Ben I'd like to start my work in Downtown Central and he says, "Let's tour a couple more jails first."

Two weeks later we head out to Descanso Men's Facility, mostly a men's minimum-security unit. Next, George Bailey, a modern prison-style men's jail.

During tours of four San Diego jails, Assistant Sheriff Ben McLaughlin talks about life as a street cop, the transitions through the ranks of sergeant, lieutenant, and captain. He was appointed to the position of assistant sheriff during his stint as captain at Las Colinas Detention Facility in Santee, California.

4/6/95   First jail tour
         Downtown Central Men's Facility (DCMF)

9

9-10. Downtown Central Men's Facility, 1998

Jails are locally operated correctional facilities that confine persons before or after adjudication. Inmates sentenced to jail usually have a sentence of a year or less.

Jail populations . . .

From 1995 to 2005, the number of jail inmates per 100,000 U.S. residents rose from 193 to 252.

From midyear 2004 to midyear 2005 the 12-month increase of 4.7 percent in the jail population was slightly less than the average annual increase of 3.9 percent since 1995.[4]

National statistics . . .

At midyear 2004
The nation's prisons and jails incarcerated over 2.1 million persons.

In both jails and prisons, there were 123 female inmates per 100,000 women in the United States, compared to 1,348 male inmates per 100,000 men.

A total of 2,477 state prisoners were under age 18.

The number of inmates in custody in local jails rose by 22,689; in state prison by 15,375; and in federal prison by 10,095.[5]

5/4/95 **8:00 a.m.**

Fifth jail tour with Ben McLaughlin, Las Colinas Detention Facility (LCDF)

Ben is late. I bring an assistant and we wait for Ben outside the women's jail. At first it looks more like a school with razor wire and cyclone fencing than a correctional facility. It's a single-story facility and doesn't appear large from the street. I imagine the tour will be short. When Ben arrives, he moves quickly into the jail. The clerk is friendly to him and releases the grills of the sally port door from inside the Control Room. We enter a small space and the door automatically encloses us inside. Ben signs a book indicating the time-in, asks for my driver's license, and tells me that we must have my ID each time we enter the jail. He talks to the clerk through the barred window. "Sorry to hear about Marian," he says. The clerk responds, "She'd complained of abuse and told everyone she worked with that he [husband] was going to kill her one day. I don't understand why she went back to him."

The door on the opposite side of this closet-sized cubicle is released, and we move into the main jail, a simple and cold place. At first glance, it is not as intense as the men's older high-rise facility.

Ben talks to sergeants who pass, periodically stopping them to introduce us and explain my project. Deputies and sergeants greet Ben with enthusiasm and respect. Women gawk behind glass and steel doors, a different scene from the other jails we have previously toured. The sounds and cries of women bounce off the walls.

I ask the clerk from the jail-side of the Control window if a woman named Chelsea Donnelly has ever entered the jail. She tells me, "Oh yes, three or four times since I've been here." Ben laughs, remembering some of my photographs of Chelsea on the streets. "I think you've found your home. It's a good starting place."

On our way to the housing units, Ben opens a large steel door and tells me, "This is the Safety Cell. Step inside." A harsh yellow light turns on overhead when he closes me inside a space resembling a big vat with

11. LCDF, Receiving sally port

a drain in the middle of the floor. There are no bunks or benches. I can barely hear Ben talking to my assistant and laughing, but I can see through the narrow window in the door. I can't imagine being locked inside this space for very long.

We move through housing units. The place looks more like a jail as we enter A housing, the high-profile unit, where an inmate leaps off her upper bunk and calls out Ben's name. Ben talks briefly to her through the glass portion of the locked door and then explains to me, "This inmate is difficult. She made my life miserable when she was here last, and I was Captain. She's back on violation of probation. Her name is Shelby Roland." Another inmate rushes to her door and begs Ben for a sheriff's parole; she's about to have a baby. Ben recognizes her, too, and says, "You had a baby the last time you were in here. Who's taking care of him while you're in here this time?"

We move deeper into the jail and enter a separately locked unit, B housing, maximum-security. Staff and inmates recognize the former Captain. Ben describes the unit as housing the more sophisticated criminals. "B1 and B2 are the felony, hard-line inmates who have been around the block. The level of criminal sophistication breaks down into many categories, not the least of which is predatory." This unit also has B3, the reception center, where all inmates are housed before classification, during the time they await arraignment.

"We let deputies determine classification based on hard and fast criteria set by the National Institute of Corrections. We look at the crime they are charged with, any other crime they have been charged with or convicted of, or both. Just because they were charged with a crime and not convicted doesn't mean that they didn't do the crime. We're in law enforcement, so we kind of look at it with a different perspective. Just because they got off doesn't mean they're innocent."

"Back in A housing, our special handling [unit], inmates could come from any other housing unit. Primarily they are mentally deficient individuals. ADA (American Disabilities Act) requires that we screen people for disabilities. But some of the inmates in A housing obviously are not mentally deficient.

"Shelby Roland, on the other hand, is in A housing for special handling due to her case. She's another issue, another side of the coin. It's not just people with mental disabilities in A. It's also people who are behavioral problems, disruptive problems in the jail for one reason or another. Shelby worked her way in there because she is such an advocate of other inmates and ultimately she creates a disruption in the system. I wouldn't have

A housing is a maximum-security unit, designed for high-profile inmates or those unable to remain in the general population.
33 inmates

B housing is the maximum-security unit for serious felons capable of living in a dorm environment during the day and sharing a room with one other inmate.
132 inmates

C housing is a medium-security unit, covered with a razor-wire cage over the roof. It is located on the minimum-security yard.
100 inmates

D housing is a minimum-security unit for trusty workers.
83 inmates

F housing is a series of three minimum-security dorms enclosed by fencing and razor wire.
147 inmates

E housing is the voluntary psychiatric and counseling unit.
12 inmates

Lockdown refers to (1) a disciplinary section of cells for two inmates where there are no windows and no TVs, and (2) a disciplinary action taken by deputies that locks inmates in their cells for extended periods of time.

Safety Cells are cells for inmates requiring the most severe form of isolation.

put her in there, personally. I'd have her in B, with the general population of maximum security. Other staff are more intimidated by her, so she worked her way into A housing, Protective Custody (PC). Frankly, she's a good one for you to start out with. She's manipulative and dealt me a lot of headaches. Her probation violation is for credit card fraud, plus she's filed a suit against the county. We're not geared for someone like her. She's the best. Yeah, she's a good one to start out with."

We exit the main jail and enter a yard surrounded by the main jail itself, as well as cyclone fencing and razor wire. The first brick unit is C housing, considered medium security, with a cage over the unit, yet located on the minimum-security yard with D, E, and F housing. Minimum-security houses the less sophisticated criminals. "Those are the basic, entry-level, low-security-risk classification inmates, in for minor crimes, comparatively speaking."

F housing is a set of three connected dorms with closed-in patios. This is a drastic contrast to the main jail, which houses A and B inmates, Disciplinary, and Safety Cell Lockdown units. Women mill around in the

heat on the concrete patio. Some talk to one another, others complain and shout at the deputies.

After we tour the landscaping area and GED classroom, Ben introduces us to Carmen, the chief of the kitchen. She tells us to find a spot on the patio and help ourselves to the staff buffet of turkey and salads. My assistant isn't comfortable eating food prepared in the jail. Ben helps himself to tuna salad and I take the turkey. At this time, Ben talks openly.

"Keep in mind, there is a phenomenal thrill in America for women committing crimes. Coming from a culture and society based on the reverence for women and motherhood, it is a cultural shock. It is a cultural dilemma. I get reports of women in prison and it's more and more statistical. I don't see many people studying it. What you're going to do is a personal, up-close assessment. Gloria Steinem dictated what feminists should do. Go and act on it; do it. Women want sex and not marriage. Women want married men. Where's the moral anchor? Do you throw it all out the window? If so, what will replace it? 'I can do what I want to do!' 'I can; therefore I will.' 'I'm going to get even!' Women fight."

He explains that most captains are hardcore when it comes to inmate treatment and that they believe men and women should be treated the same. "They aren't the same," he says. "The women are quite different as inmates. They tend to idealize their outside relationships while they are inside. They fantasize a lot and once they get out they return to the same sick relationships."

Ben took his former position as captain of a women's facility very seriously. He finds motherhood at a serious crisis level when we're having to lock up so many women, most of them mothers.

"Society has been built on the family unit in the tribe. That's our nature. Family is the tribe and tribe is the family. You can look anywhere in ancient history and that's what's made a society strong. We lost that—our government has passed law after law that has destroyed family and the tribe. We became urban and mobile. A society where nobody knows their neighbor anymore. We don't care because no one is going to be there long enough to worry about it. A society of gangs."

After lunch, Ben steers us back to the Professional Visit area, a section of eight booths used primarily for attorney-client visits. "Pro Visit" is a short distance from the Control Room and the sally port. Ceiling mirrors make both professionals and inmates visible to Control. Outside professionals don't enter the jail beyond this point.

Ben introduces us to Lieutenant Jenene Milakovich, one of two lieutenants at the jail who reports directly to Captain Pierce, the captain who replaced Ben. Milakovich explains that the nine sergeants and hundred deputies are divided into teams to work day and night shifts. The sergeants report to the lieutenants. Ben says the jail has a cap rate set at a maximum of 500 women, but due to increases in female criminal activity, the number of inmates is usually about 600. He says that 70 of the inmates have "trusty" status, and these trusties in the jail save the county thousands of dollars in operating expenses.

Ben tells a deputy to bring Shelby Roland to the Professional Visit area and then he excuses himself, saying he's late for a county meeting.

We take a seat in the first booth and set up the recorder and camera. The place is somber, cold, and gray. Behind me, an attorney instructs his client to cop a deal and plead guilty. The interview halts and a woman shuffles along, handcuffed and in a strong-arm hold by the deputy. My assistant appears wary of being inside the jail. She's curious what Shelby Roland will be like to interview and photograph.

entrance parking

Breaker

Deputies

sgt · Lt · Watch Commander · info

Hold Tank · Hold

chains

Control

Bkg.

Rel

Release · Sally port

Rel

Visiting Room · Visitors Inmates

parking

offices/

Pro Visits · Secure pro visits

Receiving Sallyport · P.D. td.

Test/Hold

Cells

Hold · photo/print · Rel Hold

strip search

showers

property

Discipline cells

clothing/ laundry

Dispensary

Kitchen

Disc. patio · MPR · couns.

B-3 · B Control

A patio

A · A · A

SICK CALL

Psych · Dr. · exam · inst.

Line up area for B transport

B-1

E

Ch

Drawing of LCDF contributed by Kath Anderson.

Stepping inside the jail, hearing the clanking of the steel doors and getting questioned by clerks and guards in offensive ways . . . the difficult part was actually coming face-to-face with the reality of incarceration. I had the opportunity to meet the inmates, photograph them, and interview them. How was I going to interpret what they told me? Truth or fabrication? Reality or manipulation? What about the staff? Now that I was inside, could I gain an appreciation for what jail is? How is it different from prison? What about mental hospitals? Is there a similarity?

By the time we get permission to see Roland, we learn it's mealtime. Hours go by as we watch staff move inmates from one locked place to another. Roland appears with a disgruntled deputy escort. Roland tells the escort she can leave. Confidently, the slim, 5'10" tall inmate takes a bucket chair, pulls herself up close to the recorder, and crosses her long legs.

Would it bother you to be photographed for a book?
Roland: Heck no. I don't feel embarrassed anymore. If it can help somebody else, it's worth it. What can I do for you?

You jumped from your bunk when the assistant sheriff and I were outside your door, and called out, "Captain!"
Assistant Sheriff McLaughlin's a wonderful person. He was the Captain when I was here in '93 and still the Captain when I was brought back 11 months ago. You should've seen his face when I returned. I thought I'd never come back again. I'm back here on a violation. I'm automatically going to prison.

Why are you in A housing, maximum security?
I have a civil case against the county, a really big case against the [San Diego] Sheriff's Department, so I'm a high-profile inmate. It's real different in A housing. There are a lot of fights. I'd never seen women fight before. There are 13 women in here for murder. Eleven of them used crystal methamphetamine. Ninety percent of the women have homosexual activity. I could do my time standing on my head; I'm serious. I've watched this happen. I've watched deputies with inmates.

So you violated probation and at the same time you sued the Sheriff?
I did something really stupid. I violated probation by going to Mexico for a business reason. You aren't supposed to leave the country when you're on probation. The case against the Sheriff is for excessive treatment: $6,000,000. I was in Vista [Jail] because Las Colinas was overcrowded. I had a Professional Visit with my attorney, and the staff decided to strip-search me in front of all the inmates and deputies. The deputy had a personal vendetta against me to the point where I'd have to sing "The Star Spangled Banner" to get a roll of toilet paper. It got really absurd. On the 15th of August she got me up at 3:00 a.m. and took me to the exercise yard up on the roof and stripped me again and beat me. I was sent here for my own protection. I was glad to be back with Captain McLaughlin. Then he was made assistant sheriff in January. Next I go where Betty Broderick is, California Institution for Women (CIW).

Tell us about jail.
The male deputies are so much kinder than the females. Captain McLaughlin never would've allowed us to be strip-searched in that manner. Strip searches are very degrading. Deputies check your underarms, have you bend over, cough, everything. I was beaten with a flashlight and kicked. I still have the knots on my legs from where I was bruised. I've never been beaten before by anybody in my life.

What was your original charge?
Grand theft with credit card fraud. I had my own interior design firm. I worked with an architect, and I used his card, charging up $48,000. It was a felony, and I did a year on a six-year sentence.

I got out and returned to work. We were building a house in Rancho Santa Fe and ran out of tile. The owners were flying in from back East. I didn't send my guys to Mexico to pick up the tile because they would end up signing off and getting extra stuff for themselves. So I crossed the border myself. This was really an honest mistake.

An honest mistake?
I picked up the tile, signed the receipt, dropped off the tile, and, dummy me, I sent in the receipt to my probation officer instead of my accountant. I was picked up and sent to Vista Jail.

Being locked in a cell is a lot different than being an interior decorator. How do you adjust?
Every time I hear keys at night I bolt up because I'm still jumpy. That deputy came in, and rolled me up, and I still have nightmares.

Last time you were in minimum-security, and the Captain assigned you a job. Is that typical?
No, but there're no programs for me. I'm highly educated and I don't use drugs. So, they didn't know what to do with me. I made requests for books and access that was out of the ordinary. Other inmates will sit around and read the Harlequin love stories. There's a small legal library but hardly anyone uses it. I did and I caused problems by helping inmates do court research. Many can't read or write. They need a beginner's program, not just GED. Some of them can't spell. They have no idea where to begin because it's so overwhelming. I get my attorney to bring forms and I help the women do court research and file motions.

Then they leave and a couple weeks later come back. They have no one to take care of their children and so CPS (Child Protective Services) takes them. There's a lot they can do, and they don't realize it. They're intimidated by the paperwork. They don't have money on their books. The first thing they do is go back to drugs. Repeat the cycle. It has to start with literacy. The Captain put me to work with Dar and Sal in counseling, tracking inmates on the computer. I loved it.

How do you feel about yourself now?
I've never been mixed in with all the different backgrounds and associations, and it's given me a taste of something I'd never seen because I'm so removed. My life was so upper-middle-class white Catholic. This was good for me. I knew nothing about drugs. Eighty percent of the women in here use drugs, so I've learned a lot. When I get out, I think I'm going to go back to school and get my Ph.D. in child psych. I have three boys. I feel blessed that I have a very good education in child development, so I'm able to talk to them in ways they can understand.

Deputies give us looks of disapproval. Roland warns me that a lot of the staff won't be receptive to our visits. She's escorted back to A housing.
   Another deputy asks, "Why are you talking to Roland? She's manipulative and causes the deputies a lot of problems."
   That night my assistant says she has to work closer to her home due to family conflicts. I realize the jail visits have troubled her. I request permission to have a clearance check made on another assistant.

That evening I contact Roland's attorney to inform him that we're talking to his client. He says there's a 99.9 percent chance she'll go to prison, but he hopes for an appeal. When she violated probation, she was maxed (given maximum time) by the judge, and he revoked probation. The attorney suggests that the judge made an example of her because she isn't like the typical drug-abuse or misdemeanor case, poor and uneducated. He says Roland is like the Lemming character in Cool Hand Luke. He says she's capable of standing up for herself.

12.   Inmate Roland

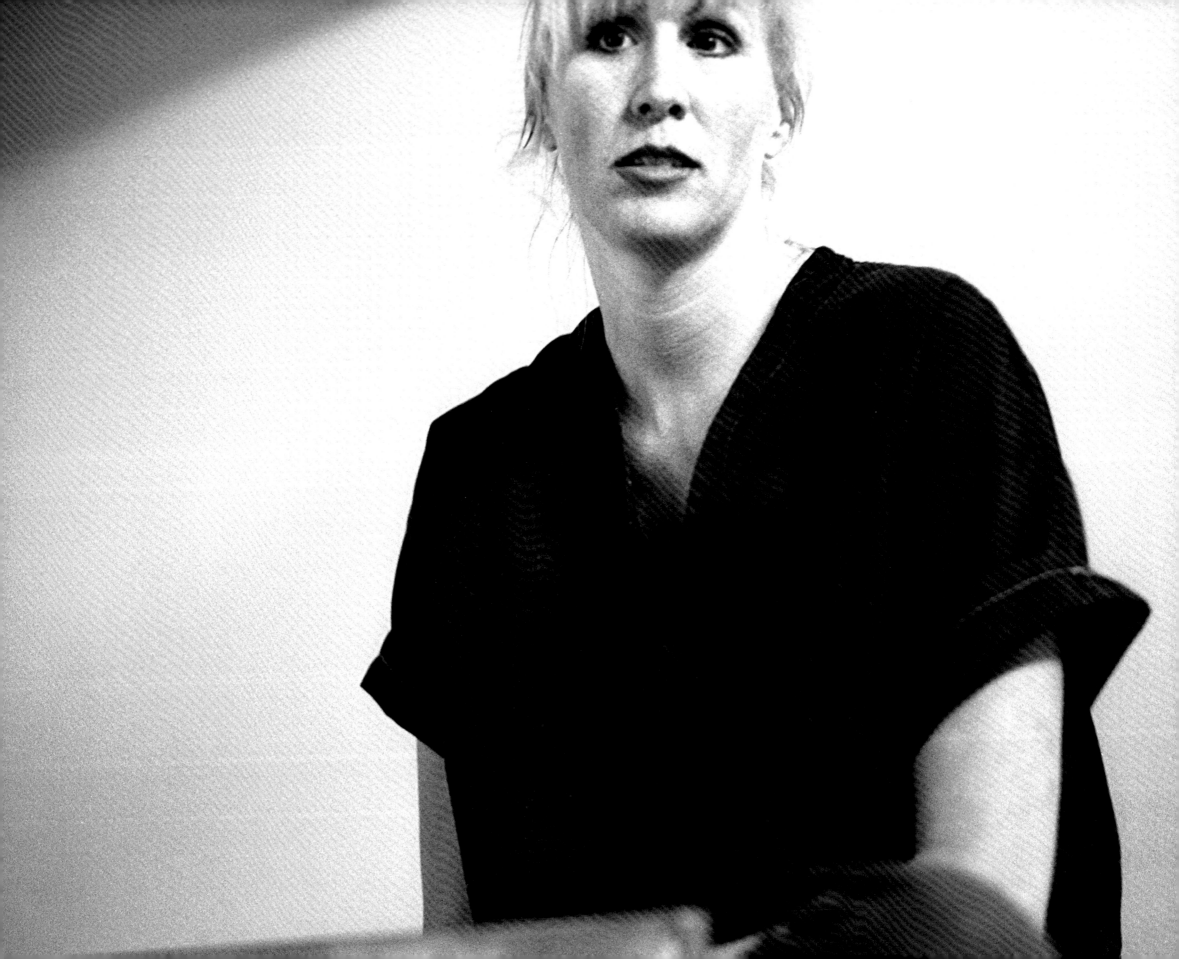

5/6/95 8:40 a.m. Pro Visit
Inmate Shelby Roland

Two days later, Ben McLaughlin tells me my new assistant, Barbara Jackson, has been cleared to enter the facility. We enter the sally port. The clerk doesn't like the change and leaves us in the sally port for 20 minutes while she locates the lieutenant. The clerk returns and points to the sign-in sheets and holds out her hand for our IDs. Without a word, she releases the grills on the sally port entrance to the jail.

Deputies move up and down the corridors with inmates at their sides. I take the same booth and go to the Control window and request Miss Roland. The clerk says, "You'll have to talk to the lieutenant."

Deputies look disapprovingly when we ask to see Shelby Roland again.

The clerk dials up the lieutenant and turns to me, "She's not in." An hour passes. I go to the window once again. Same clerk dials up the lieutenant a second time. This time I hear her say, "Someone's here to see Roland."

Roland arrives and takes her seat.

Roland: It's good to see you again. I was afraid you might not come back. People don't come in the jail and want to talk to inmates to create a change.

I talked to your attorney.
He told me. He liked you.

You said that you were married and have children.
Was married. I'd been married for ten years when I first came to jail. I'm the first in the family to get a divorce. My mom and dad have been married 37 years, and my grandparents had been married 72 years when my grandfather died. It's been real difficult for my children.

However, they know where I am. I tell them I don't know when I'm coming home. I always tell them the truth.

She pulls out photos of her mother, father, and three sons. She tells us the children's ages and shows us some of their artwork. Drawings of guns I question. The conversation dissipates. Shelby is becoming an expert on captive women.

Most of the educated people in my category you don't find in jail. You find them in prison. Felonies are crimes against society. Manslaughter resulting from drunk driving is a year sentence, whereas I got six years for violation of probation.

Were you always a risk taker?
No, I didn't start taking risks until I was out of school. I was always the perfect student and the perfect athlete. I was a competitive swimmer. I'd get up at 4:00 a.m., drive 45 minutes to the pool, come back, and get ready for school. I went to an all-girl Catholic school. When I got to college, it was like, gosh, there are guys here and new experiences. That's when I got a little more rebellious. School wasn't that important to me all of a sudden.

You see other inmates as recidivists, yet you, too, came back through that same door again.
The biggest thing that I faced in the last couple of years was my ex-husband getting remarried. I divorced him, but then it was like, he's going to marry somebody else and the two of them are with my kids right now. I just lost it when the guy I was working with–who I felt should be supportive–talked to my ex-husband behind my back. I found out and the trust was gone. It was his card I used for $48,000 of credit card fraud. I've learned there are other ways to deal with anger. How can you put a price on missing a child's birthday? I was so involved with my kids: room mother and sports.

How do you feel about what's happened?
I'm embarrassed that I'm here. My mother wasn't a drug addict or a prostitute. My parents were great. I had a nice home in La Costa and I drove a Mercedes. I just got angry and lost it. It's funny. My mother can't say the word "jail." Like good parents, they blame themselves instead of me. But I can't blame this on my childhood.

When you look back, what contributed to you breaking the law?
I'm very hyperactive. I was such a tomboy growing up, always crawling up in trees, breaking bones. I mean you would've thought that I was a boy, beating up the kids in the neighborhood who picked on my little brothers, and then I woke up one day, and they were 6'4" and 6'5". I didn't have to defend them anymore. I think my dad wished I'd been a boy at first. Then when my brothers came along, they took up the slack. But I was the best athlete. I never wanted to disappoint anyone.

We hear screaming.

Sounds like Kim Gardner. She's a volatile person. You see people in green, and they're either violent, or they try to escape. I've had roommates who were heroin users and sick. I'd have to take care of them. Now I have a roommate, and I helped get her divorce. I said, "Why hire an attorney, like I did?" I spent a fortune. We can do it ourselves. She has the same educational background. She lives in the same area I do and she's also white-collar crime.

The lieutenant is best suited to getting things done. In fact she'll let you come back to the housing later. You need to ask her if you can come to my Contact Visit with my kids tonight at 7:00 p.m.

There're some things that you guys need to know about these women. They still get drugs in here. They can't shake the cycle. The sexuality. The number of women who lose their children . They don't care if they go into foster care. Their way of coping is by using the drugs to hide how they feel. It's a pattern. The same children of these women are the kids in Juvenile Hall.

How do your children feel about you being in jail?
My nine-year-old has times when he's most affected and sad. We're writing a children's book together. I have a connection with Random House and got a bid. Whereas my nine-year-old understands the concept of jail, my seven-year-old doesn't understand, and my four-year-old asks if he can come and spend the night.

What will you do your dissertation on?

I can't believe you're asking me this. I want to do it on the impact separation has on children from divorce, incarceration, or death. The real prisoners are the children and members of the family who don't know what's happening to you behind these walls. I think it's [jail] more of a prison for them than it is for us.

13. *Inmate Roland*

5/10/95 8:00 a.m. Pro Visit

The halls break out with activity. My assistant tells me she thinks this work's going to be impossible because several deputies question us about visiting Roland. Dep. Sisco overhears their complaints and stops to chat.

Deputies seem upset when they see us talking to Shelby Roland.

Dep. Sisco: I don't have any problems with Shelby Roland. Once people have broken the law and come in here, I'm the boss. Roland wanted to be treated like she was in a hotel. It's like this: I'm the deputy, and you're the inmate. We're like a giant babysitter. It's staff and inmates. We can't make it work without each other.

How has this work affected your life?

It's hard not to carry your work home, but you gotta leave it. Actually I have guys who won't date me because of what I do. Deputies tend to be dominant people. Deputies seem to fight change. My kids tell me that I've changed for the better. I was a hard-line deputy. Deputies tend to associate with other deputies. I don't do that now. I got investigated for excessive force on an inmate, and I didn't even start the confrontation.

Are you bitter toward the system?

Bitter? No. I just let it go. It starts early, in childhood. I was a dominant child, and that part of me came out in the divorce. Pretty soon you're just there, and the marriage is gone. I have a dog now. She's spoiled rotten. I'm going to be 48 in a couple months. If I wrote a book, it would be about here, about me. Males are becoming goofy because females are becoming powerful.

14. *Corridor to Intake Receiving*

10:00 a.m.

Lt. Milakovich makes it clear that she doesn't make it a practice to know each inmate, but one inmate that we may want to talk to is Rolenda Banks, a young woman who struggles inside the jail. This time the lieutenant tells us that we need to have names and numbers of inmates for the deputies to be able help us. I try and tell her that we don't know any inmates other than Roland. Ben must've known this would happen. From now on it will be up to us to find the inmates we want to visit.

I ask the lieutenant to allow us to visit Roland in A housing, and request that we get some exposure to other housing units and not be restricted to the Pro Visit area. She says she'll have to look into that. In the meantime she tells us to call out Rolenda Banks while she checks with Captain Pierce.

15. Lieutenant Milakovich

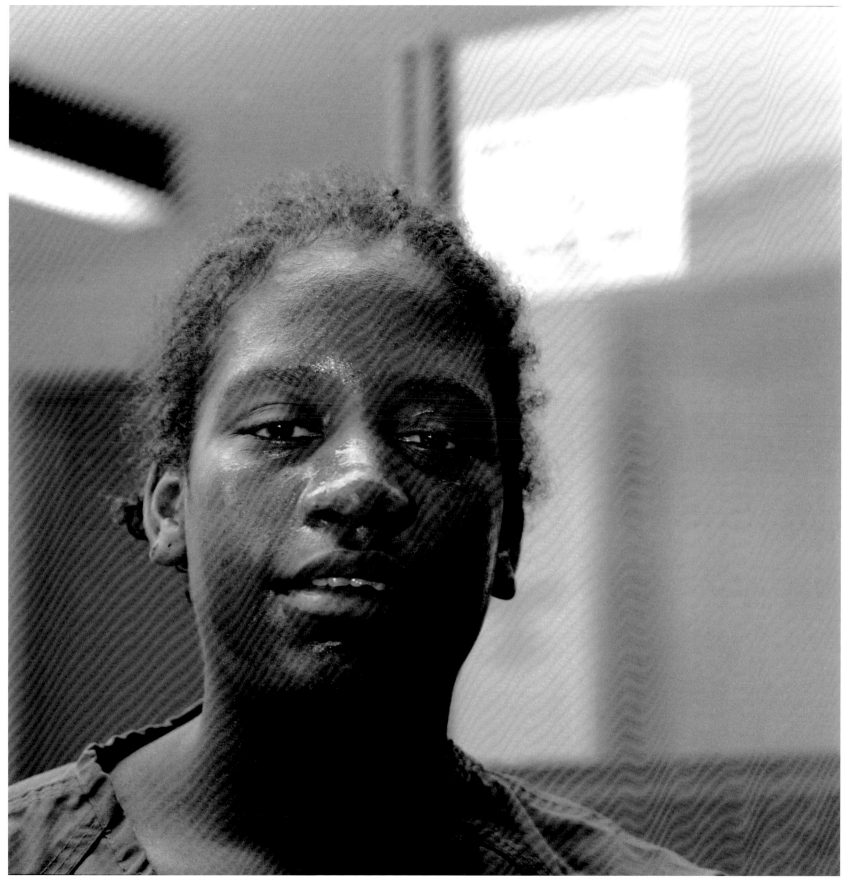

16. Inmate Banks

2:30 p.m. Pro Visit
Interview with Inmate Rolenda Banks

Pounding and screaming make it hard to hear. The lieutenant tells Dep. Phelps to bring Rolenda Banks up front from A housing.

Dep. Phelps: (Yells down the hall) Is that you screaming? (Screaming stops)

Is that Banks?
Dep. Phelps: No. The one screaming now is a pain in the butt. The lieutenant said you want to see Miss Banks? To be perfectly honest, she's my child. If anybody in the facility can handle her I can.
Another Dep.: Banks got meds a half hour ago. She just sat down and she's starting to nod off.
Dep. Phelps: I'll talk to her.

Phelps leaves to talk to Banks. Moments later she returns with a pregnant inmate who slowly shuffles into the Pro Visit booth. Phelps tells Banks to sit.

Banks: I'm on medication.
What meds?
Banks: Thorazine, tryptophan, and something else. Plus vitamins.
Dep. Phelps: Sometimes they give them to you, and you don't take them.
Banks: Yeah.
Dep. Phelps: She was refusing them.
Why are you in jail?
Banks: I stole my daughter from a foster home.
You look too young [noticing the inmate is pregnant] **to have another child.**
Banks: I got two kids already. One is one and the other is two.
Are they in a foster home?
Banks: One is with a friend and my son is with his daddy. I ain't having no more. I didn't know I was pregnant with this one before I came here.
What do you do in here? Any reading?
Banks: No. I been acting up pretty much. I been in trouble a lot. I'm in Lockdown. Deputies have to come and get me.
What kind of trouble?
Banks: Knocking on doors. Not today. I guess the meds are in my system, and I'm feeling kind of mellow.
Dep. Phelps: She quits taking them.
Banks: I'm shaking. They make me real tired. I took them once when I was in a nut hospital.
Dep. Phelps: Nut house?

Banks: In San Bernadino.
Is that where you're from?
Banks: No. I'm from Cleveland. I been out here for six years by myself.
Your mother?
Banks: I haven't seen her since I was 13.
How did you live by yourself?
Banks: I was selling drugs and living on the streets.
What kind of drugs?
Banks: Marijuana. I'd sell weed and sherm, that's cigarettes dipped in embalming fluid. It's an upper.
You like that feeling?
Banks: I just did it because others were doing it. Sometimes I get depressed, and I don't look forward to anything. I just don't care.

Her son was born prematurely because she got into a fight, and he was delivered at seven months, weighing almost five pounds. He was on a breathing machine three times a day.

Do you take meds when you aren't in jail?
Banks: No. I don't need them.
Are you threatened by confinement?
Banks: No. I came in here when I was 16. I lied and told them I was 19. They'd have put me in Juvenile Hall, and I'da been there forever 'cause I ain't got no family. I been coming here, back and forth, for a couple of years.
Dep. Phelps: Miss Banks wasn't kidding about getting into trouble. When she wasn't on her meds, she was in the restraining chair. She fought the deputies. They strapped her in, and she'd bite her lip so bad it would bleed. She spit blood everywhere. She's got a really bad reputation. I'm a corrections deputy, not sheriff's deputy. Everybody starts with the jail. Sheriff's deputies go out in the streets. I've got two kids. I don't want to be out there. In here, too many deputies treat her like they shouldn't. Just because inmates are in jail doesn't mean they should be treated like shit. You'll see when I take you out to housing.

Rolenda points to Dep. Phelps when asked who she gets along with. It's clear that the deputy cares about this young woman.
Rolenda's release date is June 26. Where will she go?

The most valuable natural resource in the entire world is our mothers. These incarcerated women are symbolic of the disintegration of Motherhood/Parenthood and the inexorable developmental perpetuation of it.

We live in a society of developmentally-arrested individuals, whose functioning is characterized by extreme immaturity across a wide range of functioning. Add drugs and alcohol to this and you have a societal time bomb.

These women are all victims of fundamentally improper and/or inadequate care. They are made visible by this work to a society which would seek to keep them invisible, and unchanged, to prevent the realization of the need for personal and social visibility and change. It is therefore incredibly important that when we are assaulted by these photographic images, that we not look away. Hope and change are possible only through increased consciousness.

When young girls' fundamental needs are unmet in early mothering, they must turn to their fathers for their esteem. When their fathers are destructive or unavailable it sets up a very self-destructive patterning in relationships, which leaves many of these women very vulnerable to ongoing victimization and diffusion.[6]

Scott Brandt, Ph.D.

17. *Deputy Phelps and Inmate Banks*

4:30 p.m. Pro Visit
A Housing, maximum security

The lieutenant returns to tell us permission has been granted by Captain Pierce to visit Roland in A housing at 4:30 p.m. She adds that Roland is difficult because she expects a lot of extras. She has sued the Sheriff. If she wants an extra shower, she'll probably get it because the deputies don't want her to add them to her list.

Dep. Lemos and Dep. Phelps appear for A housing escort. I load my cameras and gather equipment to relocate. Headed down the long corridor, inmates turn their faces to the wall as we pass. Inmates' hands must be tucked inside the waistband of their pants so they can't pass any contraband.

Dep. Phelps gives a more complete description of A housing than we've had to date. It's multipurpose housing that includes medical and psychiatric inmates, disciplinary-isolation and administrative-segregation inmates, as well as high-profile inmates, child killers, and escape risks.

Midway down A housing unit, Lemos stops and unlocks Roland's cell. Inside the six-by-nine-foot cell is a built-in bench, paper bags full of commissary items, bunk beds, and a ceiling-mounted TV.

18. A housing cell door

Dep. Lemos: Did you ladies do this to the inside of your door?
Roland: Heck no. Do we look like graphic artists?

We step inside. The deputy stands outside the cell. Roland introduces us to her roommate, Julia. Lemos warns us that it's going to be busy in the hall; it's feeding time and there are a lot of sick inmates in the unit.

Roland: Most girls gain 30 pounds in here. Julia and I are non-drug users. So our metabolism stays the same. I've been sick in here though. I had an ear infection, and long-term antibiotics gave me a full-blown colitis. I started losing my insides. You don't ever want to get sick in this place. There's only one Isolation Room. You have to get referred to go to a hospital. Nurses determine if you're an emergency, and if they don't like you, then you're not an emergency.

Deputies rush around the food cart as doors are opened, and trays handed over to inmates.

Roland: You know what's funny? Since I'm suing the [San Diego] Sheriff's Department, as a group the deputies will really talk cruelly about me but, individually many of them come to my room to see how I'm doing. It's so hypocritical.

The cart moves along. Across the hall an inmate begs for assistance. "Can you help my roommate? She's having a seizure!" Roland is preoccupied and ignores the other inmates.

Roland: One gal has three personalities, and one of those killed somebody. You ought to spend time on the A housing patio.

We look into the hall. Roland draws our attention back to the cell.

Roland: This is where Betty Broderick was when they photographed her on the top bunk, wearing nothing but her underwear. Remember that? My roommate got 13 years. She embezzled two-and-a-half million. She worked for an insurance company.

Roland's roommate says little. I move toward the door to check out the activity in the corridor.

19. Deputy Lemos in A housing

Roland: We're PMSing right now, aren't we, Julia? We're both eating chocolate and yelling at each other. Julia's from Jamaica, and she's worried that after sentencing she'll be extradited. She's not a citizen.

Roland jumps off her bunk.

Roland: So many people are immune to what goes on here. Look at all the people who watched O.J. Our justice system isn't fair. It's who you are and how much money you have. Look at Heidi Fleiss. They gave her a bail bond while she was on appeal.

Intensity rises across the hall. I can see a woman yelling for help through the narrow pane in her cell door.
"Help! My roommate's having a seizure on the floor!" she shouts.
The food cart cranks along the opposite wall, in spite of the chaos. Two trusties dressed in white have a job to perform delivering food, and it has to be on time. Roland stops one of them, insisting they have given her the wrong meal.

Roland: I don't have deviation!

The overweight trusty holding Roland's tray doesn't pay any attention and hands it to her. Roland takes a good look and thrusts the tray at the trusty's stomach.

Roland: Can't you hear? I don't have deviation tonight. It's hamburger night and I don't have a special diet when it's hamburgers! Usually I have a special diet due to my intestines.

She turns back to us.

Roland: They neglected to treat me for a bacteria, and now I have a permanent condition. You'll have to check out the commissary list. This is all the items we buy. Sundries, hair care, skin care, greeting cards, real generic brands. I have a court order so I have Chanel and all of my special brands. Toothbrushes fall apart here, so I have my Oral B.

You learn how to cope. I'll never wear this color again.

I take a photo of the room, and Shelby Roland quickly turns toward her roommate, Julia Trainer.

Roland: We've stepped up our exercises lately, haven't we, Julia? We're working out real hard 'cause it's bikini weather, even though we're not going to be in bikinis, but still you've got to think like that. I do 800 crunches, 200 squats, leg lifts, dips, daily.

Dep. Lemos moves in closer to secure the doorway as hallway activity picks up. Roland shouts at Lemos. The deputy ignores her and stays focused on the hallway and our safety. Dep. Phelps leaves her duty by the food cart and rushes to the corner cell. Lemos signals for us to exit the cell. "Come to my Contact Visit tonight," Roland shouts as we leave. "You'll love my boys."
Lemos calls us out of the cell. Things happen fast. We follow her to the corner of the corridor where she joins Phelps. "Crawford, did you OD on Motrin again?"
Phelps calls into the cell from the door. The inmate is in the shape of a cocoon, tightly wound up inside her cotton blanket. The roommate says, "Crawford won't come out." An emergency call is placed on the walkie-talkie to the infirmary about the Motrin overdose. At the same time, deputies load the other inmate across from Roland into a wheelchair for transport. The inmate's red hair is wet and uncombed. Her face is ashen, and her body flaccid.
"The redhead was tweaking. Probably heroin and alcohol," Phelps explains. "Crawford, however, is something else. She has done this before and never taken a lethal dose."
A housing is intense.

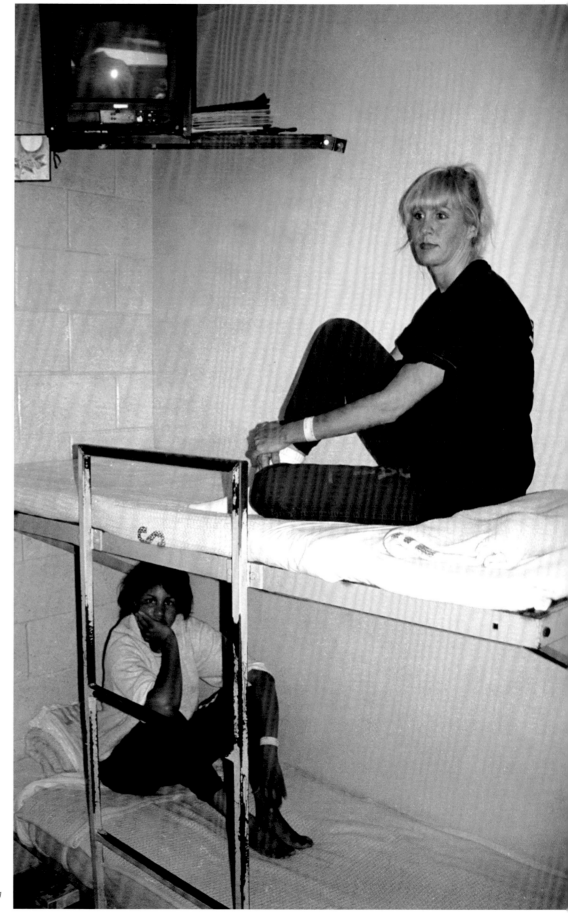

20. Inmate Trainer
21. Inmates Roland and Trainer
22. Deputies Lemos and Phelps
    in A housing

22

5:00 p.m.   Pro Visit

A spirited woman wearing white jeans, shirt, vest, and thick glasses comes to our booth and asks what we're doing. Her name is Ellen Conner. She is a counselor, the PIP (Pregnant Inmate Program) leader.

Conner: I have a sick little puppy back in maximum-security who needs to talk to someone. Her name is Kristina Edwards. She has no family, is pregnant, and is only 18 years old. I'm headed back to her housing unit there now to see some clients. I'll get back to you in a couple of hours and let you know if she'll come out and talk to you.

Interview with

Inmate Kristina Edwards

Ellen Conner returns from B housing with a message from Inmate Kristina Edwards.

Conner: Little Kristina said, "Yes." The deputy will bring her out. Remember she's in for a mega-crime and hasn't gone to trial yet. Chances aren't good for her getting out before her baby's born unless a miracle happens. Good luck.

A deputy arrives at Pro Visit with a short, young, pretty Kristina Edwards, from B housing. She wears heavy makeup, which makes her appear years older.

Ellen said that you may want to talk to someone outside the jail.
Edwards: Yeah. I guess. I've never been in jail before and talking to these girls isn't that easy. You just got to learn what to say to inmates. Trying to confide in people, and I'm facing life-without. I went to the wrong place, and it occurred there. I'm facing murder in the first-degree along with three other people because I was there, and I didn't stop it. I been on the streets and don't know where my mother is. I haven't known where she is since I was 13. My dad's just got out of being incarcerated for four years.

You spent nights out on the street?
Behind Hilltop Liquor in Crestline and behind dumpsters, you know. I'd just go to sleep. I had no place else to go. I slept all around.

You weren't in school?
Well, for a while in Big Bear. I didn't go afterwards, I mean not for long, not since ninth grade.

What about clothes, food?
I'd go to the thrift store and shoplift.

Did you ever try to go to a shelter?
No, I was too embarrassed. I just was out, you know, being high.

You didn't go to a shelter because you'd have to clean up and not use?
Well, it's just because I wouldn't be able to do what I wanted to do. You know what I'm saying? When I was out there, I wasn't in my right mind. I didn't care where I slept.

Were you afraid?
Yeah. I was too scared to go to sleep. So I did drugs. I've never did heroin. I've just done speed. Just watching people with no food, kids wanting to leave their homes. If I could go back home, I would. Some kids had so much denial and hatred from what happened to them. Now I have Chlamydia. They said it could blind my baby. I don't even know what it is, maybe from the drinking water.

Where's your mother today?
I don't know. Last I heard it was Pendleton, Oregon. One time I did thieve when me and my boyfriend had theft a truck to go up to see her, only for her to slam the door in my face. That was four years ago. My mom's life was more conservative, sophisticated. I could never ask her questions about things like sex or drugs. She didn't have time for that, you know. I went to live with my dad at 13 in the San Bernardino Big Bear Mountains. Two weeks later he went to prison for heroin, and I ended up on the streets.

When did you first use drugs?
My first drugs was IV needle using with my dad's girlfriend. Then I was too high all the time and I'm Catholic. I guess God put me where I'd stay away from that stuff and not harm myself. I just had to tell someone, you know what I mean? I get a lot of stress. My dad says, "They got you in there mixed with regular people. It's harmful for pregnant people to be in with regular girls."

Regular meaning maximum-security?
Well, yeah. General population, not Isolation or A housing where there's not so many women.

Do you talk to inmates in B housing?
No. I ain't got nothing in common with those women. I don't have nobody to talk to.

Her eye makeup smudges as she wipes away tears. Suddenly, her anger and fear overcome the youthful desire to trust.

Everyone in here thinks I'm in here for grand theft auto. Since my vehicle was used, I am just as guilty. So I'm facing all this because I was there. What's a pregnant girl supposed to do when she's with older guys? You can't really stop this. I'm not Wonder Woman, and now I'm going to trial. One girl just got the death penalty, and she didn't even do anything. She's only 20 and had the same public defender I got. I couldn't live with it, and now I'm going down. Well, they're the ones who did it.

We need to talk to your attorney and make certain it's OK to see you.
He's a public defender. We call them public pretenders because they really don't care what happens to you. I just went ahead and told them, "Go arrest these people because if I'm going down, they're the ones who did it." (*She's crying*) Two of them are in the downtown jail, and one's in Juvenile Hall. I have nightmares about it. I went to the police, and they tricked me and made me feel like I was going to be protected for ratting. Then I got hauled in, too. It was a murder here in San Diego. I had brought a friend of mine here, and he got killed by a couple of guys I had met because I drove this guy here to score. The guys didn't like him. They beat him up real bad.

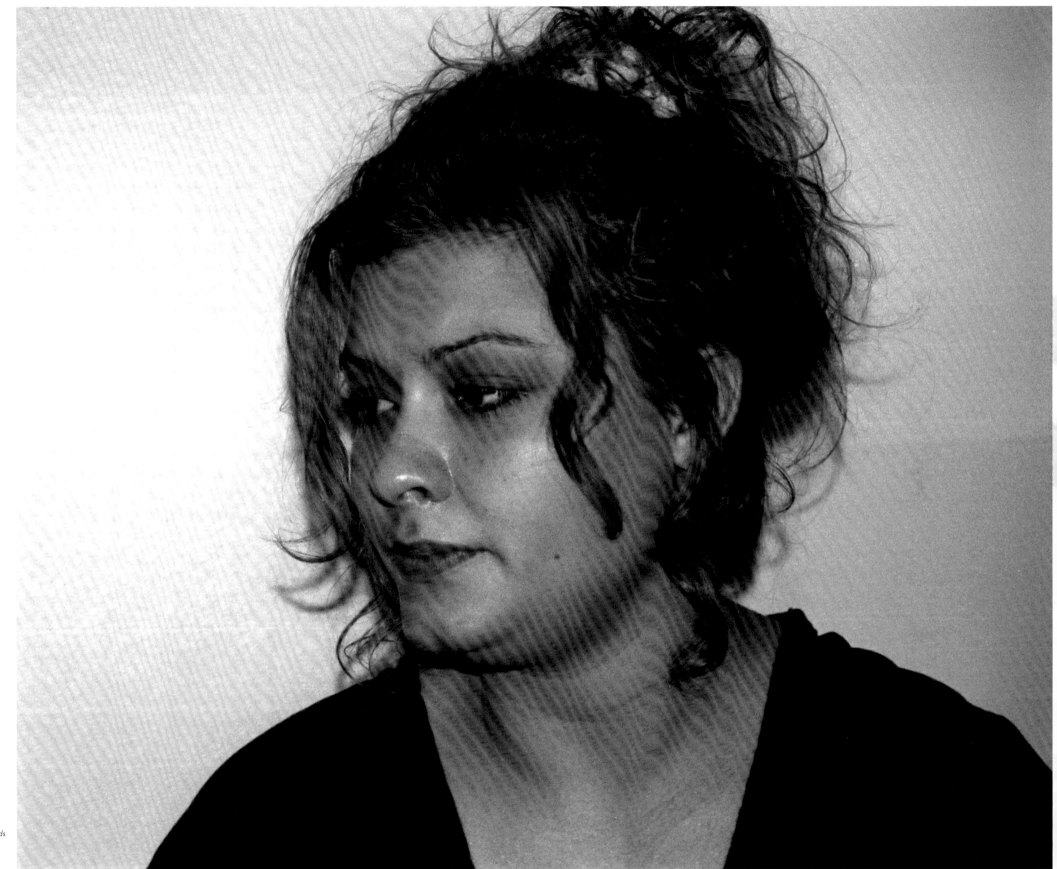

23. *Inmate Edwards*

5:45 p.m.   Phone call

I tell Ben that I have permission to talk to Shelby Roland and Kristina Edwards from their respective attorneys. Although Ben's not familiar with Roland's attorney, he informs me that Edwards' lawyer, Alex Landon, is one of the best. Ben talks about Contact Visits.

How do you feel about the children coming to the jail to see their mothers?
Ben: It's traumatic, and I want to get the trauma out of it. I don't want them coming through locked doors. I want them to come in to a play yard, a green grassy area, someplace where they can feel comfortable, and it doesn't look like a jail.

As it is now, the children must feel like they're in prison too. We see women coming from the visits, crying, weeping, only to return to handcuffs and cells. It's not a good situation. The jail, as it is, it isn't the place for children.

So how would this information get out to the public?
Develop a speakers' bureau within the jails to make presentations to high schools and colleges.

6:00 p.m.

We take a break outside the front of the jail and snack on leftover cheese and crackers and fruit from sack lunches. An SUV pulls up and three young boys jump out and rush to the maple tree in front of the facility. We realize they are Roland's children, arriving for the 7:00 p.m. Contact Visit with their mother.

*24. Inmate Roland's children
before Contact Visit*

Back inside by Control

We see Roland sitting on the bench waiting to see her boys. She has signed the waivers permitting us to attend the Contact Visit and witness how the children react to an incarcerated mother.

The lieutenant had told us earlier that women have Contact Visits for bonding purposes, since many won't see their children for a long time. Typically, a social worker or family member is asked to bring the child. Contact Visits are conducted in an effort to help both parent and child, so when the mother gets out of custody, she's not a total stranger.

25

25-28. Inmate Roland and children at Contact Visit

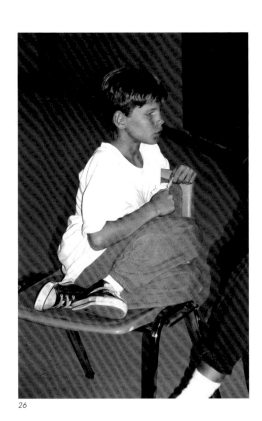

Childhood is a dangerous time. For infants and children, survival is dependent upon adults, most typically, the nuclear family. It is in the family setting that the child is fed, clothed, sheltered, nurtured, and educated. Unfortunately, it is in the familial incubator that children are most frequently manipulated, coerced, degraded, inoculated with destructive beliefs, and exposed to violence.[7]

Bruce Perry, M.D., Ph.D.

What we are as adults is the product of the world we experienced as children. The way a society functions is a reflection of the childrearing practices of that society. Today, we reap what we have sown. Despite the well-documented critical nature of early life experiences, we dedicate few resources to this time of life. We do not educate our children about development, parenting, or about the impact of neglect and trauma on children. As a society we put more value on requiring hours of formal training to drive a car than we do on any formal training in childrearing.[8]

Bruce Perry, M.D., Ph.D.

Since I had contacted Kristina Edwards' attorney, Alex Landon, and received permission to visit her, he now acknowledges the fact that she has no one to talk to and that this may be of help. I ask permission to attend court proceedings. He informs me that they are open to the public.

5/31/95 10:00 a.m. Pro Visit

Ten days pass since we first met Ellen Conner and saw Kristina Edwards.

Conner: How'd you like Kristina? She came to a PIP meeting, and they used her to pass notes from hall to hall. That's how inmates try to communicate. I had to tell her, "That's not OK, bringing this crap in here for someone else." They did it right in front of me. She thinks she's doing someone a favor. I said, "Read your rules." You have to understand: for the inmates, once you're used in here, you'll always get used in here. Now she's trying to survive.

You said you teach classes in this jail.
I work for recovery homes and teach seven different programs through the McAlister Institute. It's county funded. Before this, I was in and out of here for three years. I've got eight years in recovery. That's why my program is so successful. The women don't listen to everybody, but they listen to me. They understand. I can show them that it does work.

Kristina arrives. She looks upset.

How are you doing?
Edwards: It's real bad in here now. We were in Lockdown eight days, locked inside our cells. No phones, nothing. I was really stressing. I don't know how to handle this. I mean, my dad warned me, but it's like I just wish it were a long time ago, and I could see my mom.

I talked to your attorney.
Yeah, he told me. He said it's OK. I talked to him on the phone this morning. I'm pretty upset.

She pulls at her hair. She looks down at her lap and says she's scared. I can only imagine. A pregnant child (18) without the emotional tools to deal with such huge events. A child about to have a child and, on trial for murder.

Do you have any questions you'd like answered about pregnancy and birth?
I have lots . . . Back in B, they tell ugly stories about what happens. It's not like on the outside. I'm just glad that my dad's out of prison and can take my baby once it's over. He can't be here now 'cause he doesn't have plates for his car. He gets upset because of rumors in here. The girls start up saying, "Oh, you talking to the newspaper?" Three girls were walking back to my dorm when the sergeant walked in here and they were bringin' me up. See, there's been shit in my dorm this last week, and if they get raided, they always try to nail the first person. People shouldn't talk to anyone. The deputy said, "If I was you, I'd be refusing visits. If it's not your lawyer, don't talk to them."

So how do you feel about your dad today?
He's having problems and had to throw his girlfriend out. She brought heroin into the house. He wasn't doing it. She stole all his money and his car.

Your trial starts soon?
No, not soon! The 22nd is my Prelim. You don't get it! Trials take up to a year. There're girls been in here for ten months, and they've barely gone to Pretrial. The Prelim is my hearing to decide if I'm facing life-without [a life sentence without parole]. They bring up all the charges against me to see if they're gonna have the evidence to go to Superior Court. This is the day I've been waiting for to see what the hell's goin' on . . . the man's family, his friends, they're older biker people. The guy was in his 30s. I was the last person the guy was seen with. They can't take my life away from me for something I didn't do, but everyone in my dorm has had the book thrown at them: they got 35-to-life. These judges look at me and it's, "You did the crime." See, I'm pregnant, 18, not married, doing drugs, didn't graduate from high school, on the streets. Know what I'm sayin? It doesn't make me look good.

Your attorney has advised you as to how to conduct yourself?
You're not supposed to talk about your case to anyone in here because a lot of these women turn on you. They just go off and lie about you. That's how a girl just got the death penalty. People said they overheard her saying she killed someone, shot her up with battery acid. The one I told you about, who's 20, had my attorney.

Yes, I remember.
I'm scared. I've gained 30 pounds and all they give you is beans and a stack of cookies. I'd like to buy me a bunch of radishes if I had 40 cents in my pocket. The deputies are mean. They wrap the chain around my stomach when I go to court. I say, "Hey, I'm pregnant!" They say, "Yeah, so am I." How rude.

30. Inmates at court bus Line-up

The deputy bus drivers arrive for inmates' transport to court.

On the other side of the partition, voices are rising. Deputies are rushing around. I stand to look over the booth's partition and see ten inmates lined up, all wearing regulation sweatshirts and blue pants with "SD JAIL" emblazoned on a pant leg. Deputies shout, "Face the wall and put your hands over your heads! Lean into the wall and spread your legs!" One of the deputies steps around the partition, upset that we had earlier talked to Roland. Before I can respond, the deputy returns to her post.

Edwards: They're getting the women ready for the court run. They do this twice each day. We get body-searched, cuffed, shackled, and bussed to the courthouse. We're gone most of the day. It's no fun, going to court. I hate being chained to other girls, dragging you along.

Kristina grows uncomfortable and wants to return to her unit. The deputy arrives and stands between Edwards and me. The deputy explains the Line-up search is to check for contraband. She says, "They sneak shit inside all the time. Contraband is a big problem. They keister it—put it up their vaginas. Cigarettes, drugs, weapons. They wrap them in plastic and aluminum foil. You can't assume anything."

An inmate in the Line-up turns her head as if to see if Edwards is behind her. She says, "Nice going, Kristina, your roommate just tried to slit her neck." Edwards tenses up and glares at the woman. The deputy tells Edwards to move along.

The stern female deputy straightens the informer against the wall and shouts.

Dep.: And what's that?
Inmate: Huh?

The inmate looks over her shoulder in denial.

Dep.: That!

The deputy points to the girl's arm.

Inmate: A letter.
Dep.: Mail? Really! Yeah, I always carry my mail inside my shirt sleeve!

The deputy takes the envelope and stashes it.

Dep.: What's that on your neck? Your lipstick?

Dep. Harper moves in and explains that inmates don't slit their necks and wrists with serious intent during busy day schedules.

Dep. Harper: If someone really wants to kill herself, she'll do it at night after final night check. We've never had someone slit their throat to commit suicide. They try to cut their wrists, horizontally. When they decide to try suicide, it's usually for attention. Mostly it's a half-assed job. If the girl were going to do it, she would have done it with Edwards in the room as well. If someone's going to kill herself, you can't stop her.

"OK!" The other deputy signals Harper. She commands the shackled and handcuffed inmates to move along. The inmates scuff along single file through the Inmate Receiving sally port to board the bus.

Ellen Conner stops at the booth.

Conner: The sick little puppy [Edwards] . . . What's happened to her back in B housing isn't good. It's tough back there, and the girls are using her as a snitch. It's sad. She got herself into this predicament, and there's nothing that can be done about it. The inmates are rough in here now [B housing]. They're predators. She's in for a long time, and she's got to learn to survive. Her crime is too big to be a snitch. Chances are they'll ask her about talking to you. No one can let these guys get control.

Alarms go off and we freeze. Conner has to take a seat with us. We're ordered to remain in the booth. Deputies scurry around, but then the jail becomes silent. No voices; no movement; deputies are out of sight. Five minutes pass. Another bell rings. Activity resumes. Conner continues.

Dep. Harper explains to us that the bell goes off if there's concern about an escape or if a fight breaks out that's a threat to the facility. Dep. Phelps turns up at Pro Visit and says the lieutenant has authorized her and Harper to escort us to F housing.

We pass a wall of security cells, each with two inmates. A frantic inmate claws at the cell's narrow side window, screaming. At the end of the corridor, we stop in front of a steel door. The deputy inserts an oversized key and lights go on and off in a side panel. The door is released with a loud clanking noise and we step outside the main building onto what's called "the yard," another world.

31-32. Deputy Parra, court bus driver

11:00 a.m.   F Housing

The hot sun is blinding compared to the lighting in the main jail. Women roam the patios attached to dorms. Cyclone fencing enhanced with razor wire secures each unit.

Dep. Harper and Dep. Phelps stand next to the F housing unit.

Dep. Phelps: We can set you up outside the fencing, and you can talk to inmates in minimum-security.

Dep. Harper moves along the cyclone fence with her walkie-talkie, communicating with the Control Room. Inmates rush her with questions. Others move toward Barbara and me.

Dep. Harper: Listen up ladies and hear me good! Anyone who talks to these visitors has to first sign a consent form.

Helicopters fly overhead. The women ignore the noise, adding their own chaotic sounds. Harper tells me not to photograph the razor wire.

Lane: Why not! Those wires are a part of us.
Jennifer: Hey! You remember me? I knew you on the streets in southeast San Diego—working with the homeless. I sure remember you. I remember that camera too. How did you get here?
Lane: I've been here since April 15 for manufacturing.
Jennifer: I been in here ten times, each time for only three days until this time.
Lane: I'm not using drugs now. I got four kids: five months, fourteen years, seven years, and eight years. One of them is on the streets. The others are in foster care. My kids are Puerto Rican and black. My parents have nothing to do with us.

Where are your parents?
Lane: Del Mar. I went to Torrey Pines High School. My dad's the fire chief. They call him Bake. I grew up with my father and stepmother. We had everything we wanted except love. My parents thought it was normal life. When we went to bed at night, it was "I love you," but it wasn't the kind of love you get all through the day. My father buried his problems by being a workaholic.
Stokes: These women aren't violent. I'm a housemother in this dorm. Nights are hell because they sleep during the day a lot. Plus there's a lot of lesbians.
Lane: Look around you. You don't have the freedom to leave. You can't walk out. It's scary, don't you think? They won't even let you inside the patio because they're afraid we're going to hurt you. Come on. We want to talk to you so you can learn.
Jennifer: I just found out that I have ovarian cancer.

Dep. Harper moves in closer to the fence.

Dep. Harper: We have a lot of women die in here: AIDS, cancer.
Jennifer: I'll have surgery at UCSD. It's because of what I did on the streets. My mom did speed, heroin, everything. Now she's a school bus driver. Ha, ha, ha. She's the best con artist I've ever seen.

34

36

37

38

Dep. Harper: This is the first they've been outside for a couple days. They've been in Lockdown.

Lane: Yeah. Because one person did something wrong, we all get in trouble. There's a lot of fighting. They're not rehabilitating anyone in here. I've learned more in here than on the streets. I'm going back out to the streets real soon.

Why? What about your kids?

Lane: We're all addicts. We all have compulsive addictions. We're always going to be addicts.

Francine: I quit school right after I got my driver's license. I was born and raised in Chicago. I was a cheerleader and in pom-poms. I never got below a C grade until we moved to California, and it was easy for me to fit in real quick with the fast crowd. They're giving me a year. When I get out, I'm going to isolate myself and start a new life. I'm engaged. Now he's going to prison. He got busted with me. I had a gun on me, and he took the rap to set me free. He was a felon at the time. He'll be doing quite a few years. I think he loves me.

35

33. F housing inmates; 34. Inmate Stokes; 35. Deputy Harper on walkie talkie and F housing inmates; 36. Inmate Jennifer; 37. Inmate Lane; 38. Inmate Francine

The Safety Cell is occupied. Someone wants to kill herself.

I have learned that the jail deals with mental illness regularly. I go to E housing, referred to as the psych unit, to talk to contract staff psychiatrists. I am informed that for over 30 years, under the Lanterman Petri Short Act, penal code 5150*, for institutions, an inmate has to be a threat to herself or to others and unwilling to accept treatment for mental illness for the jail to transport her to EPU (Emergency Psych Unit), located outside of the jail.

I ask the psychiatrists to explain further who is considered voluntary or involuntary. I am told that this LPS law and Title 15** make it impossible for the jail to impose treatment on inmates who may be talking "word salad" (a term casually used to describe unfocused communication) and going "sideways" (unable to be compliant during the incarceration) in the jail. Someone in A housing who is "looney tunes," won't accept meds, but keeps her clothes on, eats food, takes showers, is considered voluntary. She may be "talking to the wall and singing to the floor"—evidence of a psychosis coming on, caused by drugs or chronic mental illness like schizophrenia—but eventually, she will be released, untreated. In these instances, jailing is little more than warehousing, as in an asylum. Other inmates may agree to treatment and get out of custody with good intentions, but most of them head back to the street again, discontinue treatment, and return to drugs. Often they will mix medication drugs and street drugs.

Outbursts are common in the jail. I have witnessed many daily. Women clawing at the slivers of windows flanking the steel door to their cells. Women trashed out, dirty, and snarling at guards only to turn and smile at someone who might listen to them. I wonder what each of them has done to end up in this place. I ask the doctors what role they play in helping these women deal with their personality problems and drug behaviors, and I'm told they will medicate those who voluntarily accept meds to help them comply with confinement and authority. Guards tell me that many inmates will act out to be given drugs so they can go through their incarceration numbed or sleeping.

More and more women are incarcerated with drug histories. One of the doctors discusses women and drug abuse. He addresses the subject by referring to the drugs the women take outside the jail—"street drugs" and the ones they are offered in the jail—prescription drugs, which, he says, have "no street value" to individuals using crystal meth, heroin, and cocaine.

Among the many types of manipulation inside the jail are suicide threats to get on Valium or Xanax. The doctor states that an inmate typically enters the facility and goes through detox before she is placed on medication.

An inmate may ask for Valium or Xanax, but she is not given such a drug because the tendency for drug dependency is great.

"Most people don't click," he says, when it comes to drug addiction and behavior. "They have to hit the gutter." A user, he explains, comes into the jail on Friday night after 5:00 p.m. and goes "sideways," freaks out, tells deputies that she plans to kill herself; protocol is that they will put her in a Safety Cell, without any clothes. The cell is a concrete cube. She has no place to sit other than the floor. There is no sink or toilet, only a hole in the floor to "pee in." A sickly overhead yellow light remains on at all times for the staff to monitor the inmate as they make rounds, checking through the slit in the door. Once the contract doctor appears on Saturday morning a decision is made whether to send her to EPU. Often, one night is all it takes in that cold cell, naked. If the inmate turns around, she goes to a high-profile A housing cell until another level of change or a court action takes place. An inmate who does not turn around quickly, smears feces on the walls and yells in hysterics, has to stay in the Safety Cell another day and may, if she still does not turn around, be transferred to EPU.

Inside the jail, the staff deals with many types of personalities. The psychiatrists describe degrees of mental disturbances, from drug-induced behavioral problems to suicide threats and antisocial personality disorders. Addictions are driven by "shame and blame." In turn, acting out develops into more severe behavioral outcomes. A personality disorder is described as "an ongoing behavioral pattern or style of dealing with the world. Someone who disregards the feelings of others, who starts fires, who is cruel to animals, and who runs away at the age of 15, is a concern."

Clearly, not everyone in the jail has a serious personality disorder; however, those who do and do not wish to receive treatment, make it difficult for the jailers as well as other inmates and staff. The doctor impresses that because someone steals doesn't mean she's mentally ill. The decision to steal outweighs the reality that she might get caught or punished. He says when a minor incident turns into a more serious event and the person shows no remorse, it becomes a sign of antisocial personality disorder. "A classic example is a sociopath, an antisocial individual like Robert Alton Harris, who shot a kid and then ate his hamburger."

Since deinstitutionalization, all of the resources have dried up and County Mental Health (CMH) is out of funds. More people enter the jail for mental reasons as a result.

Given the history of mental health treatment in California, as well as other states, there is little reason for surprise when our jails are occupied by a high percentage of mentally ill inmates. In the mid-1800s mental hospitals were opened and by 1963 Cal State Hospital population peaked at 33,757. With the advent of the Community Mental Health Act, arising from the Short-Doyle and Lanterman Petris Short Acts, basic patient's rights were put into law.

Now it was up to the individual to seek her own rehabilitation and re-entry into society.

It is little wonder that recidivism is so high among females once they have entered the criminal justice system.

* Code 5150. Dangerous or gravely disabled person; taken into custody; application; basis of probable cause; liability.

** Title 15. Use of Safety Cell. In no case shall the Safety Cell be used for punishment or as a substitute for treatment.

Human beings are strongly dependent on social support for a sense of safety, meaning, power, and control. Even our biologic maturation is strongly influenced by the nature of early attachment bonds. Traumatization occurs when both internal and external resources are inadequate to cope with external threat. . . .

When there is no access to ordinary sources of comfort, people may turn toward their tormentors. Adults as well as children may develop strong emotional ties with people who intermittently harass, beat, and threaten them.[9]

Bessel A. van der Kolk, M.D.

39. Safety Cell

The effects of child neglect can impact every area of a child's functioning, and can result in a multitude of adverse consequences for the child, family, community, and society. Neglect may actually have a more significant effect than other forms of maltreatment, affecting basic physical and psychological structures necessary for later development and adjustment. Because of its insidious nature, neglect can often go unchecked for a longer duration than other types of abuse. While difficult to isolate, future empirical research on the long-term effects of neglect in its various forms is greatly needed. Studies focusing on social, cognitive/academic, physical, emotional, and developmental implications of neglect will be necessary to better illustrate its impact, and give essential information to professionals and policy makers regarding the formulation of effective intervention and prevention strategies. Increased discussion among professionals about this pervasive influence on our nation's children will ideally create a growing awareness, a more concrete definition, and better assessment and intervention in American families. Until then, we all continue to pay the price for our past "neglect of neglect."[10]

Bruce Perry, M.D., Ph.D.

We attend Kristina Edwards' Preliminary Hearing at the downtown courthouse.

Preliminary Hearing: Legal proceeding used in some states in which a prosecutor presents evidence to a judge in an attempt to show that there is probable cause that a person committed a crime. If the judge is convinced that enough probable cause exists to charge the person, then the prosecution proceeds to the next phase.

6/22/95   8:30 a.m.
Courthouse

My notes of Kristina Edwards' Preliminary Hearing.

The judge arrives and puts on his robe. The ambience of the room is much like the back rooms of The Omaha Stockyards Livestock Exchange Building, with the good old boys gathered around and making decisions.

The DA, Rick Clabby, a short, balding man around 40 wearing wire-rimmed glasses, nervously paces and listens to the judge make bold, manic comments about a TV show.

The judge, dressed in a white shirt and tie, light tan gabardine slacks, holds center stage. He's balding, too, but his sandy hair is combed over the top of his head and appears dyed. His eyeglass rims match his hair, and they're thick.

Alex Landon, Kristina's attorney, enters the courtroom. At first glance, he looks like a young Willie Nelson because he has a ponytail. He takes his seat at the defense table and opens his files.

The bailiff announces, "The Honorable . . ."

Court business is handled and the names of the defendants are announced: Grant Bellows, Jamie Ryan, Kristina Edwards. (There's no mention of Julian Price, the juvenile codefendant.)

The prosecution begins the direct examination of homicide Detective Albert Collier, witness for the People.

On April 6, the detective went to San Bernardino and met with Kristina Edwards and discussed the death of Marcus Klotz for one hour. The detective then brought her to San Diego to locate the murder site, but she couldn't remember much. She was confused and only knew the general area. Codefendant males sit, calm and unbothered. Every now and then they look at her.

Collier talked to Detective Pete Shepherd on April 8, looking for the body in the hills of Poway. They found an item of clothing and wanted to confirm what the victim was wearing. Collier went to a plateau on Jacinto Way and underneath two wooden pallets was a blue and gold UCLA tennis shoe.

He says he noted the odor of a decaying body at 1700 (5:00 p.m.), by a high powerline. He spotted a car key, loose change, and a Copenhagen container of chewing tobacco. He later used the key on a Mr. Dick Bidwell's white Dodge. When he talked to Bidwell, he discovered that Bidwell and Kristina were good friends. Bidwell said that he unofficially adopted Kristina. He said he gave her the car to go to the store and she was gone four days.

Alex challenges the court, calling this hearsay. Under new law, hearsay evidence is noted and overruled.

April 9, cadaver dogs went into the canyon. They found the body in five minutes. The body was cannibalized. The arms had some flesh, but parts of the body were mostly gone. The medical examiner, Dr. Super, and a medical investigator were present.

Now we see overhead photos of the plateau, photos of the decedent's body, cannibalized, mostly bones; the victim's legs, the pants down around ankles, the arms still with some flesh on them. Close-up photo of the decedent's skull, detached from the body, 15 feet away.

Rocks are found with blood on them, consistent with the decedent's, and hairs, the same as those attached to skull. Criminologist's measurements indicate this is a male. Rocks examined appeared askew from the indentations under them.

Dr. Super told Collier that facial bones were missing and it appeared the victim suffered blunt trauma to head, the cause of death.

(K. Edwards' hair in tendrils, very pregnant, skin looks lovely. The male codefendants glance around the courtroom.)

Judge requests the autopsy report—he wants to cut through all the questions.

One marshal stands behind Kristina and one behind the codefendants.

Clabby: When you spoke with Kristina, was she in custody?
Collier: No.

Did you suspect her of being involved in this particular homicide?
No.

Danny Wallace and Robert Greenberg are called as witnesses for the People. They represent the location, the Donner Ranch, a house in Poway, California, the location of the onset of the crime and a house occupied by young adults and teens who gather for the purpose of using drugs.

Arraignment—July 11, 2:00 p.m. "All we do is plead not guilty. That's what everyone does."

40. San Diego Hall of Justice

2:00 p.m.   E Housing

41

42

41. Counselor Sal; 42. Counselor Dar

We meet with counselors, Sally Quigley and Dar Inman.

Thank you for meeting with us.
Sal: What were you most affected by when you first came here? The visual impact of the cages, the women locked in rooms? How did they get here? Who are they? Where are they going?
Initially, the sights and smells. And the overwhelming question— how did these women get into this situation?
Sal: They're innocent until proven guilty. We're the holding place. They are falling into the criminal justice system where they are at the mercy of the games between the other people. We call this justice. There are state, federal, and Title 15 (laws of humanity)* laws which tell us how to take care of and house the inmates.

Kristina Edwards is mentioned.

Sal: You've trusted the attorney to let you know what he thinks. Are you going to use your judgement when you see the inmate?
Dar: And if she's a powerless-appearing individual in B housing, she can be taken advantage of by women who are stronger, more knowledgeable.
Sal: Predatory inmates.
Dar: Experienced in jail mentality.
Sal: If she's perceived to have power, influence, money, or drugs, then inmates manipulate her to become part of that. In men's jails, it involves the issues of same sex, violent sex.
Dar: There's an assumption that when people get into jail they're not going to act the same as they do on the streets. However, they bring the same personality traits, behavior, and manipulative skills with them. It's not different because of the confined space. I've been in this business 14 years. Since the '70s there's a different type of offender. The offenses we're getting from women are more violent—more gun activity, more heavy drug use, and drug sales. Women have had opportunities to change and rehabilitate but can't. Once you're drawn into the system, there are obstacles to overcome to get children back and to stay on probation.

The ones we get now have done something serious with no prior offenses or have a history of minor offenses leading them to prison. Middle-aged women come to jail. "What happened to you?" "Well, I was using and lost my job." Critical things happen to people! It's difficult for them to get back to a functioning level. Take Shelby Roland, who was in our counseling service. Perfectly rational reasoning on her part to go against her probation order, but she got nailed. They get less compliant and more institutionalized each time they violate.
Sal: I've had mothers and daughters in the jail at the same time with the third generation visiting. Sisters and cousins, of course. Shelby Roland's children have been torn for years between their mother and father. I'm surprised the father still brings them. We begin by making opportunities available. As we loosened up the system, children came in with relatives and not with agency employees. Contraband appeared in diaper bags

or diapers. We don't have institution rooms for children. They meet in concrete places. Through Contact Visits and other acts that complement county and government systems in an effort to give children time with their parents, have we conditioned some children to feel that this is a normal part of life—with nothing to be feared, nothing to be taken seriously?

It becomes part of their expectations for life. To them, the bad guys wear uniforms and represent society and expectations for conformity: it was authority figures who hurt their mom or dad. I deal with the reaction of the children after the visits, because sometimes the relatives call me and say they're not really sure if they should bring the child. I reply, "You, as the caretaker, certainly have the authority to determine that. Let me just tell you some of the pros and cons and give you a little insight into what it's like inside and what could be the values or maybe the deficits of a visit."
Dar: When I talk to the women who come from good homes, from educated homes, it reinforces in me that drugs have permeated every level of society. I was in corrections in the '70s when there was treatment going on. Then in the '80s, everything just kind of dried up. We had to take a hard stand and lock them up and throw away the key. Drug addiction is permeating every aspect of society, and it's snowballing. There's no end in sight. Not just the sales and use of it, but the prostitution, the lifestyle. Generations of families are into the lifestyle.
Sal: There've always been wealthy people and people who've used wealth as a cover for illegal income. There've always been those prone to and vulnerable to the lure of women. People have used prescription drugs for years and years to self-medicate. Our society represents the quick fix in advertising and sexuality in advertising. Society as a whole, including the legal profession, plays a part. There've always been backdoor deals in the world of high finance. When you talk about basic issues for women, it was clearer 20 years ago.
How many books and movies glamorously portray women involved in crime?
Sal: Women were always dull criminals. They didn't have the opportunity to be exciting. The reasons—poverty in the inner city, matriarchal families, single parenting, lack of resources, and low income. Women using drugs leave their kids on the streets who then make their peers their new family. There's no rehabilitation with very young gang-oriented kids. It's habituation. They were not parented! They don't have the basics. They need to be taught to wash behind their ears and brush their teeth.
Dar: Children who've been abused or molested at young ages often end up as addicts. There's a direct connection between later life behavior and early childhood trauma. Now the majority of women in jail are white. It used to be mostly low income.
Rolenda Banks?
Sal: She's very fast-paced, not your average inmate.
Dar: The psychiatrists get the severe emotional and drug-abuse cases: dual-diagnosis types. I have strictly alcoholics or addicts. In a short time we know their life story and are involved with codependency, low self-esteem, poor choices, addiction. The worst punishment for them is to be separated from their families and children. Their main issue is, "I miss my kids."

* Title 15 use of Safety Cell. In no case shall the Safety Cell be used for punishment or as a substitute for treatment.

Many women resort to rocking, thumb-sucking, and other immature, childish behavior. Without the tools to self-soothe, they are not capable of grasping the pressures of working, raising a family, and problem solving. There is a tendency to revisit and reenact the intense experiences without a conscious memory of the event(s).

43

3:20 p.m. Pro Visit, Inmate Rolenda Banks

Dep. Harper delivers Rolenda Banks to Pro Visit from a Disciplinary Cell. The banging on the door that day is indeed from Rolenda. I am surprised that Harper allows the visit.

Banks: I get so angry I just wanna die. They don't understand me here. I can't stay in a closed room. It drives me crazy to be in Isolation. That's why I bang on the door 'cause I want out of there!

She changes from sad and depressed to more animated and connected.

Banks: Your shirt reminds me of the clothes I used to take from Nordstrom's. I walked around, picked up underwear, shoes, socks, went into dressing rooms. I want to get out of here and go to a hospital. I got problems. I don't know what they are but I got them. Remember "Barbie" [Roland]? You know "Barbie" with the six-million-dollar lawsuit? You should've seen her when she first came here. She wasn't "pretty Barbie." Her face was black-and-blue on the sides, her arms swole up. She left on the bus last night for prison.

What contributes to your acting out?
Flashbacks of me and my daughter at home. Of me in a foster home. Of my foster dad burning me on my leg with an iron when I was ten. Then my mom found me in the McClaren Children's Center so she could get her check. She didn't like me. She used to tell me I was a mistake.

How far back can you remember?
Seven or eight. I had a great-aunt who took care of me, and she cooked dinner for me. My daddy's aunt. My daddy picked me up on weekends, bought me toys and clothes. My little girl's birthday is in three days. Can you get her a doll and send it from me?

What would you say to your daughter?
Give me a piece of paper. I'll write something.

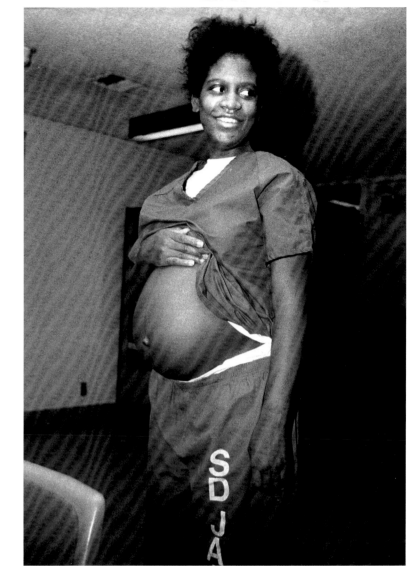

44

45

46

47

48

43-47. Inmate Banks; 48. Inmate
Banks returning to Lockdown

Dep. Harper: Let's go, Banks.

Rolenda's led by Dep. Harper down the hall to Lockdown. Rolenda turns back and smiles. Soon we hear shouting, banging, and then wailing breaks out. Harper jumps into the corridor and yells back to us.

Dep. Harper: She's suicidal now. What did you do to her?

Stunned by the hollering and pounding, we look down the hall. A deputy says, "Banks assaulted another officer earlier."
   Harper shouts up the hall, "You wanna tell her something now?"

Tell her I won't get the doll if she doesn't quiet down.
Dep. Harper: Hey Banks, Susan won't get that doll if you don't shut up!

The screaming escalates to horrific wails, echoing throughout the halls and corridors of the jail. Rolenda was engaging with us. She held a decent conversation. She tried to take a photo with my Hasselblad. Why is she doing this? The screaming grows unbearable. Another inmate joins in and Harper shouts at her, calling her Miss Trenchmouth. Harper returns to our booth.
   An interested nurse stops on her way back to Sick Call.

Dep. Harper: It's not you. It's the day. Remember I said she hasn't taken her meds? She did this to me yesterday. She bites and spits blood at us.
Nurse: She took her meds.
Dep. Harper: This is a ploy to go to the hospital. She wants a free ride in the car to [County] Mental Health to get medicated and a ride back here floating. She tears her wristband apart, and swallows the metal pieces so we'll be concerned.

Is that what she was sucking on?
Dep. Harper: Yeah. Yesterday I said, "Give it to me." She goes, "No, I'm going to swallow it." I said, "Swallow it," and she did. The nurse told me to check her poop the next day. She passed it. Kids swallow keys. I hate this house! I can do so much more good for girls out there in F housing.
Sounds as if her life has been pretty horrible.
Dep. Harper: Everybody has problems. I talk to her about her baby, and one minute she goes, "Oh, my baby," and the next minute she's punching herself in the stomach. We give people respect, and they tell you they don't want it. She's in the Safety Cell three times a week on the average.
What about B housing population instead of Isolation?
Dep. Harper: She failed housing regulations . You can't put a volatile person where she not only wants to hurt herself but also becomes homicidal. She wants to be medicated to the max and not think about past, present, or future. If she really wanted to hurt herself, she'd bash her head into the brick walls in her cell, but she bangs the walls to make noise, not hurt herself.
Not much consolation.
Dep. Harper: You were giving her attention. You're doing what she wants. Another one's yelling at me now because I won't put her on the patio. It's childhood tantrums. I'm going to write up that Banks had a nice interview,

4:00 p.m.   Phone call

I talk to Ben and let him know that Roland left for prison only after she encouraged us to visit A housing. Ben laughs, "Good. See, that's all calculated on her part. She sets those scenarios up, depending on how she reads you and what's going to reach you. She's good. She picks up so quickly."

7/13/95 8:00 a.m.
Step Study with Counselor Dar

We have an escort to the Step Study. Inmate Tiffany sits at the front desk; part of her trusty duty is to monitor the inmates entering the program where they deal with the 12 Steps of Alcoholics Anonymous.

Dar stands in front of the blackboard and begins the day's discussion.

Dar: Today we start Step 2, Acceptance. The process of accepting begins with a conscious decision to accept a higher power. Instead of just hearing it, you make a process out of it. We have two guests today. Does anyone want to contribute?

DeeDee: I sat with a rig of drugs, not wanting to use, crying, and I still got loaded. Your body fights you, saying, "I want to have this." Your mind says, "I shouldn't and I don't want it." But your body takes it.

Dar: You're sitting here. Can you tell me this was supposed to happen?

DeeDee: Yes. I'm grateful.

Dar: Most of you must've said, "I didn't do this. This is a mistake."

Sue: I can't wait to come to jail to get a vacation.

DeeDee: Three meals and a cot. I was homeless. It's not prison, and it's not death. It's recovery.

Gwen: Wild horses couldn't drag me here again.

Dar: You didn't plan this six months ago?

Gwen: I bet none of us realized we could spend months on the same paragraph.

Sue: I need to concentrate less on what happens in the world and more on me.

Dar: What a revelation: I am the problem. The world isn't screwed up. It's not what happens to you, but what happens in you. After starting with drugs, little things become big.

49. Inmate Lorinda, F housing

Fourteen women in a circle give their name and state their drug of choice.

My drug of choice is . . .

Dar: Let's get your name and addiction of choice and finish the sentence. In my recovery it's hard for me to accept . . .

My name is **Tiffany.** My drug of choice is <u>crystal</u> and it's hard for me to accept feelings. My biggest problem that I'm learning [to deal with] is not my addiction to drugs, it's my addiction to men.

My name is **DeeDee.** My drug of choice is <u>rock cocaine.</u> The thing I have a hard time accepting is that underneath all of this is a beautiful child and that someday that child's going to grow up to be a beautiful woman.

My name's **Dottie.** My drug of choice is <u>crystal</u> and the hardest thing for me to accept is that I've let <u>crystal</u> ruin the last three and a half years of my life.

My name's **Debbie.** My drug of choice is <u>crystal</u> and I'm having a hard time accepting what <u>crystal</u> has done to my life, too—over four years.

My name's **Colleen.** My drug of choice is <u>crystal.</u> It was really hard for me to accept that I'm always going to be fighting off the addiction.

My name's **Gwen.** My drug of choice is <u>alcohol</u>, <u>cocaine</u>, and <u>crystal.</u> They're one and the same for me now. I can't think of anything that is hard for me to accept right now except for that it's a life disease.

I'm **LeAnn.** I'm a <u>crystal</u> addict and it's a hard thing, like Colleen said. I was a pipe user—I smoked it and I can't look in the mirror yet and say that I'm not going to get high. That's a hard thing for me to accept. It's scary.

My name's **Julie.** My drug of choice is <u>crystal.</u> It's hard for me to accept that I'll never be able to make up the years with my kids. (She cries)

Hi, my name is **Antoinette.** My drug of choice is <u>alcohol</u> and <u>cocaine.</u> I can accept I lost our son . . . it's hard to accept you can't turn and go back . . . I mean he'll be graduating, age 18 . . . .

My name is **Sue.** My drug of choice is <u>crystal.</u> It's hard for me to accept all the years I took away from my children.

I'm **Darlene.** My drug of choice is <u>alcohol.</u> In my recovery, it's difficult for me to accept that I do have to work in a program every day and it isn't anything I can go to sleep and wake up and it'll be done.

Nicotine has the fastest tissue adaptation of any drug. There's no smoking in jail.

Dar: Families are in denial. They need specific boundaries. They aren't going to recognize their problem, and oftentimes they sabotage treatment. My task isn't to fix the family, but to have them understand that family relationships are toxic. I define boundaries. There's usually one relationship that's loving, more difficult, because it's more dependent. For women, this is a big reason why they relapse. They have the resolution and determination to change, but they get out of jail and the influence is so powerful. Boyfriend, husband, kids, mother-daughter relationship.

Tiffany: After two drinks all I want to do is get high. I can deal with not getting high, but if I pick up a drink, I have to have two. As soon as I get the buzz, I want that sensation that alcohol won't give. I want to get high.

Dar: It's either an emotional or a chemical connection. Society feeds it. Research shows that addicts have a higher need for these types of brain chemicals.

Tiffany: I know girls in here who have been nurses at Children's Hospital. They put those kids' lives at risk.

Colleen: I'm scared to death to leave. I'll walk out the gates and run into somebody I know. They'll hand me a bag.

Dar: In prison there are more drugs and gangs. Each time you come before the courts and you've been to prison, the punishment is more severe. You become institutionalized. Three Strikes passed because there's money on the drawing board, yet nothing for rehabilitation. At the Criminal Justice Conference, people were amazed that the governor was not educated as to what this law would do to the state. It was a political move to get reelected. We get high-functioning women, professional women, in here for cocaine. Cocaine has permeated every level of society. Heroin is used as a depressant. There's not a moral conscience about behavior. There's no remorse.

More classes are being taught today by people who are in recovery. I've had a lot of training, counseling, and been in therapy and worked the steps. I couldn't teach a class on 12 Steps without having gone through it.

What is the most dehumanizing point when you come to jail?
Colleen: The sally ports, the search. Straddle, bend over, cough.

Dar: It's hard to see the older ladies who drink too much get picked up and go through this. After a Contact Visit with your kids, the visit's almost over, and it's here we go again. You have to take everything off; other inmates are around;

---

deputies stand in front of you: they take you in a room—all three, four, or five of you—you take your clothes off, bend over, open your mouth, show your ears, cough, turn around, and the deputies stand there with the door open to the hall, other deputies walking up and down the hall.

Why won't the mothers protect molested children?
Dar: Because the mothers are probably in denial.

So a mother's love isn't great enough to transcend that denial?
Dar: You have to understand that there're a lot of women who're passive and very needy and it has to do with their own childhood. They know the way their mother handled it.

I've talked to women who say prostitution is the way they dealt with conflict.
Dar: These are the women who fall through the cracks. These are the women who're in all the social services. It isn't a surprise story in the social services.

When do these walls get formed? How does a three-year-old child make sense of molestation as a part of life?
Dar: Through their beloved parents. They are the people who protect and feed and clothe them. The child is taught not to tell. The child must deny it to anyone who asks. They're taught that it's their fault.

I've heard that mothers may ignore the behavior.
Dar: Sometimes the victim senses the mother knows and sometimes she doesn't. Sometimes the father or the relative says, "If you tell your mother, I'm going to beat her up."

And girls who've been fondled or molested by their brothers . . .
Dar: That behavior didn't come out of nowhere. We want to think it's exaggerated, when in reality there are those who cover it up and are rigid. There are people who are less self-disclosing, but you accept them because they seem to have it together.

What about the theory that prostitution gives women an opportunity to have power over men?
Dar: I'm finding women who are guilt-ridden simply because they participated in the act and maybe even enjoyed parts of it. There's power over the perpetrator. Once they get to the point where it's their fault for participating "voluntarily," it gets very twisted. It's the same kind of twisted [thinking] when talking to a prostitute about love. Who got tricked? Who victimized whom? If you have no concept of love, you've got no concept of limitations. You have no boundaries. Try defining love to someone. It's a very complicated dynamic.

Methamphetamine

Methamphetamine is an addictive stimulant drug that strongly activates certain systems in the brain. Methamphetamine is closely related chemically to amphetamine, but the central nervous system effects of methamphetamine are greater. Both drugs have some limited therapeutic uses, primarily in the treatment of obesity.

Methamphetamine is made in illegal laboratories and has a high potential for abuse and addiction. Street methamphetamine is referred to by many names, such as "speed," "meth," and "chalk." Methamphetamine hydrochloride, clear chunky crystals resembling ice, which can be inhaled by smoking, is referred to as "ice," "crystal," "glass," and "tina."

Health Hazards

Methamphetamine releases high levels of the neurotransmitter dopamine, which stimulates brain cells, enhancing mood and body movement. It also appears to have a neurotoxic effect, damaging brain cells that contain dopamine and serotonin, another neurotransmitter. Over time, methamphetamine appears to cause reduced levels of dopamine, which can result in symptoms like those of Parkinson's disease, a severe movement disorder.

Methamphetamine is taken orally or intranasally (snorting the powder), by intravenous injection, and by smoking. Immediately after smoking or intravenous injection, the methamphetamine user experiences an intense sensation, called a "rush" or "flash," that lasts only a few minutes and is described as extremely pleasurable. Oral or intranasal use produces euphoria—a high, but not a rush. Users may become addicted quickly, and use it with increasing frequency and in increasing doses.

Animal research going back more than 20 years shows that high doses of methamphetamine damage neuron cell endings. Dopamine- and serotonin-containing neurons do not die after methamphetamine use, but their nerve endings ("terminals") are cut back, and regrowth appears to be limited.

The central nervous system (CNS) actions that result from taking even small amounts of methamphetamine include increased wakefulness, increased physical activity, decreased appetite, increased respiration, hyperthermia, and euphoria. Other CNS effects include irritability, insomnia, confusion, tremors, convulsions, anxiety, paranoia, and aggressiveness. Hyperthermia and convulsions can result in death.

Methamphetamine causes increased heart rate and blood pressure and can cause irreversible damage to blood vessels in the brain, producing strokes. Other effects of methamphetamine include respiratory problems, irregular heartbeat, and extreme anorexia. Its use can result in cardiovascular collapse and death.[11]

Influx of New Drug Brings Crime and Violence to Midwest

"This is the most malignant, addictive drug known to mankind," said Dr. Michael Abrams of Broadlawn Medical Center in Des Moines, Iowa, where more patients were admitted during the past year for abuse of methamphetamine than for alcoholism. "It is often used by blue-collar workers, who feel under pressure to perform at a fast pace for long periods. And at first, it works. It turns you into wonder person. You can do everything—for a while."

Methamphetamine causes psychotic and violent reactions, he said, because the drug throws out of control the production of the brain chemical dopamine, which plays an important part in movement, thought, and emotion, as is the case with schizophrenia. Over time, the drug damages the brain.

"A person addicted to this stuff looks and acts exactly like a paranoid schizophrenic," he said. "You cannot tell any difference."

Indeed, the use of methamphetamine goes back many years, perhaps to the 1920 or 1930s. But today's form is far more powerful, and deadly.

Years ago, the authorities said, a typical street dose of methamphetamine consisted of perhaps 20 percent ephedrine, the ingredient that delivers the kick. New methods that emerged in the late 1980s and early 1990s, often using a synthetic, pseudoephedrine, have yielded a much more potent substance. Now the drug contains over 90 percent of the active ingredient.[12]

Although inmates do plan release binges and may keep an hourly count of the time until their release date, those about to be released very often become anxious at the thought, and, as suggested, some mess up or reenlist to avoid the issue. The inmate's anxiety about release often seems to take the form of a question put to himself and his friends: "Can I make it on the outside?" This question brackets all of civil life as something to have conceptions and concerns about. . . . Perhaps such a perspective is demoralizing, providing one reason why ex-inmates often think about the possibility of "going back in" and one reason why an appreciable number do return."[13]

Erving Goffman

50

51

52

According to the Women in Prison Project, at y jail, or on parole or probation in the United Sta offenses (almost 80 percent in 1999), prostitutio

The Self. The generic definition of addiction I use is "the chronic neglect of self in favor of something or someone else." Addiction can be conceptualized as a self-disorder. One of the first questions women in recovery need to begin to address is "Who am I?" Women in our culture are taught to identify themselves according to role: mother, professional, wife, daughter. One of the first tasks for women in recovery is to find words to describe who they are from a deep, inner place. In addiction, one loses the sense of oneself and, with it, the ability to have a real connection with others. Recovery is about expansion and growth of the self, both the inner and the outer self.

Many women enter the prison system with a poor self-image and a history of trauma and abuse. As we have seen, prisons actively discourage relationship. Creating the kinds of programs that help incarcerated women to develop a strong sense of self, an identification that goes beyond who they are in the criminal justice system, is vital to their recovery.

Relationship. Some women use addictive substances to maintain relationships with using partners, some use them to fill up the void of what is missing in the relationship, and some use alcohol or other drugs to deal with the pain of being abused (Covington & Surrey, 1997). One of the tasks of any recovery program is to teach women self-soothing techniques in order to deal with the myriad of feelings that surface when abstinent.

Women in the prison system often have unhealthy, illusory, or unequal relationships with spouses, partners, friends, and family members. For that reason, it is important for recovery programs to model healthy relationships, among both staff and participants, providing a safe place and a container for healing (Covington & Beckett, 1988). Our greatest challenge is to overcome the alienation that is fostered within prison walls, and replace it with a greater sense of relationship in community.

Stephanie Covington, Ph.D.

50. Inmate Henderson; 51. Inmate Tiffany; 52. Inmate Teena; 53. Inmate Celeste; 54. Inmate Ameerah; 55. Inmate Sanders; 56. Inmate Lopez; 57. Inmate DeeDee; 58. Inmate Mindy

2002, an estimated 1,040,000 women were in criminal justice custody, either in prison or majority of these women were incarcerated for non-violent crimes such as drug-related perty offenses including larceny, burglary, and fraud.[14]

NOW PBS

After the first visit to Step Study, I contact Ben McLaughlin. I tell him that we've spent time on the minimum-security yard and I'm curious: Is there a difference in the intelligence of low-risk felons compared to the inmates in maximum-security?

Ben describes the difference between maximum- and minimum-security: "There's an element of criminal sophistication and it affects the classification and housing of inmates. Inmates in maximum-security are generally the more sophisticated. It's my experience that it's not about IQ or inmate intelligence. It's all about a low level of education. Ever hear of the Prado Principle? The 80/20 rule? It's like this: 20 percent of the people do 80 percent of the crimes. Today most charges are drug related. Women carry the drugs because they're less apt to be searched as thoroughly as males. They're committing more violent crimes."

We watch the women file into the small library space. Dar shows impatience with their tardiness. One inmate, Tiffany, steps up with an explanation and Dar is particularly upset with her and claims that she oversleeps frequently. Dar sends another inmate, Gwen, outside for an interview at the picnic tables while class continues.

59

Gwen: I'm actually super self-conscious. I have an addict personality.

To what do you attribute the development of this addict personality?
It wasn't so much the drink as it was the explosion of late-blooming stuff that crept up on me. I was a rebellious kid.

Before I ever took a drink, I was super-structured with tunnel vision on tennis. I grew up in La Jolla with a tennis racquet in my hand and had a sheltered upbringing. My girlfriend was an outcast from La Jolla High because she had a pregnancy in junior high. We were both alike. I was shy. If it weren't for alcohol and drugs, I'd never have come out of my shell. I could dance all of a sudden. I could talk about things that were bothering me.

When did you discover alcohol and drugs?
When I was 22. I saw a billboard advertising Tanqueray's for a dollar at a bar called Diego's. I went there with my girlfriend, and I drank several vodkas and did an eight-ball. No one could understand how I could consume so much at one time.

So this was a switch in behavior for you?
Yeah. I never drank or did drugs. I'm a maverick. The first time I took a drink I said yes to coke. That's how competitive I am. I never had a hangover. I did three Family Fitness commercials, and I was up for 14 days on crystal meth. No one had a clue.

You were an athlete?
I was number four in the nation in tennis, and no matter what I did, I didn't think it was good enough. My mom is easygoing, but my dad is super controlling and frugal. My mom didn't put pressure on me, but when I'd go to national tournaments, I'd get pressed. If I left a crumb on the counter, I'd be restricted for a week. I had a nine o'clock curfew even for Homecoming, and I was Homecoming Queen. I couldn't do other sports or go skiing in case I broke my ankle. That's how my dad is. I didn't have the key to my house. Never did anything wrong. My mom and dad were always home. We had a tennis court in the back yard. Growing up in La Jolla there were snotty people in cliques—sororities and the ditty group, the brainy group and the druggie group, and the surfers. I hate cliques.

Were there other ways you didn't fit in?
My dad races cars. I even have my SCCA, Sport's Car Club of America. I drive around 110-130 mph. So on the freeway, clean and sober, I drive around pretty hard. I'm doing my death wish. I'm 32. I'm always the one to not want to wait in line. I've been married, had a miscarriage, and came here because I took the plea for something my husband did. I was here for eight days last December. That was the dumbest thing, because when I came in under the influence this time, they gave me 90 days. I have a boyfriend who bailed me out the first time, and then I missed the court date with the probation officer. Now my bail is $20,000. I have to stay until October.

DeeDee comes out of the annex for an interview. Gwen returns to the annex.

DeeDee: I have a favor to ask you. Please take my picture from the waist or neck up 'cause I gained 30 pounds.

How old were you when you started drugs?
Fifteen. I started crack with my son three years ago. All of the processing we're doing in Step Study helps to bring this awareness out. I was on prescribed pills to make me eat when I was five. I was having trouble with molestation that was going on.

Who was molesting you?
My dad, of all people. My first molester was my uncle Frank when I was two. Now that I'm older I don't think my father was aware of my uncle's involvement. I can remember waking up on my uncle's couch, my dad and his wife in the other room playing cards together. My uncle would say, "Quiet." My aunt and uncle had ten children, and there was always a chance of a child coming into the house or into the room as time went on. And later on he actually became a john.

The uncle?
I punished myself saying, "If I hadn't been such a bad child, he wouldn't have molested me." Then the perversion, the addict side of me was saying, "He thinks I'm attractive and I have nobody in my life who says I love you, who thinks I'm attractive, and wants to get close to me. Why not date somebody I know, that I've already had an intimate relationship with?"

How old were you when you were thinking these things?
Let's see, I'm 40 now. Probably 27.

Were you in love with him?
Not in the least. The sad thing is that because of me this guy started smoking crack.

Someone you met on the street?
Yeah. He tried to take care of me. Now he's an addict. We can't be together because all we're doing is killing ourselves. He took me right off the streets as soon as I agreed to be his lady. He was a date. He wasn't a john.

Why do you feel you became a prostitute?
To be loved. See, I took care of my family from the time I was eleven. I cleaned, cooked, did laundry. My grandmother had spinal meningitis when she was young. I took care of her. My dad was my grandfather's stepson. My dad would pull me into the bedroom when he got home from work and ask if I'd talked to my grandfather. If I said yes, he'd knock me upside the head. I'm not supposed to talk to the man who feeds me, who takes me out on Sunday nights to dinner, who pays for my tuition at school, who gets my uniform, pays for my books?

When did you become a prostitute?
In 1990. I was on crack. I wasn't about to ask my family for money for food. I'd rather sell my body. The only way I could be a Catholic and a prostitute is by doing drugs, because that numbs everything. We don't love ourselves. We seek the gratification of prostitution and drugs.

60

61

62

A young girl walks out of Step Study to replace DeeDee. DeeDee introduces her as Teena, and says Teena is like a daughter to her. She says the girl needs help.

63

Teena: I was the child in our family who went into an orphanage. Then I went from family to family. I was born in Baltimore, and raised in Boston. We got split up into different families. I was three years old when my real mom was put in a hospital, institutionalized for a nervous breakdown. She couldn't deal with eight boys and five girls.

How old are you now?

I'm 24. I contacted my real mom about two years ago when I took the bus back to Boston. She got out of the institution and we got together with my family again, but it was weird. It was like, who are these people telling me that I'm their sister? I was kicked out by my adopted parents because they couldn't deal with me. I was on drugs. One tried to teach me a lesson and broke my arm with a baseball bat. I was molested by him at 13, and I had three girls by him. I love my kids though.

Why are you in here?

I agreed to do something for money: prostitution. I've been doing it since I was 12. Pimps and prostitutes are my family.

You're in Step Study. Do you think this will help you?

I finally accept that I need help for drugs. I've been doing drugs since I was eight. I started on rock cocaine, heroin, and ice. I'm tired of it.

64

Cindy Mulloy shares with us how her habit led to prostitution.

Mulloy: It was quick, but it wasn't easy. In '86, I was 23. The others knew I made a lot of money so they wanted me around. But anyone who wanted to get close to me and find out about "Cindy," they scared me. As a kid, my mom and dad's relationship was weird. There was alcohol in the house. We lived with my aunt and uncle for a while. They had a keg in their garage. I was eight. "Cindy, fill up my beer." I'd drink a beer and deliver a beer. I was mad at my mom. I was smoking pot and hanging out. I'd say, "You can't save me. Please don't try."

I had a 105-degree fever, and the jail thought I was crazy. I never before had a fever while kicking. It was last year when I had just gotten back from the hospital from having the mitral and tricuspid valves in my heart replaced. I was in the hospital for almost three months.

McGlothlin: Cindy's special. I had just come back from burying my 91-year-old mother; I saw Cindy in the Holding Tank. I said, "My mother looked better than you." This time Cindy looks better. We've got to retrain her. She's intelligent and lovely.

65

Barbara McGlothlin, the GED instructor, steps out of her classroom to see Cindy Mulloy.

66

Chuck heads up the GED program across from Step Study where McGlothlin teaches classes.

Chuck: I think the problem with women in here is empowerment. I think they don't feel like they have any power. When they accomplish something, they can say, "I did that myself." It might be a microcosm of women in society, but it's a calling for me. I think people on the outside want to simplify this place and say the women are all alike. It's not true. There are women who are cons and there are others who shouldn't be in here. They come in and say, "I'm back." I say, "OK, here we go again. You will make it this time." You keep the hope alive. You have to believe that maybe they'll make it this time.

59. Inmate Gwen; 60-62. Inmate DeeDee;
63. Inmate Teena; 64. Inmate Mulloy;
65. GED Counselor McGlothlin;
66. GED Counselor Chuck

The most damaging sexual molestation is the one perpetuated by someone the little girl trusts and considers a protector such as her father, an uncle, the boy-friend of her mother, and sometimes her mother. Sexual abuse obliterates the child's sense of identity. She does not know if she is a wife or a daughter, if she is girl or a woman. The demarcation between reality and illusion becomes blurred. To escape the shame, the guilt, and the confusion the little girl begins thinking of herself in the third person, as though she were someone else. In her own eyes she becomes an object, a thing of no value.[16]

Maryam Razavi Newman, Ph.D.

67. Inmate Teena;
68. F housing razor wire

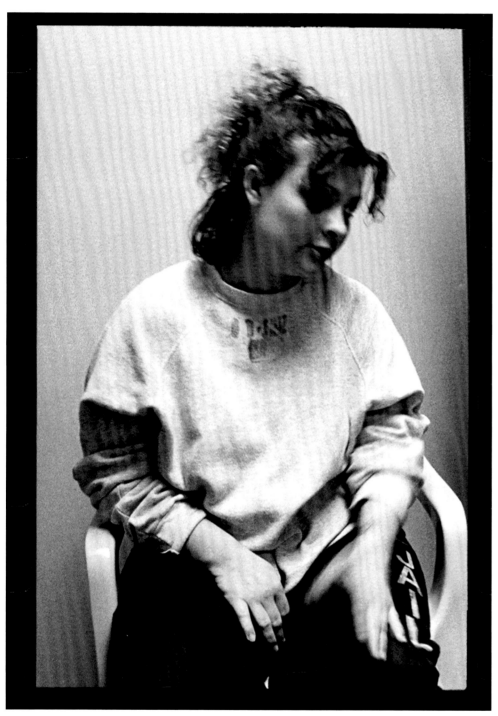

69. Inmate Edwards

7/28/95   10:30 a.m.
Pro Visit Room

My assistant, Barbara, and I wait outside the clerk's Control Room.

An inmate appears, comes around the glass wall, hands in her pants, stone-faced. The deputy bows back and asks, "Are you comfortable talking to this individual alone? She's from B, maximum-security." I nod and Kristina Edwards drops into a red plastic bucket seat. The screws are loose, and she adjusts herself in the seat and checks the wobbly aluminum legs of the chair.

How are you doing?
Edwards: Fine.

You look more down today.
If you had to deal with that deputy you'd be down, too.

Things are pretty rough back there?
Drugs were found in my room. Everyone goes into Lockdown when they raid us and find drugs. I haven't seen you since my Prelim. My attorney reminds me of a stoner-biker guy. What did you think?

I like him.
I don't know about that. Anyhow, they think you're my mom. Ryan and Bellows. There wasn't anybody talking against me, just my statement. The detective didn't start the tape clean. It wasn't a confession. I think I said something like, I don't remember, and then the tape started. I picked up a rock and threw it in the guy's face.

I don't want to ask you any questions about the court.
Twilla Donner's dad owns the house, but the judge said, "I take it there ain't never been no parents there at the house." She's right. Hey, my dad's back in jail. Now I'm worried about my baby. I'm gonna do some time.

Getting your GED, showing interest in education would be good.
The whole thing was bad. I was disgusted and almost puked. I didn't even know half the stuff that happened. I wasn't all there. I never knew about the dog chain being wrapped around his neck, I was in the car crying at the time. We had stopped on my way to Oceanside. I wouldn't have said, "Finish him off," like that kid told the judge. Ryan still hasn't made a statement. He never did make one to the police. You can't use what codefendants say against each other. Ryan will keep his mouth shut through the whole thing. He's like that. Bellows obviously said Ryan had did it. He's the one that brought up the thing about Ryan and the dog chain. Ryan's been to the pen before for robbery.
He's 25.

They all look like shit now. He didn't have no hair when I knew him before. He was a Skinhead. White Supremacist Tattoos all over. I wanna know when they're gonna bring in that juvenile. He's the one that tells the story like me. His case is separate from ours. He was with me in the car. He didn't drop no rock on the dude, but he threw rocks at him and beat him up. He didn't kill him. He's in the same position I'm in, but he did participate.

When you get out of jail what will you have learned?
Not to come to San Diego. I'm not going to get involved in something like this again. I'll go back to Cedar House recovery. I wouldn't be in this predicament if I woulda stayed there the first time. This happened three nights after I left it with my boyfriend. I just want to go home. Now inmates say, "We didn't go run around murdering somebody with a rock like you did. Hope you get the death penalty." They're thinking everyone's snitching. It's fucked-up. It's just they're fucked-up on dope back there, and they're always worried. I don't know where my mom is or I'd a called her a long time ago.

Sgt. Miller introduces Dep. Purdy to escort Edwards back to B and to take us to D housing.

Dep. Purdy: You need an escort? I'll take you wherever you want to go.

We walk back to B housing with the deputy and Edwards shyly says good-bye to us and quietly enters the housing compound. We have a few seconds to look through the glass into the unit. This is the most we've seen of B housing. Edwards goes to another door inside and waits for a deputy to unlock the B1 unit.

We exit the main housing and move out to the minimum-security yard.

I see women coming in over and over again under the influence. I'd say 98 percent have drug histories even if that isn't what they're arrested for.

Deputy Purdy

Dep. Purdy: We had one girl tell us, "When I get out, I'm going to Louisiana." That was a couple weeks ago. This morning I saw her again in here. It's a running joke when they say, "I'm not coming back." I don't think rehab works for a lot of these girls. Eighty percent come back. In here, they're in a structured environment. F1 housing is geared toward Stepping Out. Inmates are selected for the program based on strict criteria. These inmates in F2 and F3 are just doing time, walking and talking on the phone, collect calls. They're lower-class criminals and drug users. They're not the murderers.

We have our codes for breaking the law. You get a speeding ticket, it falls under vehicle code. Use drugs, it's under public safety health code and penal codes for basic violations. You could talk to 400 inmates and get 400 stories, yet all their charges are related. They're in here for being under the influence of drugs, petty theft because they stole money to get drugs, burglary because they went into a house to steal things to get money for drugs, or assault with a deadly weapon because they were under the influence of drugs. If you're looking for a solution to a problem, it's to solve the drug problem. Three Strikes on a drug charge . . . going to jail for life doesn't work. We need to revise the judicial system.

The yard's hot, no breeze. We move along the walkway to D housing to meet trusties.

Dep. Purdy: This house is where the women are most likely to succeed. It's the minimum-security housing for trusty workers.

We see an oversized TV, long white plastic sofas, and a handful of women sitting together and watching a soap opera.

71. D housing trusty inmates

D Housing, trusty

Inside D housing, Dep. Harper's on duty behind a counter that's inside a steel cage. Three other deputies mingle behind her. Harper calls out to us, "Rolenda's escaped from CMH." The other deputies act as if they don't hear the announcement.

What did you say?
Dep. Harper: Rolenda tore her water bag the day you saw her, and we took her to the hospital. She was supervised for three days by two deputies, but her charge didn't warrant $1,400-a-day guard duty to the county. They released the deputies, and Rolenda wanted a cigarette. The nurse said, "You can't smoke inside," so Rolenda left the hospital.

We're shocked at the news, but can't stand around and talk about it as Dep. Purdy moves us along to meet more inmates.

The unit's calm. Inmates are returning from early work shifts. Caroline, a trusty, enters a quiet room where we can talk. She tells me that she isn't a groupie and doesn't mix with other inmates. She does her time staying cool—working and not fighting the system.

Caroline: I was in jail for six months for a first violation, a drug charge and possession. This time it was just for a violation, five years for heroin.

You have any children?
I have a boy in Dallas. He's 13. He doesn't know where I am. I send him cards saying I'm at work, and I can't get off of my job, or I'd come and visit.

How'd you get started on drugs?
I went straight into heroin. I went to a bar when I was like 19, and the first person I went up to said, "I know where to take you." Nobody twisted my arm.

Were you using a needle?
Yeah. It seemed exciting. I've always been a little apart from people, not necessarily because of drugs, just from trying different things. Good heroin is a relaxed, speedy high. I used to have a heavy drinking problem. I went to Kaiser as an outpatient, and I stayed clean for several years. Then I broke up with some-one, the usual thing. I did some prescription drugs over the years and a little coke here and there, but other than that I didn't do heroin until I broke up with this person. I got into speed, and to get off of speed I got into heroin.

Heroin has power over you.
You just want it. Most people lie about how much they use. Most people say they have a $200-a-day habit. I haven't shot $100 a day ever. I don't believe nine out of ten people. I don't know why people choose to lie. I'm no saint, but I don't lie.

I've been married twice. My son's from my first marriage. My father has always bailed me out from jail. My mother says, "When you get off drugs, go to the airport, and call me, and I'll tell them to put it on Visa." I just can't picture myself doing normal things anymore. I don't know what it is. I don't steal. I never have. I don't like to associate with those people. You get used to something more exciting and avoid going back to something that's boring.

I'm always having thoughts and fantasies of a life that's different. At the same time I want a normal life, a straight life. But I don't like being told what to do. You hear a lot of girls talking about drugs in here. They want to use when they get out. Just because you're in jail doesn't mean you want to quit. I won't get anyplace if I don't stay straight. It's a Catch-22. There're a lot of things I want to do with my life. The things I could've done with the money I spent on drugs. I wanna get a passport. I wanna travel.

Where did you get the money to spend on drugs?
Men! I don't have too much trouble getting money from men. I mean it's not even a sex thing all the time. You get close to them, and they offer. You don't even have to ask.

Not all guys are exciting.
No. It's very degrading. I don't feel good about myself. I met them wherever a situation evolved. I had this one person I'd been seeing for four years and he's been more emotional with me. He said I had gotten almost $30,000 from him. He knows I've been in jail both of these times for drugs. He found out and still gives me money.

You think this person really loves you?
Yeah, he really loves me. I don't care about him, but at the same time I don't feel I encourage people. I don't tell them I love them. I tell them there's no future. As far as I'm concerned it's business, and it always has been business, you know. I guess a lot of people steal.

What kind of protection did you use out on the streets?
Condoms. That's the only kind of protection to use.

Did any of these guys abuse you?
I've been very lucky. I don't go out with young people, black people, very few Mexicans. I don't even talk to the girls about working on the street.

Do you worry about HIV and hepatitis?
I don't wanna give anything to anybody. It's too easy to get new needles. They say bleach works. I still don't like doing that.

How do you feel about legalizing drugs?
Why legalize? I could've gone and gotten on methadone. That's legal. I didn't. People are gonna use.

Did you experience severe withdrawal?
From alcohol. I've had four alcoholic seizures in the past. The last one was the worst nightmare of my life. DTs, shaking. I was in the UCSD hospital for three days with a 103-degree temp. I shook for a month after that. My nerves to this day are shot. My liver is borderline. I drank several bottles a day. I'd sell jewelry for alcohol. You shake. The next day you take a drink to get over the shakes. I've been obsessive-compulsive for as long as I can remember. One of anything has never been enough. I suffered horrible guilt trips from drinking. I'd drink, forget, have black-outs. You can control your drug use, but with alcohol, you'd wake up and you don't know who you're with or where you been. I'll never drink again, never. One time I woke up in the middle of the night in the woods with somebody I didn't even know. I'd been to a bar with him. I didn't even know where I met him. I was 24.

Do you think you'll change?
I think the reason a lot of people get back on drugs leaving here is the weight gain. I weigh 30 pounds more. That's one thing that's depressed me more than anything else. Even my dad, when I talked to him on Father's Day, said, "You haven't gained any weight have you?" It's always been a big deal with my parents. He wanted me to be Miss Alabama. He told me nothing I'd ever done in life had impressed him or made him happy. He's a perfectionist. One time he flew out here, and we drove to Reno where I've got relatives. I thought we had a really nice trip. He said he didn't think it was a very good trip at all. My mother used to say, "Why do you say such crazy things?" when I'd try to express my opinion. Nobody in my family on either side had ever done drugs or drinking.

You sound as if you've taken an independent path.
I have a real estate license. I remarried when my son was three years old. If my ex-husband hadn't been so excited about me being pregnant, I wouldn't have had my son. I never wanted children. My parents separated when I was about ten. My mother worked. My dad was out of town a lot. A lot of times I started getting bored in life, and I'd start looking for something.

Like getting married and having a child?
I don't have any patience with kids. I never did babysitting. I never knew how to put a diaper on 'til I had my son. I was 25. There've been times I've asked myself, "Do you really love him?" I equate

72. Inmate Caroline

it with how my parents loved me, an overflowing thing. I'm not a very emotional person or sentimental. I never wanted a girl. I was happy he was a boy. I like him because he's mine, not like other kids, but I treat him more like a little adult.

I don't like the way he's been raised because he's been given too much and been too pampered. He's growing up to be a sissy. If I had him, I'd throw him out there and let him sink or swim. When he was little, we'd walk to my father's. It'd be hot. He'd want to ride in the car. I'd make him walk with me and build up some stamina. They'd say, "Oh, let him ride." I'd get so mad. It was no different than when I was little. I was never made to make my bed. I was waited on hand and foot. It upsets me when my parents say they don't understand why I can't do certain things or pay a bill on time. Why didn't you teach me? Teach your child how to climb a mountain when he's ten years old or something. I say let him build up the confidence.

Listening to these women talk about prostitution so matter-of-factly, I realize there is unfocused history that contributes to their lack of self-image. Caroline exits and a young woman steps inside and takes a seat.

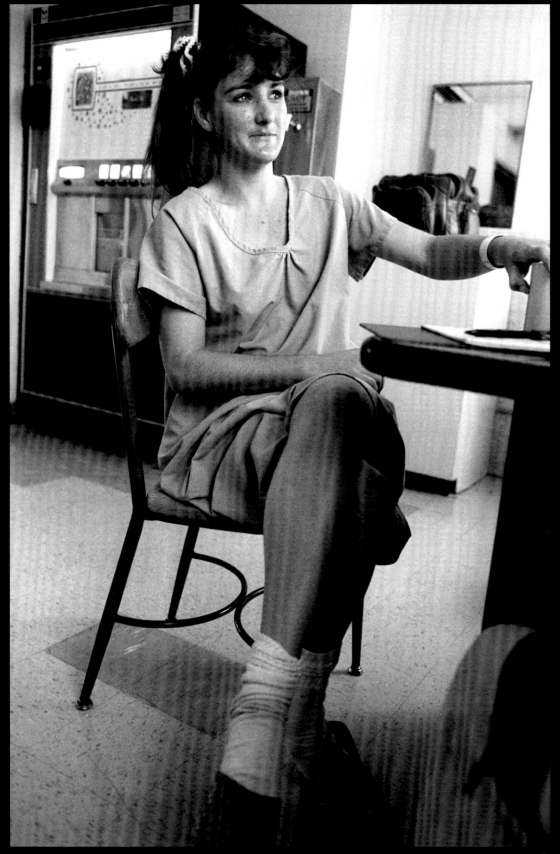

The next inmate is young. Her name is Kathy.

Kathy: Everything I'd say and do involved being around drugs. This is my third time in jail, all for the same offense. I got into trouble in '91 for violation of probation. I've been doing crystal since I was like 14. I have this problem with older guys. It just happened. My first love, everyone thought it was puppy love. I was 14 and he was 26. I used to babysit for him and his girlfriend. They were our neighbors. I felt sorry for him. The girlfriend treated him bad. It started out with my sister telling him, "Hey, you know my sister's really in love with you."

The neighbor started you on drugs?
Actually, he only did that to me like two or three times with a needle. He quit seeing me and I started using a needle without him. He'd hear about it. I was obsessed with this guy. I'd cry into a vial and save my tears. Everyone thought it was a big joke.

I never really thought using was cool because I had to hide it from everybody. I remember I was wearing long sleeves in the summertime, and everyone was staring at me, wondering.

I still have this little demon in me. I hate sleeping alone at night. It's not the sex part. I'm like the kind of person who goes to bed and likes to be held and then falls asleep knowing that someone's waiting for me out there who loves me.

That's what I feed off of. I'd never give my heart to him again. I just wish I could quit thinking about him.

73. *Inmate Kathy*

Tiffany, an inmate we met in Step Study, walks into the room as Kathy is leaving.

Tiffany: I wanted to get to talk to you in Step Study, but I couldn't. Dar was a little upset with me. I wanted to tell you that the high from drugs you can't get with anything else. The only thing you can compare it with is sex. It's the feeling I get when I'm shooting dope. When I was 16, I married a 32-year-old Hell's Angel. My sister left home at that time and joined a religious cult called God's Country. She turned over all her worldly belongings because she found family.

I went to the Hell's Angels because I found family. They took me under their wing. I developed a terrible addiction to dope, and in order to support it I had to sell it. Later, I did three years federal time, and my husband did six years. I got out, got a job, and stayed clean for five years. I remarried and had a straight life, two daughters and a beautiful home. But things fell apart two weeks after my second daughter was born. My sister was run over by a drunk driver and killed.

My parents didn't fly back to identify my sister's body. They didn't want any part of it. They didn't press charges on the drunk driver. They burned her body and threw her ashes to the wind. My parents dismiss everything. They don't care to see their two grandchildren.

I was doing real good. My second husband was using and running around while I was working. I took care of both my daughters while I worked in La Jolla at a mortgage firm. I sold everything I had and went back East with another guy. Next thing I knew this guy brought his girlfriend out there and sent me and my daughters home with nothing. I got back in town, called an old friend and said, "I wanna get high. I want to shoot dope."

My mom and dad were always fairly wealthy. They worked every day. When they weren't working, they were going on weekend vacations to Santa Isabel, San Luis Obispo, Palm Springs, wherever those little golfers are. I haven't seen a family situation. I want to tell my daughters that everything's going to be OK. It's like I still need to learn. My biggest problem that I'm learning here is not my addiction to drugs; it's my addiction to men.

74. Inmate Tiffany

"Women's self-esteem is tied up in their identity with men and their relationships with men."

Counselor Dar

1:00 p.m. F2 Patio

Inside the F2 unit we talk to Dora and Patty on the patio.

Dora: I came here from Hawaii when I was ten. I was used to farmland with a lot of cowboys, space, mountains, and beach. I'm 43. I've been locked up every year for the last three years. This will be the last time. I was 20 years old when I got locked up two years in prison. I didn't get into using until I got out of prison. My husband and I got into dealing. I haven't been in prison since '75.

I have two children, a daughter 22 and a son 24. He's doing fine. My daughter uses. She's going through the same thing I did. Last year she was up here for a month. She's immature for her age, no self-esteem. Kind of hopeless. She was molested when she was the same age I was, three or four. It's happened to her like it happened to me. With me it was my uncle. Who knows, maybe it happened to my mom, too. She loved her brothers, but maybe they got to her when she was growing up. It's secrets, you know. I'm glad my daughter could tell me, but she already has trouble with men.

Anytime I relapsed I started on alcohol. I don't connect with AA or NA. I don't have problems with groups; I just don't like walking in and talking right away. A lot of people don't like the structure of this program, but I will go from here to a sober-living house and live with other women and then look for a job.

75. Inmate Dora

1:30 p.m.   F2 Patio

Patty: I didn't think my child was going to end up in the emergency room. I didn't think someone would feed my five-year-old child dope. I didn't think I'd be incarcerated. I was woken up by my daughter tapping me, saying there were bugs all over her. She started to hallucinate. Her pupils were dilated. I got dressed, gave her a glass of milk, scooped her up, called my friend, met him at the street corner, got in the car, and went straight to Grossmont Emergency Room. As soon as I got arrested, drug friends broke into my apartment and stole all my clothes. They cut up all my blankets and everything that was in my room.

    I'm 25. I had a very abusive marriage. For five years I had a man who beat me constantly, and mentally tortured me. I was 16 when my boyfriend gave me my first dope. I thought I was dying. Since then I couldn't put the needle down. I can't have any more children either. It's rotting my body. I had kidney failure with the birth of my son. I have rotten teeth from dope. Crystal methamphetamine eats at you from the soul out.

76. Inmate Patty

Dep. J. Bilyeu quizzes us outside Patty's housing. I remember Ben McLaughlin had said that he assigned her to Stepping Out.

Dep. J. Bilyeu: That one you talked to is a breeder for the White Supremacists. She's blonde and has blue eyes and will have babies with blonde hair and blue eyes. Sounds crazy? They have to increase their population. They don't care if they can't take care of themselves. Welfare will take care of them. It's scary. A woman came in, and I said, "Are you pregnant?" And she said, "No, I just killed her," with an evil look on her face.

Then take Rolenda, she's maybe having a child just for the love. There's a mindset. They get high, and they aren't thinking about safe sex. These young people think the babies will give them love. It's sick. Some women, it's their third time here, and they should be sterilized. I'm seeing baby five or six. And the county pays for it. The kids get put in foster homes. This one girl was totally ballistic. We said, "You're in no place to take care of these children. You can't give any help to these kids until you learn to help yourself."

After F housing we run into Counselor Dar who asks us, "How's it going?"

We're finding differences in the personal motivations of inmates inside various housing units.
Dar: You must remember some of these people don't know right from wrong. The consequences led them to the criminal justice system. Psychiatrists prescribe meds, and they have clinical guidelines. I try to get across to women, after they become clean, that they're going to be stuck with the same personality they had before unless they work on that personality. A personality disorder is a thinking disorder—the way people think and perceive the world and their role in it. We have the ability to change the way we think. We just don't always have the willingness. In the case of Kristina Edwards, she's dust in the wind.

Responsibility for parenting

Most drug-abusing women offenders are of child-bearing age. Most have children, and most are single mothers. Prior to arrest, most of the women had custody of their children, as compared with about half of men involved in the criminal justice system. Many of the mothers receive little or no help from the father(s) of their children, and most of the women expect to live with their children after release from prison (Bureau of Justice Statistics, 1990, 1993). Many drug-dependent women lack supportive family and social networks and have limited financial resources. Often the children of these drug-abusing women carry their parents' childrearing practices into adulthood and frequently become drug abusers themselves, thereby perpetuating both drug abuse and dysfunctional parenting across generations (Bekir, McLellan, Childress, & Gariti, 1993; Burns & Burns, 1988).[17]

The Prison Journal

We return to the Pro Visit booth and wait for Dr. Hillary Bennett, a contract psychiatrist. She exits the sally port and heads over to our booth, carrying two coolers. We move into the private Pro Visit Room. The doctor closes the door, takes a seat, and says she has to eat lunch, as she opens the Igloo coolers. I ask her a couple of questions as she sets up her lunch of yogurt, diet soda, and cherries.

Dr. Bennett: How can I help you?

We would like to talk to some of the inmates you treat.
It's a confidentiality thing. I don't have a problem with you talking to them if they sign a release. That's OK. I work Wednesday and Thursday, and every other Saturday I come in. There's a list, and I see the people on it.

Tell us a little about your job. Your badge says that you're a volunteer?
(Looks at her breast pocket) I don't know why it says that. I work for the county. I should have one like everyone else does in mental health. I'm a psychiatrist. I don't have a private practice. I only do contract work.

So you order the meds for the inmates.
Right.

Rolenda Banks, who's at-large now, was on Thorazine in confinement.
Yeah.

She's out, probably not on prescription drugs. How does this work?
I don't know. The system works reasonably well. It would be nice if we had the facilities available here at the jail to hospitalize people, but what we need to do now is refer them to the county hospital to be hospitalized. Sometimes there are communication problems between the staff here and the staff at the hospital. They don't keep people we think they should keep. We don't have control over it.

The medication you prescribe is to help inmates survive this confinement. Does your treatment extend beyond the jail?
I'm not sure I know what you're asking me. Are you saying is there a need for extra treatment outside? First of all, I don't know if you think that everybody I see is floridly psychotic. They aren't. The most common thing I see is not being able to sleep well, or depression.

Or coming off drugs.
Well, many people are on drugs. Most people do not present themselves with a complaint of "I use drugs." They say, "I'm depressed," or "I'm nervous," or "I hear voices." Of course they comprehend that there's treatment. I give people information about places they can go to follow-up on the outside. Some people get their lives together, and some people don't.

If a woman is a repeat offender and is medicated inside, what treatment will she get outside?
I don't have any influence over what these women do when they leave here. I'm real clear from the very beginning what I can offer and what I can't offer. I'm not in a position to control other people's lives or their choices. I establish some kind of rapport and make recommendations. Then they're on their own. This is the United States. You're permitted to screw your life up completely if you wish. A lot of people do. That's what I tell them. I'm not going to get all

excited about whether or not they're going to go back to using. I can't. So, you want a cherry?

She opens her Tupperware container, offers me some fruit.

Do you see any positive results in people who leave here?
Yes, I do. Money would be a positive solution. There's a funny attitude that many staff have: the inmates don't really deserve anything. It's, "Hey, you fucked-up. You pay the price." People with any kind of authority trying to help someone feel good about herself is seen as mollycoddling, pandering, and giving into manipulations. I see that as being a big part of the solution.

There is an interruption. The psychiatric nurse approaches Dr. Bennett. The nurse questions the doctor's prescription for lithium for an inmate.

Dr. Bennett: Actually it's totally wrong. You're right. That's more like it. Thank you.

I try to ask the doctor more about Rolenda Banks. I explain that it is perplexing how someone can be sweet and compliant with us, and yet go into wild rages with the deputies. Although Banks is not the doctor's patient, the inmate is well known in the jail.

Is this like a return to childhood?
Children manipulate a lot, don't they? They manipulate for some sort of a reason. They don't do it for amusement. There's some sort of emotion or underlying need, and it doesn't mean that it's appropriate. You know she's not a child, and she's not capable of taking action. But she's expected to take responsibility for her own behavior. It's a reasonable standard. I don't know her that well. I don't want to even get into discussing her.

She's the only one we know who is on Thorazine.
She's quite an exception. She's difficult to manage. I'm not sure if that's the most helpful thing for you to do, to pick someone who stands out in the crowd. She's not representative. The person I have in mind is more representative of the large number of people in here. Rolenda's obviously ill, and she's a very primitive person in terms of her defenses: her way of thinking about things, and her way of seeing things. She's exceptionally bad in all of these areas.

That primitive thought, what does that stem from sociologically?
There're many things to consider. Consider her baseline intellectual level. How bright is she? Is she retarded? Does she have an I.Q. of 80? Then you think about how much drugs and alcohol has she done. What kind of damage have they done? The brain goes through changes that eventually can result in people losing their inhibitions and their control. Chronic alcoholics, for example, can experience this. She may never mature psychologically beyond the status of a small child, or develop adult coping mechanisms.

She was abandoned at an early age, put in an orphanage.
She's like a train wreck. In other words, everything's wrong. You can't even say, "Doctor, why did she come out this way?" It's like, who knows? If you want to focus on how to keep people out of jail...

In the case of Rolenda. . .
Forget her!

Just to put a closure on our concern—is it a case where she'll end up in a mental hospital?
Or dead.

I believe in civil liberties for people. To take away someone's civil liberties, you have to have a damn good reason. Just because you don't like the way she happens to be living her life, you can't impose change. A person has to be literally incompetent. People who are chronic drug users or schizophrenics aren't necessarily incompetent. But someone like Rolenda, I don't know. I think her prognosis is very poor and I think that if we want to talk about what can we do to make things better, I think it's a waste of time to talk about her.

The jail introduced her to us. She was attentive and non-threatening.
(Laughter) She attracts a lot of attention. She's more of a maintenance type. You should put your energies into maintaining her in a condition in which she's as functional as possible, where she's not suffering, where people around her can get their work done. She's a maintenance issue. On the outside, she'll be a maintenance issue. There are a lot of people inside who aren't in that category. There are a lot of people here where things can be done.

They can learn to get into self-help groups?
The waiting lists are way too long. You're talking four-to-six weeks. When somebody's in here for spousal abuse and can't get into the domestic violence class for six weeks, they go right back to what they came from. That's absurd.

They get into the convict-inmate thing?
They have nothing to do. There's no corrective experience for a long time. It's money that it boils down to, isn't it? I'm sure you realize that mental health doesn't get much priority.

There's going to be even more of a need with crack babies.
Depression might be the presenting complaint, but the real problem is personality disorders, people with borderline personality disorders. I'd say it's the single diagnosis that describes people who don't have what it takes inside to say, "I'm going to go help myself." Being able to determine their destiny or future isn't in there. People have to get away from the mentality that they're helpless, that they have to constantly be searching for somebody to fix them, or some medicine to fix them, or some drug to fix them.

Feel better . . . get high?
Even when they say, "OK, I don't want to get high anymore, I want to get well," they still don't understand. The power's within them. We have to teach people.

We should teach our young children.
I think decent parents do. Parents who have it transfer it. Take the kid who's getting molested or beaten at home and the rest of the family's in or out of jail, prostituting, or doing drugs. Put the kid in a little drug education class in school? That's not going to change their reality. Basically, it's going to make them feel more isolated. I don't think it's going to make much difference. I try not to think about drugs so much from the big social picture. I don't worry about that too much. I'm not driven to mentally work on a solution for the big picture. I have my little piece that I can do and that's what I do.

We discuss a date to work in Sick Call. The doctor wants us to learn about other issues and not focus on Rolenda.

78. Sally port door

I talk to the lieutenant and ask her to talk about serious offenders, some of whom we've met.

Lt. Milakovich: You were saying the DA said some people are just bad. Did you ever see *The Bad Seed*? No matter what you do or what you try, some people are just not gonna comply. In the movie, a little girl wanted a penmanship medal that another kid won. It irked her and she took off her shoes and beat his head and shoulders until he fell off the pier. No one could figure out how he died. She was a perfect little girl when you looked at her. She answered her mother politely, yet the groundskeeper found her bloody shoes. He went to her at the piano where she played the same tune over and over and told her he'd found the shoes. She clubbed him and set fire to his room and went back to the piano.

Or take the publicized story of the three teens who tooled around with a paraplegic and got high. They started going, "Does this hurt?" They were putting cigarettes out on his legs, making little cuts to get a reaction, hitting him. Then they dumped and left him for dead.

I was trained in the academy to consider these personalities as volatile and capable of doing violent crimes. We've come across a grandmother type who'll blow you out of your socks. I don't think women have always been doing the serious crimes that we see today, but they're getting more independent. They don't need to rely on a guy to carry out criminal acts. In general, human life means so much less. Today kids see actors get shot in movies, and the next day they see the same person in another movie. "There's really no danger to me." There's no fair fight like in *High Noon*. Nobody in the corral or having a sword fight where someone says, "I may not have this fight."

79. Polly Doll

MINIMUM SECURITY

As I read the stories of these women, it strikes me that this book is about hatred, the damage that incompetent, cruel parents can inflict, the responsibility of society and the responsibility of the individual. A baby girl is born with an innate ability to love and to be aggressive. She needs the energy of her aggression to master the skills and knowledge she must have to become a civilized and productive member of her community. She also needs the soothing caress of love to learn to be kind to herself and make an attachment to her caretakers. Her innate love and aggression must come together to create a balance so that her aggression does not become pure destruction, and her love does not become pure hedonism. To accomplish this enormously complicated feat, the little girl will need the love of a caretaker with whom she can build a stable, consistent, and long-term relationship. It is the caretaker who will allow her to experience just enough frustration to develop emotional stamina, but not so much as to become overwhelmed. It is the caretaker who will build the little girl's self-esteem by helping her to achieve and then admire her achievement.[18]

Maryam Razavi Newman, Ph.D.

Confinement

The place is cold and dark. The staff seems disingenuous at times. There is an understood voice—the public—everywhere. And I feel as guilty as if I had committed a crime by the mere fact I am inside. The staff treats me as if I am guilty of some crime. "This doesn't happen," the sergeant told me. "We don't let cameras and tape recorders in here. You're invading a privacy." Power.

Inmates squealing and staff talking about the dead end. The system doesn't want to recover. It's a thriving business with protective walls. The judges control one center. The sheriff's department acts respectfully, but does whatever it pleases with the inmates it jails.

Jail is a holding tank. It houses all the broken-down dolls who were objects to so many abusive family members, spouses, even themselves. They are lacking the tools to sustain themselves outside of the criminal justice system. The big bucks we spend on their incarceration are not changing them.

80. F housing fence

The mind is more vulnerable
than the stomach, because it
can be poisoned without
feeling immediate pain.[19]

Helen MacInnes

My assistant, Barbara Jackson, meets me at 6:00 a.m. There's no traffic on Highway 52. A dense fog changes our mood as we chat about Kristina Edwards and her upcoming trial. We drop into Santee. It's 60 degrees at 6:30 a.m. By noon it'll be 90. At the jail, a mist covers the ground. The air is fresh.

7/28/95 6:30 a.m. Sally port

We're told to go to the minimum-security yard exit and push the red button on the door. Once we arrive at the door, the clerk shouts out through the speaker to "Push the button now!"

Clerk: Turn the knob. You're on your way.

Outside, the housing units are packaged neatly, patios empty. Through the windows we see bodies lying asleep on bunks. A couple of birds chirp. An eager trusty approaches us, headed for the main jail with her hands obediently tucked inside her pants. She directs us to the kitchen where Carmen, the chief of staff for the kitchen, waits for us at the entrance.

The nation's prison industry now employs nearly three-quarters of a million people, more than any Fortune 500 corporation, other than General Motors. Hundreds of prison-generated products end up attached to trendy and nationally-known labels. After deductions, many prisoners . . . earn about $60 for an entire month of nine-hour days.[20]

New America Media

81. Minimum-security yard sidewalk;
82. F housing

83

Carmen: You're late. You missed it all. Deliveries and clean-up are done. We're getting ready for inspection, but I can give you a little cook's tour. I used to cook in big kettles, making macaroni and cheese, the à la king right there. I'd cook the meat and everything from scratch. I've been here for 13 years. But now the food is cooked in a bag at the central kitchen in Otay Mesa, where they do a procedure called "chill-blast." The food arrives here in trays and immediately goes into our refrigerators. It can stay there for up to six weeks. Only lunch is prepared here at Las Colinas, mostly bologna and cheese sandwiches, or what we call "circles and squares."
The count today is 518 just for this jail. We got diets for diabetics, low salt, even gastric-soft. Also, we have clear liquids when they're kicking. Ladies kick coming off drugs. They're throwing up, and so we give Ensure a lot. It takes a doctor's order to change a diet. To get everybody fed, it takes a 16-hour day. For the main jail, breakfast is at 6:30 a.m., lunch 10:30 a.m., and dinner at 4:30 p.m.

Do you have personality conflicts among the trusty workers?
They fight with each other. They're lazy and slow. Every day we push. It's like pushing a piano, and the turnover is a killer. You train them, and another drug charge arrives. I have to be right there with my girls. I got my salad girl chopping vegetables for the staff lunch line, and I have to remind them we're at Las Colinas. They'll make a party out of everything. They're adult women who act like little kids. We pick out the responsible ones right away to be a cook. If it wasn't for my cooks, I couldn't run the place. They're the ones I can trust.

Carmen introduces us to trusty inmate Esperanza, who is carving into a side of beef for the staff lunch.

Have you ever been hurt by an inmate?
Carmen: No. But I've been threatened by female deputies! They say they won't take care of me if I don't take care of them! I say, "I'm not afraid." They think that because they're correctional officers they can tell me when they want to eat. "No, no," I tell them, "You go to momma's and raid her kitchen. I've been here for too long." Staff meals are served from the 1100 to 1300 hour. The inmates take liberties and put stuff in their pockets, like lemons and milk for facials.
It's all about drugs and the hold drugs have over them. They have babies and more babies, drugs and bad relationships; so much pain.
This is the cold storage.

If it wasn't for my cooks, I couldn't run the place. They're the ones I can trust.

Kitchen chief of staff,
Carmen

84

85

We follow Carmen inside the walk-in refrigerator. Freezing cold air blows over us. Carmen pulls a tray off one of the baker's racks and points out a sample breakfast of white bread, creamed eggs, and oatmeal.

Carmen: Zucchini and rice tonight. Tomorrow they're having peanut butter, oatmeal, and grits. This is Saturday's. Here's Sunday's breakfast: scrambled eggs, ham, and bread. We heat this in the ovens. This tray will be zapped before it is delivered to the unit. It takes careful planning.

83. Carmen; 84. Trusty Esperanza;
85. Refrigerators

86

We leave the kitchen and re-enter the yard. The sun has broken through the early overcast skies. Santee is baking. Carmen directs us to the food hall across from F housing where deputies direct the breakfast line-up. One of the inmates turns away from the line and vomits in front of us on the sidewalk. Barbara jumps to the side.

Carmen: That girl's kicking heroin. The inmates will have to clean it up. Watch. It'll happen fast. Clean-up's very important around here. Girls are kicking all the time. They still have to go to the food hall, sick or not.

Inside the food hall, five deputies share private jokes as the women receive food trays from the cafeteria line and file off to tables and benches in orderly fashion. Breakfast is short and quick.

86-87. Minimum-security breakfast line-up;
88. Trusty worker clean-up

87

88

There are many reasons for the growing numbers of women in the criminal justice system, but the primary one is the increase in drug-related convictions and the advent of mandatory sentences for these offenses.

The issues of addicted women are, for the most part, invisible in the criminal justice system. Historically, treatment, research, and recovery have been based on the male experience, often neglecting women's needs. While this neglect has a serious impact on women and treatment programs in the free world, the problem is magnified for women in the criminal justice population.[21]

Stephanie Covington, Ph.D.

89

91

92

93

90

Back in F3, several inmates call us over to the fence.

Stokes: Come over here!
Lorinda: Yeah, we want to talk to you.

Stokes and Lorinda linger at the fence. They want to complain about Dep. Barnes, the deputy on duty.

Lorinda: I said the "f" word and the sergeant took away my stores for three weeks.
Stokes: Yeah, their commissary, that's all they got to look forward to in here. Look at them now standing around and waiting. Today is delivery.

Dep. Barnes moves in.

Dep. Barnes: No, it isn't.
Stokes: Yes it is! It's Tuesday.
Dep. Barnes: Doesn't come on Tuesday.
Stokes: Does too! You don't know. You been on another yard. Look, there's the truck!

Stokes turns away from Dep. Barnes.

Stokes: We like Harper. Barnes is a butthead. The commissary guys have been here in the morning for the last four weeks, and Barnes won't listen to any of us. The girls want their candy. Some of them only have six dollars to spend. It means a lot.

Women jam the fence with excitement.

Lorinda: There's too much homosexuality in here. If you go to the bathroom at two in the morning, you see one girl giving another cunnilingus. When you open a bathroom stall, they're doing it. They try not to do it on the cots 'cause they'll get written up.
Stokes: The deputies are glorified babysitters. They don't like their job, and it shows. They're so disgusted and frustrated that their only excitement is a good fight. They could actually be helping people. Instead there's no change. It's a revolving door.
Daisy: Drugs? Mine is cocaine. My first time in jail was for forgery, using credit cards. I was at Nordstrom's and got caught with $5,000 of gift certificates. I had all the information on the person and called it in. I had the person's checks, driver's license, everything. Somebody I know gets ahold of people's purses and wallets, and I buy things from $100 spread for The May Company, Robinsons, Nordstrom's, plus Visa and MasterCards. This time I'm in for violating probation on a drug charge. I got a year. I have a newborn baby, too. He's five months old today. Next time I'll go to prison for two years.
Elaine: I been in 13 or 14 times. I've been using heroin since I was 14 years old. I'm getting methadone now, and it gets into your bones and the back of your legs hurt real bad. Chocolate and sugar helps you kick.
Lorinda: This is my second arrest in a month for grand theft auto and forgery. I was with some people who did the crime. It's a felony now. I can't even vote. I'll miss my kid's birthday and her going to kindergarten. I'm not in here for drugs, although I do drugs, never IV,

I just smoked crystal and heroin or I ate it, or snorted it. I turned 21 in jail. I have done drugs since I was ten years old.

Stokes introduces Constance, an inmate who's bent over with her arms pressed tightly over her stomach. She's kicking heroin. Barbara talks to another group of inmates. It's hard to hear the women when everyone wants to talk into the recorder and tell her story.

Constance: I came here and couldn't hold anything down, and in this heat everybody gives me their juice. Ameerah rubbed me down with BenGay. They know what you're going through.
You've been using drugs a long time?
Constance: Yeah, I'm 39. I started when I was 21. I never wanted to do drugs. I'd get so mad at my boyfriend for using that I'd flush balloons of drugs down the toilet. Then one day, after my first son was born, I got bored and it took the edge off. Now I have an 18-year-old and two sets of twins, 16 and 8. Both sets are with my mom and sister.
Lucky your mom's helping.
Constance: No, she's a bitch. We don't have a relationship. She took 'em 'cause she wants the welfare money. I never had a loving relationship with her because my father abused me when I was young. I had a big fight with her before I came in 'cause she knew about it and never did nothing. He did it to my sister, too. Now I'm scared for my daughters. He did it to my niece. I tell my daughters, "Don't let grandpa touch you."

94

95

Have you confronted him?

Constance: My mom stood up for him when I told her. Now my children live with him.

Has he been reported?

Constance: Yes, by the people across the street, because he did it to their daughter when she was little. But then, when the counselor came to see my father, my sister-in-law told them I had abandoned my kids. Now I can't have my kids.

Lorinda: Women never believe their husbands molested their daughters. I have eight brothers. I know.

Sheila moves into the group at the fence.

Sheila: I was in for burglary. I got two new cases. My drug of choice is crystal. I started doing drugs after I had my youngest son.

How many children do you have?

Sheila: I got a 13-year-old plus a set of nine-year-old twins. I haven't seen them for five years. They're with my ex-husband. My youngest is seven.

Is your mom alive now?

Sheila: I guess, I'm not sure. I was sexually abused by her boyfriends. I'm hoping to get some kind of help for myself, and I want my oldest and youngest back. I want to see my twins.

They're safe?

Sheila: Oh yes, they're better off right now 'cause I was stuck in a pattern.

Are you doing a better job than your mom did?

Sheila: No. I totally abused my oldest girl. My oldest is 13 and my ex abused her.

How did he abuse your 13-year-old?

Sheila: From my own knowledge, he fucked her.

Was he the father?

Sheila: No, stepfather. I thought he was just abusing me. I get SSI (Supplemental Security Income), because I'm mentally disturbed. I got a slight learning disability. I got dyslexia. But I have a twin sister, and she's mentally retarded. We weren't raised together. I was in a foster home. I was abused as a little kid. I have a temper and I just go off. My oldest brother hit me and my foster mom beat me. I got a broken breastbone from when I was under three.

What does love mean to you?

Sheila: Now love means a lot, but until four years ago I had all hatred in me. When I had my oldest, I held her in my arms and cried for hours. Once I went off on her. I hit her. She's with her grandparents, and she's a straight-A student. She's in the eighth grade and I'm proud of her. She don't wanna come back with me. Her dad abused me. He was drunk all the time. I left him for her stepfather. He's got the twins, and I haven't seen them in five years. It's hard for me to accept love. I've got a fiancé right now who treats me real good.

Your fiancé is on drugs?

Sheila: He was. He's in prison right now.

You still care for him?

Sheila: He cares for me. I have to have the help. It was hard for me to show my kids love. My youngest worshipped me, and I pushed him away. My oldest kid feels rejected.

Can you work on SSI?

Sheila: No, I can't work. I'm not that smart. I'm not that good at reading or writing. I read backwards. It's hard for me to understand. I got like a third-grade level. What I'm really good at is cleaning house. I'm taking meds, so they won't clear me for no trusty job. I could be looking at two years and eight months in prison.

Stokes: After the women come in here a couple times, they end up in prison 'cause the crimes get worse. Deputies could break this pattern in here with

programs and education, and then I think the deputies wouldn't be so hardened. I look at these women, and they're children. They aren't much older than my daughter, yet mentally a lot of them are 20 going on 12. I mean, they really want you to read to them. They rock themselves to sleep. They suck their thumbs to go to sleep or to watch TV. As for me, my ex showed up here twice trying to get me five years time. He claimed I was stalking him, and out to kill him. I had to take a third psychological evaluation, a nine-hour test over two days here. Of course it proved the same thing the other two proved: there's nothing wrong with me. I'm not violent. I'm just a typical mom. The judge gave me the maximum she could give me for breaking the court order because I wanted to see my kids. Now I got to do a year.

Is it hard to sleep at night?

Lorinda: You can't sleep in here 'til 2:00 a.m. 'cause there's people talking.

Stokes: I've been getting them quiet earlier because I walk the floor until everyone calms down and goes to sleep. There's no lights at night.

Becky: I have slept three hours a night since I got here. I'm not used to sleeping with 30 people. I sleep with one person, and that's it. He doesn't make a whole lot of noise. These people snore and talk in their sleep. They moan and cry, and grind their teeth. It drives me crazy.

Other inmates from the next patio cry out.

96

97

Margene: They overcrowd it! People sleep on the floor. I've been here before. I stole a bottle of lice shampoo for my daughter and got arrested for petty theft with a prior.

Dakota: I found maggots in my sweet potatoes last week. The other morning they gave us stuff called "cream of eggs." It was eggs with water.

The chaplain, a dour woman in her 70s, pushes a cart of Bibles and stops to explain her feelings about women in jail.

Chaplain: There are women in here who have no right to be here. They get thrown in jail so they don't have to pay for the pregnancy. If they'd only stop their sassing the deputies. It's hot and muggy, and they get into trouble. Women are so demanding. I don't think men get better treatment, they just don't fight back all the time. In the Book of Genesis the command was given to Adam to not eat of the tree in the midst of the garden for the day. You eat, you will die a spiritual death, not a physical one. Then God created Eve, and I'm sure Adam told Eve all about this: don't eat from the tree. So they're out in the garden strolling, and Satan tells Eve to take the fruit and take a bite, and she hands it to her husband. His place as the man of authority was to say: Eve, don't eat. God told us not to do it. He didn't. So ever since that time woman has tried to rise against man and there's this constant battle. Just take a look at it. I didn't go to school to learn that, I just read the word, and I say that's the problem.

89. Inmate Stokes; 90. Inmates Lorinda and Elaine; 91. F housing inmates; 92. Inmate Lorinda; 93. Deputy Barnes; 94. Inmate Constance; 95. Inmate Sheila; 96. Inmate Dakota; 97. Inmate Margene

Carmen told me to check out landscaping. O running trusties maintain what little lawn there is, rotate the compost, and grow vegetables and fruit trees.

98-101. Trusty workers in landscaping
102. (opposite page) Landscaping

11:00 a.m. Pro Visit

We return to the Pro Visit booths.

I step up to Control and tell the clerk we're ready to see Edwards and would like to talk to Sal Quigley, the counselor. The clerk denies my request and says, "Next." An attorney standing behind me steps up to the window.

Attorney: My client has no money on her books. She swallowed Drano. She has kidney stones and cancer. She's been shooting heroin for eight years.
Clerk: The inmate has to pay three dollars for medical. Next . . .

Once again I step up to the window and repeat my request.

Clerk: Sally can't talk now.

The clerk closes the window. A sergeant appears. The clerk reopens the window to hear what the sergeant is telling me.

Sgt: You can't wander around here like this. I'll call a deputy to assist. Have a seat and wait.
Clerk: She wants Edwards. I'll have Harper get Edwards.

Dep. Harper hears the clerk and steps into the conversation.

Dep. Harper: I'm not working B housing.
Clerk: Get Edwards anyway.

I return to my Pro Visit booth. I see an inmate sitting on the Intake bench, looking pretty bad. She has a black eye. A deputy hands her a clear trash bag, and the woman vomits into the bag. Dep. Harper, on her way to get Edwards, stops by Pro Visit to tell us what happened to the sick inmate.

Dep. Harper: You wanna check in the jail like that girl did? Tell you what you do. After you commit your crime and get arrested, you pull a gun on an officer.

The sick inmate passes our booth with her face in the garbage bag, sick again.

Dep. Harper: The officer gave her a dot in the eye instead of killing her, so she's lucky. Another one came in the sally port, got her handcuffs on and slugged one of us. I guarantee you, that's one way to be noticed. Guess I'll get Edwards for you.

The attorney who tried to get medical help for his client sits with her in the next booth. Edwards is correct. People hear things in the jail. I hear the woman say she had left the house drunk with her two kids, got in the car, and committed a hit-and-run. Now she's up for murder.

Dep. Harper arrives with Edwards. She looks drained. Her hair is greasy. She continues to gain weight, has no muscle tone, and walks with a lethargic drop-shoulder gait.

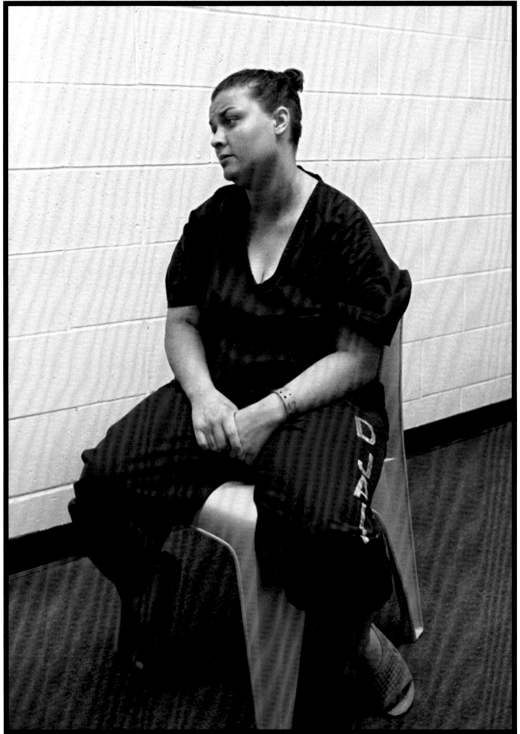

103. Inmate Edwards

11:30 a.m. Kristina Edwards

Edwards: I got four more charges at my arraignment. How come you weren't there?

I thought it was going to be a five-minute procedure.
It was, but they brought up new charges, and they're considering the death-penalty for all of us!

What was the judge's name?
I wasn't paying attention. I was too busy crying. I got murder, torture, conspiracy, special circumstances, and my codefendants got murder, torture, special circumstances, conspiracy, and kidnapping. We go August 23rd to find out if it'll be a death-penalty case. I'm just saying for a fact we're not guilty of all of those charges. I most likely will have to take it to trial and risk getting convicted. There's some people on the outside saying that the boys told them that I came back, all puffed up, bragging about it.

Are they friends of yours?
They were supposed to be.

Were Ryan and Bellows present?
Yeah. They were standin' right behind me. I just wanna find my mom.

Is Alex trying to locate her?
I don't think so. I haven't talked to her for so many years.

Where do you think she lives?
Last I heard, it was something called Beaver, California.

12:00 p.m.   Dr. Jim Bull

A tall, lean, middle-aged man with white hair, wearing jeans and a starched, blue-and-white, striped shirt, turns up at the opposite end of the corridor, holding a clipboard. He's Dr. Jim Bull, staff psychologist. We've noticed him on a number of occasions. He frequently takes a booth behind ours to interview inmates. This time, in a relaxed manner, he nods and stops.

Dr. Bull: Mind if I ask what exactly you're doing?

We explain, telling him we'd like to talk to him.

Dr. Bull: I'd be delighted to shed any light.

He warns that the jail is a pretty sad and often dead-end place to be, to work, or to be incarcerated. Bull, who holds Ph.D.s in both sociology and psychology, has years of experience in jails and prisons. He once worked in the worst men's prison in California, Vacaville. He joins us and talks openly about the inmates and how he sees them.

Inmates have mood swings often. They feel empty, alone, lost. They tend to reach out and cling to something to give them an anchor. These people have very intense relationships, and find somebody who is like a container. Then they pour themselves into the container and take that shape. They idealize that person. They find the love of their life, their savior. But it won't last long. Something will spoil it, and they'll feel betrayed again. The same thing happens again and again. Mood swings, emptiness, intense brief relationships. We call them borderline personalities.

Is this caused by a lack of bonding?
Yes. A lot of these women have severe drug habits. They've lived in such pain that to survive they require an anesthetic. They live with shame that's so extraordinary it drives them to the drug abuse. People are getting high from drugs with profound depression underneath it. I tend to see major depression and lots of abuse going on for years. Before I got this job I wouldn't have believed the stories of abuse and mistreatment. One woman was beaten, locked up in her bathroom for two days, until she jumped out of a window and ran naked down the alley to save herself. The brutality—deputies will tell us that inmates write that they're losing their minds, crying all the time, and talking to the lamppost. Some are detoxing from heroin or alcohol. Some are suicidal. Some are long term and may have a treatment history of 20 years. An incredible crisis, a divorce, a fight with her husband, and she stabs him. Some are terribly needy, and some very psychiatric. There's a diverse mix.

These are difficult issues. What can be done during incarceration to change the dynamics?
I don't even know how long my job will last. They're talking about moving the psych and having all counseling go to psychiatric meds. That'll be sad. We've worked hard to create a unit, E housing, where therapeutic work can be done. My God, I talked to a woman the other day who had been molested by her father from ages two and twenty-two. He fondled her up to the age of 16. Some of these women have incurred abuse since childhood. At a certain point they get on drugs to alleviate the pain, and we call that a cop-out? There's a survival mechanism in people, and it is more than merely using drugs to make things feel better.

When does it begin?
Young kids who are abused tend to blame themselves. So there's a sorting-out process for attributing causes, believing oneself, and eventually forgiving parents who aren't prepared to be parents in the first place. They had no clue and/or were overwhelmed by everything. They retreated to anesthesia. I come across women whose children's fathers are also the grandfathers. We disown the most impoverished levels of our society and create something that's deliberate. Still, I guess most people don't have a clue how horrific the injuries are that others have suffered. I talked to a woman who had been raped as a kid. The guy found her too tight, so he took a hunting knife and opened her up for entry. I saw her 30 years after this happened. She was still trying to work through this. We're talking about permanent disability!

How do these personalities fare with the deputies?
There's some deputies who have wonderful reputations among the inmates, and I'm sure that there are deputies who get really abusive with inmates as well. I'm sure that a hell of a lot of what goes on I never see. The other day a deputy was really cussing out an inmate in the Safety Cell. I was surprised when she said, "Dr. Bull, turn your head." Both of them continued to swear back and forth in mutual disgust. I wasn't surprised that it happened, but I was surprised that it happened in my presence. I was the observer. Yet that's the kind of behavior inmates are very willing to tell you about.

Shelby Roland had a different effect on staff.
Shelby Roland is narcissistic, self-inflated, very pathological to the point of unreality. She's very skilled, attractive, bright as hell, and she's a hell of a schemer. I almost get the impression that after she laid out this scam, she actually believed it herself, and it's her own belief in it that makes it absolutely convincing.

I don't even know how long my job will last. They're talking about moving the psych and having all counseling go to psychiatric meds. That'll be sad. We've worked hard to create a unit, E housing, where therapeutic work can be done.

Jim Bull, Ph.D.

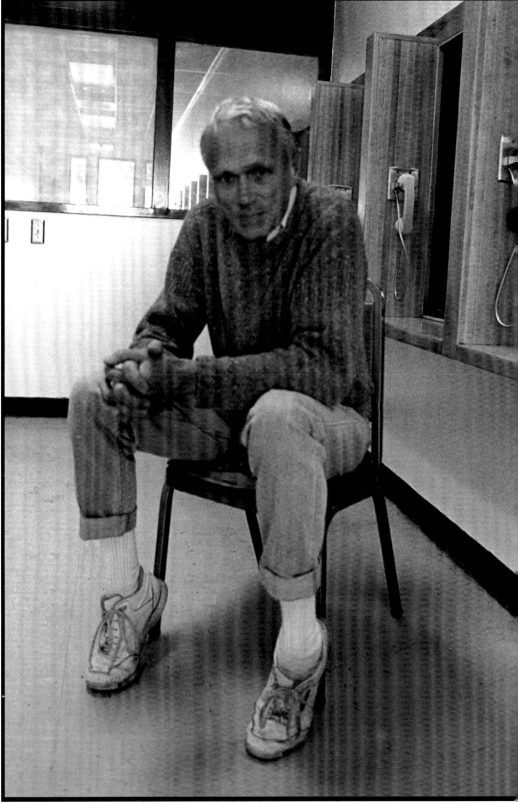

104. Dr. Jim Bull

106

7/31/95 F Housing

Workmen are on the roof adding more razor wire. Stokes spots me and cries out, "Hey, where you been?" Stokes is the housemother for F3. She yells at inmate Delano to get out of her nightclothes.

108

105

Ameerah: I have a good story!

107

Stokes: Delano's a homosexual pain in the butt. She goes to everybody's bed, pussy to pussy, in the hall. Miss Washington woke up with Delano next to her in the bed and yelled, "What're you doing?" These women don't even cover-up what they do. Plus, she's a whiner.

A new face comes to the fence. She introduces herself as Ameerah Muhammad.

Ameerah: Come closer. I have a story for you. Listen to me!
Stokes: A pussy is not my thing. I'm close to the other housemother, but I don't feel like kissing on her. I don't feel like holding her hand or like climbing in her bed to cuddle, even though we sleep right next to each other.
Ameerah: Please. I have a real good story.
Stokes: Lots of these women are lesbians when they're in jail. They were abused by men. They're all looking for love and attention. It goes on outside the jail, but in here it's more open. I've never been to jail before so I didn't know about this going on. There's a woman who just had her sixth baby. She's only gay in jail!

Lorinda: I like your jeans. What are they? Turn around and let me see the label.

Jennifer stops outside F housing to say she's a trusty worker now. She asks a woman inside the fence when she had her baby. "The baby's with CPS." Her other kids are 22, 18, 16, 10, and 5 years of age. The last one is four days old. She was 15 when she had her first child.

Ameerah: Believe me, I have a good story. I was married four times. I'm still tore up. Find a bush to sit by. Let's make this good!

Another inmate, Becky, talks about the irritations of living in a dorm, the lack of sleep. A fourth inmate, Francis, stands behind Ameerah, listening.

Ameerah: My story's interesting. I was raped, held hostage, tied-up and put in a closet. I went into a coma. My husband died in bed. I went into shock and was institutionalized for 30 days at a mental hospital. My body went into denial. I didn't believe he was dead.

Becky: I was the committee chairman for Santana High's grad night. I borrowed $1,200 to pay my tax penalties. I raised the money within a week and still got charged with grand theft. They said I took $3,100! I was a good person that did a bad thing and got railroaded. I missed my daughter's wedding. My son moved out of the house. He's so angry and confused. He doesn't understand why I'm so revengeful. It's killing me.
What's it like living in a small space with all of these women?
Becky: It drives me crazy. I'm a very quiet person.
Ameerah: She screams!
Becky: I get angry and internalize it. I don't scream at people, Ameerah!
Ameerah: You scream! Why do you all make fun of screaming!

110

A pregnant woman on the next patio, F2, paces. A cat slithers in front of her along the outside of the fence with a rabbit clenched between its jaws. I follow the cat. Confusion and shouting breaks out from the patios.

Stokes: Quick! Get your camera. She's nine months pregnant, and they're taking her to Lockdown!

The deputies pull in tighter as the shouting builds. The cat drops the flaccid rabbit to adjust its grip. Deputies shout at other deputies. "What happened?" Inmates shout. I watch the posture of the thin, scrawny, hunter cat as he proudly drags his prey. Twisting fluidly, the cat wraps himself around the end of one gate and escapes through the narrow space between the front and the back gate. Outside the jail yard, he drops the fresh kill, long enough to nuzzle it and lick it.
 The inmates continue yelling.

Stokes: You missed it? What's wrong with you? This was your chance to see them hauling Arlynn away. She's going to Lockdown and her baby's due!

I step back to F2 thinking about the rabbit, probably pregnant and dead.

111

105. Inmate Stokes; 106. Inmate Delano; 107. Inmate Ameerah; 108. Inmates Lorinda and Becky; 109. Inmate Arlynn; 110-112. Cat carrying rabbit

112

I have a real good story for you.

Inmate Ameerah

Ameerah: I cut their hair, make them feel pretty, and touch them—massage their temples, the back of their necks. I relax them because I know how they feel. They're hurting. I have them stop at my bed. They come in turns. They want me to touch them, feel them and rub their hair, listen to them. It's the gift that separates us from animals. We don't run on instinct. Animals get whatever is available. I can go as high as I want spiritually, or I can make a conscious decision to take on a spiritual death. We're the only animals that choose to commit suicide. We've been blessed with a power. I did cocaine, marijuana, and alcohol as a painkiller. Now they give me over-the-counter medication. I don't have to get trapped in manic depression. I have to take this story from the beginning. You know what it's like to hold something back and be fake?

Let me tell you. I was a nine-seat-barbershop owner in Atlanta. Five kids, married to an accountant who was in the military. We had a beautiful home. I never imagined life could take such a twist. I was a vegetarian, very spiritual, fasting and doing prayers. I ate organically-grown food I grew. I was going to save the world, and the world I needed to save was my own. Let's not go too fast. I'm gonna get confused. Psychiatrists have my files sealed! I was very happy. It all turned two years ago. Devastating.

I was a normal housewife and used to sing in dance clubs. I loved life. Crazy about everything good! An extremist. I don't eat mucous-forming foods like white flour, white sugars. Mucous is the highest killer. It kills more than drugs, heart attacks, and strokes. Food causes more disease and destruction. No pork! That's nasty, very slimy. I got a bachelor's degree in agriculture, from Spellman. I'm very educated. My father and mother were divorced. He crossed the line and married a white woman. He died last month.

Wait, I can do this in seven minutes. I went to beauty school. Let me tell you what happened. My husband died in the bed! He had a brain tumor. Before he died, he didn't know he had the tumor. The doctor said it was from Agent Orange. His personality changed. He put a gun to my head and told the children to drink my blood. He made me make him scrambled eggs on top of apple pie with cheese. Every morning he got me up at 5:00 a.m. to fix his dinner, but he had lost his mind. We didn't have any idea why he was out to lunch. I really loved him.

He became impotent with the tumor. He couldn't make love to me no more. He came to my job and beat me, threw hot water on me, and said I was fucking another man. That night, I saw him walking home in the snow. I was so happy. I went out and hugged him. I fixed him something to eat and took him to bed and he made love for real. He didn't just mouth me with no erection. Everything was normal and life was back. I was happy and then I woke and he was real wild. I was holding him. I tried to fix him. He had blood coming from his nose, ears, and eyes. All of his orifices. I tried to clean him. They said I went into shock. I wouldn't believe he was dead.

Where were your children?

Don't skip through this story. My oldest boy called the paramedics. He was the one who pulled me off of my husband. Paramedics put him in a body bag, zipped him up, and covered his head. When they covered his head, that's when I fell apart. "Don't zip up his head. He won't be able to breathe in there." They put me in the hospital and tranquilized me. I was unable to go to the funeral.

Everything started falling apart. I never used drugs. I saw a man at a bus stop. I felt like I was dying. I asked him for a smoke. I wanted some drugs. I wanted to die. I increased my life insurance policy. I wanted to be murdered. That way my kids would have double money, and I wouldn't have to live here no more. I smoked a joint laced with drugs. I had no knowledge that this world ever existed. If you have no reason to use these drugs, you have no reason to learn about these drugs. They don't exist for you. You see people on the television use the drugs and regular people watch them, but it doesn't mean a thing. It was an instant pain reliever, instant memory loss.

The reason it's an epidemic in this country is that it doesn't last and you have to keep buying more. It destroys the country's economics. It takes away morality! It gives you the feeling of a climax. You can go to bed with anybody, honey. You can, under the influence. Yes, you can go to bed with a woman! It attacks the pleasure center. It breeds homosexuality with men, too. It takes you to the most exotic place in your mind. It takes the defenses down. Some people can't live with themselves after they do it. I used the drug until I lost everything. I got involved then with drug dealers. At night the barbershop was a drug store. I was out there, feeling sorry for myself. A white man, Sunshine, dated me. I was a prostitute. He talked to me all night. He told me to heal my wounds.

OK, back to the rape . . . I didn't care if I died or not. This was a different pain. It was a physical pain. They were going to take me out of my body. They checked me off of this plane of consciousness. They gagged me. I met them buying $10 of crack. I was a nonfunctioning addict at this time and no longer making $900 a week. I felt sorry for myself. I wanted crack. They tied my hands but not my feet. They took the high away, they slapped me so hard. I was bleeding down my shirt. They taped my body. At first I wanted to do drugs and sex, but once it started, it got to be hours of sexing me. They tore my pubic hairs out. They were abusive, oral-sexing me, biting me, real cruel things, put me in a closet.

She takes a breath and pauses to explain her manic-depressive warning.

Feels like you're going to cry when you've got a manic-depressive episode. Breathe real slow and you can walk past it. When you're an extremist you constantly get stuck. It's good for me to have these feelings. Let me get through this. They uncuffed me, and the lady said, "We'll kill you!" I said, "Fuck, I'm already dead." I ran outside. I was so fucking dirty with blood. I never knew that pain in my life. It was worse than having a baby. I drank a bottle of Cisco, very awful wine, and it made me violent. I started throwing things at their windows. The man came out and broke my nose. I was mental. I wanted to kill them. By the time the police got me I was in a pool of blood. They thought I was dead. The police brought me in for an old prostitution warrant, nothing else. I have 30 days.

113. Inmate Ameerah

*On the minimum-security yard, the women struggle to bond with
each other. When the women yell at the deputies, they are united.
They complain about authority and feel strength standing against it.*
*Dep. Bilyeu steps in to talk and tells us that DeeDee Klotfelder is
back in jail.*

Dep. Bilyeu: DeeDee's been through Step Study twice. They won't let her in
again. I just wanna slap DeeDee silly. I won't even talk to her. I said, "Don't even
think about coming over here again 'cause I don't even wanna see your face
over here again." I don't go for the bullshit.
Do we know why she was picked up this time?
Dep. Bilyeu: Prostitution.

*I look at F2. Women cluster at the picnic tables and enjoy the still,
cool air. The sun is high, and it's going to get hot. DeeDee exits
the F2 unit.*

DeeDee: I thought you guys would never come and say hello!
What happened this time?
Prostitution case. Cop pulled up. I hadn't ever done this before, a half a block
away from going home. I tell him, "I really don't need the money. I'm not high."
I got in and said, "Look, I'm not a junkie, I'm not gonna hurt you. I'm just gonna
show you a couple things you'll like."
The guy was a cop?
Yeah. He was young, and I didn't expect . . . Hey, remember you asked me
about being a prostitute, and I didn't really tell you the last time I saw you. I was
very nonchalant when I worked. I treated it as a business. I didn't want to grow
up as a prostitute. I had other aspirations for myself, but as I grew, I had to do
this. I used my common sense, and my belief was you give a good service at
a reasonable price and you don't rip the dates off, and you don't put them
into a situation where they're uncomfortable. Then they'll come back and all
of a sudden it's not so hard to get into that car. You know your date. You know
what he wants and how long he's going to take. I love my guys, and that's why
it's so hard to get out of it.
There's only one time I was truly scared, and all he got was a free $20 blow
job. It was traumatic to the point I was shaking, 'cause I had a knife held in the
middle of my back the whole time I was giving him a blow job. I thought of
biting his dick off, but with my luck he'd spaz and I'd get killed. I can remember
when I first became a prostitute–I had somebody come say to me, "Were you
molested as a child?" because most prostitutes were molested as children.
Prostitution gives them power over men.

*I remember Dr. Bull telling us that our perspective gives us a different
access to the inmates than the access he has as a psychologist.
He said, "These people are going to be more honest with you than
they are with me. They don't tell me about illicit things like drugs in
the jail. You've got the freedom to obtain very private information,
and you can observe how life goes on, not only with the inmates,
but also with the deputies."*

Two-thirds of incarcerated women have children under the age of eighteen (Smith, 1991). Many feel enormous guilt about being absent from their children's lives and worry about whether they will still have custody of their children when they get out (Bloom & Steinhart, 1993). These and other concerns, including unresolved issues of physical and sexual abuse, lead female inmates to make requests for psychological counseling that far exceed those made by men. Penal experts agree that women would benefit from additional services (Salholz & Wright, 1990).[22]

Stephanie Covington. Ph.D.

We leave the yard and head back to Control for an escort to the lieutenant's office in administration. Dep. Love appears and escorts us out the Inmate-Receiving sally port, across the back professional lot where inmates are received, and to the next building. He tells us that his brother is a coach in the Juvenile Hall and that it's depressing guarding locked-up humans. Love wants to be a lawyer and experience the other side of the criminal justice system.

116

11:02 a.m.   Administration

Lt. Milakovich talks to us about incarceration. She tells us that she's out of uniform because she has a lunch meeting outside the jail.

Lt. Milakovich: You mentioned you had problems with some of the inmates?

Not exactly. I was just curious about Banks.
I don't think that her life is a success story. There are times she's really on and then times when she's impulsive and not going to think about ramifications. You mentioned the other girl.

Kristina Edwards. We are seeing her, and her case hasn't gone through court yet.
What kind of plea?

Torture—seven-to-life so far.
Was it a murder?

Yes. She's the one who reported the murder.
They may give her something for that. Was she in custody at the time?

No.
If not in custody you don't have to give Miranda. The concern is—do they think they're in custody. If she told them she was involved and she's not in custody then we talk to them. Someone says, "I hacked this person up and the body is over there." Then it's, "Well, you wanna show us where the body is?" You want to find out other things. They just tried Sherry Dale, who was drugged out. That doesn't negate the fact someone is gone! She was called the axe murderer.

Why do people commit crimes?
The reason they steal rather than get a job? Why show up nine to five, Monday through Friday, when this is easier? It takes five minutes to knock you over your head, take what you bought and worked for.

They've seen others do it.
Sure, and it's like, if dad's injuring his own uncle, then I could be expendable, too. Growing up in that environment doesn't pack. The public doesn't care. Lock them up, but we have to take care of them, and respect their rights. The public says warehousing isn't working, and they're trying to find new methods, but nobody wants to spend the money or the time. As a cop, I worked curfew sweeps. One time, Circle K called in and said a kid had shoplifted. When I got there, the kid had a smug attitude. I handcuffed him and he cried. Next thing, the mother made a lawsuit out of, "Don't touch my kid." The kid's probably at home saying, "F you."

She goes on to describe some of the most serious pathological personalities.

117-119

Sadistic rapists are the worst kind. They have rape kits and torture the gal 'til she dies. Then the totally different side of him teaches Sunday school. Society is predatory. Look at Bundy. There was a selection of victims, with no pattern to his attack, big on knives. It took the females a half-hour to die. That's what got him off, the pain.

I believe we can't warehouse people, but some crimes we have to incarcerate, and I do believe in the death penalty. I don't know what's going to make society change, what'll make the parents care. It has to be something outside of custody.

The conversation returns to the women's jail and we discuss some of the differences between the women's behavior and the men's.

Inside the jail, the women get into little catfights, but nothing crazy. With the men, when someone climbs the bars, and screams, "Let me out of here," then the others throw a blanket over him and knock the snot out of him. Men have welcoming committees, and if they don't like somebody, they throw a blanket party—the victim can't tell who beat him up or how many. A house like that's very difficult for a deputy to work. It's high tension, and it's not unusual to have three incidents like that a night.

> Sadistic rapists are the worst kind. They have rape kits and torture the gal 'til she dies. Then the totally different side of him teaches Sunday school. Society is predatory.
>
> Lieutenant Milakovich

Men and women both act on power plays. "I like your tennis shoes, and if you don't want me to take them off you, give me five boxes of Top Ramen." There's a lot behind the scenes we don't even touch on. "If you don't want me to beat you up, then give me your stores." Trading sexual favors for food forces somebody who's really naïve, who screwed up and took a bad turn, to end up in here with somebody really experienced.

The lieutenant talks about the first three inmates we'd met early on.

I know Roland, and it's sad when you think what her kids have to look forward to. She's very manipulative. Kristina Edwards is probably not going to ever see the streets again. Can you murder somebody and only get seven years? You could argue someone's not capable of doing a crime. The pack mentality is weird. There's a feeding frenzy. Rolenda? I heard she's back. She was picked up in Arizona. She turned herself in. What we have is a wide variety. Somebody wanting to be a nuisance is one thing. You can tell the difference when they're kicking the door down. If they're no danger to themselves and just petrified, I say leave them alone. We get people who stuff blankets down the toilet to be ornery. You wouldn't put them in a rubber cell for that. There are criteria for the rubber cell. Inmates have to be exhibiting bizarre or violent behavior. It's called the aggravation game. They push up to the point where they won't get physical. I used to go in the dorm and they're watching soap operas. I go, "It's gonna rot your brain." They read all this crap. You have to wonder, the type of individuals that are here. It's gonna be a rare individual that sits down and reads to learn something new.

When inmates violate a rule that's published, they're fair game. I'm pretty black and white in that sense. But if an inmate says, "I soiled my pants," I'm not going to say, "That's tough." We have rules about inmates communicating with inmates in other houses, like flagging, where they'd write backwards. They know things, and I have no clue how.

Banks goes into the restraining chair often. . . .
She has a nasty habit. Repulsive. People start backing away when you're spitting blood and biting hard. Extremely bright inmates just get bored. Genius people who get bored get into trouble in the jail. Have you met Kath Anderson yet? She was Kath Mills back when I first got here as a deputy in '82. I thought she was a nice gal. She's sharp. That's why I suggested you talk to her on the outside. She's very experienced about jail and prison. I heard she heads up a sober-living program now called Hamilton House. I hope she stays clean. She's aged a lot.

Leaving Lt. Milakovich's office, I set up a time to meet Kath Anderson.

116. Deputy Love; 117-119. Lieutenant Milakovich

We drive up to a park on Oregon, off University, near Polk. Hot, really hot. Sand flies attack the Jeep door. A woman, Native American in appearance, steps away from a group of rough-looking people. She approaches my old Land Rover and introduces herself as Kath Anderson. Her arms and neck are marked with scars. I notice her clear blue eyes and a smile that feels warm and receptive.

Anderson: Nice car.

I grab my camera equipment. Barbara hauls lunches for three. We walk to a picnic table, and Barbara spreads out the salads and Snapples from the Cheese Shop.

My history—Las Colinas had state beds, and if you were in the prison system, you could do a violation at Las Colinas instead of going to prison. I was doing a nine-month violation, and I really wanted to go to prison. It was more fun. More freedom. I was there nine times. The first time I was in was two years and eight months for armed robbery. I had a gun, but I wiped it and tossed it.

There's a lot of ties and closeness in prison because of the length of time you are there. A lot of people form romantic ties in prison. They think they do in jail, but they don't really. There are years to consider in prison. People just set up house. I had my first girlfriend in prison. She was an Apache Indian, doing 25-to-life. She escaped, got caught, and broke a cop's neck.

A rough group in prison.
Yeah, and yet some of the most beautiful souls I've ever met have been in prison. I had a couple of girlfriends over the years, but prison did that. I was 21. I grew up about three blocks down this street. My family had property. I was adopted when I was six months old into a very religious family, no drugs or alcohol. My dad invented the hydraulic lift and then he invested in real estate. I found out there are several different kinds of abuse, and one of them is overindulgence, placing too high expectations on achievements.

120. Kath Anderson

Anderson met a girl named Roni on one of her trips to jail. Once released, they spent five years together when Anderson wasn't in prison or in jail on violation of parole. They raised her son after he turned nine. They even married at a gay church and lived as "little suburban queers," according to Anderson.

The flies are terrible.

Your scars?
From abscesses. I've got them on my stomach, butt, under my arms, my armpits, everywhere. I have no veins. When the antibiotics started working, I'd run away from the hospital with a central line in my chest. Then it would get so infected that I would have to go back to the hospital. I've done several hospital trips. This trip right here was for endocarditis.

Anderson knows Cindy Mulloy. They hung around the same areas, knew the same druggies and convicts, and both had drug-related heart conditions. Mulloy's history with endocarditis required two valve replacements—enormous expenses charged to Medi-Cal. Endocarditis is often caused by bacteria from dirty needles.

How'd you come off the street drugs after you were hospitalized?
Usually a combination of methadone, morphine, Xanax, and Ativan. The last time I was in the hospital, my heart had failed. I was on my way to my connection, and he found me and took me to the hospital. I spent the first 30 days of my incarceration in the hospital, kicking. Heroin addicts, especially old heroin addicts, tend to be real snobbish. They can't stand tweakers because tweakers don't kick.

A lot of the girls are angry in F housing . . .
They're unhappy in that dorm. It's an animal warehouse. The deputies feed off of the inmate behavior. There're a lot of drugs, speed, among the deputies. Did you talk to a girl named Maxwell? God, you missed a colorful one. Edie Maxwell. She's in B. She's a stud broad with big, blue eyes and red, curly hair. She's highly intelligent. I don't even know what she's there for. She was in C. She was also in F1, D, F2, F3, and A. They hate her at that jail.

You've been in A housing?
When I was doing a nine-month violation there, I was working in the kitchen. I was the only one there that had been to prison. They were trying to make some wine in the kitchen, but they didn't know what they were doing. I said, "OK. Here's what you do, but I get to drink some." When it was ready, we drank it. Somebody told Sgt. Ziegler. We were up in A dorm serving with the cart. We were bouncing off the walls. When we came back to the kitchen, Sgt. Ziegler stood all of the girls in a half circle. She said, "Kath, would you like to tell these girls what hooch is?" I was moved immediately to A housing and left on the next chain to CIW.

Why do you think you moved into a life of drugs and crime?
I love to be scared in different ways. Like the rollercoaster. It was a power thing. I don't really think of it at the time, but I like it afterwards. I had a friend who was 6'11", one of the most intimidating dope fiends you've ever seen in your life and he's got three years clean now. But we did armed robberies together. A lot of my crimes were armed robberies because women didn't do them back then.

You were almost a *Bonnie and Clyde* without the murder?
That could've happened easily. We were just lucky.

Did you have any other means of making money?
I "signed," that's homeless hustling at supermarkets, and made $200 a day. My sign said, "Single Mom needs work." I worked when they wanted me to work.

People actually wanted to hire you?
Cleaning offices and houses; but I made the most money on the street. The La Mesa police department loved me. I wasn't a problem to them. They had no idea that I was running. They believed my alias.

Kath moves through the crowd breaking up after an NA/AA meeting. She introduces me to several of the recovering addicts, all with prison histories and hospital episodes revolving around abuse histories.

You wanted to die?
There wasn't anything left to live for. I had a daydream, just a flash-like crystal vision. It's a sister to déjà vu; one instance of clarity. I saw myself utterly and completely alone. Everybody was gone, and I was alone. It terrified me. But it goes away as fast as it comes, that clarity. My mom had died, my son had left; I sold everything that could be taken out of the house, my parent's property. I took the fireplace out of the wall and sold it to antique stores on Adams Avenue. I was running amuck. I left my family home to the wolves. I dismantled it. I sold everything. My cats ran away. One cat, Sam, even took his toys and ran away.

A bunch of strangers were living at my house. We sold the front door, the burglar bars, and the hardwood flooring. We dismantled everything that could be removed. A joint on Adam's Avenue bought the built-ins, the china cupboards, the desk, the room dividers, the cedar kitchen cabinets, and the leaded windows. Everything went. Afterward, I had the feeling I'm never coming out of this. I didn't have money, food vouchers, or bus tokens, just my head telling me "go use."

But instead I came up here to a meeting two hours early, and for some reason my roommate, Jared, came along with an old friend, Gordy. That's how I got this job managing Hamilton House. Best thing that ever happened. Now I'm doing real life and doing it OK.

You've had a lot of anger.
It's an emotion that a lot of us haven't learned to identify and deal with. You can allow yourself to feel anger. It was the hurt that scared us.

So when you feel anger now, what happens?
I don't feel anger like I used to feel it. I used to be very violent.

Describe a scenario.
My son and I and some of his friends were at a gas station at 33rd and El Cajon Boulevard. I had a Chrysler Cordoba with a sun roof. The boys were all hanging out of the sun roof and this lady drove up and stole my gas pump, and I jumped on the hood of my car, snatched her up from the pump in the aisle and started banging her head into the hood of the car and the boys are going, "Yeah, Kath. Go on Kath!" When you're on heroin, you think you have special rights.

Talk about the effects of heroin.
After using it for a while, you can function on a normal level, but my normal level was bizarre. It was extreme. I flew off the handle. The drugs created an imbalance in me. They created false emotions. There's a thing called post-acute withdrawal, and throughout the use of the drugs there's a lot of neurological damage done. Post-acute withdrawal is a very real thing, and it takes anywhere from two to six months to figure out if you're going to come out of it. Sometimes I'm unable to think clearly. I'm really good with numbers and I know I can handle them, but I have the worst time in the world keeping the books at this place.

121. Kath Anderson

122

8/8/95　11:00 a.m.　North Park

We meet Anderson at the park, and she introduces us to Gordy, an important figure in her life of drugs and crime. He tells us that the detox counselor contacted him and told him Gwen, an inmate we met in Step Study, is out on house arrest, wearing an ankle bracelet, and needing a place to stay clean. She's going to join us in the park. Gordy's heard that she's a former model and tennis player. "She's supposed to be real good-looking, but you know what? That could work against her. She's on her way over here."

Gwen arrives at the park, meets Gordy, and is anxious. She wants to know she has a place to live. Will Gordy take her into his unit? Anderson stands back with Barbara and me as Gordy and Gwen talk like old buddies. Gordy takes off on the topic of addiction, like an expert.

Gordy: If someone overdosed and died from a drug, I wanted to know where they got the drugs. The drugs must be good if someone died from them. Remember when China White was dyed brown, and people were dying like flies? I went on tour with Janice Joplin. I was the guy who got the drugs and alcohol and partied with them. We went to Devonshire Downs, Monterey Pop Festival, Palm Springs Pop Festival, and the Golden Bear in Huntington Beach. I stayed with her four months. It was crazy back then.

Why take something that kills someone?
Gordy: I've died three times. I'd shoot up with coke or speed. I was too high to know. You get mad when they bring you out of it 'cause you were so loaded that they ruined it. You're mad they ruined your high, not that they saved your life.

Even if you're so high you passed out?
Gordy: Yeah. Anything to deaden your emotions is cool. And when you get clean you start fixin' all over again with women, cigarettes, coffee, anything that takes your mind off of the problems. You can switch your addiction. Right now my addiction is Pepsi and cigarettes. I'm coming up on a year clean, and I'm going to try to stop smoking cigarettes.

He asks to see Gwen's ankle bracelet, saying he's never seen one. She coyly says, "I hate my feet. I don't show them to anyone. I lost my toenails permanently playing hard tennis."

They talk about sports and review her successful tennis history. Gordy played football, and said it takes the fun away when you have to win. He tells Gwen to get a deposit to him for a unit at his recovery operation. Gwen is flirtatious with Gordy. She's less confident in a group of recovering addicts. Inside protects and outside tempts. Gordy acts proprietary.

Gwen: My boyfriend is real supportive. He takes care of me.
Gordy: Is he a stalker? Let me make a suggestion: don't tell him where you are. It seems to me you don't want this relationship. It creates more problems for me if I gotta go up to him and say, "Hey, Pop, leave her alone and get outta here." I like a woman who's gonna speak her mind, say it like it is. I don't like bullshit.

122. Gordy and Kath Anderson;
123. Kath Anderson and Bigsly

Later we meet up with Anderson at Hamilton House to see the rehab environment and meet some of the residents. The house is tiny, dismal and dark inside, furnished with Salvation Army sofas and tables.

Anderson: Gary just called. He and I did some horrible things together. We had a barbecue at the beach one day because I knew I was going to prison. I was out on bail. I started drinking, and when Gary and I got together we got rowdy. We'd go and find somebody to fight. This guy named Cherokee and some others came up and asked us for hot dogs. We said, "Yeah," and then they wanted more. That was our cue. We were just drunk enough that Gary, with hands the size of hams, beat Cherokee within an inch of his life. He broke a bottle over his head. I kicked him so that his face was like a pulp. He ran into the parking lot of a 7-Eleven where an ambulance was parked, and he dove inside. I can hear the sirens, and someone saying, "Come on, Gary," through the haze of anger.

Alcohol and drugs are behind the rage?
No, guilt and fear. Fear of feeling things. You mask it. The cold wall of anger. You end up feeding off of each other.

We get in my Land Rover and head east around El Cajon Boulevard's unsavory section to check out Cindy Mulloy's old haunts and some of Anderson's old hangouts.

Mulloy hooked between 40th and 52nd and El Cajon. Pull over. I'll see if Bigsly's home. He's the one who took drugs to Cindy in the hospital.

Outside the small cottage, the neighborhood is quiet. Shortly, Anderson turns up with Bigsly, a drug addict for 23 years. He talks openly about his heroin use, and his petty crimes to support his habit. He got out of jail clean and started up the heroin again. Is Cindy doing tricks for his habit and hers already? He says he went into jail weighing 120 pounds, on drugs, and came out weighing 160 three weeks ago. Due to malnutrition, he has lost the sight in one eye.

Cindy's out of jail.
Bigsly: Yeah. I found her at a friend's.
Anderson: If he doesn't leave, she'll bring drugs home.
Bigsly: Cindy's my friend, and not just because she brings me drugs. I'll do anything for her. But I can't do the program. I can't take the rules.
Anderson: I'm not a program. I'm sober living.

When did you shoot up last?
Bigsly: This morning. I'll be sick by morning. I'll probably go back out and get something. It depends on how bad I want it. I don't know how bad I want it until the sick comes.

What kind of treatment do you get? Is the jail interested in your recovery?
Anderson: Law enforcement doesn't care if you come back.

So why not get clean and stop the cycle?
Bigsly: Rehab's not for me. I was in one in Hawaii, Habitat, and they tried to tie me up, shave my head, and put me on a stool with a dunce hat, yelling and screaming at me like constipated gorillas. I was in with Ryan O'Neal's kid. Five of them say, "Get your hands on the wall!" They go up and down your body and then throw you in the rubber room, sometimes five of them. Dealing with junkies, they don't care. A guy comes in San Diego Downtown Jail, crazy, talking to himself, with the back of his head partly shaved. He had head lice real bad. The tank captain tells the deputies, "This guy's got lice." The

My mind can't process numbers the way I used to be able to. It'll take months. Maybe I'll never be able to, so it takes me a long time to do the books …

Kath Anderson

123

inmates squirt chemicals all over him, and rinse him off, and he's still itching. The inmates say, "He's still driving us nuts." So the deputies put him in the hole. He was there two weeks. He didn't bother nobody, didn't tell nobody to fuck themselves. The hole is inhumane.

I was serving him food at the same time I was serving Hamilton George, the guy that raped a girl and cut her arms off. Your attitude is different in jail. You're just looking at those bars for three months. It seems like a dream that won't stop. You can't get out of it. You're not sick. You're getting healthy. You say, "I'm not going back," and then when that door opens at the end, you walk and it all disappears. You're getting yours because you deserve it.

Anderson walks with Bigsly back to the side of the house. I think about Bigsly growing up in conservative Omaha, my hometown. Anderson returns to the car.

Anderson: A lot of these girls go out and make money for the guys and give them the drugs. God knows why he isn't HIV. I count my blessings. He and I

both lived in a trailer with a guy named Terry, and we both used his needles. I used bleach on needles. But there were times we were so sick that we'd say, "Fuck it, give it to me." I know a lot of hookers are spreading HIV deliberately.

Bigsly said Cindy Mulloy doesn't have a bad habit yet.
She has a probation officer to check in with. Nobody can tell me she hasn't used every day since she's been out. Cindy needs to enter Crash. Everyone at Hamilton House went to Crash. It saved my life. She'll see Bigsly sick, and she'll go out and get drugs for her and give him half. Bigsly knows the PO (parole officer) could decide to send her to prison right now by trying to get her on a short-term run. My run was nine years before I got clean this last time after doing time. Cindy's has only been a week.

Anderson doesn't hesitate to answer my questions. Her clear blue eyes flash with great intensity.

If I didn't like what someone said, or the person, I guess it showed in my eyes. You learn to not express things in an overt manner unless you're on a mission. Talking to Bigsly I went into my old posture and physical mannerisms. I dropped into the Folsom squat.

Anderson tells me that although it's painful to know that Cindy Mulloy is out of jail and prostituting herself for drugs for Bigsly, she admits the memories are triggers. I ask her how she landed the fortunate placement at Hamilton House, a transitional, sober-living environment.

I graduated from Crash and I was sitting in North Park, seriously ready to take a hit, when Gordy saw me, came up to me and told me to go to a meeting in the park with him. I did. I stood up and spoke. Gordy knew how close I'd been to taking a hit, but he told me there was a job open at Hamilton House. They needed someone to manage the residents and keep the books. It was the job he had before he moved to another sober-living unit. Shocked that he asked me, I took the job.

He sensed you were able to step into a position of responsibility even though he could see you were thinking of using hours before?
That's right. Gordy knows me. It hasn't been easy either. My mind can't process numbers the way I used to be able to. It'll take months. Maybe I'll never be able to, so it takes me a long time to do the books, keep track of everyone, and not get caught up in everyone's problems. Mulloy is a good example. I know what's up with her now. I know what she's thinking, what she's up to, and the part Bigsly is playing in it all. She's not going to make it if this keeps up.

He didn't seem too bothered.
No, that's because he's using. That's all he can think about. It's all about the drug. Nobody, nothing's as important as that drug. You need to spend some time talking to Gordy. He's done it all and seen it all. I owe everything to him. He believed in me enough to go out on a limb for me or I'd have been back doing drugs.

Crash is a detox facility. It has long-term or short-term components. Hamilton House is a transitional housing program, an independent program, where residents are expected to remain drug free and follow basic rules, i.e., curfew, housecleaning, paying rent, attending NA/AA meetings. It's a stepping-stone from structured Crash to living on one's own. In a sober-living environment, treatment and therapy are not offered.

After a discussion with Anderson about her life at Hamilton House, she hands me a letter she had written to me. "You're seeing life inside a jail. I want you to know about life in prison."

124. Kath Anderson

I missed my entire young adulthood. I missed my son's first day of school, every first day of school. I never learned to live, work, and play, except in a closed society. I never learned to develop a normal relationship with a woman or a man that wasn't based on penitentiary values.

Kath Anderson

Kath Anderson: contribution

I remember the years best through songs, people, and trips to prison. When it began in 1976, the song was "On and On" ["He just keeps on trying"]. The women who sat me down and taught me to carry myself when I got to prison were Phillis and Reggie. I was 22 years old in the old county jail, about to take my first bus ride to Fontana. Phillis and Reggie told me, "Don't clique, be yourself, be young, and don't take no shit."

Kestra taught me how to wear my bandana. Low, so my blue eyes would blaze. Kestra was older. She didn't mind a kid tagging along. She taught me how to lean against the brick wall by the auditorium with my hands sunk deep into my Levi's pockets, with one foot kicked back on the wall. I could drop into the Folsom squat in the blink of an eye. I learned the prison posture well, and I kept it with me for many years.

The years in prison, all the different trips I made, tend to run together when I try to verbalize what made each one unique. The feel of each trip was different. The personality of the place changed with the faces. But for trip after trip, the feeling of coming home prevailed.

In 1978, I met the first girl I fell head-over-heels in love with. I would have walked on hot coals for her. She helped to shape my prison persona from that year on. She was a wild Indian, an Apache. A yangster—too old to be a youngster, too young to be a gangster. She was a painfully good artist, with pen and ink. She could bring tears to my eyes as I stared into the weathered faces of her Indians. The generations of pain, the undying pride, the strength. She taught me about the Indian side of myself. I carried it with me when I left.

She called herself Butch. Her real name was Catherine. I can still remember when her long, black hair made a tent around me when she bent her face over mine. In 1979, Butch was waiting when I returned to prison. She started coming over on long summer evenings and sitting against the tree outside my window smoking pot. She played the guitar as beautifully as she drew. A lot of folk music, "Wild Horses" by the Stones, Joan Baez songs, "Prison Trilogy" and "Diamonds and Rust."

That was the year I began to learn prison politics. I became active in the Prisoners Union, an affiliate of the ACLU. There was, even then, rampant injustice and corruption in the system. I was naïve enough to believe we could conquer it. What we did do was change things somewhat. We fought the good fight. In 1980 came the "Baby Killer" riots. Every woman on the yard with a child-related case was attacked or threatened. Anyone trying to protect them fell, along with the snitches. I remember looking around me on the grass of the circle in front of the administration building, amazed and excited by the sea of faces and the shouts of "lock arms," when the men with gas masks appeared on the tops of the buildings.

In 1980, we began to see women die. The CMO (Chief Medical Officer) was a Christian Scientist. He pulled all drugs. Epileptics had seizures, diabetics went into comas, women with migraines cried in pain, and the three transsexuals on the yard began growing beards. Butch and I were no longer together, but we were bound to each other by cause, by experience, by belief, by spirit. We filed a class action suit against the medical department and won. But we paid a price. When I slipped a disc in my neck, I was left to suffer. My name was automatically erased from the Sick Call list through the end of that trip and the beginning of the next.

In 1981, I met Robin. We sold weed on the yard. We were Butch's competition, but we worked with her as well. Robin and I worked for our prison mom and dad, who spoiled us rotten. We wore gold and silver. Whatever we wanted could be bought for weed. Our pads were bizarre and beautiful. We lived in a haze of Valium and hash, and, of course, there was heroin. After I left that year, Butch escaped from CIW (California Institution for Women). When I returned again, there was a void I couldn't fill. New friends, other girlfriends, but no Butch.

I clung to Butch's friend, Norm, and to the spirituality of the Indian culture. We witnessed the construction of the sweat lodge. We carried on in the United Indian Tribes Organization. Norm and I walked and walked in the sun, the wind, and the rain. We felt the power of nature in the field behind the canteen. We collected feathers, and the giant crows of Prison Valley followed us as we walked. Norm taught me to look up whenever I walked out of a doorway. Look up to the sky and the tree tops and feel the power stirring. She taught me that birds keep the same partner for life. Norm walked me to the gate six times to wave goodbye before she couldn't do it anymore.

In 1982, Butch broke a cop's neck in Arizona. She was sentenced 25-to-life. I went nuts on the yard in California. I bought and sold and wheeled and dealed. I spent that year in a fog that lasted 'til the morning I paroled. I was so angry, so cheated, so sad.

I'd met my wife that trip, Roni. I continued to go to prison. Nothing compared to the heartbreak of doing time with Roni. Her second trip to prison was my seventh. She needed to run the yard and play. I needed to do cell time. Watching Roni play nearly broke me. I ceased to function, except to score and slam. Ronnie and I were married for nine years, but never again would I let her "crime." I never wanted to go to prison with her again.

In 1984, the Baby Killers [a riot ensued between prisoners and women who were found guilty of murdering their children], still in PC (Protective Custody), filed their class action suit with the ACLU. And I was there again in 1985, when they won the suit and came flooding back on the yard.

I saw a Baby Killer burned in the face with an iron, another sexually assaulted with a hot curling iron, another hit in the head with a board full of nails. I felt nothing. I was there when Jenny left. The Bag Lady of CIW, she used to find kittens in the yards and break their necks. When I paroled, she burned down a hotel full of people. A little insurance that she'd never have to parole to that nasty, unfamiliar real world again. I met the Manson girls at CIW. In Receiving there's a hall that housed them for years. The rosebushes they planted so long ago still bloomed, last I knew.

The Manson women were different people. Leslie, Susan, and Pat never had reason to associate with each other. Leslie was the student. She'd have her master's now if they'd just let her out to take the necessary courses. Many others have done it. But as long as the Folger family breathes, there will be no small favors for any of the girls. Pat was the darkest, the most private. Our birthdays are both on December 3rd. She went to prison when LSD was the hard core drug. Knew nothing of meth, heroin, or coke. Pat was a thinker and a brooder. Susan was a character, a calculating would-be capitalist. The last I saw her she was into weight lifting, trying to get her pictures in a magazine.

I got quite close to Emily Harris, while she was doing her ten years. She introduced me to the first trilogy by Stephen Donaldson, *The Chronicles of Thomas Covenant: The Unbeliever.* On one of my return trips, I brought her the second trilogy of the series. I often wondered if she read the third trilogy.

The spirituality of convicts is fascinating. It's almost as if those with lots of time under their belts have tapped into an awareness, a plane that most people don't know exists. It's funny how violent I was on the streets. But in prison, I was different. It was a time to be calm, to learn.

In 1987, my last trip was to CRC (California Rehabilitation Center); I can never fully tell of the beauty in that place. It's a paradox. Beautiful badness. Originally built by Al Capone as a sort of gangster retreat, it had a man-made lake, murals on the ceilings, marbled walls and archways, sculpture. Anyone who has stood there can tell of a spot that's the gym. The silence is so awesome; it's overwhelming. Even the wind doesn't stir the trees. The presence is utterly real. Images of lawn parties and champagne, beautiful women, powerful men at leisure, money. Ghosts of the past, felt by many.

I missed my entire young adulthood. I missed my son's first day of school, every first day of school. I never learned to live, work, and play, except in a closed society. I never learned to develop a normal relationship with a woman or a man that wasn't based on penitentiary values.

The song was "Stranglehold":

I'm breaking that hold now.
And although I wouldn't change this new way of life for anything,
there are many things I'll hold dear.
I still look to the sky.

Between meetings on the outside with Anderson, we visit the jail. The personalities are complicated by the survival tools they have acquired. They find themselves in the jail society, only to be released to society-at-large, which they are ill-equipped to handle, and so they return to drugs and, eventually, back to jail again.

8/9/95   1:00 p.m.   Jail

Dep. Barnes, a red-haired male deputy, approaches me at the fence and asks, "Do you want to come inside and do your stuff?"

He opens the gate to the patio. Stokes is surprised we can enter the patio.

Barnes says that Ameerah's real name is Maya Brown and she's in for the second time this year.

Ameerah comes forward and admits her alias. She takes us to the corner where two plastic chairs are set up. She comes closer.

Ameerah: I thought of something else I wanted to tell you. When I was little, I was told I wasn't pretty. Most people who end up in this type of life were abused. I would say my mother and father raised me to the best of their ability. I loved to dance. I could see something on television and get up and do it. My whole soul took over. My father used to say, "Don't let no one take your smile from you." I never knew what it meant. He said, "Your smile will heal your soul." My father took all of the walls away. He said, "Truth will set you free and take away the ugly." It'll help you understand a murderer.

I was married to . . . 16 years, and all the time he was in the closet. One day I found dildos, rubbers, and dirty pictures of men in my husband's closet. I thought the brain tumor was AIDS. This made me so scared, so sick. I think about the Oprah Winfrey shows, and they never talk about how it feels to know that your husband is homosexual. Your world is upside down.

I think of all of the women who hurt like this. Yesterday, I went into the bathroom, started crying in the toilet, and shut the door. I didn't want to share my pain with them because they're hurting bad enough. I isolated myself, and then came out with a big smile. I like to sacrifice for people.

But that pain I experienced with finding dildos, rubbers, and dirty pictures–just looking at them, and when he wanted to climb on me, it was like a rape. I lived in hell. And you know what else? I wished him dead. For a while, I believed I caused his death.

125-127

128

Women gather around Dep. Barnes and Dep. Wildenberg.

Dep. Bilyeu shouts at an inmate outside the fence, "Go back and bring that disinfectant back inside the gate. You act like your arms are painted on!"

Lani Kale walks up next to Barnes and tells us she's in jail for assault with a deadly weapon, a hammer—a Tommy-hawk, as she calls it.

Dep. Barnes: These women are different from the ones in the big house, the main jail, who are the stronger personalities and power players.

Dep. Wildenberg: They try and push you around. These women don't. They just see how far they can push before they get a reaction.

Dep. Barnes: Women in here are sentenced up to six months. In B housing it's for a lot more time.

What about Banks?

Dep. Barnes: She's still on the run.

Dep. Wildenberg: I never had to fight her. She knocked off the crap with me.

Dep. Barnes: I did. We had three cell extractions with her in one night.

Dep. Wildenberg: Never give her the opportunity to get close without someone else right there.

Dep. Barnes: She's gone, and there's somebody else to replace her. Ms. Pace bites. These inmates could have AIDS, but legally, medical services aren't supposed to tell us. Being tested for AIDS is voluntary. Why are we dealing with these people? County Mental Health is packed. Many of them don't have enough sense to commit a crime. The women get away with everything, and they know it. You tell men one time what to do, and they do it, but women are manipulative.

There are women who are very dominant and those who are docile and afraid of everything until someone shows them the ropes or they end up in PC (Protective Custody) A housing. Women throw things at you. I got covered with food the other day when an inmate shoved it back through the slot at me in A Lockdown. She was psycho. That night she was bailed out. But she had many counts of assault against her: assault with a deadly weapon, battery, stalking, and possession of a concealed weapon. Now she's on the streets.

Inmates fry their brains with drugs. More and more women are coming into the jails. Ninety percent of the charges are drug related, stealing for drugs or holding drugs. Some of them don't have roommates. Docile ones get hit up for stores, robbed of their commissary items. We don't have room to isolate them unless they get beaten. They get used to us babysitting them. I want to work with men and get out of here for a while. Men know they can't get away with name-calling deputies, talking back, or walking with their hands out of their waistbands. They can't break rules.

Inmate Mindy turns up on the patio. She's been in Lockdown.

129

How does she go from A housing to F housing? The deputies act friendly toward her.

Dep. Barnes: Her time was up in Lockdown, and we had to find her housing.

Dep. Wildenberg: She likes to call deputies names.

Mindy: Yeah, that's right.

Dep. Wildenberg: Tell her what you called me.

Mindy: A bitch.

Dep. Wildenberg: More than that.

Mindy: A fucking cunt. But I didn't mean it. I'm sorry. I did two days in Lockdown. I'm on strong medication that makes me sleep all day. Mellaril, Trazodone, and Tegretol. I don't like it. I get negative reactions from it. I want out of here. I want to find my mom.

130-131

125-127. Inmate Ameerah; 128. Inmate Kale; 129. Deputy Wildenberg and Inmate Mindy; 130. Deputy Wildenberg; 131. Deputy Barnes

132. Disciplinary Cell

I ask Dep. Barnes if he knows Edie Maxwell, remembering Anderson's suggestion that we look her up in the jail.

Dep. Barnes: You want to see Maxwell? I'll take you to her.

We leave F housing, enter the main jail, and make a turn I haven't made before. We are somewhere behind the laundry room where three inmates in blues fold clothes. In a short, dark, narrow hall, four cells are aligned, opposite a polished concrete wall. The place reminds me of a small Midwestern cellar. Barnes opens one cell door with a small slit in it.

Dep. Barnes: Maxwell, someone's here to see you.

The dismal yellow light overhead stays on day and night. Maxwell rises from her pallet and acts pleased, in a sleepy sort of way. The bunkmate hides beneath their cotton blanket.

Maybe we shouldn't bother them.
Dep. Barnes: You want to see her? She's yours after she has a shower.

Barnes delivers Maxwell to us at Pro Visit. Maxwell sits down and talks comfortably and intelligently on her own.

Maxwell: I'm in Lockdown now. Lockdown is Disciplinary Isolation. I hate it. It's horrible. Normally I'd be in the main unit with other people back in B housing. I guess I extended my visit a little with all of the write-ups I got. I take chances and I give the deputies a lot of crap. I'm a clown. I entertain a lot of the girls and it usually costs me a day or two in the hole. I was standing up outside on the planter box when you were talking to Rolenda, which is a big "no-no." I was peeking in the window, another big "no-no," and I was waving in the window, another big "no-no." Those three acts cost me 23 hours in the hole.

This is my second time in this jail. I've been in others. Maine and Florida. My favorite was Mendocino. I don't come to jail continuously, like one right after another or for long stretches. I'm 40 years old. I've had an ongoing heroin problem since I was 20. With periodic bouts of incarceration, I'll stay off drugs maybe six months to a year. I'll be real healthy then I'll go down and just get involved with the criminal element and drugs. I'll get busted, and then I'll clean up in jail. Jail does me a world of good. I look at these jails as my angels because they drag me in off the street, and they clean me up. Then things will start eating at me, or life will get too good, and it's time to sabotage the situation a little bit.

County time is different from prison. It's limited and petty. All kinds of personalities come through here. They're angry, depressed, and distraught. It's constant. There's a lot of women who keep coming back here as a home-away-from home.

Drug addiction always stems from somewhere in the deep recesses of your damaged mind. My parents separated when I was a year old, and my mother left. My dad raised me. He had a lot of groovy friends, and he was a groovy dude. He dedicated himself to raising me. I'm an only child. My father was a marine biologist and had a couple boats of his own. We went on trips all over the Bahamas and West Indies, sailing. There was a lot of beauty, but that one element of not having a mother really devoured me. As wonderful as my father was, he could never be that maternal, and I grew up with this intensive craving.

I saw my mother when I was 12. She's gay, and she turned me on to the exciting life in the gay world. I'm gay. The cycle of a search for a mother manifests itself in my relations with women. I'm convinced there's no resolving it. If you miss something as a child you are pretty much going to miss it forever.

I remember as a child all the other kids had mothers, and their mothers would put their coats on or pull their skirts up tighter. I would just watch, and I would have this incredibly painful longing to have the same attention.

Sex is like the fundamental root of all acting out, but basically, all sex is about the fundamental need for love, attention, comfort, and nurturing. This man told me that his wife left him, and he was devastated. He said all he ever wanted in life was a woman who would nurture him and screw him at the same time. I said, "You go, dude." Men want their mothers, and they want their sex. I'm the same. Nurture and screw me at the same time. I'm not a nurturer. I attract women looking for more of a male. They miss their dad, boyfriend, or brother.

I entertain fantasies of being thrown in jail with 500 women. I also have a fantasy of being completely free of all responsibility and having somebody take care of me. I got a taste of it in Las Colinas, and it was wonderful not to have to deal with anything. I got very comfortable with people telling me when to go to bed, when to get up, when to eat, and when to put on clean clothes. Perhaps the worst part of being in jail is the boredom. Jail's so boring and, ultimately, the punishment of living in Las Colinas is death by boredom.

Except for the trusties and the few who seriously attend the drug-rehabilitation programs, inmates have nothing to do all day. They watch TV in the dayroom. Lockdowns are torture: no television. Any distraction is welcomed. Tricks played on the deputies and acts of defiance, covert or overt, are entertainment.

Boredom, overcrowding, and just being with other people all the time brings out the bellicosity and prejudices characteristic not only of those who wind up in jail, but of humankind in general.

Despite the complaints, the daily miseries, and the abusive acts by deputies, many of the women are not discontented. Indeed, like Maxwell, they often welcome their respite from the struggle on the streets. They are detoxed, fed, given medical care, and allowed to sleep at night. In jail they receive the welfare services that were unavailable, or difficult to obtain, outside.

133. Inmate Maxwell

Around the age of two, a little girl begins experiencing a physical and emotional separateness from her mother. She becomes very attached to her blanket or a favorite doll... This object creates in the little girl's mind the illusion of the comforting mother when she is physically not available and helps the little girl to learn to soothe herself and carry the comfort experienced with her mother within herself. For these women, the doll representing their mother is broken, ineffective, unable to soothe, and so these women cannot self-soothe. They become brittle and don't develop resiliency.[23]

Maryam Razavi Newman, Ph.D.

134. *Polly Doll*

The Next Morning
8.10.95 F Housing

Two daily inmate rosters sit on the check-in counter at the entrance of the jail. The sheets are designed for visitors and staff to scan. Barbara and I see an inmate directory on the visitor side of the sally port. We fill out our blue cards, listing the inmate numbers and housing units. An escort takes us to F2 housing.

8:30 a.m. F3 Housing

Dep. Mentes opens the gate for us and allows us to enter the unit. The inside of F housing feels friendly, in spite of the lines of metal bunk beds and wall of tiny lockers. The women take pride in their belongings.

Mindy Sanchez jumps off her bunk to show me her locker.

Mindy: I'm off those meds. Doctor didn't want me to look all drugged up like the others. I have Jerry Garcia posters. I love to play chess, but nobody wants to play. I got a haircut from a girl named Red.

Dep. Mentes, tall and statuesque, appears sympathetic to the inmates' realities. She says that Mindy has been in several of the jail's units. Another inmate, Dena, says she is scared and pregnant. The last time she was in she was placed in Isolation, where she delivered her baby on the cold cell floor. The baby died.

Dena: I've been desperate to get my story out. I remember all the dates and times like it was yesterday. Now I'm four months pregnant, and I don't get out for a year. Take these papers. I wanna get on *Hard Copy* with what happened.

136

Dep. Mentes: Violence doesn't happen in here. They rely on each other for support. They're too docile to go all the way. Women are too disorganized. When the men riot, it's not something that happens for just two minutes.

Thirty percent of the women in jail at any given time are pregnant. The deputy moves us to the main house and secures a Professional Visit booth. Mindy looks over her shoulder to see if the deputy is going to stick around.

Mindy: Is she gonna listen to everything? Let me read you my poem. I wrote it sitting in Jack in the Box downtown on Broadway, tweaking. I had just lost my kid to his father. I've been with two guys in my life, and both were very abusive. This place has taught me how to deal with my anger. It takes a lot for me to become violent, but in here I just wanted to knock one of those deputies.

What happened?

Mindy: I asked to be taken off the meds so I could go to the recovery home. You can't be on drugs there. The doctor said OK. Then it was like a set-up. It was the week I was supposed to be a trusty with Dep. Delgado. You knew about my mother dying? I wanted to go to the chapel. Dep. Delgado was standing in my face. I asked, "Can I go to church to go to confession?" But they let some other girl go. I had to roll up my belongings. I was punching the window because I was pissed. Sgt. Henderson put me in Discipline for 24 hours.

Later, Dep. Condon put me in the restraining chair. He said I kicked him. Four hours they kept me there and then they made me do chores. I had to clean out cells, go back to Discipline for a couple days, and then I ended up in F3. I love my mom.

You said your mom was a drug addict.

Mindy: An abuser, but I had to learn to forgive her to get on with my life. CPS (Child Protective Services) took me because they found needles all over the floor and beer bottles. Me and my mom shot drugs together once. She actually gave drugs to me. I wanted to try and see how it felt. It's not cool, but it's better than doing drugs with a stranger. My mom was like my best friend.

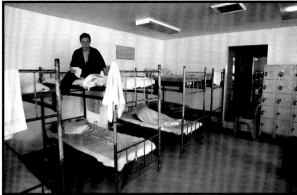

137

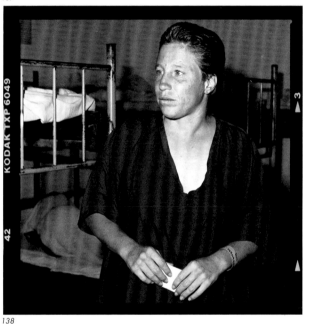

138

139

135. F2 housing bunks   136. Inmate Dena; 137-138. Inmate Mindy; 139. Deputy Mentes and Inmate Mindy

8/12/95 7:15 a.m. Sick Call

We leave for Las Colinas early Saturday morning to meet Dr. Hillary Bennett, the psychiatrist on duty in Sick Call. The medical unit is located in the main jail. An inmate from A housing sits on the bench next to an inmate from F housing. A large female deputy sits in the hallway. Upon our arrival, she leaves her post, heading off in the direction of the screaming and yelling. A labyrinth of cubicles lies beyond the corridor.

The doctor calls us inside her office, a space the size of a small closet. One inmate sits next to her waiting for a prescription. The doctor notifies me that she's already seen the women who signed our release forms. We're relegated to taking our chances with random inmates who enter Sick Call.

Passing by the tiny rooms, I see a woman in labor, and next to her is the infamous Isolation Room that Roland warned us about: "You don't ever want to get sick in this place. The one Isolation Room has four beds."

One inmate paces in front of the Isolation Room. Tuberculosis and other airborne diseases are easily spread throughout this facility. The existing ventilation system is not set up for contaminants. Vents suck in air from this unit and pass it throughout the jail. Until the county funds can provide for separate ventilation systems, contagious cases have to be sent to another jail.

A registered nurse is on duty at all times. A visiting physician appears for a few hours daily to see women who signed-up for Sick Call. The OB-GYN doctor makes two visits per week.

Women sit handcuffed to the bench, waiting to be seen by available contract doctors. We join them, asking if they'd be interested in talking to us. The guard reappears and takes her seat.

Dep. Houck: I'm sittin' here all fat and happy. I went to the doctor and I have low cholesterol, low blood sugar, and everything's normal. He said I'm just grossly overweight. There's nothing wrong with my blood or my urine. I always worry 'cause diabetes runs in my family. I'm the only one in my family that's fat. My whole family is lean. They drink those diet colas and eat fat foods. I've only been fat for the last few years. All of a sudden I hit 45, and I just gained.

Do you work in Sick Call everyday?

Dep. Houck: Five days in one spot and two days off until the shift rotates. We get off at 6:00 p.m., but after 3:00 pm I'm a walking zombie. We work a shift and just get a handle on what people are doing and who's here, but not enough to where you say, "Nah, I don't want to come back here to work." I'll tell you what does bother me. It's my feet. End of the day they're killing me. I'm going over to Foot World and get $150 boots that are good for concrete.

Celeste: I'm 48. I didn't get into any trouble before I was 46. I've never been in any trouble in my life! Never even had a parking ticket. The judge said, "What happened to you?" I said, "I guess I had a change of life, I don't know." I've gone bad with these girls in here.

We hear more screaming from around the corner.

Dep. Houck: That one's been going like that for hours.

Where's the inmate who's screaming?

Dep. Houck: She's in the Safety Cell. They've been working with her a long time. She's been down to CMH (County Mental Health) and she's really young. She's worse than Rolenda. And this girl's not that stupid either. We go to the door with pepper spray and she knows to get back and stay away.

42   KODAK TXP 6049

140

141

142

140. Deputy Houck; 141. Inmate Celeste;
142. Inmate Marlo; 143. Inmate Candice;
144. Inmate Eloise

The screaming escalates. Wailing echoes. The psychiatrist arrives in the hall shaking her head.

Dr. Bennett: Maybe Kale would like your attention. It would shut her up. She's been flipping me off.

Was Kale in F housing last week?
Dr. Bennett: Check with the sergeant. I wanted to brief new people for you, but I had no choice because I had to greet charming Miss Kale. We don't do involuntary medication. We offer the medications, but she refuses them.

What's wrong with Kale?
Dr. Bennett: Her diagnosis? I don't really know, to tell you the truth. I'm sure she has some chronic psychotic disorder like schizophrenia or a graphic disorder. I'm sure she also has a substance-abuse disorder. She's raising hell.

Inmates on the bench communicate.

Marlo: I'm in for a drug case. I leave for CIW next week for 11 years.
Candice: I've never laughed as hard as being in here, when they were smashing that girl's face up against the wall. The cuts she got! I'm here for petty theft because my daughter lied. I didn't do anything to her or hit her, even though she lied and said I did. I can't ever see her again. She's 16. She's with my dad. But it's still not the point. Since I been gone, she brought a loaded firearm to school without the safety on. I'm going to prison for a dirty urine test. She's been doing everything wrong.

Candice sees an African American inmate on the A housing patio.

Candice: The blacks are what bug me in here. If you don't watch their TV show, they get loud. As long as they control the TV, they're fine. I love what happened in the L.A. riots. They were running around and blowing each other up, destroying their own businesses. I loved it. I loved every minute of it. I hate 'em in my heart.
Marlo: Definitely, they have more control in here.
Candice: It's a black sheep house we're running here. They sit there, and they whine. They have to sit there and pretend. I mean, I'm not prejudiced, but I sure as hell know what color I am. I'm full-fledged German and I loved November 1943! I wish they'd do another sweep like they did to the Jews.

Pardon, could you explain that?
Candice: Hitler. I don't have my makeup on. I've been crying because I'm going to get three years. I shoulda went up there and wrote bad checks and beat up old people for their SSI checks. I shoulda done that. I probably woulda got only a month or two. But I don't do that kinda stuff to people.

More women arrive. There's a lot of hall noise. A large African American woman sits quietly as another inmate, Eloise, is seated next to her on the bench. I ask if they'll join us.

African American woman: No!
Candice: Why not? She wants to know what's going on.
African American woman: My name's Ruby.
Marlo: I jumped off the bed, off the top bunk. I'm getting a sling. I've been getting pain pills.
What caused the hole in your arm, Eloise?
Eloise: Shooting dope, cocaine. It festered real bad. It got to be where I couldn't sleep with any pill. They lanced it. It used to be real big. I see the doctor every day. They put on a bandage, and it comes off in the shower. I came in on 85 milligrams of methadone and a double habit. They don't help any drug addicts in here. I'm too old to be coming back here. I'm 42. Look at them. They're children, aren't they? I mean, you can't sleep. You gotta go hit them on the head at night and shut them up.
Ruby: This is my first and last time.
Eloise: They're dirty. I mean, nasty. Dirty Kotex lying around in the bathrooms—gross. And they think it's funny.
Ruby: I'm here for forgery. I never put myself in a situation like this. This is the pits.
Eloise: Don't put your name on nothing that don't belong to you. Ha, ha, ha.
Ruby: It's terrible. I don't see how these people can come in, go out, come back.
Eloise: I been in here twice. When I get out of here, I'm not coming back again. I get Social Security.
Ruby: Isn't that something? All those people out there can't get nothing to eat.
Eloise: I got seven grand when I first got out, retroactive, 'cause it took me eight months to get on it. I get $615 a month. I just got my check yesterday.
Ruby: They pay you for being a dope fiend? You really feel you gonna stay clean? How long you been using?
Eloise: Twenty years. I'm going to go to a program, NA, AA. Let's just take one day at a time. See, I don't hang around with friends. If I want to get dope, I call my connection and he'll come to my house and deliver. I'll do my shit in my house. I sit in my house and drink my beer and watch TV. I don't go out and party. I don't roam the streets. I'm content being at home with my grandkids. It's my daughter that drives me nuts and that's another story.
You do this with your grandkids in the house?
Eloise: No, I don't do it if they're there. They're staying at my girlfriend's house. My daughter is there. She's a speed freak.
Your daughter takes care of her children?
Eloise: If that's what you call it. I don't know. (Laughter) You know she's a good mother but she doesn't clean house. She's got her priorities a little fucked-up right now. I only hope that when I get out I can help her and she can recover. I mean it hit a lot of buttons with me. The kids are seven months and three years old.

> I mean, I'm not prejudiced, but I sure as hell know what color I am. I'm full-fledged German and I loved November 1943! I wish they'd do another sweep like they did to the Jews.
>
> Inmate Candice

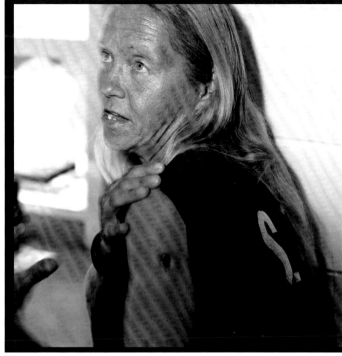

144

When your daughter is out of it and . . .
Eloise: She gets high and then she sleeps all day and the kids have to fend for themselves. They scream and scream. I've walked in there, and the kids are lying on the floor with cake all over their fucking face, and it's a wonder the baby hasn't choked to death. I get my daughter up, screaming at her to get up, put a diaper on the baby, and take care of her kids. She tells me to get the fuck out of her place.
What's going to happen to these children?
Eloise: I'm going to take them. To my apartment!
Ruby: Oh great. How can you say that you're clean only two months, after twenty years?
Does your daughter get money also?
Eloise: Yeah, she gets AFDC (Aid to Families with Dependent Children) for her children. It's $1,400 a month, and we don't get along.
Ruby: Amazing.
Eloise: See, I can't live with her and keep her in check. She's got to do that on her own.
Ruby: Why don't you take those kids and call CPS on her before one of them gets hurt?
Eloise: They gonna get hurt anyway. Child Protective can walk in and I can say, "Get out of here." They gonna come to me 'cause I'm the nearest living relative. The government knew I was a junkie when my kids were little. They didn't take them away from me, as long as there's food and they're getting taken care of. I was scared to death to tell anybody I was a junkie.
Why do women have children when they know they are junkies?
Eloise: I don't know, sweetheart.
Were you using cocaine?
Ruby: Yeah.
Eloise: I like my beer.

Ruby: I smoked it. Cocaine. My child called 911. He was five. My kids are my life!

Eloise: My son said, "You ain't gonna use, Mama," and I left Chicago and came back here. I didn't use for almost seven or eight years. Then I started hanging around with the wrong people. I was with my girlfriend, and she was getting high every day, and I thought I had to. It's crazy. Because it's there, you wanna do it. The next thing, you're out on the streets selling your ass. Next thing, you're back here again. It's ridiculous. It's a vicious cycle. I don't know if it's pressure or just wanting to do it. I'm not craving dope. Granted, it's hard if somebody lays it out here in front of me, and says "Take it or leave it." I got priorities right now. I'm still messed up in the head, fighting alcohol, too. My daughter don't smoke in front of them or nothing. She's always in the bathroom. The kids see mom in the bathroom all the time. He's maybe three now. He'll be six pretty soon.

Dep. Houck: Your hands and feet were swollen, too [talking to Ruby].

Nurse: How much soup and goodies are you eating from the commissary? That soup's loaded with salt. I'm gonna grab you by the ears and shake that blood pressure down.

Deputies escort more inmates to Sick Call.

Dep. Houck: New arrivals, sit down.

Candice: I wanna go home. I got full-blown AIDS. I had it last time here, too, and they just told me. I want out of here. They can't take care of me in here. People are harassing me in the dorm. They tell everybody to get away from me.

Dep. Houck: How'd you get it?

Candice: I was a caretaker for an old man.

The deputies know that you have AIDS?

Candice: Yeah. Overhearing my conversation. I got a 19-year-old son. I've got an 11-year-old daughter I gave up when she was seven. They tested her as genius at three, and she was too much for me to handle. She's in a Christian private school with a Christian family. Thank God. That was the Lord's way of taking care of her. My foot's bad. It hurts inside. It started with a little cut on my fourth toe, and then the infection just got really worse. The doctor, a black guy, thought there was a fracture because the skin was so purple and rotten. I sat in here suffering. Charging $3—it stinks. All that some of us have on our books is $20 a month. I like to have my goodies. Especially now. I need to eat more. I got $15 on my books the other day and they're already going to take $6 out of it for this shit. I'm an AIDS patient. I think they should take care of me free. I don't think they should have me in F housing. I think they should have me in the Infirmary. I'm contagious. I have open sores that are bleeding and have pus. They tell me to stay in my dorm. Goddamn them.

Dep. Houck leaves to check on new patients. When she returns, she breaks out in laughter.

Dep. Houck: All of a sudden you're quiet 'cause I walk in.

Candice: At least the doctor gave me a shot in the foot, painkiller, and antibiotics. He cleaned it. It was so swollen I couldn't walk on it. He told me to soak it in a plastic bag in Betadine.

Dep. Houck talks to us about her life as a guard.

Dep. Houck: Tonight I'll take a shower, wash my hair, read the newspaper, talk to my kids on the phone, spy on them, you know. My one son has a 30-day leave. He's in the army, a paratrooper. He does Europe and flies all around the United States. So it's been a good military experience for him. He's really athletic, doesn't drink, doesn't smoke, doesn't do drugs. He's Mr. Joe Clean all the way, yet my other kids have experimented. I have a son who's been in and out of jail four or five times. Yeah! I was working in the men's jail when that happened.

Candice: Oh, don't go to jail and have your mom be there! (Laughter)

Dep. Houck: Yeah, the first time it was terrible, a fate worse than death, but that's his choice. He was on the roof of the jail playing basketball. I got on that microphone and called out, "Why do you do methamphetamine?" He told me it makes him feel powerful. He was in four times. The fifth time I wasn't there. He's done anywhere from six to eight months each time in all of the men's jails. He knows better, but he's chosen another way. I said to him, "Don't come around the house, because you're contaminating my family." I love him very much, but I don't like him. I don't like what he's doing. "See you on the holidays, Bud." When he's out, he can only hold a job for about six to eight months.

Angie comes in from the A patio.

Dep. Houck: Angie had a baby, named Octavia. Her sister's watching the baby. You had to bring another Angie into the world? It's not going to a foster home with someone strange, I hope?

Candice: Angie's a lot better person in here than she is out on the streets.

Angie: I'm in A housing because in B housing I'd get into a lot of fights. There's a lot of drugs in there, so I just got into A.

Kale, in the Safety Cell, yells louder and louder.

Dep. Houck: Funny. That girl's screaming for a cookie.

Dep. Houck shouts into the hallway, "Give that girl a cookie!"

What are you in here for?

Angie: Assault with a deadly weapon. A hammer. It was a man. He made me mad. He wouldn't pay me my money, so I beat him.

Candice: Yeah, they'd kill me for $15 on the street.

Kale screams even louder.

Dep. Houck: Will someone give that girl a cookie?

Candice: Waiting for the AIDS results was scarier than hell.

Eloise: I've had four tests. I get scared every time. I don't share needles. I get fresh needles from the pharmacy, and I'm a bleach fanatic. I wreck the needles soaking them so much. I haven't been to bed with anybody in two years.

Ruby: Maybe you should do that instead of drugs.

Eloise: It's better to have an old man than to fall in love with an oxygen pump. I had a good old man, but I left him a few years ago. I shoulda stayed. My life's gone to shit. I been on the streets with my kids, and been in jail for my drugs. I mean, I had it made. Then I screwed up and started in with drugs. You can't make a life with drugs. I have to wash my hands of my kids. I got a son in jail in Chula Vista for domestic violence.

145-146. Deputy Houck; 147. Deputy Houck and Inmate Angie; 148. Deputy Houck and Inmate Eloise; 149-150. Inmate Angie

148

What kind of attention did you get as a little girl?
Eloise: I didn't. My mother died when I was 12 years old. I been on my own since. I was in a couple of foster homes, but they couldn't handle me. I don't remember being a child. I remember being shuffled from place to place and having a drunk mother passing out all the time. I'd come home to a cold house. She killed herself. At least with my kids, I didn't do drugs when they was little.

It was better being on the streets than at the home with your mother?
Eloise: Sure, I'm street smart. My kids are street smart. My daughter thinks she can go get a job. I'm not going to knock her, but at 19 with no education, dropping out of school at eighth grade to have kids, what's she going to do? Work at Jack In The Box? I'd rather sit at home and clean house and watch kids than get out there in the working world. But that's me.

Do you worry about neurological damage from drug use?
Eloise: Sure. I got a bad memory. I don't even know what I did

yesterday, much less a week ago. I've had a lot of daytime blackouts, not just going to sleep. There's nothing more frightening than to have somebody tell you the next day what you've done, and you can't remember. I used to say it was because I slept so hard I just couldn't remember but I think it was from drinking and taking pills or drinking and doing drugs. At one time I was doing methadone, heroin, Xanax, Dalmane.

Where did you get all of the drugs?
Eloise: From a doctor. They were legally prescribed. I was doing methadone and shooting heroin at the same time.

What did you tell him you needed methadone for?
Eloise: That I was coming off. I didn't tell him that I was still on heroin. I've OD'd from drinking and shooting dope. I've been lucky as far as jail time and using drugs. I won't even go home when I first get out, because I know the rat race at my daughter's house. It'll just piss me off, and I'll go out and use again. I have to be in court on the 31st, and I'll be goddamned if she's going to drag me down to her level.

A girl outside the Sick Call window on the A patio stomps around in circles. Houck says it's 112 degrees in the shade.

Someone in green is a psychiatric issue?
Dep. Houck: Escape threat.
Rolenda Banks wore green. Will Kale?
Dep. Houck: Sure, if she ever gets out of the Safety Cell.
Eloise: I've heard a lot of deputies say they'd rather work with the men than the women, because women whine.
Candice: I'm ready to go to sleep now.

Candice wiggles into a more comfortable position like a child medicated. The handcuffs don't seem to bother her. She's had her meds and lunch.

Eloise: Women are pigs.
Angie: Most of these women are from the streets. They don't have property, and they're not used to a house or a roof over their head. They misuse what they have in here.
Candice: You had an assault with a prior.
Angie: The forgery charge was an assault. I got my first strike this time.
Eloise: You too young, honey. You better curb that anger.
Angie: The L.A. riot. I was in that one too. I was there stealing clothes.
Looting things to sell and get money?
Angie: Oh no, I was just doing it 'cause I liked it. I got a whole bunch of new clothes. I wasn't even thinking about drugs. It's a wicked world out there. It was just anger.
Do you think something like the L.A. riots could happen again?
Angie: Certain people own L.A., like the Iranians, and Japanese. It's not black-owned. What's not, the blacks burn down. I think the world's being taken over by the Japanese and Iranians. They own all of the businesses and never want to give black people a job, but we're their biggest customers.

149-150

Eloise: Yeah, and we get AIDS. I wake up in night-sweats, with my glands hurting and I'm kickin' the dope.
Angie: It's so weird to just think about it. I know someone who has AIDS. We lived together for months and months, years.
Candice: Yeah, I know her too. She's only 42. She's not going to make it through the end of the summer. I'm 36, and it's scary. I think I've had AIDS for six years. That's how long I've known the guy I got it from.
Angie: That's a lot of welfare.
Candice: It's been that long, and I been doing drugs and living in the streets. I'm allergic to sulfa and a lot of the AIDS drugs have sulfa.

Kale starts to scream again. Dr. Bennett enters the hall.

Dr. Bennett: It's good to be here on Saturday because there's a lot less other shit going on. Let them chat with Kale.
Nurse: We have to clear it through the deputy.
Dr. Bennett: They wouldn't even open the door for me. She's smearing feces. She's not predictable.
Nurse: I'm sure you're aware that everything has to be cleared with the sergeant. Kale is completely without garments. I don't know if you can photograph that. It's real messy in her cell. Be prepared. The doctor is checking if Kale will see you.

Oh, yes; I like Maxwell! She's a very intelligent person. She was in Lockdown, and she's back in B now. She reads constantly. She has beautiful penmanship and good communication skills . . . She could do anything.

Deputy Houck

Is Maxwell still here?
Dep. Houck: Oh, yes; I like Maxwell! She's a very intelligent person. She was in Lockdown, and she's back in B now. She reads constantly. She has beautiful penmanship and good communication skills. She sticks out like a sore thumb. She could do anything. She has some of the nicest photographs of her hiking and vacationing. I never have any problems with her. I mean, at least some times with these girls, by the grace of God they'll die. OK. They're discussing if you can see Kale right now. You can't go over there yet until the sergeant says you can. Sit here.

A trusty inmate will be expected to clean up the Safety Cell when Kale is removed.

Dep. Houck: They take a spray bottle, disinfectant, and mop. The sergeant won't give you permission to see Kale. I can't go against what he says.
Dr. Bennett: They aren't comfortable letting you see Kale because of all the crap she's been doing, but I told Kale you're here to see her. She's decided she's not going to hurt anyone or herself. So when you're back next time, check in with the administration.

Sheriff's Department vs. Correctional Department

9/1/95 11:00 a.m. San Diego Sheriff's Department Headquarters, Ben McLaughlin

Ben McLaughlin tells us more about jail and law enforcement.

McLaughlin: I was afraid you were going to identify with the inmates too much at first. You're the set of new eyes. I don't care about what the inmates say.

Inmates label themselves to create order in the tank, cell, or group. Shelby Roland was always in charge of a group during her first stay. A deputy may pick someone with power and persuasion, and say, "Get all of these guys together for court," and then hand the inmate the list. We pull morning courts at 5:00 a.m., and afternoon courts at 10:30 a.m. We haul them all over the county to various courthouses where we pass them to the marshal. The marshal takes them to holding cells where they stay for eight-to-ten hours at a time. They may only get a three-minute audience with the judge. They sit on a hard bench or cold cement floor until we bring them back.

There are a lot of forces at work in these dynamics. I've seen many deputies and staff crack, usually in the form of alcoholism, drug abuse, or abnormal sexual behavior. In fact, one of my former partners on patrol turned out to be a stalker and rapist of go-go dancers. He ended up in prison for a lot of years. Joseph Wambaugh's *The Choirboys* is about this: "Let's go have a drink, tell stories and laugh and get healed." Police life creates a lot of alcoholics. It's a hook. Pretty soon your emotional release is alcohol. I used to tell deputies, "You're no different with alcohol than the inmate is with drugs. It's a choice."

I want to train them to learn the correction's perspective, not the cop's. We have to change the mentality. It's a tough transition to go from law enforcement to corrections. I'm a babysitter. If inmates commit a crime in the jail, I'll deal with it. The idea is to train people how to work in institutions.

As we become urban and mobile, we lose our sense of place. We feel like we live in a vacuum. Prisons have become the place where the good element of society puts the bad element, so society doesn't have to deal with it. The prisons are full. Gangs are replacing family.

There's no real way to explain it. Bottom line is we're raising a whole generation of killers who haven't gotten to legal age. At 14, they carry automatic weapons and shoot people. What's going to happen when they turn 18? People are starting to realize we have a very violent juvenile population rising. We say, "What did we do wrong?" That's simple. We passed laws that destroyed family cohesiveness, taxed families so that both parties [mothers and fathers] have to work, and then wonder why kids don't have more supervision at home. The culture has destroyed any incentive for families to stay together. It's too easy to get divorced. The 60s said everybody ought to run around and do what they want. We introduced drugs and pop culture since then. The movies have glorified all of this.

It takes a commitment of the federal government, like putting a man on the moon, the kind of commitment you're never going to forget. It has to start with the president of the United States. We tax programs that work against the family. Kids go to school wearing black, getting tattoos and body mutilations. Even if they have good families, they feel the pressure of the media. The popular culture dominates. It has an attraction, a lure. It's illusory. Our society is focused on 20 percent. The teen who is pregnant can have an abortion, go back to school, and the parents don't know. The teen falls down the stairs and needs sutures, but can't get them unless the parent gives permission.

You're a paranoid parent if you question the public school system. Liberal elitists get into the schools. We're warehousing a generation and we haven't done anything to help the next one. Society can't function with random, extreme kids. It was, "I don't want to bust anybody's legs. I just want to kill them."

It's a whole different ball game and a whole different society than we've ever had before. We could deal with it if we enacted legislation that empowered families. Congress isn't passing good laws.

You can tell how civilized your society is by how you treat your prisoners. It's not just a humanitarian perspective, it's how you help them get out of this life of crime, this mentality of criminality. That's a mark of society. I think everybody has the ability to change from a life of crime. A certain percentage never will, but a vast majority can be turned around with the right programs.

You mention the inmate Rolenda, and you ask good questions. The judge has zero control when he sentences her to state prison. He sentences the inmate to the custody of the Sheriff and we don't do what he told us to do. They have absolutely no say-so about the way the law is set up. He'll say, "Send this one to honor camp." Honor camp is full or doesn't want the inmate, so there's no obligation. The court can't mandate what we do with the inmate once they sentence the inmate to our custody.

151. Assistant Sheriff Ben McLaughlin

Well, we make an erroneous assumption that because we care for somebody they will care about themselves, and it isn't true. Bottom line—you can't force people to care about themselves, and if they think so little of themselves, then somewhere along the line you have to teach them to think better of themselves.

Assistant Sheriff Ben McLaughlin

Kath Anderson has called and asked us to drop by Hamilton House. She has a surprise. When we arrive, little Cassie sits outside, waiting. She is the daughter of one of the female residents.

152

9/8/95   12:00 p.m.   Hamilton House

At Hamilton House, Anderson leaves us in the front room with Justin, who, I've been told, likes to play with knives and guns.
Justin and 13 other men and women live at Hamilton House.
When Anderson appears, Maxwell is by her side. Maxwell looks worn-out and down. It's a hot day, but Maxwell's wearing a down vest. She takes a seat on the sofa. Anderson sits next to her. They tell us that Maxwell wants to share what's happened to her since we saw her in jail.

Maxwell: In Las Colinas, they kept me on a daybed and wouldn't give me a room 'cause I had a big 'H' for homosexual on my sweatshirt. In a room with other women they thought I might have too much fun. All night, lights were on, lousy. There was no privacy and you have to stay on your bed, too. They played the night owl game every night. They'd get me up to handcuff me, take me to Control, and then handcuff me to the bench for a whole shift. I'd fall over asleep and bump my head, and the deputies would laugh. They were bored.

153

Gordy enters from the kitchen. He tells us that he's visiting Hamilton House to see how Anderson is going to deal with Maxwell. Maxwell fondles a sickly kitten that followed her to Hamilton House. She appears oblivious to the concern Gordy has, saying she wants to sleep. Anderson tells her she has to go to VOA (Volunteers of America), a detox facility. Crash, another facility, is full. Anderson places a call to VOA. They're full unless someone has $50 for her entry.

Maxwell: I've used up my nine lives. Speaking of nine lives, where is Cindy Mulloy?
Anderson: Out on the streets.
Maxwell: She knows that suicide is real for dope fiends. Dope is a really peaceful way to go. I got a ride out at midnight, freezing cold, with a bunch of crazy girls in a taxicab. They dropped everybody off, one by one. They dropped me off in North Park and I spent the night in the front seat of this guy's truck. I froze my ass off. He's a tweaker.
Anderson: Next thing, she was on a motorcycle at two in the morning outside this house.
Maxwell: I'm supposed to be on probation but probation doesn't pay attention to me. I'm supposed to be in a recovery home. So I wrote Dep. Houck a letter. She's wonderful even though she tortured me. I was in Receiving four days puking my guts out 'cause I relapsed. Harper loves it on duty outside the Release Room. Heil Harper! The deputies don't like me.
Anderson: I knew Milakovich 20 years ago. She's watched me all these years. There're a couple of good programs in the jail, like the one with Crandall. Nobody affected me like Crandall in his class. You've talked to Donnie, Joe, and Gwen, graduates of Crandall's program. He has no funding. He's a clinical psychologist with a master's degree. Crandall's a recovering addict who earlier was declared institutionalized. He says 80-85 percent of inmates are incarcerated for drug or alcohol crimes, and there's a 50 percent recidivism in the first six months alone. He told the Board of Supervisors he'd take a $7,000 cut to keep his program going. Programs geared toward 12 Steps are going to fade. He doesn't feel that the higher-ups know the real depth of the problems.
Gordy: You gotta listen to the addiction.

Crandall, recovering addict, enters the living room along with several other residents who had been in the kitchen.

Crandall: You take on the characteristics of those you hang with if they're using dope, and they're destructive and violent. Those behaviors become your skills. I came out of jail at 34 knowing how to use dope, how to be violent, and how to be destructive. Recovery taught me otherwise. There's no such thing as a stupid dope fiend. We never failed to get our dope. We're not stuck on stupid. We're stuck on uneducated, fear of failure when you grow up. Failure becomes a part of your lifestyle. You're programmed to fail.
Maxwell: Jail creates dependency. There're all these inmates and female deputies telling you to go to bed. It's past your bedtime.
Anderson: When you're messing with women and you're in jail or prison society,

> I'm supposed to be on probation but probation doesn't pay attention to me. I'm supposed to be in a recovery home.
>
> Maxwell
> Hamilton House

154-155

156

that girlfriend or old lady is gonna be your mother. It's a codependent web, little families.

Prostitution is a part of addictive behavior?
Maxwell: Prostitutes are fascinating to me. My roommate could make so much money. She'd go out of that room at the Berkshire that cost $22 a day and walk down that block and come in with a date. I'd leave and sit on the step for approximately seven-and-a-half minutes. Then he'd come out with, "I'll see ya." I'd go in, and she'd have 20 or 40 bucks depending on what she did. If she gave head, she'd get $20; if she had intercourse, she'd get $40 and more sometimes. Like last night before she got arrested, I walked her down to her date. Then she walked away. She was gone approximately 20 minutes. She came back with $80. All day long she does this.

Maxwell's voice fades in and out, Gordy observes.

Maxwell: My addict behavior stems from Mommy, the absence of. The women I hook up with cannot take the place of Mother. They nurture the child in me.

Anderson: And they spoil you and pamper you and press your pants. They make your soups. I did that too, in prison.

Maxwell, how do you see yourself?

Maxwell: I don't have that maternal, female side. What drives me is the male, learned behavior. I think it's conditioning and genetics.

Maxwell tosses the kitten onto the floor.

Maxwell: I'm sick from the heroin. You can call me whatever you like. Whenever I have a kitten I torment the hell out of 'em. I wind 'em up and then let 'em go; they run all over the place.

You said you challenged the staff at the jail.

Maxwell: It was entertainment. It's terrible, but any form of demented or unstable or left-field behavior is entertainment.

Did you room with Rolenda?

Maxwell: No, and there's worse than Rolenda. She had a problem in her mind, but she wasn't violent. A lot of those women are so violent you can't glance over at them without starting a fistfight.

Gordy: It isn't anything like prison, where inmates make shanks out of sharp objects and stab each other to death.

Maxwell disappears to a bedroom. Anderson has placed several calls for placement for Maxwell. VOA is the only option.

What happens if you keep her at Hamilton House?

Anderson: She's exhausted right now. Out like a light, but it's not going to be very long before she wakes up.

Gordy: Did she get high today?

Anderson: Early this morning.

Gordy: That's enough to hold her 'til she wakes up. How long a run did she have?

Anderson: Ten days.

Gordy: She's clean two years. It's more psychological. She doesn't have much to work out.

Does heroin work like alcohol?

Gordy: I seen people who kicked alcohol just tear their insides, but heroin is more of a mental and physical thing. You can't eat and you can't sleep. The best way to describe it is as a real intense flu. Your skin crawls. You pick at yourself 'cause you're loaded. Heroin addicts do that, they scratch a lot. I used heroin for 25 years.

Anderson: She's really close to me, and that worries me.

Gordy: She's only got a ten-day run. She's gonna snivel and complain. If you got her and she wakes up, she's not gonna stay. I don't care what you do. She's gonna go out and get what she needs. She doesn't have the willingness to quit. Detox is controlled, and has facilities to prepare for something like that. They'd rather put them in prison than help them to get connected.

Anderson: She's looking for strength. She wants to bond with a female in a loving way and find the kind of nurturing she never had. She does this in jail. She said that she goes into every unit and gets close to another female. It's a supportive, not just a sexual thing. She gets close and then feels too good or too happy, and the whole thing kicks back in and she uses.

Gordy: Here's how they do it—when I got out of prison, I didn't know how to get clean. So I used. I went to the parole officer and said, "Look, I used, and I know what's gonna happen. I know what's ahead. You don't have to tell me. I've done this too many times. I know what kind of fool I am and I want some help." It's the first time I asked for help. I'm tired. She looked at my file and goes, "My God, you're willing to go into a drug treatment facility? I need to put you on a list." I said, "I won't show up. I need to go now." She said, "Be here tomorrow morning." I did and I've been here every day since.

Maxwell needs to get the same basic structure. She doesn't have the foggiest notion. Until you've experienced and worked it out for yourself, it's not going to stick. If somebody told me, "You use because of how you feel about yourself," I'd look him in the face and say, "Get out of my face, stupid. I use because I like to use." All throughout life you go reaching for the love and making bad decisions. Addicts aren't bad people. They just make bad decisions. Some of them are worse than others. I believe most addicts are overly-sensitive people.

I hear you talking about drugs. What about alcohol?

Gordy: Alcohol numbs everything. I've seen alcoholics when they got clean after many years. They were just numb. They couldn't feel. They didn't have any feelings or show any emotion. A place like Betty Ford wouldn't work for me. It wouldn't work for Kath. I'd tell 'em what they wanted to hear. I'd start to control it, but then I would need somebody to sit me down and say, "Hey stupid, sit down and shut up."

What was kicking like for you in jail? Did you go through it?

Gordy: Many times. It's not something that would stop me from usin', 'cause you seem to forget those bad times. Jails, institutions, and death, I've done all three. I've died, I've OD'd. I've been brought back to life. I've been to every institution in California. I've been to mental institutions.

Next morning. Anderson calls. Maxwell's been asleep 17 hours.

157

152-157. Photos at Hamilton House
152. Cassie; 153. Maxwell; 154-156.
Maxwell and Kath Anderson; 157. Gordy

158   159   160

9/12/95   10:00 a.m.   Pro Visit Room

I go to the jail to see Kale, with the image of her screaming from the Safety Cell, and a curiosity about why she was spreading feces on the walls. I haven't talked to Dr. Bull in several weeks and I see him at the sally port.

Dr. Bull: Some people are really harder to love than other people. I would like to think that the people who are the hardest to care for are the ones we can learn the most from. They're like messengers who tax us and teach us.

Would Rolenda qualify as a messenger?
Yes. I don't think there's anybody here who isn't understandable and worthy of our compassion if we just get close enough. We don't have psychiatric units in the women's jail, but the men's jails do. If E housing were a 24-hour-a-day, full-fledged psychiatric unit, like the men's jail, then the women in psychiatric crisis wouldn't have to go to the mental hospital. The Safety Cell, with the Turkish toilet, is for someone who is exhibiting bizarre or violent behavior. It's a protective environment for them, not for us. The Detox Cell is a little different. It has a toilet. It's for the intoxicated person.

What about someone like Kale, smearing feces on the wall of the Safety Cell?
She gets an automatic trip to the mental health ward. Most sane people don't play with that.

Dr. Bull has an appointment. Dep. Ford arrives to escort us to the showers where they'll allow us to see Kale.
We pass the Release Room, and a woman in a red silk slip with cuts on her face and a weather-beaten expression smiles at me. Her blonde hair is matted. She sees Dep. Ford and shouts that she got clubbed with a 2x4. He stops and corrects her, "No, you fell."

161

Kale shakes my hand through the cuff-release hole—a strong warm hand, and sits on the shower tile floor, Indian style. Her hair is slicked back and combed wet.

How do you like A housing?
It's kinda nice. I have TV. I listen to anything I want. I don't have chaos. Back in F and C housing it gets radical. Especially in F housing, they're a bunch of babies, and they have two housemothers, supposed to be like the caretakers. The day you took pictures of me, I was in F housing and got pulled back by Dep. Barnes. He took me in that day because I had my pants rolled up. I was brought to Isolation. I got mad and tore up a couple jail cells. Finally they put me in without a bunk. I had to sleep on the floor without a mattress. I had to go to the hospital. I overdosed on the Ibuprofen pills, two days ago. I wasn't going to say anything, but I know some first aid. If I were gonna stay, my heart would slow down. So I told the deputy. They took me to UCSD and put an IV in me and gave me charcoal. That didn't make me sick. It just flushed me out. Then they took me to CMH (County Mental Health). I'm manic-depressive and claustrophobic.

Confinement is difficult for you?
I got mad last night. I'd been up all night, and they wouldn't let me go to the CMH to get more prescriptions or to see the psychiatrist. I'm taking everything–it just isn't working. Ativan, lithium, and Resperdal, a new neuroleptic. I'm like in a manic phase right now and they're not doing anything. I want to sleep but I can't.

Are you describing mania or claustrophobia?
Claustrophobic. In my room, I said to the deputy, "If I don't get out, I'm gonna burst." When I was little I was always sent to my room, at bedtime, you know?

Maxwell was your roommate?
Yeah! She knows the deputies were tormenting me.

I heard you yelling, "I'm a prostitute!"
Ha! I was making up this song, 'cause I've been involved with drugs and I've worked in Long Beach for Parks and Recreation with blacks, Mexicans, and Samoans. I learned a lot about the SOS, Sons of Samoa. On the west side of Long Beach there were a lot of Bloods and Crips. I learned about the gangs. The little kids would be in gangs, and they taught me a lot of dances. I got rhythm.

Where was your home?
We moved around a lot. I was born in Long Beach. When we moved to Thousand Oaks, my dad worked for McKesson Chemical Company. I was in second grade. Then we moved back down to Huntington Beach, and my father started working with my grandfather at the Mail Delivery Service Company. I got curious and went dancin' at the gay bars. I learned a lot about being a woman. It was interesting. I'm a bisexual. I have a boyfriend right now.

Looking back, what was growing up like for you?
Craziness. Growing up with ballet, tap dance, soccer, school, and the swim team. My brother could've gone to the Olympics as a water polo player. He chose USC over Berkeley for a scholarship. He's younger, 23. I was jealous of him because he was on the swim team. I have a beautiful swimming stroke. I was a lifeguard at the beach, and worked for the state teaching swimming for 12 years. That's when I got involved in meth. I got fired from my job 'cause I had to be at work at six-thirty in the morning, open up a pool, teach swimming all day, and go to school. It was too much to do. I crashed. My grades went down. I started failing classes. My GPA is like 1.4 at Cal State. The only way I can even get back in school is with a note from my psychiatrist. Once I'm in school, I have to take Ritalin to concentrate. Using speed was like using Ritalin.

When did you start taking street drugs?
The very first time was when I was on the ski lifts at Mammoth. This guy goes, "You want a bullet?" I did it and felt good. I took a class at college in logic and my teacher said, "If you go with a bunch of friends and get stoned, you'll understand logic." And it's true. Logic is like, all dogs are cats, all cats are dogs, therefore all dogs are animals. I liked coke too much and I never tried it again.

What frightens you?
My fear of success. I haven't completed things. I'm afraid of Isolation. I went to the rubber room in Anaheim. See this scar right here? I was at my boyfriend's house. I was pissed. I was in a manic stage. I busted out of his window. I got the cut right here. He wanted me arrested for being drunk in public. They took me to jail and I tore the jail cell apart. I took the phone, and busted it apart. I tore the mattress apart. I flooded it out. They put me in the rubber room. I was still on the speed. I was spinning around inside the rubber room. The ambulance came and took me to the hospital. I was put in the psychiatric ward. I've had to be in the chair like seven times.

The restraining chair?
Yes. Your legs are strapped. Your arms are strapped. Your chest is strapped. You have to stay there for hours. I had no circulation whatsoever. I was screaming and crying. When they removed me, they took me to CMH.

What about your parents?
I worked with my dad at his company but he fired me when he found a pot pipe in his car. He knew I was doing drugs. My drug dealer, I called Mother. She's 47. I'd go to her for advice. She's been married, had kids, and now she's gay. She's what they call a bull dyke. She's helped me in so many ways just getting through life. Giving personal advice. You can't just go over to a drug dealer's house. You gain trust by gaining a friendship, doing drugs.

Where will you go after court?
I'm going back to live with my boyfriend and our dog, Sparky. If it doesn't work I have a grandmother who speaks five languages and lives in a mobile home. My parents kicked me out and put all my stuff in public storage. Everybody thinks I'm violent, and I'm not violent.

Kale, smiling and wanting to engage in more conversation, spins into a manic state. Out of nowhere she starts out with a strange story, more dreamlike than real.
She stands behind the grated metal door and waits for another question.

165

158. Halters; 159. Inmate shoes; 160. Inmate Kale
locked in showers; 161-165. Inmate Kale

162-164

I try to locate Kristina Edwards' mother by talking to a phone operator who searches through directories in several counties in California.

Kristina's grandmother answers and says Kristina's mother isn't there. Although concerned about Kristina, the grandmother says Kristina wasn't willing to live with house rules.

9/12/95   2:00 p.m.   Pro Visit Room

At the jail, Kristina arrives.

I talked to Ellen.
Edwards: I hear you talked to my mom.
Initially I talked to your grandmother, and discovered that you have many aunts and uncles.
I don't get along with them. They don't like me.
How do you feel?
Like shit. I didn't have a check-up or nothin'. It costs three dollars every time you make a request. But they rescheduled me. I was in the shower. You can put money on my books, really.
You know we've been over that.
So the death penalty was dropped, and life-without [parole] is where it's standing now. The DA's trying to make deals non-negotiable and that means there's no deal. The juvenile's going to jail for seven years. Man, I would take that in a heartbeat. My lawyer even told me he doesn't want to put me up on that stand because he's afraid if he puts me on that stand the DA will bury me.
You're going to have a baby soon.
I went into a car with them and I seen them treating him that way, and then I got out of the car for no reason, and I handed this guy a rock. Aren't you going to be there?

Kristina hears from her mother the next week.

10/6/95   11:00 a.m.   Pro Visit Room

It's been three weeks since we've seen Kristina. Barbara rides with me in my old Land Rover to the jail to visit Kristina Edwards.

Is it lunchtime?
Edwards: Yeah, I was just eating. The whole unit's been in Lockdown for two weeks. I was in the Infirmary for three days. I gotta go to court on the 24th for my motions. At 8:30 a.m., Department 9. That's when they're gonna drop the charges of kidnapping and torture. My mom can't make it to the court. She's got two little babies, and her boyfriend works. I don't feel good about my attorney.
Your hair is growing out. Your natural color is pretty.
I'm ugly. Call my mom and tell her I love her. I'm in Lockdown. The whole dorm is. I can't call.
You talked to your mom?
It was weird. I had my roommate call. I had false labor. I might go in a week. I mean, I got an approval from the sergeant for my mom to come, and you can come to the hospital. My mom doesn't understand anything that's goin' on. She's thinks I was really involved. That's why I'm really comfortable with you. I can't explain it to her on the phone. She goes, "Well. You did it, or you didn't do it." "I didn't do it, I'm telling you." She said I was out chasing after drugs.

166. Inmate Edwards

10/16/95   9:00 a.m.   Phone call

I call Ben McLaughlin to make certain we have permission to enter the hospital and go into Kristina's delivery room. He says, "Just let the Captain know."

Captain Pierce has been replaced. The new Captain says, "This is highly irregular, but since it's already in place, just talk to the lieutenant." The lieutenant says, "Fine."

12:00 p.m.   Lunch at the Roadside Café with Deputy Bilyeu

I sensed on the yard that you had more to say.
Dep. Bilyeu: I couldn't talk to you and do my job at the same time. I'm glad we could meet here. Things are getting out of control. We're getting early releases because of overcrowding, and we have to shove them out the door. There's a lot of mental illness, but much of it has been caused by progressive drug use. One woman, a wonderful singer, very talented, drank the mercury out of a thermometer to get high. Her brain fried. The popular drug today is crystal methamphetamine because it's less expensive than cocaine, and it's more accessible. Women today are stealing to get money for drugs. They prostitute themselves to pay for their drug problem.

No one's immune to having someone in his or her life with an addiction. Deputies have or have had alcohol problems. Some people come from very wealthy families. Maybe they take prescription drugs, like painkillers that are addictive, but go unnoticed.

It's like getting rid of roaches. When inmates leave jail the first time, they go back home to their mothers or boyfriends, into a dysfunctional situation. They slip once, and it starts all over again. I can relate to it. I tell them, "Just because I have this badge doesn't mean that I've had fewer experiences. It's not really any of your business to know about me, but I've been there. I was sexually and physically abused." Recovery isn't automatic. Had I not been given the opportunity for therapy, I wouldn't be where I am today. Women need a transition from the jail structure to the outside world.

Women in jail are looking for affection and attention because they tend to be more open and sensitive than men. They bond in jail, or what we call "switch hit," while they have boyfriends on the outside. We can provide the lumber and concrete to build the house, but if you don't have the tools, nothing's going to happen. There are women who have learning disabilities. There are women in here having babies and using drugs. It's progressive. Our teachers haven't been trained to handle kids adopted at birth with physical health problems and disabilities. The teachers are frustrated with all of the hyper kids. At the same time the kids are taught that it's abuse if parents yell or spank. The kids run the parents.

We had a girl come in who had cut her boyfriend. She was felony-stupid, pregnant, and acting dumb. She was using crystal meth, and pregnant. Today her child is three, and the child can't put two words together. The mother has gone to rehab and walked out. She wants her drugs. The courts are swamped. We feed inmates, give them exercise, follow Title 15 requirements. We have no time to sit down to work with these people. The Stepping Out Program is the only way we try to correct behavior.

Cindy Mulloy was good at the game. These aren't ladies. They're females. They have children because they're looking for love. Even if they can't keep the child, it's a mindset. Kids are now using drugs and popping out babies. They get high and start shooting people with no conscience. They're accustomed to not having boundaries and values. "What are you gonna do to me? Put me in jail?" I tell them, "Nobody can take away your recovery unless you allow them."

167. Deputy Bilyeu

Neurons in your brain release many different neurotransmitters as you go about your day thinking, feeling, reacting, breathing, and digesting. When you learn new information or a new skill, your brain builds more axons and dendrites first, as a tree grows roots and branches. With more branches, neurons can communicate and send their messages more efficiently.[25]

National Institute on Drug Abuse (NIDA)

The Great Disruption

Perhaps the most obvious prediction from a Darwinian view of parental motive is this: substitute parents will generally tend to care less profoundly for children than natural parents.[26]

Francis Fukuyama, Ph.D.

In order to understand the origins and impact of interpersonal violence, it is essential to appreciate how violence alters the developing child. The child and the adult reflect the world they are raised in. And, sadly, in today's world, millions of children are raised in unstable and violent settings. Literally, incubated in terror.[27]

Bruce Perry, M.D., Ph.D.

Anger's a damn good cover-up for hurt.

Inmate Mindy

168

169

168-169. Inmate Mindy

10/24/95 9:00 a.m. Pro Visit Room

It's been over one month since we've seen Mindy. She has been removed from F housing and placed in Discipline. We call her out for a visit. Mindy has a third-grade education and has lived on the streets since the age of nine.

Mindy: I'm here on a 459 [assault with a deadly weapon]. I'm an alcoholic-addict. Some deputies are assholes, like Dep. Wildenburg. They want to fuck with someone. Yeah, I called her a cunt. She was being a cunt. It's a bad word. It means like when you call a guy a fag. You'll call a chick a cunt. If you call a straight guy a fag it's gonna piss them off. Some deputies don't like me. I've gotten out of A housing and Lockdown and been back in F. They treat me like an animal. Some of the deputies favor the hardened criminals. Maybe because they envy them. The criminals are the heroes! Anger's a damn good cover-up for hurt.

I have compulsive thinking. I don't think before I act. I asked Daniel, my husband, who died, not to do drugs. I found out this other guy he was with was a scumbag, making porno flicks of young girls and young boys. I gathered up my friends at St. Vincent de Paul, and we went to his pad and had some fun. The guy goes, "I don't make porno movies." I knew he made a porno of him and Danny. I wanted the tape. I go, "Yeah, you do, man." My friend goes into the kitchen and gets a beer. I'm sitting there in my red-and-white. That means that I'm down from my white pride. It's like I'm the leader because I'm the female, the dominant one.

We all go to the kitchen. We're all checking out the pad, and he's got an electric guitar worth money. This guy's never done anything wrong to me, but my notion is set that he went to bed with my old man. The guys bashed his brains into a wall. I'm not in denial about it.

My mother told me my dad said I was an ugly kid when I was born. I think that was a fat lie. I think my mom was screwing around on my father, and my father was screwing around on my mother. I never knew my dad. I don't know what he looks like.

I was in a place called the Mercy Home from six years old to eight. My brother was there with me when I was six. I remember one time going home with my babysitter, Stephanie Mills, the singer. I like being a woman, but I'm a woman that likes women. I love men's clothing. Women's clothes, you have to be all sucked up with cleavage coming out. My mom made me mad. I didn't want to hit my mother. I respected my mother. My mom goes, "You're not coming home," when I put my hand through the window. I was nine.

I won't take medication. What a person needs is another person. Here's the abuse, the molestations, the rapes, and the substance abuse. I remember [the lyrics] "Running down the road just to loosen my load." I sat in a classroom with a bunch of kids from truancy. Then we'd walk down the street together and next thing you know, cops swiped us all in a little van to Staten Island. I was in and out of Childville, 440 East 88th, Brooklyn. Mrs. Barnes was my counselor.

One time I ran away and met this construction worker in Mayor's Park. This guy was really cute, and I was only a bitty tot, nine or so. He had Jack Daniels, and I'd already smoked weed by then. He's at work, sitting there on break; big, buff, blonde, blue-eyed stud of a guy, and I walked up and said, "I'm Mindy." I bought him a ring out of money he gave me for doing things you wouldn't want to know. In the park I stood up on the picnic table, and I said, "Till death do us part," and I put the ring on his finger with construction workers around. They went along with it. They took it as a big joke. Later I met him and he said, "Kid, you want to smoke this joint?" I said, "Fuck, yeah!" This guy was the nicest, prettiest, most muscular guy with brains, and he took the time for a kid. He kissed me on the cheek.

I have a responsibility to my daughter. I'll be the most adventurous mom, like Robin Hood. I'm never coming back to this place. I've wanted to be Bonnie, like in *Bonnie and Clyde*. Now I'm going to get my education. I'll be in a recovery home. I'll get a job. I'll get my GED and be a substance-abuse counselor. I want to own a business and have a '66 Shelby Mustang parked outside. I can cook. The only red meat I eat is steak. I can sing. I can do art and dance my butt off. I write poetry. I have talent. I'm 28. I've made it this long. I can't go into the military, join the corps, and grovel around on the ground blowing guns off at anybody. That's really negative. My uncle was a Top Gun pilot in the Air Force. He was my idol.

There're women in here who really want to change their lives, yet the fear of the unknown is stopping them. They need something that isn't rejection or people saying they're addicts. If they weren't addicts, they wouldn't be in here. Talking about it helps them get the monkey off their back. Being around violence brings about violence. I had to learn how not to put the fist through the window. I can hold back now. I've walked away from so much this week, people calling me dyke. I'm powerful enough not to listen to them. Just like my parents, who said I was a fuck-up, a screw-up, and demented. I fell into believing all that shit.

Maybe at times I was a depressed child. I'm not going to let anybody label me. It's normal to feel hurt and feel sad. It's normal to feel anger, but not normal to go outburst your anger with violent behavior. I can punch a punching bag, play the piano, or guitar instead. Someone says, "Hey, you fuckin' this or that," I go, "Listen, you fuckin' piece of shit, leave me alone." When I get out, I want a really good fruit salad, Deluxe Crème cookies, and soup.

Tell us about the differences between men and women in confinement.
Dep. Mentes: If a male inmate asks a deputy a question and gets a no, he leaves it at that. Women ask "Why?" They want a full explanation, and they play games to get what they want. The inmates have nothing better to do but watch us 24 hours a day. They know personal things about us because they listen to our conversations with each other. We have to be careful.

Minimum-security housing offers this.
We don't take misdemeanor offenders in the jail anymore, only offenders with felony arrests. Sometimes people come in jail on a misdemeanor, but it's on top of a prior offense. It's called a commit. We don't take prostitutes or batteries. There's no room. We don't have enough money to house all these people. We have to cut the lesser crimes to house the higher crimes. Laws need to be more stringent. Drug charges keep rolling through the court system.

It's alarming to see how many women are in jail who'll lose their children.
With female drug addicts, CPS yanks the kid out of the home. One gal, Lamb, is in here for killing her child. CPS had taken the child from the home three times!

How do you see inmates relate inside the jail?
Older inmates tend to mother a lot. Younger ones are taken under their wings. At night we get lots of complaints—stomach aches, people acting up, and suicide attempts. There was an Oriental lady who was embarrassed to get arrested because of her culture. She was diabetic and stopped taking her insulin. "I refuse." What are you going to do? You gotta handle it. You do first aid. She was in the Detox Cell. She had taken her clothes off. She was HIV positive. She hung herself.

It was the worst thing I'd ever seen. I cut her down and she had oozing abscesses. She was very vesicated. She fell on my shoulder. I plopped her down on the ground and she didn't have a pulse. I didn't have my mask because they're a big pain in the butt. It happened so fast. If they vomit, we get it. With this one, I tilted her head and started blowing. As soon as I did, she started coughing. She made it. We have a TB test every year. We also have hepatitis vaccinations, and I get yearly HIV tests.

What changes have you noticed in the jail during your career?
The crimes are more violent. There were three murderers, female, when I started, and now there are 15.

Inmates tell us they have to be strip-searched.
You have to check all their cavities: ears, nose, mouth, anus, and vagina, without touching them. You make them bend over and spread [their labia] 'cause they keister drugs. I gagged on my first strip search.

We had one girl who swallowed a baggie, and it broke. So when they come in we ask, "Have you swallowed any packed drugs? Do you use drugs?" "No." You know they're high, of course. You say, "I'm asking you because if you start flopping around like a fish, the nurse wants to know what she's dealing with." Sometimes they'll say, "Well, I did this or that." Mostly they deny everything.

Have you witnessed any inmates who've turned their lives around?
I had this girl, Suzy Fast, talked a mile a minute. She amped out. She was hyper all of the time. At the Del Mar Fair, she ran up behind me and said, "Hey, look, I have a job!" She'd been clean six months and was proud. She said, "You helped me. I hated you, but you helped me."

You seem pretty sensitive to the predicaments of the women. What's it like for you?
It's dealing with this element all the time. I'd rather be in law enforcement. I'm getting burned out dealing with the worst of the worst. I'm totally different at work than I am off duty. This job takes its toll. I've had people I work with commit suicide. This job has made me stronger, yet a more calloused person. That part's not good. I have a lower sympathy level in my family. Where I used to blame things on how people were raised, now I say everyone's got to have control over their actions. When I drive home, I'm grinding my teeth, I turn up my radio. If I had a bad day like yesterday and I get a tension headache, I go home, open a beer, sit on my bed. I look at my hockey cards and do other mindless things. I don't answer the phone. I pour a glass of wine and take a big bubble bath. Read. I like to read children's books, like "Winnie-the-Pooh."

173

171-172

170. Deputy Mentes; 171-173. Inmate Donnelly

We wait to see Edwards. She's getting close to her labor-and-delivery date. I look down the corridor that leads to the yard. Dep. Thomas is escorting a familiar face. It's Chelsea Donnelly from the downtown San Diego streets. I last saw her on the streets of downtown San Diego when I was interviewing and photographing the homeless. A self-proclaimed "street-person," she tried to convince me that she chose to live on the streets as her lifestyle. She said the homeless people have no choice. During the time I knew Chelsea in downtown San Diego, she disappeared for two or three months at a time, only to return to the streets healthy, heavier, and with the pitch that she was clean and going to stay that way. Now, when she sees me, she forgets she's in jail and reaches out for a hug.

Dep. Thomas: No physical contact! Can't you read the sign?
Donnelly: (Interrupts) Don't worry about her. Hey, how are you guys? I wondered how long it'd take for you to find me in the jail!
Are you ready to quit the streets?
Donnelly: Hell no! The street's my home. I told you that many years ago. Would you like it if I asked you to leave your house?

Another deputy lets us visit with Chelsea in the Pro Visit booth. Chelsea leans back in the bucket chair and stretches her legs.

Donnelly: I went to Wackenhut Jail with a dime [of crack] in my mouth and two pipes. I don't smoke like I used to when I couldn't go 15 minutes without a hit. They brought me here and gave me 150 days for hooking. I had three cases. Just being in here makes you feel like you are in the twilight zone, doesn't it?

There's no one thing that starts a person to be an addict. It could be stubbing their toe and someone saying, "Hey, bet this will take the pain away from your toe. Smoke some marijuana." There is nothing you can blame it on. I didn't try drugs 'til I was 28. Now I'm 36. I wasn't forced. I did it 'cause I watched someone smoke cocaine. I tried it and liked it. Two days later I saw someone use crystal. I tried it and didn't like it. I saw someone shoot up. I tried it and didn't like it. I enjoy smoking.

Chelsea reminisces about the other street people I had photographed. She tells me most of them are still around. They go in jail to clean-up and get strong.

We remain at Pro Visit waiting for Kristina Edwards when an inmate shouts at Dr. Bull in the next booth, "I'm scared, OK?" We wait another hour, uncertain if Kristina will come out for a visit. We haven't seen her in over two weeks and her baby is due soon.

The smells and sounds oddly stay the same, day after day. The reality of locked-up minds is troubling. While we're waiting, another inmate, mother of four, tells her attorney that she wants a plea bargain on her second strike that will take her to prison for a long time.

1:30 p.m.   Pro Visit Room, Kristina Edwards

Edwards returns from court.

Edwards: I had two charges dismissed today. My lawyer told me not to worry, that I got the torture and the conspiracy charges knocked off. It doesn't really mean nothin' new to me 'cause I came into jail without those charges.

How are you feeling?
Fine. My mom wants a photo of me, but I don't wanna be in it alone.
I don't want no pictures in black-and-white of my baby though. I wanna see what my baby looks like. I want a Dr. Pepper. My attorney gets me one all the time when he comes here.

She's happier today. She laughs, teases, and plays until she thinks about her mother. Then her mood changes.

My mom told me she asked you for $4,000 to buy a car so she could come to court. I can't believe she did that. She's not coming. You're going to be there, aren't you?
Next court date is tomorrow for Continuation of Motions?
I just had status for my Readiness Hearing, that's when they dropped the death penalty. My lawyer said I'm going to do a lot of time, 15-to-life. The worst is life-without. Alex is telling me honestly, from his view, that he thinks I should put my baby up for adoption. A girl in jail let another girl named Sandy, who's rich, adopt her baby. She'll take my baby, too. She's coming to visit me. I just wish things were different. These guys [Bellows and Ryan] made sure I'll be sent up north, to VSP (Valley State Prison for Women). They had me do as much as I did so if I ran my mouth off I got in trouble. My Readiness Hearing is October 30th.

Barbara changes the subject and talks about Kristina's pregnancy.

Inmates get a pill for breast milk, since we can't nurse our babies, 'cause we don't get to keep them with us. Plus they handcuff you to your bed. It's embarrassing. I don't sleep at night. I don't like to think about where I'm going. I wanted a double mattress 'cause of all the weight on me, but the Captain says, "Don't come to the jail pregnant!" He's an asshole. I went to UCSD the night before last 'cause my baby wasn't moving on this machine here. It looked like I didn't have no liquid in there. They thought I had been leaking fluid, but at UCSD they said I had enough fluid. I told my mom I won't be tooken to the hospital 'til my water breaks. I have to put a name on the birth certificate. Pamela Edwards is pretty. Can you leave money on my books so I can buy things?
We can't do that while we're working on this project.
All you have to do is make out a money order and leave it at the front desk with my name and number on it. I need things for court. I need makeup and my mom won't send me any money. I'm the only one back there who doesn't have anything on her books. I clean people's rooms to get some of their commissary items.

Kristina stands for escort back to B housing.

You have an excellent attorney.
Yeah. He got hired for another case in the courtroom today. Some guy walked in and said, "We need you!" I just hope that doesn't interfere with my case. I was worried about the torture charge, 'cause torture gets life-without. Next time they're gonna do what they didn't do today. Ryan has a new lawyer.

174

Ellen Conner, the counselor from the PIP, passes the Pro Visit area after Edwards is returned to her unit.

Conner: She's extremely immature, and she's dealing with a mega-charge. She's scared of getting close to anyone who might leave her. Her mother and dad have drug backgrounds. I know she's not motivated. With her charge and her housing . . . see, B housing is full of predators. Anything she says about B is accurate. They're vicious. Kristina told me you were in court, and she wants you there for the baby, to get pictures of the birth. Everyone leaves her. She only does things for money or for drugs. She's doing time. The baby has to be adopted.

I stop the lieutenant on the run and ask her how we can talk to Kristina Edwards and Rolenda Banks in a place not in view of the general population. Lt. Milakovich tells us she'll see if she can get us into B housing. She'll talk to the Captain and the sergeant in charge, San Filippo.

174. Inmate Edwards; 175. Sheriff bus at courthouse

10/25/95 8:20 a.m. Courthouse
Kristina Edwards' Motions Hearing

It looks like there's no hearing; there's no one around, and there's no sheet tacked on the sidewall stating the cases.

We go to the clerk's office. Motions are to be read this morning. I look through a crack in the torn paper taped to the entrance windows and see the marshal organizing the courtroom.

Kristina Edwards' attorney, Alex Landon, arrives, smiling. We enter the courtroom.

Ryan enters in chains with a deputy. He looks severe and strong and has grown a trendy goatee. He's compliant and non-communicative. The marshal takes off his chains and seats him alongside his attorney.

Kristina enters with chains pressed against her bulging belly. Her hair has been washed, combed, and hangs in loose curls. Her makeup has been applied tastefully on her olive complexion, with special attention to her eyes. Alex talks to her, and she strains to understand his words. Ryan's attorney is talking with his client as well. He's a new attorney, appointed since the last court date. The deputy district attorney sits straight, reading documents. No one, other than her attorney, is present for Kristina, except Barbara and me. No one, other than his attorney, is present for Ryan. Bellows, another codefendant, isn't present at all. Kristina turns around, sees us and smiles.

The judge enters. The conspiracy and the torture motions are accepted. Kristina's attorney stands and pleads for the motion of kidnapping against Kristina to be dropped. He cites several arguments. He says there's no evidence that his client did anything other than drive with Klotz to the house to purchase drugs. There's no evidence that suggests she had anything to do with Klotz's being jumped on. There's no evidence to suggest Kristina Edwards wanted to go with Ryan and Bellows when they took Klotz to the plateau to kill him. Ryan hit her on the side of the head to get the keys. Her attorney says Kristina was ordered to get in the car and was taken to the plateau.

Landon: Bottom line, in order for there to be a kidnapping charge, there must be activity on the part of Kristina Edwards in felony murder kidnapping. There must actually be death as a direct result of the kidnapping. Illegal kidnapping is when there's been a removal of the body (Malleck vs. Superior Court – 142 CA2d 396). Our position is that there is no more evidence…it implies there's some other interpretation than the evidence for special circumstances and I feel the kidnapping charge should be dropped.

The prosecution says this was a brutal act of torture and that Kristina played a larger role than her statement suggests. "This is a crime of significant violence." Edwards supposedly was part and parcel of everything going on there.

Kristina starts crying. By the time the judge denies the kidnapping motion, she's weeping.

Landon: The kidnapping charge is the movement of the body–no evidence says that she was involved.

The judge asks to hear from Ryan's attorney.

Ryan's attorney gets up and talks about recently being appointed to the case and not fully versed. He says he has spent many hours

175

talking to Edwards' attorney to get caught up, but still is behind. "I feel like I am doing a lateral arabesque." He says there's no credible evidence to convict his client. They're dealing with witnesses who are liars and drug users.

Kidnapping motion is denied.

The inmates are handcuffed and taken out, one by one. Ryan's attorney talks about Kristina in Dick Bidwell's car—the car she took from Big Bear—"putting on makeup, listening to the Doobie Brothers, and she yells, 'Fuck that. I'm putting on my lipstick.'" Ryan's attorney senses Bellows' attorney doesn't show up in court on purpose: to get the other two defense counsels to fight it out with the prosecution.

Edwards' attorney approaches us. I tell him I don't understand what happened. Was the torture denied? "No, that was granted, but the kidnapping was denied." He's surprised and says this is an unusual situation for the young girl to be in. He's compassionate and says that she needs us and thinks that our support helps. He'll go for a severance so that Kristina will be tried separately from the other codefendants. Price was sentenced in Juvenile Hall courts and will go to CYA (California Youth Authority). Alex Landon appears dedicated, smart, and dignified, a man with his own style.

Noon . . .

Barbara and I meet Ben McLaughlin at P.F. Chang's restaurant to fill him in on our work. Barbara's curious about the number of women committing crimes. How can so many women risk the time away from their families and adopt this way of life?

We hear that women are more manipulative than men as inmates.
McLaughlin: We try to treat male and female offenders the same, but we can't. Women challenge authority more than men do.

Why do women come back to jail?
You have to ask about what is the reality of her life. It's like childbirth. "I'll never go through this again," [they say] right after delivery, and not too long afterwards, "Maybe we ought to have another one. . . ." Inmates forget the pain of their relationships. They idealize them when they're in jail. Then they walk out of the door remembering only the good part. The jerk shows up, and it's not long before they're back here again.

   As humans, we tend to forget the bad and idealize the good. Inmates are looking for the best, and they have the worst. They fantasize a lot. A normal person who hasn't had something to do with jail or crime can relate to what the inmates say on some level if they listen. At one point in my life I could've been on the other side of those bars.

So we're talking to some who had serious misfortune early on and missed opportunities to thrive, and we're also talking to some bad seeds.
Right. It's hard to believe the crime when you meet a person like the one you mentioned, Kristina Edwards. It's surrealistic to find out later what she did. I've known Alex Landon 20 years. He takes the toughest cases. He makes a career of it.

This case represents a higher level of criminal activity?
We call it criminal sophistication. The difference between inmate personalities in different housing units is their criminal sophistication, not the least of which is predation against other inmates. The lieutenant has the right of review over the deputies who determine the classification of inmates. The National Institute of Corrections developed the criteria for all jails in the U.S.

10/26/95   8:00 a.m.   Juvenile Hall

The pigeons mostly sit close together on the high power lines above Meadowlark Lane in front of Juvenile Hall. It's crisp outside. The sun shines on the birds. Several fluff up. Some sleep. Others preen. I look over my shoulder at the cyclone fencing around the juvenile detention facility. Inside, cells are organized into groups according to criminal behavior. Price, the fourth codefendant in Klotz's murder case, is probably in the 1,000 group, maximum, for individuals alleged to have committed assault, rape, kidnapping, murder.

   I enter the Juvenile Hall on several occasions for self-defense classes and meetings with the director as standard procedure. My assistant, Barbara, will not be accompanying me on this project. Initially, I'll be on my own. I am curious how many youths have family in jail or prison.

I have another meeting with the director of the Hall to make certain I understand protocol when I visit the units. Once inside, I discover my meeting has been cancelled. I have time to make a quick trip to Las Colinas to see how Kristina Edwards fared after yesterday's court date.

10:30 a.m.   Jail, Pro Visit
Kristina Edwards

This time, I enter the jail in a skirt and sweater, without camera equipment. The clerk has colored her hair light red to match her dress, and stands next to a male deputy wearing a "Patrol Football" sweatshirt. He acts tough at the sally port until Red says, "She's OK, let her go."
   They call up Edwards.
   I sit in the booth, waiting for Edwards. An inmate jumps above the partition. It's Chelsea. She's confident and sassy. I find her playful in the jail, as compared to her sophisticated street-person persona in downtown San Diego.
   Soon Kristina enters the area, slumped over. Her hair is wet.

Edwards: I was in the shower! I can't sleep. I'm going to lose it. I'm going to crack. I need to get some medication or I might do something. I just wanna go to prison and stay there for life. My mom can have my baby. Alex lost all of the motions. I haven't slept. My mom said I'm gonna be punished. I want it to be over.

I was in the shower! I can't sleep. I'm going to lose it. I'm going to crack. I need to get some medication or I might do something. I just wanna go to prison and stay there for life. My mom can have my baby . . .

Inmate Edwards

Part Three Maximum Security

It is the caretaker who, over the years, and through millions of mundane and dramatic moments, will help the girl know who she is. It is the caretaker who will stand solid and accepting when the little girl needs to push to find out her own strength and boundaries. And it is the image of this loving, solid, admiring, soothing, reliable caretaker that the little girl will have forever stamped in her psyche. Wherever she goes that image will be her internal "other" and she will never feel alone. And she will always see and judge herself through the loving eyes of the caretaker and be loving and gentle to herself. And as she views herself with kindness, she will view others with kindness.[28]

Maryam Razavi Newman, Ph.D.

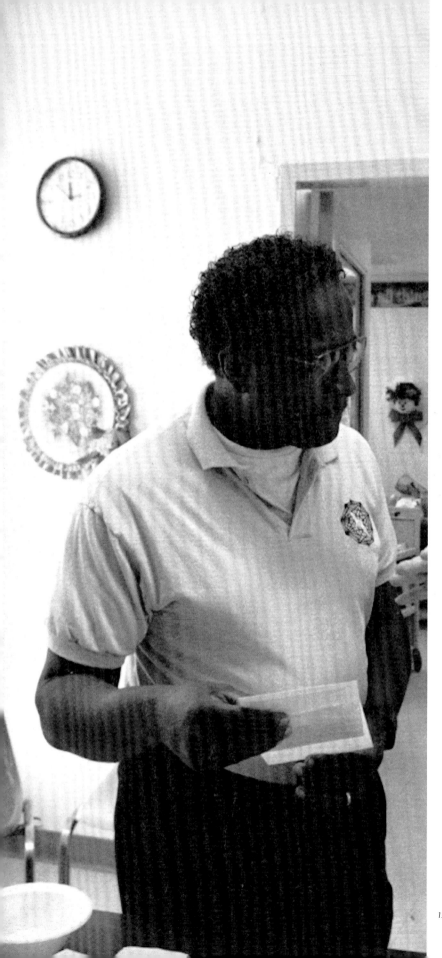

177. Sergeant Pugh

"Jail is a hodgepodge of criminal sophistication."

Assistant Sheriff Ben McLaughlin

11/3/95 Jail, Pro Visit

After talking to several inmates on the minimum-security yard, we return to Pro Visit and notice activity at the Intake Receiving sally port. It's Kristina Edwards, shackled and wearing a heavy chain around her belly, being escorted out of the jail. I ask the clerk where Kristina's going. The clerk pushes a button on her control panel and tells me to take a seat and wait for the sergeant.

When Sgt. Miller arrives, she tells us that Kristina is headed to the hospital for a sonogram.

We need to get a pass to enter Kristina's delivery room.
Sgt. Miller: I don't think so.
We have permission from the assistant sheriff. Where do we get the pass?
Sgt. Miller: Actually I've had several complaints about you from the staff. Do you realize that you're an invasion of privacy here? Have you ever thought about that?

The sergeant leaves.
We wait four hours for Kristina to return. Another sergeant I've never met steps up to the booth and introduces himself as Sgt. Pugh.

Sgt. Pugh: I just want to thank you for locating Ms. Edwards' mother. Things have been tough for her and this will mean a great deal down the road.
She expects us at the delivery. How can we get permission to be in her delivery room?
Sgt. Pugh: If Ms. Edwards said it was OK, go downtown to the central jail and tell the deputy at receiving that I sent you.

4:00 p.m. Downtown Central Men's Jail

The deputy at the downtown jail tells us we can have a one-day pass. I tell him we need an extended pass. "You'll have to talk to the Sheriff," he says. He steps away from the Control window. I tap on the glass and ask him to call Assistant Sheriff Ben McLaughlin.

The deputy places the call. He hands the phone to me. Ben sounds irritated and wants to know how long I'll need the pass. I tell him a week or two. He tells me to give them an hour to process the extended pass.

It's early evening when I get to my studio and call the jail to see if they have news about Kristina. A woman in the medical services says she can't give out information on the inmate.

Later, Kath Anderson calls. "Gordy's phone has been disconnected, not unusual for rehab clinics to not pay their bills, and Gwen relapsed a week ago and is back with her ex-boyfriend, a La Jolla architect."

The most important property of humankind is the capacity to form and maintain relationships. These relationships are absolutely necessary . . . to survive, learn, work, love, and procreate. Human relationships take many forms, but the most intense, pleasurable, and painful are those with family, friends, and loved ones.[29]

Emotional Glue.

Bruce Perry, M.D., Ph.D.

11/5/95 Sunday morning, Phone call

The phone rings. It's still dark outside. No one's up yet at my house. It's Kristina's mother. Her voice is raspy and broken. She tells me that I have to go to the hospital immediately. She'll meet me, but it'll take her and her husband and their two small children a couple of hours to get there. My daughter has a special event at 11:00 a.m. at UCLA in Los Angeles, a two-hour car trip the opposite direction. There are animals to be fed, and preparations for my youngest child. Also, my car is low on gas. I scramble, and get to the hospital in 45 minutes.

6:45 a.m. UCSD Hospital

It's a chilly and damp November morning. The yellow street lamps have halos. I pass a police escort vehicle on my way to the entrance. Inside, the fluorescent lights are blinding. A blue stripe on the floor directs me to the elevators. A security guard, not a sheriff's deputy, sits outside Kristina's labor-and-delivery room. I show the guard my credentials and paperwork.

A nurse arrives and punches in a code on a lock box. We enter the tiny private room. Inside, I'm surprised to see Dep. Thomas, sitting on a stool next to the head of Kristina Edwards' bed. She's the one who had shouted, "No physical contact. Can't you read?" the day we first saw Chelsea Donnelly in the jail.

Kristina's left hand is chained to the bed. She reaches out for me with her right hand. The deputy adjusts the chew in her mouth to say, "It's OK." She laughs, remembering the incident at the jail. Kristina's pained expression breaks with another smile for a moment, only to get angry as she exclaims, "Imagine how I felt, walking in the hospital this morning, little kids seeing me with with chains on my feet, walking in to have my baby? Damn . . . is my mom here yet?"

It's a tight area. I put a wide-angle lens on my camera. The deputy admires my equipment and says, "I wanted to be a photographer. I wanted to study at the Brooks Institute."

The outside guard enters and says, "Let's throw a leg chain on her." Kristina grows anxious, and asks me, "Can you find my mom? She's probably here and doesn't know where to go."

A mild contraction registers on the monitor, and I realize it'll be hours before the delivery. Kristina begs for pain medication. A young female resident says Kristina can have some morphine. She examines Kristina to see if her water has broken. Kristina complains throughout the exam, and pulls on the chain with force, tugging and thrusting. She shouts, "Fuck!" as the doctor withdraws a gloved, bloody hand. "She hasn't dilated to three centimeters yet, but I think her water has broken." A pretty nurse arrives with the morphine. Her name is Joan.

"How long will it take?" Kristina asks desperately.

"A couple of minutes," Joan says, soothingly.

Kristina grimaces. "This hurts."

I ask Joan if UCSD Hospital receives all of the jail's pregnant inmates. She tells me the hospital has the county contract. There's always a sheriff's car outside the hospital.

As the pain eases, Kristina starts joking with the deputy. "Harper was in the hallway when I left the jail and I told her I might change sexual preference after this is over.'"

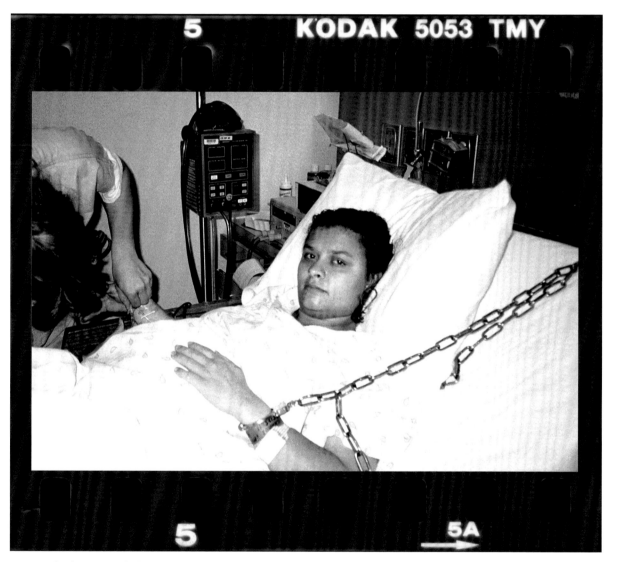

180. Inmate Edwards, UCSD Hospital, Labor-and-Delivery

Dep. Thomas whispers, "She's not going to have much choice."

The deputy picks up the wall phone and calls the jail. "When is the relief coming?" She hangs up the phone and says, "I arrived on shift this morning, and they handed me a pair of gloves, a pair of scissors, and a plastic bag and told me to take Edwards to the hospital."

Kristina receives constant attention. They don't want her to feel any pain, and they keep the room calm. She's asked for her mom several times. It's time for me to leave. What if her mother doesn't arrive?

"My mom looks like she's 60. I used to go down another aisle in the grocery store because my mother wore bell-bottomed pants," Kristina says.

Commotion breaks out in the corridor.

We hear someone arguing with the guard. "It's my mom!" Edwards cries out. I recall Kristina telling me her mother had 17 living siblings. One died young, after eating bug poison.

Her mother enters, pushing a stroller with a young child into the crowded room. Kristina sees her mother and cries out, "Oh, my God. What did you do to your hair?" The mother's petite, appears older than her years, and has long, dyed hair. Her snappy dark eyes, outlined in black eyeliner, tear up when she sees her daughter. She steps in front of the small child to give her daughter a hug. Then she steps back from the bed, nervously talking about Kristina's appearance. Her husband enters with another stroller and child.

I leave for L.A. During the trip, the image of Kristina Edwards and her mother lingers as I try and imagine how things will turn out for the baby.

On the way home from UCLA, I call the hospital. Edwards still hasn't had her baby.

Two-thirds of incarcerated women ran away from home at some time as children, and about one-fourth attempted suicide previously. About 65 percent of incarcerated women were victims of severe and prolonged physical and sexual abuse, primarily as children, but for many continuing into adulthood. For most of these women, the abuse occurred before the age of 14 and was perpetrated by a male member of the family. Three-quarters had histories of alcohol abuse, and one-half had histories of drug abuse. Many had previously participated in drug and alcohol treatment programs (ACA Task Force on the Female Offender, 1990, pp. 17-19).[30]

The Prison Journal

6:00 p.m.   UCSD Hospital

I arrive back at UCSD Hospital. The moon is full. Everything is calm outside the hospital. I notice Kristina's family entering the building. We ride up in the elevator and enter Kristina's room together. Edwards is highly stressed and restless in spite of the epidural drip. She rubs her left leg with hard strokes, semi-delirious. Nurse Joan asks me to push against Kristina's right leg and places Kristina's mother on the left leg. Kristina's mother makes a crack about her daughter having gained weight. Kristina cries that she can't take it anymore. "One more big push, the baby's head has crowned," says the doctor. It happens fast. The baby is born and now is crying. Kristina cries as her mother reaches over to kiss her. They both cry. The baby wails. I notice the chains are gone. "I made the guard take them off," the nurse whispers. As the doctor prepares to deliver the afterbirth, Kristina's mother heads out the door. She can't stand the sight of blood.

Kristina strains as the doctor tells her he's delivering the afterbirth. "Susan," Kristina says, "you take her. Hold her." I'm stunned, and uncomfortable. The nurse nods, "It's fine." Blood is everywhere. The nurse lays the bare babe in my hands. She's warm, damp, and alive. One of life's greatest moments is all fouled up. I look into the infant's face. I see the purest of innocence; her tiny chest rising and falling as she takes her first breaths of life, her eyes open and searching my face. She's calm, lying in my hands. The only newborns I've held were my own. I look at Kristina. She's distracted. Her eyes are vacant. The doctor brings her back to focus with instructions. I hold her baby, careful not to cuddle the unwrapped child, hoping Kristina will take her.

The nurse doesn't seem to be interested or concerned that the new mother's a jail inmate. The only thing concerning her is the bonding between the mother and child. She offers the infant once again. Kristina takes her this time, naturally and softly. She brings the baby close to her own face. It's dear and touching. I tear up and swallow hard. Kristina repeats, "I'm sorry baby, I'm so sorry. I love you, baby." She turns from the baby and cries out, "I'm still hurting." The infant slips down Kristina's belly until the nurse readjusts the mother and baby once again. The baby opens and closes her eyes. Kristina cries, "Oh, this hurts!" The doctor explains he has to get the clots, and he slithers the afterbirth into a specimen tray. Kristina doesn't realize what's going on or why her mother has left the room. Holding her child, she drifts off into a distant gaze and restlessly tells me, "Find my mom!"

I go into the corridor and ask a rough-looking guard if she's seen Kristina's mother.

"I have no idea! All I know is that I lost the head gasket on my car, and now I have a double shift outside the room of a criminal. I don't need this. Fuck!"

Re-entering the room, I encounter a distinct smell, one I recall from days working in the Baylor Bacteriology lab. It's the smell of warm bacteria on agar plates inside large incubators. Something is wrong. Kristina complains. She's not feeling well. She's feverish. The room is hot.

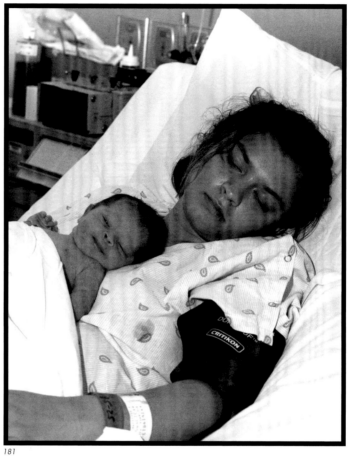

181

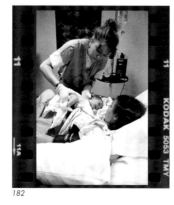

182

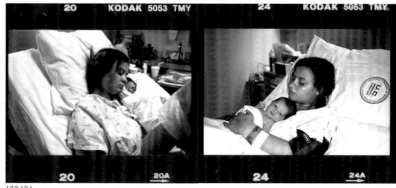

183-184

Birthing is biological, mothering is not. And, all too frequently, these mothers come from families that were themselves in crises or that are still in crises–that were mired to poverty, drugs, violence, and homelessness.[31]

The Prison Journal

181. Inmate Edwards and baby; 182. Inmate Edwards, baby and Nurse Joan; 183-184. Inmate Edwards and baby

Attachment is the capacity to form and maintain healthy emotional relationships. An attachment bond has unique properties. The capacity to create these special relationships begins in early childhood.[32]

Attachment is an enduring emotional relationship with a specific person, one that brings safety, comfort, and pleasure; loss of that person evokes intense distress.[33]

An emotionally and physically healthy mother will be drawn to her infant—feel a physical longing to smell, cuddle, rock, coo, gaze at her infant. The infant will respond with snuffle, babble, smile, suck, and cling.

The acts of holding, rocking, singing, feeding, gazing, kissing, and laughing are bonding experiences.[34]

Bruce Perry, M.D., Ph.D.

I got to have her all last night. Me and
her slept in the bed, but they just took
her back for her stats.

Inmate Edwards

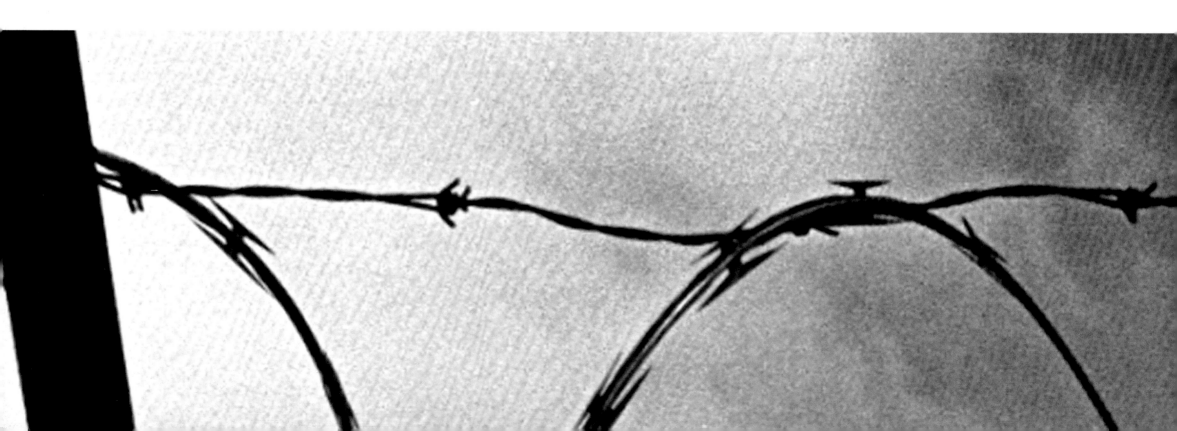

11/6/95 8:00 a.m.   Phone call

Kath Anderson calls me and tells me that inmate Cindy Mulloy is in Mercy Hospital. Her boyfriend, Bigsly, is supplying balloons of heroin to her there. She is in serious condition and may not survive.

11:00 a.m.

Edwards and the baby remain hospitalized for infections. I pick up Barbara at the airport, and we head off to UCSD Medical Center. We find Kristina shackled and moving around in a spacious single room. Her guard seems to be enjoying his duty and provides a relaxed atmosphere.

Edwards: I got to have her all last night. Me and her slept in the bed, but they just took her back for her stats. Go see her. CPS was all over the hospital. They may not let my mom have the baby. They said since I'm up for murder-one that my mom may not be fit to raise the baby. They let Sandy hold her. They let them go in the nursery, but I want my mom to have her.

After viewing the baby, Barbara and I leave UCSD Hospital to visit Cindy Mulloy at Mercy Hospital in the Cardiac Care Unit. She had another attack of endocarditis. This time the infection wasn't isolated to her heart valves; she had a life-threatening seizure caused by an infection in her brain.

Mulloy's not in her room. The nurse tells us she's down the hall having a cigarette.

We wait in her room. Soon Mulloy enters, surprised and happy to see us. She talks about her near-death experience. We ask why she left Step Study in jail and went back to drugs on the street.

When you were released, you didn't go into a rehab?
Mulloy: No. At first I thought I could do it on my own. I went to an NA meeting, and there was a lady I knew from the streets. We had lived the same kind of life. Her name is Kath Anderson. She and I have parallel lives. She's a hope-to-die dope fiend. She got out in May and runs a sober-living house. She knows Bigsly, too.

What happened? How did you end up back in the hospital?
I've used heroin for years. Last year I got endocarditis; one of my heart valves was leaking. The cardiologist said, "The valve is destroyed, Cindy. We have to replace it." I had a temperature of 105 degrees for five days, and the jail thought I was trying to play crazy. I was vomiting–like with kicking–but I've never had a fever from kicking. If it wasn't for Dep. O'Neal, I'd have died in Las Colinas. I couldn't see using drugs anymore. I started a relationship with my family again. My mom let me spend the night at her house. Then one day I thought, "Why am I doing this? Nothing's going to be any different. I'm really uncomfortable with myself. I don't see anything changing." So I went back to my same drug group. I thought they were more caring. In reality, they like me because they know I make a lot of money. I support my drug habit by prostituting. I relapsed at the end of September, and came back to jail in October for two weeks for possession. The jail cut me loose from the hospital because of my hospital bills. I started using right away, and I got arrested again.

Were you molested as a child?
Not overt sexual abuse, but my parent's relationship was weird. My mom was cruel to my dad. Looking back, I think she was jealous of the relationship I had with my dad. I'm the first daughter, daddy's little girl. I can do no wrong in my dad's eyes. I think I created a lot of animosity and resentment with my mom. I wasn't my dad's actual lover, but I think there was emotional incest. They were divorced, and my mom and I were never the same. I acted out. I have a younger sister, who is 30 years old now. She and her six-year-old daughter live with my mom, who accepts everything my sister does. I was terrible growing up. My dad would laugh,

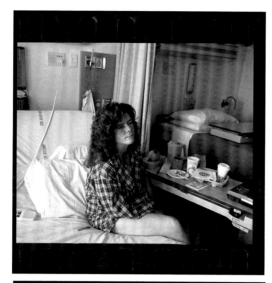

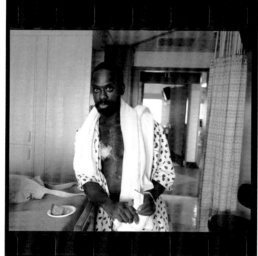

186-187

and my mom would say, "Cindy, I'll give you something to cry about."

Did you ever live on the streets?
I'd go to somebody's house or a hotel. I lived with a trick before I came in here. The guy who's been putting money on my books has got feelings for me. Over the last ten years, I've had more tricks than I can count. I don't even know half their names. I wouldn't recognize them if I saw them.

What happened the first time you had a trick?
The first time was really weird. I was staying at my mother's. My boyfriend was in jail downtown, and I was hitchhiking. This guy who picked me up propositioned me. It was really easy. All he wanted to do was look at my body. Then it just progressed.
Why?
I didn't feel like I deserved anything. I didn't want anyone having a hold on me. I didn't want to be obligated.

Mulloy's friend, Harold, strolls into her room from across the hall and wants to talk.

Harold: I'm an IV drug user. I was in the hospital last summer with endocarditis. I'm on my Third Strike. If I do anything against the law, it's all over. They'll lock me up for the rest of my life. Two grams of powder, and I'm going to the pen. I never had a real close-knit family growing up because of the drugs and being a gang-banger. My mother was a single parent. I left home at 13 when she said, "If you can't respect the rules of this house, you're out of here." I'm 41, but I started marijuana, alcohol, pills, and PCP at 16. I was cracked-out the last five years. Never got into speed. I had a pound of it in the ghetto and couldn't give it away. Youngsters smoke it. It's white boy's drug of choice.

Mulloy: This time I had a seizure caused by little abscesses in the brain. They put me on Dilantin. My cardiologist is a great guy. He said, "I'm not going to let you die." I told him that I got to the place where I didn't care. My neurosurgeon said they might have to cut my head open. He warned me that if I went back out, I'd die. He was real abrasive, but I didn't care.

Do you want to stay alive now?
Yes, I do. But I feel like I don't deserve it. I'm a monster. I couldn't go out and consciously take my life, but, subconsciously, that's what I'm doing. My friends thought my parents had the perfect relationship. Looking back, I didn't get straight A's, but I was in gifted classes. I had all these wonderful opportunities. Now it feels really good to sleep at night and know I don't have to go hustle. I don't have to jump into some strange man's car and do something I don't wanna do. I've lived my whole life in a fantasy.

How much does this cost Medi-Cal? I hear daily, on the news, about transplant expenses and organ availability. Do inmates receive priority services?

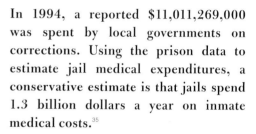

In 1994, a reported $11,011,269,000 was spent by local governments on corrections. Using the prison data to estimate jail medical expenditures, a conservative estimate is that jails spend 1.3 billion dollars a year on inmate medical costs.[35]

Needle Exchange Programs

11/7/95   9:00 a.m.   Pro Visit
with Courtney, psych nurse

Ellen Conner introduces us to Courtney, a registered nurse with psychiatric certification.

Drugs are a common denominator with these women.

Nurse Courtney: We'd benefit by training additional custodial deputies in the jail. We need to work with women in the therapeutic community to have a better acceptance of their problems and disease. We need a mix of ex-offenders and chemical-dependency counselors who have been through recovery. They know the problems and the barriers. County nurses refer inmates to psychiatrists who often give women meds to make them lie on their bunks, eyes closed, with even respiration. It makes running a facility with 500-600 inmates possible, but these meds can keep you from a REM sleep and make you groggy the next day.

More and more women are using drugs.

Women have been abused by our society. Doctors prescribe Valium for their anxiety. If you have a couple kids to raise and housework to do and get a little goofy on Valium or Xanex, that's all right. But would a doctor prescribe those for a husband who's a machinist? No, the guy could lop off his finger and the doctor would be liable. It's a mindset. Xanex is grossly over-prescribed, and it has the longest withdrawals. A small dose creates a gradual tolerance. When you stop the drugs, the anxiety you experience is much greater than the anxiety you had before starting. If you're a heroin addict, drugs like morphine and Demerol aren't going to work as well.

How can you determine whether you should prescribe an inmate a drug?

I ask, "Do you think you didn't have the problem before because you were using drugs? Is this anxiety a part of being clean? Is this what you're going to have to deal with everyday?" In F1, a smaller environment, I'll tell inmates to not sleep or lie down on their bunks during the day. It is difficult because the bunk is their home, their condo. I ask them to avoid certain foods and cut down on their fluids. I suggest they do a series of bio-feedback meditation and relaxation exercises. I give them things to look forward to when they get out instead of that fix.

How do inmates make the move from F3 and F2 into F1?

We get referrals from the counselors and the psychiatrists. It's a voluntary program.

So what creates addiction?

It's based on physical genetics, and on life experiences.

Talk about alcohol addiction.

Some studies show that alcoholism varies with ethnic groups. Some groups have a gene that better metabolizes alcohol. The better you metabolize it the more you can drink. The more alcohol you can drink, the higher your blood alcohol gets. So you become alcoholic. We see a lot more alcoholism in the American Indians and the Irish. On the other hand, alcoholism is rare in Japan because the Japanese don't carry that gene. A small quantity of alcohol makes them sick. They can't drink enough to develop tolerance.

Does information on addictions scare people away from using drugs?

Heck no. Most of the heroin addicts are IV users. They kill all of their veins. I've worked in hospitals where I had to start IVs on addicts, but there's nothing left of their veins. They say, "Go for the carotid." It's the only way they can get drugs in anymore.

The veins weaken with IV use and addicts can develop something called endocarditis, don't they?

Yes, they end up injecting bacteria. The bacteria enter the blood stream, puddle in little rest stops, and get lodged in the heart. The addicts have recurrent bouts of this infection. Once you've had endocarditis, your heart is weakened. Even if you stop doing drugs you're not going to have everything go your way. You need to learn alternative coping mechanisms, something else to provide comfort for you. One of the reasons the 12 Step Program works is the sense of community and concern. You walk into any group that has the initials NA or AA and there's always a bunch of people that care. Learning to open up, share, and connect is critical. Studies show people who have friends or a significant other do better after surgery.

What about giving a drug addict methadone?

It's another drug. I don't see any difference between methadone and some of the psychotropic drugs. Your personal bottom is wherever you stop using. You might not have to go to jail. You might not have to lose your family. Recovery starts when you've gotten to your lowest point.

What changes have you seen since the enactment of the Three Strikes Law?

I don't know if we can build enough facilities to house all the people eligible under Three Strikes. If we're going to look at people whose crimes are shooting up, being caught under the influence, and violating their probation because they go to the wrong place, we destroy any rehabilitation. Three Strikes should be for rapists, murderers, and armed robbers, not for somebody whose felony is the accumulation of three misdemeanors.

If Three Strikes isn't working; what should be done?

We need alternatives. If we let an inmate out of jail, where will she go? How will she take care of her child? We need to develop programs and provide work experience and training; have jobs that they can do. People in recovery take care of people in recovery. It's a pyramid. We need to cross-train those who succeed in recovery. It's simple economic logic. You have to be able to work to take care of yourself. The disease [addiction] leads to institutions and death. In jail, there are extremes of pain they haven't had before because they were so doped up. I'm willing to listen to them. The first time women enter jail they may not be susceptible to help, but by the third time many will practice what we tell them. It's called molding.

185. *Razor wire;* 186. *Cindy Mulloy, Mercy Hospital;*
187. *Harold, Mercy Hospital;* 188. *Pro Visit booth*

188

Later that day, we see Dr. Bull. He's curious about Kristina Edwards' childbirth.

It was un-birth-like to see baby Pamela enter this world without a nurturing parent to love her.
Dr. Bull: Un-birth-like. The baby will go through society with screwed-up attachments: a mother up for murder and a grandmother who is unstable.

You have seen similar instances in the jail?
An inmate who is very sociopathic, what the DSM-IV manual calls Antisocial Personality Disorder, has a terrible impulse-control issue, a capacity for violence, and no conscience or capacity for remorse. There are people in group therapy here who become aware of their feelings and begin to talk about their soft side. There are also people here who are sufficiently dangerous enough that they shouldn't be allowed in society. They're going to hurt someone. My feeling is that Kristina is one of the latter. One criteria for serious juvenile problems is a history of getting expelled from high school. Another example might be, "Oh, yeah, we used to throw pet rats out windows, or tack pins to cats' tails, or start fires." These are conduct disorders.

I'm here as a psychologist; my other Ph.D. is in sociology. I'm imposing my perspective on your project, but I hear you say that statements made by these inmates may be taken as commentary to what's happening to our society right now in a much larger sense. Describing the jail environment, you're describing the American environment; products of our society right now.

The lost child.
Ah, yes. Lost child. But there's an opposite pattern of distorted early life that leads to adult dysfunction or over-control. One example: A 16-year-old daughter of a marine left a sock on the floor of her room and he battered her for six weeks. I saw her years later and she was still furious. That type of absurd over-control leads to rebellion. The rebellious impulse is best expressed by, "Fuck you, I'm outta here."

I heard that line often on the streets with the homeless.
Yes. They are the other extreme. We need to look for the figure in the middle that's supportive and controlling, but not punitively so. You're doing a portrait of America that's illustrative, using the jail and inmates. You're going to get information that reflects the setting you're looking at. Knowing you were looking on the streets, it'll be a different picture. I talked to prisoners at Vacaville who worked to transform their lives. When I worked on my thesis, I pushed until things fell into place. It was a study of despair. But people run a course so they can live. The whole concept of time-out is a cultural thing. We don't think of it as alone-time in our society. We think of it as punitive, people in Lockdown. I've occasionally seen people who've asked to go into the Safety Cell because they've needed to have some alone-time. I'm told that the Japanese put people in contemplative solitude as a rehabilitative method. Instead of being punitive, it's done so the person contemplates or meditates about what the hell's going on.

I have inmates in E housing with histories of bad youths. They work through some of that injury and discover some positive things that happened to them as kids.

Dr. Bull doesn't give up. He searches for hope when given a reason to search.

190

191

Whether it hits Rolenda today or ten years from now, it's gonna hit her. You can't recover somebody else for them. She's got to want it herself. As things stand right now, the chances of Rolenda going to prison are good. This is a second escape.

Counselor Conner

11/15/95   8:30 a.m.

A week later, Barbara and I stand in front of the sally port door once again, like a couple of Pavlov's trained dogs. The clerk arrives at the window and surprises me with, "You're OK to go." The clerks are consistently inconsistent. Dr. Bull is waiting on the other side of the sally port.

What's happened?

Dr. Bull: Rolenda's been picked up in Arizona and extradited here. She's got to start over with her social worker. Dr. Bromley wants to scan her chart. Rolenda said she's interested in taking medication and will let me help her get through this difficult thing. She's very sad.

Dr. Bennett's view of Rolenda as a train wreck is coming true.
When we make our best efforts with our best candidate and she isn't ready, everything's wasted.

We follow Dr. Bull to his office next to B housing. Ellen Conner sees us and waits outside Dr. Bull's office, shaking her head.

Conner: It isn't wasted. We found out that people care about her. Whether it hits Rolenda today or ten years from now, it's gonna hit her. You can't recover somebody else for them. She's got to want it herself. As things stand right now, the chances of Rolenda going to prison are good. This is a second escape.
Dr. Bull: I wish I'd done some testing. I'm curious to see what kind of mental capacity she has.

It's pretty obvious that we need to get approval to enter B housing on a regular basis. It's another rung on the ladder.
  Sgt. Pugh stops and asks us about Kristina Edwards. He tells us the jail is full of controls. "There are people," he says, "who have trouble with authority and power, and are lost souls."

Sgt. Pugh: Some of the women return to jail more frustrated. I remember Stella. Every time she came back in jail, she became more depressed; her attempted suicides were more serious. I was powerless. I watched the regression. A number of people end up dead on the outside and several commit suicide on the inside. One inmate refused her insulin in an attempt to get back at the staff. Then one morning, she was dead.

As a sergeant, how much influence do you have with inmates?

People like to talk, but they won't talk if they can't trust you. Inmates like to show you that you're not so smart, and they're not so dumb. I'd sit in that Pro Visit Room with an inmate, and as people walked back and forth, she'd tell me everything she knew about them—the staff, other inmates, visitors. I'd say, "I'm putting you here so people don't see you and think you're a rat." They think they're milking the system, when I'm really the one there to collect information. They tell me which trusty is running contraband. You have to detach yourself from being a sheriff. You didn't put these folks in jail or pass sentence. You can't parole them or give them life. You have none of that authority. Unfortunately we have a mentality that says, "I'm going to make you do this." Inmates think about it and say, "You can't make me do anything." We hear those ultimatums given all the time.

11/17/95 Pro Visit

Kristina Edwards returns to the jail four days after her baby's birth. She arrives in a relatively good mood and laughs when she sees the clothes my assistant, Barbara, picked out for her for court.

Edwards: I got very upset with my mom. I said, "What's wrong with the baby?" and she said, "Well you can't do nothing about it anyway." I said, "Well it looks like you got what you wanted. Now you can go and get on with your life." She's got my baby and doesn't even come to court for me. CPS is peeking in on my trial, on my charges, on my past. They don't know if my mom should have my baby. Alex is being a dick. He told me the baby is over and I have to be thinking about my trial. He's not getting any deals for me. Half of these girls say the public defenders work the case the day before the court date.

He's not a public defender, Kristina. He's appointed by the court as an alternate to the public defender's office.
I'm just saying I hope he's working, 'cause I don't wanna take this thing to trial. He's got this last week to fight for deals. Ryan's lawyer's fighting for a murder-one with a chance for parole. Bellows' lawyer is fighting for murder-two, and Alex is fighting for manslaughter. The DA's not offering it. The only thing the DA's offering is murder-one, 25-to-life. If our cases go to trial, we're screwed. The DA's not going to budge.

Maybe some of the other kids who were at the Donner Ranch?
Why would they stick up for me? I just want the deal. I don't wanna take it to trial.

You have no write-ups since you've been in jail?
Yeah. I got one for a syringe and a crack pipe in my room. The girls that were in my room had it, but all three of us got write-ups.

Edwards leaves with an escort. Ellen Conner steps into the Pro Visit booth.

Kristina's mother's not coming?
Conner: Her mother's unreal. I think this situation is going to get worse. Her mother's gonna tell that baby someday, something bad. She's just gonna make that little girl feel like dirt; make her another addict.

Alex is going for a severance of Kristina's case from the other cases, at the hearing on Monday.
I have trouble with her trial going first. They did this to my friend, and she got fried. They said they wanted somebody guilty for the case, and she was an accessory. She got 25-to-life, and the ones who committed the murder got 12. They're gonna be out of prison in six years. All they wanted was somebody to blame. The other two people weren't even in the newspaper. They totally punished my friend even though the other two admitted to doing it. Kristina's gonna take it. You watch. Is she in Lockdown?

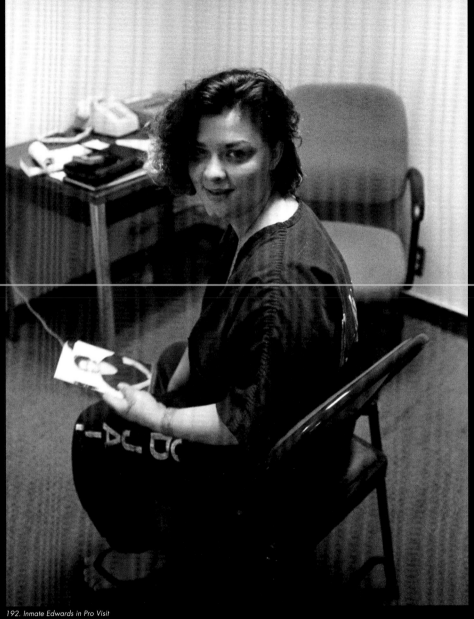

192. Inmate Edwards in Pro Visit

11/18/95

Kath Anderson calls at noon and says Maxwell is in rough shape. "She drove around Hamilton House on a motorcycle around 2:00 a.m., loaded on heroin." I tell her we're going to see Gordy.

1:30 p.m.   Gordy, rehab counselor

Anderson: You need to spend more time in B housing, maximum security. White Dog [Gordy] knows it all. He'll send you in the right direction if he feels you can handle it. Talk to him about prison. That's what maximum's all about. That's what we're all about, Susie.

It's a long drive to Lemon Grove. Gordy's rehab looks like an old motel. His rottweiler sits in the back of his pickup truck outside the place. He says it was hard to get used to larger spaces after so many years in prison.

Gordy: I tried to make each space a cell when I first moved in here. Come on in, have a seat. I was in prison 30 years, off and on. I'm 45 now. I was born in Juvenile Hall actually. Then she (mom) came up with these foster parents when I was five days old, and I lived with them 'til I was 13. Foster mom died, and my foster father was too old to take care of me. I went back into the foster-care system and couldn't handle that. They put me in Juvenile Hall for running away from home the first time. I stayed there six months. That's where I learned these behaviors. I never stole before. I was real protected as a kid, brought up in a Christian environment. But I made the kids in the Hall my family, and I went out the first time and stole a little motorcycle. I got arrested, and it went on from there.

Back in the early '60s it was a whole different story. It wasn't gangs. I later got involved with the Hell's Angels and Aryan Brothers. I got involved in drugs and went to San Francisco, the Haight Ashbury district, did the music trip, and all of that. Then I came back to San Diego. When I was in county jails and prisons, they have what they call a "tank captain." Whatever the tank captain said, went. You held the tank together to make sure nobody killed nobody. The sheriff can't keep everyone under surveillance all the time. Back in the '70s, cops used to be scandalous. They'd come in, and somebody they thought was really tough, they'd pay the tank captain to mess 'em up.

Say you got a guy that's a real asshole. He's pressuring people, taking things from people, and thinking he's a real guy. They'd say, "Hey, Gordy, we got this guy who thinks he's a real tough guy and I wanna put him in your tank"—'cause I was in a high-powered tank—"You straighten him out for me." First I'd talk to him and tell him, "Look, that stuff you did in the other tank? That behavior ain't happening here." Then I'd beat him up.

High-powered, meaning?
Where they put the Hell's Angels, Aryan Brotherhood, Crips, Bloods, everybody that's in there for robberies and murders.

Did they have any fear of you at all when they came into your tank?
Not fear. Respect. If people are really crazy, they don't fear too much. It wasn't physical; it was another type of fear.

Physically, county jail—you're talking about 40 to 50 in a cell?
Yeah, sleeping on the floor and everywhere.

Prison?
When you're in prison, you're somebody. We had got what we called the San Diego Car. The leaders are called the "shot callers." Say I go to San Quentin. I'm from San Diego, and I've done so much time I'm one of the shot callers from the San Diego Car. So a guy "drives up," and he's a child molester. I'm the one who finds out when the bus comes in from San Diego and who knows these people. What're they in for.

How do you handle a child molester?
First thing, I go to one of the youngsters from San Diego and say, "Get this guy off the yard and roll him up." That means either stab him, or beat him up. Child molesters don't walk the yard. I've stabbed over 30 of them myself. I've got a friend of mine who's doing life right now for killing one. They used to call me White Dog. I'm from San Diego. Where are you from?" They tell me. "Who do you know? What are you in for?" and they tell me. I say, "How much time you got?"

Now, if a guy's in there for child molestation, usually he's in for 30 to 33 years. He says, "Thirty-three years and I'm in here for robbery." "Well what did you rob?" He answers, "A 7-Eleven." Well a 7-Eleven robbery carries five-to-ten years, first offense, second offense, what "You got any priors?" Then I can figure it out from there. If a guy's got 30 to 33 years, he's lying to you right from the jump. So I investigate him. Oh, yeah. They're scared.

How often did you cross the line into the criminal lifestyle?
I didn't get into no trouble until my foster parents were no longer there for me. They stick me in other foster families and I knew they didn't feel any love. Plus, I didn't have many friends to begin with. I was kinda a fat, dumpy kid, and I was picked on a lot, beat up, but I wanted kids to like me. You know how it is? I had these values that I grew up with, but still I wanted that acceptance from kids. In Juvenile Hall I was somebody.

How did you justify stealing?
I don't know. I figured it was acceptable to my friends. When you take something and nobody's there to see you take it, you don't feel like you really hurt somebody personally. You rationalize it. They got insurance, they're rich, and they won't miss it. I was a con man. My role models were good pickpockets and good con men. I loved trying to make people believe in something, putting their money up, giving it to me, and have them think that they're fucking me over in the long run. All throughout my criminal history has been property damage. I never thought I ever hurt anybody.

> Well, they're cutting back on programs for kids. It's going to get worse, and people aren't going to care. They institutionalize adolescents and make money off of institutionalizing them. The biggest industry in California is the Department of Corrections. It's making money.
>
> Counselor Gordy

One thing that I did that still bothers me was when I was an addict in Texas and I was real sick, dope sick, and I snatched this lady's purse. First time I ever done that. She fell down. I felt so bad about that. I thought, oh, my God. I felt like shit for years: Look what I've become. I'd have nightmares. I'd see her face, and the fear in her eyes. It messed with me.

Were you into white-collar crime?
Sure. Very few people did what I did. I thought I was pretty good. I made a lot of money. On the street I used to play Three-card-Mollie. I learned poker in prison. I spent time thinking how to hustle and make money. I used to pop cars. From my motor home, I'd see with my binoculars people who got out of their parked cars. I'd put my little girlfriend in little skimpy shorts, and she'd bend and stretch. While they're watching her, I'd hit their car. I'd get their wallet. I'd run their credit cards quick as I could, 'cause they're only good for a few hours. Then I'd buy some gold, clothes, a TV, a VCR, and load it in my car. I'd rent a hotel room, 'cause you only have to use the card once.

OK, so, say you got a 24/7 teller card: I'd find out your name and number from your purse or wallet, and then I'd call the cardholder. I'd say, "Hello, I work for Johnson and Johnson Security Service and we just apprehended someone here using your 24/7 teller card. We'd like to know if this person had permission." They go, "It was stolen?" We go, "Yes, ma'am. We'll have this person placed in custody. But first, I have to prove that you're the owner of the cards. Give me your numbers so I can verify this is your card." They go, "Oh, well, my numbers are blah, blah, blah," and I say, "OK, thank you very much," and for days I'm punching in all their money out of their bank, and I did that forever.

He pulls out his wallet and removes a credit card.

I'm just real proud 'cause I got the first Visa Card I ever had in my life with my name on it. I've never used one with my name on it before.

What problems did you have with recovery?
I had a problem when I first came to NA. I always felt I was different because I had spent so much time in prison. I had a hard time reaching out to other people and saying, "My name's Gordy." By managing a rehab, I brought the people to me, instead of going to them. It's good to get up and share. Now Kath's doing that job and she's good.

She called us about Maxwell.
Chances aren't too good. Chances aren't good at all.

Maxwell's relationship with prostitutes is about getting drugs for them?
When you're an addict, you don't really have friends. It's, what does this person have to offer me? If I can't get nothing, I'm useless. They take from their families. They steal from them. They manipulate.

Some women in the jail I talked with started drugs as early as nine years of age. What's going to happen?
Well, they're cutting back on programs for kids. It's going to get worse, and people

aren't going to care. They institutionalize adolescents and make money off of institutionalizing them. The biggest industry in California is the Department of Corrections. It's making money.

Now there's not enough room or enough judges.
They tell you that. There's plenty of room, plenty of judges. They say, "If you don't get us more money we're gonna have to start letting these people go 'cause we don't have the judges." You're thinking, we don't want this guy on the street, so, you're saying, spend taxes and build more facilities. They build so many new prisons and then they come up with Three Strikes but what's it going to do five years down the road? You're being pressured into this and you just don't know it. So now we can build all these prisons and put everybody away. There's no rehabilitation anymore.

What about medicating inmates to keep them compliant?
That's all they're gonna do—put him on medication. Because of my size, and my attitudes they say, "Give this guy a pill, give him anything he wants just to keep him quiet." They don't care if there's a psychiatric problem or not. "Ah, Doc. I've a hard time getting to sleep." Give him Ativan. That's the solution to everything. The solution to my problem is another drug. A girl told me, "I want to go see Dr. Rand." I told her, "He's gonna give you a pill, tell you that you have psych problems and need sober living and SSI." So she goes to him, and pays for her sober living.

It's a big hustle, a scam. I could name a whole bunch of doctors I used to go to. I'd take carloads of gals with medical stickers and I'd say, "OK, Doc. Here's the scrip I want." I'd get all these scrips and I'd give the girls like 20 bucks apiece. I'd get all these pills. I'd make a lot of money.

Did you ever have a relationship?
I was married for seven years. It was the only relationship I had that meant anything to me. She just got tired of me goin' to prison. Cut me loose. I was an addict. I was a bouncer at a biker bar, and we started this business with her sister. We ran a massage parlor.

Your wife opened a massage parlor with you?
It was all-sex, all-massage parlors. They go in, you rent the room, I owned the company. I have these cubicles. Guys can go in and just get a straight massage, but that's not why they go there. I pay the girl minimum wage. Whatever negotiation she makes with the customer is her business. Your biggest worry was gonorrhea and syphilis.

She was in love with you and you had a sex parlor on the side?
For a woman to be in love with an addict she had to be a sick person. She met me as somebody else. She didn't get loaded. She didn't smoke weed. She didn't do any kind of drug. She drank very little and she tried everything she could to get me away from the drug thing 'cause I wasn't the same person she fell in love with. I had escaped from a prison in Riverside. I came here under a new identity.

How did she feel about the crime?
She'd know I'd leave and come back with all this money. She never questioned how I got it. I told her not to question and then she'd have nothing to tell the police.

Were you scary then?
Yeah, I was. I was real scary. I had to be this person to get what I wanted. I kicked people's doors in—other addicts, not normal people. I'd take their shit and leave. I felt justified when I got out of prison. I felt that the beach area was mine. Mission Beach and Ocean Beach. I controlled the drug traffic in that area. I'd get Skinheads working for me. I'll always be an addict.

How do you relate to these recovering addicts?
You couldn't do it. It would overwhelm you. They'd take advantage of you. Even though they're clean, they'd take advantage of you. There's a lot of places in San Diego that call themselves sober living that allow people to use. There's one right down the street. When I went over there, I seen two kids smokin' marijuana by the pool, drinkin' beer, all in the name of recovery.

People scamming people.
Whites are so busy doing what they want to do, establishing what they want, going further and further. It's money . . . we got to have it. I've hung around blacks and Mexicans all my life. I couldn't let a culture barrier stop me. I felt like a chameleon, able to fit into any situation. Whites don't place culture in the family as much as Hispanics do.

But our families are not getting along and our children are not getting along. . . .
We're not there for each other anymore. People don't give the one thing that everybody's looking for in life—themselves. Dad will go to work and make money and be miserable as fuck. Kids go, "Dad's never here." Moms might never be here, either.

Your mother went to prison?
She was in Juvenile Halll. I don't know what for. I was born in Juvenile Hall. It's been almost 20-some years since I seen her. I remember going to prison, getting out, and looking for my sisters and my mom. They had moved. I didn't know where they went.

You don't come across as threatening now.
I do hang out with more women. I can't say I'm this big macho Don Juan. How could a guy that's spent as much time in prison with guys say that they know anything about women and be honest about it? That's one of the things that I missed while I was in prison. Like the girl that I got here now, Cathy; I knew her husband in prison, and he's doin' life. She was an addict, and we went through treatment together. She was one of the ones that was real with me. She was using and hookin'. She's as old as I am; sweetest thing in the world. I mean, she's just a good friend and I wanted to help her, but I wouldn't hesitate a minute if she used today to tell her to pack her shit and get out the fuckin' door!

I know what kind of addict I was. I didn't have any friends. I've got friends now that care about me. My sense of what a true man is has changed. Before it was what I had learned—a man can't cry. Bullshit. That's what's instilled in children. A boy cries, and the first thing his father tells him is, "Don't cry." Now my sense of a true man is a man that can show his true emotions and still feel secure about who he is. I cried when I gave Cathy her 30-day token last week.

194-195

194-195. Dr. Bull; 196. Lieutenant
Milakovich and Deputy Price

Dr. Bull clenches his clipboard and paces as we wait for the door to open. We enter the jail.

Rolenda was in the Safety Cell?

Dr. Bull: She went into a complete temper tantrum: screaming, biting, and spitting. They put her into the restraining chair. It started all over again. When I talked to her she was crying, tears copiously streaming down her face. She talked about losing her children. Here's somebody who's absolutely empty and lost inside. She keeps having children, and she's only 18 years old. Maybe people like Rolenda are messengers who come to tell us things we really don't want to hear. Her ugly behavior creates the great wall between her and others. When she's in the chair and spitting blood all over it's pretty hard to have any understanding of what might've been the cause. When she was put in a Safety Cell, she calmed down.

Something happens to her when she's threatened, and something even worse when she's tightly confined. The psychiatrist identified her behavior as primitive. What provokes this?

Many of the inmates can't focus. Professionals can't reach them because we don't know what causes uncontrollable urges and behaviors. The damage is deep in the recesses of their minds.

The reason they become alcoholics, heroin addicts, or addicts of any kind is to have an anesthetic to ease their pain. A lot of the pain eases when people become institutionalized. A lot of the stresses change. Alcohol was once used as an anesthetic drug; ether was once used as a recreational drug. Alcohol is a disinhibitor, a permission giver. This inhibition is a really important issue. I used to say, "You've got a kid in a cage, and alcohol's the key. It unlocks the cage." The really heavy one is heroin, and every time users shot it up, they said they wished they could die. My sense is that people who use powerful drugs in powerful quantities have some very serious reasons to want to dump those kinds of chemicals into their bodies. Most of the people we have locked up are here for drug-related crimes.

Even if we locked up all of the Rahemas, their spirits would eat through the cracks and crevices of society.

Americans have a love/hate relationship with drugs. They love to get high; yet they don't want to admit it. So we make drugs illegal. There's an economic structure that provides commodities and services that Americans want. If you want a prostitute you don't go to the Yellow Pages and find it under "P"; it's under "M" for massage. If we banish people for the things we want really, we are in conflict. Our relationship with violence is the same thing. We satisfy it vicariously through film. Immigration is another example. We create circumstances that are attractive to illegal immigrants to do work we don't want to do.

Is our society mature enough to deal with drugs? Isn't pill popping part of our culture?

Dr. Bull: You could make a good argument that it could work in Holland, but not here. Drugs aren't supposed to be in our culture, so we have foreigners supply us with what we want. Organized crime is an American institution that provides us with the things that we want, but don't want to admit. If you're going to create rigid rules, you can expect people not to go by them. The biggest problem with legalization of drugs is that you knock the profit out of the whole industry. There's a large population of people who use drugs and alcohol recreationally, and not problematically. There are many people who smoke pot to unwind without appearing addicted. It's true of gambling, football games, and Black Jack. On the other hand, I've talked to people who simply smoke pot all day long, and are high all of the time. I find that as frightening as someone who stays drunk all of time. It's very self-punishing and destructive. Most of the people in F3 talk endlessly about going and getting high. Once in a while I talk to someone, usually around 40, who's going to make a change. There's evidence this is a turning point. It's, "I'm sick and tired of being sick and tired."

Sex, drugs, rock-n-roll?

One whole area that's rarely mentioned to me is sex. I know women in jail are sexually active. The ones who mention it to me are the ones who find it repugnant. Americans' attitudes toward sex are very conflicted. The same thing, however, more powerful, is drugs.

Ameerah told us, "They love me to touch them with my hands."

I suspect that she's telling you something quite profound. I talked to a guy in prison who said something drove him to have some kind of contact. What I hear her telling you is that not having physical contact, hugs, strokes, in a close proximity like this, is absurd. I know there's a whole world going on back in B housing that I don't have access to, because I'm doing essentially psychiatric interviews.

What's behind prostitution?

A pattern of rebellion against authority that sometimes leads to prostitution. Then the prostitute ends up in a position where she has power over men. They are the object of the rebellion in the first place. It's connected to a lot of dependency on other people. Drugs and prostitution are connected to living on the edge. That brings on a great deal of tension, excitement, and risk. The risk encompasses lots of sources; the tricks they're meeting, the cops, the possibility of getting beaten up . . . the whole thing's very exciting.

So, in many cases, these women haven't developed tools to cope with society, and they have developed sick relationships with men and drugs. What's the solution?

This is not a treatment facility. Neither is prison. We're more into banishment. But banishment isn't a good strategy. The only thing that works is working through the problem. Incarcerated, many get clean, yet they don't attack their underlying issues. At F, D, and C housing, the women seem to get close.

I've read about the powerful hormone, oxytocin, referred to as the "bonding hormone," that's responsible for the close attachment of mother and child, but also present at times of intimacy and touching. It's activated by estrogen. I'm curious if the women, sharing time and space, secrete this hormone, and feel a sense of safety during their incarceration. As much as they say they hate jail, in many ways they seem to receive some pleasure from incarceration. If healthy bonds weren't formed early in life, could a visit to jail be an attempt to return to early conditioning? Interesting. You see so much more than I do with these women. A guy named Erving Goffman, 40 years ago, used to hang around inmates to experience what they did. You have this wonderful freedom to collect this very private information, and you can observe how life goes on here, not only from inmates, but from deputies.

In psych interviews, what're you looking for?

I'm looking for how serious a depression is. For example: is there a loss of appetite, are they not sleeping, are they crying all the time, are they having suicidal thoughts, are they lonely?

It's very infrequent that we get anybody who's very educated in here. The only ones that come to mind right off hand are Betty Broderick and Shelby Roland. A friend brought Betty good-quality books. I remember once Broderick asked me for some books on meditation. It happened that I had a couple of them. Shelby Roland did that same thing.

Deputies say Rolenda belongs in CMH (County Mental Health).

Rolenda is very manipulative. But I'm sure people would have no concept of the injury she has gone through. There are staff who want to medicate her into a sort of oblivion. They want to banish her with sedation. Wipe her behavior out temporarily. When I heard that you worked with Rolenda, my first reaction was, "My God, why did they pick her?"

I sense a change with Kristina.

Maybe she's showing movement. I think that when she was under a lot of stress she might have had some psychotic features. Once in a while we get to see some change, and it's the loveliest thing to see happen. People begin to allow themselves to cry, acknowledge somebody within who's soft and has a tender self.

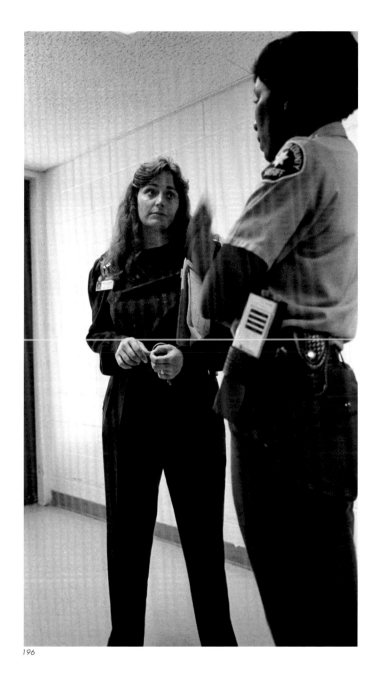

196

Permission is granted for us to see Rolenda during her Disciplinary Lockdown as long as it's done in B housing. She's a green-bander and considered to be an escape risk.

We're escorted back to the unit. Beyond a locked security door are the B1 and B2 units for serious felons. B3 is for all new pre-arraignment detainees awaiting classification. The B housing unit smells like vomit. Clear plastic trash bags contain orange rinds, bread crusts, and gravy. The deputies are sullen. "Something's different," Barbara whispers. "Things are worse." I look around. Women pace inside their units and look through glass-wired doors. They look like caged animals. B housing is intense.

Inside the private Pro Visit Room next to B housing's separate Control Room, Dep. Price joins us. In charge of classification of all inmates, she explains that CMH doesn't have funds to handle "mental" cases for more than three days and says "the jails are loaded with mental cases." She excuses herself to make room for Rolenda and her special escort.

I think, in general, the human life means so much less now. It's so easy to take a life. It's like drive-through banking. You drive through and shoot.

Lieutenant Milakovich

We move deeper into the jail - maximum security.

11/22/95 11:00 a.m. B Housing Pro Visit

Nine deputies flank Rolenda. They halt in the B housing doorway and prepare to remove her shackles and handcuffs. Two of the deputies maintain a tight grip on Rolenda's arms. Heavily drugged, she recognizes me and smiles sweetly. She sees Barbara and beams. The deputies close, but do not lock, the door to the B housing Pro Visit Room as they leave us to interview Rolenda.

This is quite the entrance you made.
Banks: They big bad deputies need all this shit [shackles and handcuffs], and here you are alone with me in this room. The door's not even locked. They just do shit to aggravate you here. They ain't got no reason to mess with me. I was talking to another girl, and Harper said, "Don't fucking communicate." I said, "It's not in the rules we can't communicate." She said, "Well it's in my fuckin' rules." Then she started yellin', "You ain't getting no water again tonight, Banks, for your soup."

She leans back in her chair after a few moments of complaining about the staff.

You know what? There's a girl who got life for abusing her baby. The baby had gangrene 'cause she was left in a car seat forever. Can you believe a mother would do that? It's sick in here. My roommate smells and has got this thing coming out of her face, above her ear, she don't clean. It's got white shit, and it smells. She eats my food and talks all the time. She's crazy. These people are crazy. I just wanna be here in B housing where I can walk around until they send me to prison.

Why would you have to go to prison?
For leaving the hospital. They had my wrist and ankle chained to the bed. Two guards were there 'round the clock. Then about six days before my release date, they got a phone call. They came back, and they uncuffed me from the bed. I asked if I was going back to jail. They said, "No, we're going back. Nice meeting you, Banks. You're on your own."

I had heard the story from Dep. Harper several months earlier.

Then you asked for a cigarette.
It was set up. I've been in the hospital four or five times before, and they never left me alone before, even when I went to CMH. This time, after they left, I asked the nurse if I could smoke a cigarette and she said, "Not in here." So I went down the hall. My friend brought me clothes. I put them on, I combed my hair, and we left. The next day I was in Arizona, and about a week-and-a half later I had my baby.

How did they find you?
I called the police on my boyfriend. I was tired of him dragging me all over. I didn't do no drugs. I just wasn't eatin' right. The night I came back into the jail, Sgt. O'Brien gave me ten days in Lockdown for flipping-off a deputy. They wanted me to carry my big bed with chains on. I couldn't do it, shuffling in leg chains. They locked me in my room without apparel. They sang barn songs, "Row, row, row your boat . . ." in the speaker box. They were yelling at me, "Banks, that's not your head is it? Bang it a little harder so we can hear you." They're doing things that I can't control.

7:00 p.m. Phone call, Kristina Edwards

Edwards: You know what my mom said when I told her I needed her? "Well you shoulda thought of that when you were on the top of that hill murdering that guy." It's obvious, she skirted everything that's had to do with me. She's never taken any responsibility with me. Why should she start now? I'm through with her. I'm not calling her anymore. Plus, now the DA won't take my deal. He said that he'd bring back the torture count.

197

197-198. Inmate Banks

11/24/95   9:15 a.m.   B Housing Pro Visit

Rolenda, upset. Her skin's broken out with sores.

You're agitated and tense.
Banks: I ain't done nothing wrong, Susan. They chained me next to this smelly girl who had chicken pox. Now look at me. I'm broken out with chicken pox. Look at my back. They got me on meds that make me think crazy. I can't take this place no more.

She drops to the floor, animated and restless. We talk to her quietly until she settles down. Suddenly she begins to describe a part of her childhood we had not heard about before.

My half-brothers took me from Aunt Etta. My mother put me in a chest that was long enough for me to get into. I used to tap my legs as many times as I could to concentrate inside it. I didn't ever tell nobody about it.

Did you tell Dr. Bull?
No.

The courts?
Nobody. The rest of the time she kept me in this dirty tent with an old white dog that had bugs on it. The tent was out in back behind the shanty she lived in. She stole me several times. We finally ended up in California.

Rolenda has a nasty cough. She's rational in spite of her drugged appearance.

They still got a $100,000 bail on me. Last night, I got mad 'cause they wouldn't let me out of my cell, and I banged my head on the mirror. A board came down and leave some big old hole in the wall. They woke me up and said I caused the board to come down.

Why were you hitting your head?
I couldn't eat. I had fever. At first, they tried to use the excuse, "There's nothing wrong with you." But I had a 103 fever. My throat was all swollen, and I was broken out all over. I got them in my head. My hair's falling out! I hate it here. I'd rather do six months in prison.

Now you're in jail with priors.
That don't mean nothin'. I have priors for taking my daughter from the foster care. That's it, and that don't mean nothin'. I love Chantia. It won't help to talk to the attorney 'cause he's gonna talk to the deputies and the deputies aren't gonna admit what they said. Any excuse to put me in the chair and leave me there for hours, strapped down.

198

1:15 p.m. Pro Visit, Kristina Edwards

We return to the Pro Visit area in the main jail for a visit with Kristina Edwards. We don't have clearance to stay in B housing and conduct other interviews.

Kristina arrives and takes a seat.

We thought you didn't want to come out and see us.
Edwards: My roommate had to come and get me. She said someone had been yelling for me for a half-hour.

Indentations from her pillow mark the left side of her face. She pulls her ponytail tighter, exposing the new dark outgrowth.

You're upset.
Alex came by and told me to not get my hopes up and to not get too down. Back in the unit, we had no TV for three days. They took away hot water and patio time for having too many sanitary pads and toilet paper in the dorm. We're only allowed two pads. My mom hasn't written. I sleep all of the time.

Kristina talks about her life as a little girl, her father's history of drugs and prison, and her mother's siblings. She worries about her child being in her mother's care. "Once my baby can talk back to my Mom, that's when it'll all begin."

2:00 p.m. Pro Visit, Dr. Bull

Bull stops at our booth.

Dr. Bull: You saw Rolenda. How'd it go?

I tell him about Rolenda's story about being locked in a small chest when she was little.

It's as if she's compulsively driven to return to the small space.
Dr. Bull: Ah, yes. If Rolenda were trapped in a chest at the age of four by her mother, it could be very traumatic. The smaller the cell the worse, I'd have to agree. When people come here, various symptoms seem to emerge. I had two women the same day with PTS (Post Traumatic Stress). Both women were rape victims. I'm perceived as a source of help. I'm a chance to unload. They'll sit, talk, and cry, but it's also manipulative. It's the disadvantage that you don't have. I imagine that these women tell you things they'd never tell us. I'd imagine that could be helpful, and they don't feel threatened.

So what's going to happen with Rolenda?
She wanted to go back to B housing. They didn't go for it; clearly not a good sign. I cleared her from Lockdown back to A housing and asked her, "How do you feel on these new medications?" She said, "I don't feel anything. I just feel normal." I thought, God, this is the best thing she could've said. That's how you're supposed to feel.

What medication did the psych put her on?
Lithium and Resperdal. None of the usual antipsychotic drugs which she had before. Resperdal is antipsychotic.

Will this prepare her for the outside world?
She needs to go into residential housing. Hopefully Kiva.

Rolenda has Bull, Ellen, Barbara, and me pulling for her. Her attorney, as well as her PO, hadn't realized she was abused and tortured as a youngster.
Dep. Sisco overhears part of the conversation and steps into the booth.

Dep. Sisco: Rolenda's a green-bander. She's attacked deputies too many times. Kiva won't happen.

11/27/95 8:45 a.m. Courthouse

Ryan's attorney recognizes me outside the courtroom. He complains that the court is overburdened by the Three Strikes Law. Another attorney says there are so many serious offenders today. "I just got one off, and I had to go home and take a shower. I felt like a sewer."

We step inside the courtroom where many attorneys have gathered and are waiting for their cases to be called. The defendants are held in a glass cage. Private investigator, Marian L. Pasas, sits behind us. She says she has two big cases, and she's exhausted. Several family members are present for Kristina's codefendant, Bellows. His mother walks along in a trance, handing carnations to several young female friends and family members.

The judge calls cases one by one. Prisoners are removed from the glass cage to stand before the judge. Kristina's handcuffed to the inmate bench outside the cage, waiting for Alex. She isn't dressed-out. Why did we bother to get clothes for her when she shows up in jail pajamas? At least her hair and makeup are reasonable. She smiles and tries to tell me something about her clothes. I'm unable to understand and signal to her to look at the sign. It says, Do Not Talk to Inmates.

The judge begins questioning the attorneys on the Bellows, Edwards, and Ryan murder case. Alex Landon arrives. The DA announces he has a new discovery. McKenzie, Bellows' attorney, says he's ready to go to trial. When the DA requests another three months to build evidence, Landon simply states, "My client's ready to proceed. We don't need the discovery. It really doesn't pertain to her case."

The judge appreciates the attorney's being ready. She says that the Severance Motion for Kristina Edwards will be heard on the 29th. Alex takes a seat next to Kristina and talks to her in a sensitive manner.

Edwards is hauled out of the courtroom to a cold, dark basement in the courthouse, where inmates are forced to sit on hard concrete benches for hours. In some cases they have to sit there day after day.

Outside the courthouse, several people are grouped around Alex. He looks past the crowd and sees us. He excuses himself and approaches Barbara and me. He asks us to stay involved.

11/28/95 10:30 a.m. Jail, Pro Visit

Barbara takes a few days off. I go to the jail to talk to Kristina Edwards.

Edwards: Did you see Bellows' wife and Ryan's girlfriends in court?
I saw some girls with carnations, dressed like little hippies. They were dirty, and their eyes were puffy.
And what's with the carnations? I'm sweatin' this trial so much. I got an earache. Right now we're in Lockdown. I just wanna go home. My little baby's already gonna be a month old. Did my Mom call you and ask what happened at the trial? Tell her that she should be there. She said, "Kristina, I can't believe you expect me to go down there." If she wants to know anything then she shoulda come. I need another outfit or two for court. Alex said, "I thought it was up to your mom to get you clothes for court."

You hear about that lady who tortured the three-and-a-half-year-old girl with her husband? The couple locked the brother in a room. He watched through the keyhole as they burned his sister with scalding hot water. They wouldn't give her no food. They threw hard balls at her. Her skin and toenails was found on the bottom of the tub. I don't understand a mother hurting her child like that. I just keep thinking about my baby's little face lookin' up at me, her suckin' on my finger, and I hate myself. She's gonna forget all about me.

199-201

202

Inmates have mood swings often. They feel empty, alone, lost, and tend to reach out and cling to something to give them an anchor. People like this have very intense relationships and find somebody who is like a container, like them. They pour themselves into the container and take that shape.

Jim Bull, Ph.D.

After Kristina leaves, Dep. Smith sees me sitting on the inmate bench and says, "Here, let me handcuff you." The handcuffs, attached to the bench, are more isolating than walking around handcuffed. When she releases them, she chuckles and says they'll bring Rolenda into the Pro Visit Room.

B Housing, Pro Visit, Rolenda Banks

Banks: I haven't been in any trouble since I been in Lockdown. The sergeant denied me going to B housing, and I have to stay in A. This medication makes me so anxious, I gotta walk around. I got a junkie roommate who sleeps on the floor and I can't walk. She smells bad 'cause she don't take a bath. She don't brush the little teeth that she do have. They gave us Christmas bags. Two packs of peppermints, two granola bars, two beef jerkies, something with cheese, and a little pencil, and bubblegum. She got all the stuff out of the bag, and ate all of her stuff, and some of mine. She keeps unwrappin' the candy and wrappin', rattlin' that candy and chewin', smack, smack, smack. I can't stand it. We got into trouble cause she's got milk cartons, Styrofoam cups, orange peelings, wrappers, everywhere. It's nasty. Everything I own, I keep right under my mattress in one little pack. I'm up there with six girls in for murder, and this lady across from me that coughs all night long puts butter in her hair to make it oily. But it makes her hair sour. She got a No Butter sign on her door. That smell, plus, the girl in my room farts all day and all night. It stinks.

199-201. Inmate Edwards; 202. Bench with chains;
203. Inmate Banks
203

11/29/95 8:30 a.m.
Courthouse, Motion to Sever

It takes an hour and a half to get to the courthouse in the fog (Californians panic on the highway with fog as well as rain).

Outside the courtroom, the Bellows family mingles. The younger sister, with honey red-blonde hair, pulls out miniature playing cards. The dad, dressed in beige, polyester, flared trousers and a brown sports coat, paces. He's short. His groomed beard emphasizes his round face. He takes a seat next to me. The mother is unable to stay focused.

Mrs. Bellows is passing out carnations to a group of young women outside the courtroom, presumably Bellows' friends and family.

Ryan's attorney opens the door to enter the courtroom. We follow and see Kristina enter and sit on the inmate bench. She's dressed in her new clothes and she smiles proudly. There is a lot of commotion as more attorneys arrive. The men pay special attention to a handsome black female attorney and joke with her about fashion. The courtroom is casual. The bailiff is keeping his eyes on me as I take notes.

At 9:00 a.m. the judge grumbles about individuals being late and holding up the court. She calls for Edwards. Ryan's attorney files a Motion to Sever. Bellows' attorney isn't present and hasn't filed. The judge says that she wants another judge to hear the Motion for Severance. The judge asks Alex to carry the Motion to Sever to Department 28.

Rolenda enters the courtroom. The marshal seats her on the bench next to Kristina. They laugh and point to me. I worry about their excitement. The court calls Rolenda's case, but her attorney isn't present.

Alex tells me to join them in Department 28 so I can hear the Severance Motion, but I have to find Rolenda's attorney. Alex asks the bailiff to help me out, and says he'll meet me on the fourth floor. I can't locate Rolenda's lawyer.

I take the wrong set of elevators and am unable to find Department 28. Lost in a corridor, I hear a marshal in front of me shout. "Hold it! Stand right where you are." People freeze. An enormous African-American male, dressed in a pea green suit, handcuffed and shackled, steps out in front of me. He's holding a briefcase. I recognize him from the tour at Downtown Central Men's Jail. It's Hamilton George, back from prison on appeal and trying his own case.

"Follow at least ten steps behind," the marshal instructs those of us standing close by.

I remember Ben telling me that the Sheriff has to provide computers and law books for those who want to defend themselves. George was considered a big headache.

I miss the entire Department 28 experience and return to Department 9 to check on Rolenda. I learn that the judge has trailed five cases, continued two, and denied bail on one. Ranting and raving about how people who are late are "screwing up" her schedule, the judge exits the courtroom.

6:00 p.m.   Phone call, Kristina Edwards

Edwards: I'm just lucky I made it in one piece. I got two girls after me. They came in my cell last night and tried to drag me into theirs. When I go to court tomorrow, I'll be in a dungeon. They'll be there. One of them said she'll "do it" in court. Girls go, "We wanna help you, but you're in the wrong. You're going to prison." All she has to do is pass it around that I'm a rat and I'm gonna have a hard time. I don't wanna walk in the courtroom with a busted-up eye.

11/30/95 Pro Visit

Dr. Bull walks by and signals us to follow him to his office.

Dr. Bull: Come in. I talked to the other lieutenant, not Milakovich, about moving Rolenda into E housing, the psych unit. The new psychiatrist felt E would be the ideal placement. There's more space, and lots of hard emotional work. Dr. Bromley has her on new meds, and it looks like they're working. Her spirits are up. I watched her yesterday, on the patio, and she was singing Christmas carols with a bunch of other women, her hair all poofed out. She had a wonderful childlike quality. When she's up, she's very endearing. E housing is a very intensive type of group therapy, and it's especially geared for women who have very abusive backgrounds. They use John Bradshaw dynamics. If she were to be judged just on the face of her current behavior, anybody would say, "Hey, this is great." My boss went on vacation; I called him up right before, and said, "I want to try this." It's difficult because she's in green, but I'm absolutely willing to vouch for her with any credibility I have.

12/1/95 Pro Visit

Dr. Bull waves. I step up to the clerk with a blue card for Edwards. I'm told the inmates are eating. Bull joins me while I wait for Kristina.

Dr. Bull: Rolenda's case is complicated by the fact that there's a volitional component to her behavior. She'll do things to get what she wants. If she thinks she can be sent to CMH by behaving a certain way, she tries. Sometimes spitting her blood works. Then she'll be nice and compliant. Last time she spit blood at deputies, I talked to her. She laughed good-naturedly and said, "Yeah, I did that." She dismissed it. It's a deliberate behavior, the very opposite of what deputies would like to have inmates act like. It triggers all kinds of deputy responses: "We'll fix her ass and we'll take care of her," banish her or whatever. So she gets punished a lot. All of the punishments she gets from authorities are only going to be reinforced.

I call Rolenda's attorney's supervisor and tell her that the attorney hasn't returned my calls. The super tells me that Rolenda is viewed as an "escapee." Dr. Girsch will do a psych evaluation, she tells me. She guarantees me that Dr. Girsch will be told about Rolenda's early abuse.

12/7/95 Rolenda Banks

What's this I'm reading in your report about San Bernardino Mental Hospital for four months?
Banks: That's where I was in San Bernardino.

Attempted suicide, when?
I don't even remember, but I was there. I cut myself. I had a big scar. You can't see it no more. Dr. Bull don't come and talk to me no more. You be around here on the 18th 'cause my baby's gonna be coming here for a Contact Visit.

12/14/95 8:45 a.m. Pro Visit, Chelsea Donnelly

Dep. Harper: You here for Banks? She's in court.

Chelsea Donnelly stops on her trusty duty.

Donnelly: I was supposed to get out Saturday, but I'm getting out tomorrow morning. They'll release me at 12:01 a.m. I refuse to leave Las Colinas again in the middle of the night. I refuse to leave in the dark. My mother-in-law used to always say, "Whatever you do in the dark will come back to you in the light." I'm going to wait 'til later in the morning.

What did you do when you got out of jail last?
Got me some drugs. But when I didn't want to be bothered, I slept for two or three days in a doorway. I coulda cared less.

How about settling down?
With a man? All men are dogs. My daddy's a dog. A man's gonna be a man. I take that back. There're men, and there're boys. I'm always thinking about my daddy, the bad and good. He's still my daddy, and I love him. I don't care what he did. I'll always love him and respect him.

You're going to get some crack when you get out of here.
You shouldn't say that! I'm not afraid of walking out that door. I've no intention of doing drugs. I don't give a fuck about you or anybody else. Listen to what I'm sayin'. I don't need anybody tryin' to put anything on my mind that might confuse me or put me into a state. And what I'm tryin' to say to you is it takes me two to three hours to get a rock, but you know how long it takes me to find a rock when I walk off from the welfare department? Two seconds. All I'd have to do is step off of the bus.

   I get a check and a food stamp check because I've been incarcerated. I see people that I got high with over the last eight to nine years.

How many times have you been in this jail?
I don't know. This may be my fourth or fifth time.

Donnelly laughs. Dep. Harper steps in on the conversation.

Dep. Harper: She's been in here how many times? It's public record. You can look it up at the courthouse. Remember, it's people like Donnelly that are my job security. Three squares and a cot. Her family is the streets. So she goes back to the same people and gets back into the same trouble. The same arresting officers see her. They crack down on her, and boom, she's busted. Why work when you can make money selling dope and stuff? She's the only one who can change her life pattern. She's got to hit the brick wall to make a change in her life. The majority of them actually end up

205. Inmate Donnelly

dying before they hit the brick wall. They get into heroin. They start losing limbs and other body parts.

During the time I knew Chelsea in downtown San Diego when she was a street-person and I was working on a homeless photo-essay, I met Chelsea's grandmother and her daughter. Chelsea had set up a time for all of us to meet at her grandmother's house, where her daughter lived. I arrived and Chelsea never came. Her daughter and grandmother were not surprised. Chelsea's daughter, at age 13, was quite composed and responsible.

207-208

206. Deputy Houck, Inmate Banks and her baby;
207-208. Inmate Banks, baby, CPS attendant;
209. Inmate Banks; 210. Inmate Banks and Dr. Bull

KODAK TXP 6049   66   KODAK T

209

12/17/95   Contact Visit, Rolenda Banks

Rolenda's emotions sky-rocket at the sight of her baby, nicknamed Jelly Bean. The CPS attendant matter-of-factly hands over the baby to Dep. Houck, who can't resist gently squeezing and caressing the infant. Houck lovingly passes Jelly Bean to his mother and instantaneous joy takes over the cold climate of the inmate side of the Visitor's room. Rolenda hugs, kisses, and rocks her baby. She places him on the floor and plays pat-a-cake, gets down on ground level and squeals, making Jelly Bean laugh, his tiny body bouncing to his mother's actions.

Fifteen minutes pass only too quickly. The CPS attendant, ignoring Rolenda, steps in and takes the baby from Rolenda's arms. Rolenda grows silent and steps back, a huge tear plops from her eye onto her cheek. She watches the attendant carry her baby and black bag containing necessities, out of the Visitor's Room. Rolenda steps up to the windows to glean a last moment's view. This is the last time she will see her baby.

Dr. Bull meets Rolenda's eyes from outside the room when she turns her face in his direction.

It is another moment of intense emotions—for both doctor and inmate. The awareness of creation and loss is profoundly disturbing. A child's beginning is in the hands of CPS.

12/25/95   8:00 a.m.
           Phone call, Kristina Edwards

Edwards: I wanted to call and say Merry Christmas.
What's jail like on Christmas?
Edwards: Just an ordinary day. No turkey. I got up and thought about the little kids by their trees. I had to be put in Isolation again 'cause my mom said that she'd never let me see the baby. She makes me go crazy. She told the police I was a murderer! Who does she think she is? She said she'd fight me and I'd never see my baby again if I try to give my baby to Sandy.

1:00 a.m.

The kids are in bed and I can't sleep. I walk around outside our house. The temperature seems to rise a few degrees between one and three in the morning, and it's quite comfortable. Christmas lights along the balcony give off a warm, colorful feeling. The North Star is alone and bright. Creatures cry out. I play back in my mind some of my experiences with Kristina, realizing that I witnessed her pregnancy, her childbirth, her separation from the infant, and her trial anxiety. I think about Rolenda and many of the other inmates at Las Colinas. How have we failed so many women?

12/26/95   8:30 a.m. Courthouse
           Records Department

Between court hearings for Kristina and Rolenda, we pull up the files on Maxwell, Anderson, Roland, Chelsea, and Mulloy. We learn Chelsea is on her 25th visit to Las Colinas. She cleans up in jail, and she returns to her life as a street-person. We look up Ryan and Bellows, and we note that Ryan pled guilty to first-degree murder with parole.

1/2/96   9:00 a.m.   B Housing
Pro Visit, Rolenda Banks

Banks: The jail cleared me for B housing. I don't know why they want me to sleep so much. My attorney hasn't come either.

What happened at the courthouse?
Banks: Nothin'. Just like all the other times. I get up, get drugged, and take that bad bus–only to sit around in a cold cell for hours. Now I'm afraid because my PO (probation officer) had me have a psych evaluation. The psych asked me questions like count from 100 backwards by seven and I said 93, 83, 73. I knew I did it by tens. Then she asked me to name the five last presidents, and how's water and air the same. I got Bush, Clinton, Reagan.

Were you able to tell her about being locked in the chest?
Yeah, that's what she asked me. Then she asked who raped me and stuff.

Dr. Bull enters and wants to ask Rolenda some questions about court.

Rolenda, talk to Dr. Bull.
Banks: I don't want to. I got nothin' to say to him, but you know what? My cousin was on *Comic View* a couple nights ago. The deputies thought I was just crazy. They didn't believe Don T. Banks is my cousin.
Dr. Bull: Rolenda. Sign this form, and I'll talk to your PO. In my note to the lieutenant I said that we'd like to move you on the 26th of this month. I might as well be up-front with you. I'm not terribly optimistic. I think you'd be an opportune candidate to live in E housing, but you'd have to really do a lot of work: group therapy everyday, a lot of searching and crying, a lot of getting well and healing.

211

Bull leaves. Rolenda doesn't want to talk to Bull about E housing or jail.

He's trying to help you, Rolenda. Don't you think you were a little rude?
Banks: Yeah. Well he don't have to do that no more. I ain't going to that E house. You don't get it. Nobody does. They won't do nothin' here to help me. I'm stuck in the system.

211. Dr. Bull and Inmate Banks

1/3/96   7:45 a.m.   Pro Visit

It'll be an hour before Kristina Edwards can be brought up for a visit. I return to the booth and overhear a PO talking to a woman charged with murder. She doesn't want a trial. No one, it seems, wants a trial. Inmates want deals so they can leave jail and go to prison with a reduced sentence.
Edwards arrives with an escort.

You seemed pretty upset on the phone.
Edwards: Did you hear? Sandy went to take my baby, and my mom and her had a fistfight! I'm giving my baby to Sandy! She's wealthy. She owns a playground equipment company. She'll let me see my baby. My mom won't.

Can you really trust this woman?
I just want someone to care about me. I'm in here, and I have no one. I want to see my baby a couple of times, and have some pictures of her.

She leaves crying, shortly after the visit begins.

4:00 p.m.   Phone call

Alex Landon tells me Kristina can't be expected to make a rational decision about the child seven weeks before her murder trial. That her mother having the baby reminds Kristina of her own abuse. It's important, he says, that she deal with the reality of her case. She is looking at some serious time in prison and she can't be with the child anyway.

1/11/96   8:30 a.m.
B Housing, Pro Visit

Kristina Edwards' 20th birthday. She refuses a visit. Rolenda has been moved into B housing, a step up from Disciplinary Lockdown. Rolenda enters the maximum-security Pro Visit Room.

You look pretty calm today.
Banks: Kristina's been talking bad about you. She said you don't hold to your word so she hung up on you. She's telling all the girls that you won't drive up to San Bernadino and bring the baby for a visit. I said, "Kristina, just shut up!"

I'm gonna get drowsy in a minute. They gave me more Lithium and Klonipin. They never give it to me three times in a day before.

How does it make you feel?
Like I can't put my cheekbones down. I keep having to clench my teeth. I chipped my teeth on Lithium. My PO's gonna recommend me for Kiva. Meanwhile, the deputies have been trying to get me. You know I'd get three write-ups a month in A? I came to B, and they give me three write-ups in two

days for eye-fucking the deputy, and for yelling. They came over the loud speaker in A to another girl and she thought she was hearing voices tell her she was a slut! She went crazy. She's in Patton State Mental Hospital.

I watch Rolenda as she enters B2. I see her with Kristina and then Rolenda comes to the window and shouts, "Kristina doesn't want to see you. Tell her Happy Birthday, anyway." Dep. Tooney hears Rolenda and comes to the B housing Pro Visit Room. He's a strong-looking, friendly deputy who deals with the maximum-security inmates every day.

Dep. Tooney: Wait, Edwards doesn't want to come out? You want her out? I'll get her.

Dep. Mores enters and stands next to Tooney.

Dep. Tooney: You guys working on a book. You're here a long time ago. We could tell you some tales. I get along with Banks. She'll fight deputies and spit blood, but she won't do those things to me. She knows better. So what kind of book are you writing?

About incarceration.
Dep. Mores: A children's book. Ha, ha.
Dep. Tooney: I've actually been accused of having sex with inmates in exchange for favors.
Dep. Mores: Excuse me. Can we talk? Don't tell them anything.

Dep. Tooney doesn't seem concerned and chuckles.

Dep. Tooney: This one's a pushover with inmates.
Dep. Mores: Watch that tape recorder. You never know what they'll do.

Sunday night   Phone call,
Kristina Edwards

Edwards: Rolenda got beat up. She was put on the bench for going on and on about B2 housing. She kicked at the deputies and went off. Dep. Price maced her in the face. Dep. Condon came in, stood her up, and popped her in the spine. She dropped to the floor on her face, passed out. When she came to, he got her up and popped her again. It was terrible. I don't know why she acts like that. It's awful. Why doesn't she learn? She brings it on herself. Everyone saw it.

Where is she now?
Last I knew she was back in A, but they had her in the chair, and she was spitting blood again.

Kristina talks fast, doesn't mention how upset she had been on her birthday, and adds that they were all strip-searched in B housing on Saturday.

Monday morning   Phone call, Dr. Bull

Rolenda is back in A housing.

1/18/96   B Housing,
                Pro Visit, Dr. Bull

Dr. Bull: Yesterday I saw her in the visiting room, and I saw her on a Contact Visit with the most adorable, glorious baby in the world. She's just in heaven, kissing and nuzzling the baby. Later, I saw her back in her room, and she was screaming. She said, "I gotta talk to you." I asked the deputy to bring her up here so I could talk to her. The deputy said they need some back-up. About six-to-eight deputies marched her up. She sat down and said, "I can't make it. I'm about to lose control. I can feel it happening. I'm not going to spend the rest of my time in A housing." I said, "Are you taking your meds?" and she said, "No. I stopped taking them two days ago." I said, "Christ!" I got impatient. "Of course you're getting upset. This medication works for you. You need to take it."

I'm very pessimistic about her chances. I stuck my neck out, and I'd stick it out again, but I need more assurance from her. A deputy called me last week and said, "I got problems with Rolenda." Sounded like an emergency. I go there and Rolenda's looking better than ever. Her hair done up in little curls and makeup on. She's really stunning, has smiles and childlike behavior. She walks in, and I say, "What's going on?" and she says, "Oh, I got into it with the deputy and got put in Lockdown for two days." She added that the deputies deliberately frightened her at night. I went to Rolenda and said, "You have to be cool. People will try to provoke you, and there'll be deputies who try to put you back into A."

Next, she had an appointment for a psych evaluation with Dr. Bonnie Hammel, down at the PEU (Psychiatric Emergency Unit). Deputies had her up here by Control. Rolenda said, "Well I'm not going to go down there." I said, "What do you mean?" She said she was drowsy and didn't want to leave. She got really combative with deputies. Later, I talked her into doing the evaluation, and she had a good interview. The report looks very accurate. Because she's been resistant, they gave her a couple days in Lockdown. Then the classification deputy wrote this long report,

carefully printed out, saying in her opinion Banks cannot be trusted in mainline, and she'd remain in A housing for the remainder of her stay.

So they bring the meds, and she doesn't take them?
Inmates can choose to not take the meds. It's voluntary here. The nursing staff delivers the medications. If the inmate refuses them, the staff says "OK." It's all voluntary here. In a psychiatric hospital they can give meds under certain circumstances, whether or not a person wants them.

1/22/96   Dar Inman,
                Step Study counselor

We head off to the minimum-security yard to check in with some of the inmates. Dar walks with us from minimum-security back to the main unit, and discusses inmate patterns.

Dar: It's a codependency. Whether it's a boyfriend or it's a mother, the lack of self-identity remains. These relationships take over. The addict has no control over it. A lot of these women have been abused and molested. Inmates have to learn they can't go back and change any of the past as a grown-up in recovery. The past has contributed to who they are today as individuals. Sally and I deal with these women. We don't even care what their crimes are. The reason? They come to us with a whole history, a life story that's complicated and intertwined. The interest isn't a focus on what did you do to get here, but what was your life like before you got here?

When you say the housing is repressive, what's the choice?
Have you been in B housing? The housing is a dormitory situation with three separate dorms. Two- or three-person rooms, with a large central Day Room. Sometimes we're so overcrowded, there're beds in the Day Room. A housing maximum-security is set up for inmates that need more supervision. In B housing, the deputies are behind a glass enclosure separated by a corridor, viewing the units. There's less deputy contact and more inmate influence. The inmates take control of their units unless they're locked down in their cells. There're a lot more games and negative stuff. The inmates aren't as likely to want a program in B housing. The deputies aren't as willing to get them to programs.

212

The jail is pounding with excitement. Kristina Edwards arrives. A shout comes from outside the Release Room.

You seem happy. What's happened?
Edwards: I'm glad to see you. I shouldn't have acted that way on my birthday. I was wrong. My mom sent pictures. The baby weighs ten pounds. She looks big. She got her shots at last. Thirty went to prison last night at 2:00 a.m. I was up all night. Alex was here two days ago. He only comes before court. I go to court for Readiness [a hearing to negotiate resolutions, confirm trials, designate judges, make decisions that could expedite the trial] tomorrow to find out about the severance and the trial date. Will you be there? My roommate's in here on appeal for murder. She got seven years at her first trial, but now after her appeal, she's gonna do seventeen years! I try to tell you, that's what happens to women on appeal.

    Then I had this dream of skeletons. One had a boulder on its head, one was cut off at the waist, and one was hanging. They were trying to make it to the top of a mountain to escape being murdered. I was crying.

    I see you and I'm trying not to cry.

I'm confused about Dick Bidwell and what he meant to you.
Edwards: I called him Mom. He took care of me.

He bought you alcohol?
Edwards: No. I took the drugs and alcohol in his place. He didn't get it for me and he never molested me.

What's the story about you stabbing him?
Edwards: I drank a liter and a half, and walked around all day long with a gallon of vodka. He made a move. He touched my arm. That's when I did it. I went to Juvenile Hall, but he never showed. Dick told me on the phone two days ago that my dad's in prison on a Third Strike.

213-214

212-213. Inmate Banks in the Release Room;
214. Inmate Banks, released; Deputy Shaw;
Inmate Edwards, and Barbara

Edwards: Look, it's Rolenda!

Rolenda calls out to us from the corridor.

Banks: Susan, I'm free! I'm out!

Inmates watch, stunned. The deputy hands Rolenda her bag of personal belongings.

Banks: You get to see my red outfit!

Dr. Bull appears. I turn back and see Barbara is staying with Kristina. They are standing close to the booth so they can see the excitement. Dr. Bull is beaming.

Ellen got her into Kiva?
Dr. Bull: That's right. Ellen worked it with Kiva that Rolenda can take Lithium there. Yes, it's good.

He clutches his files, still beaming. Rolenda exits from the Release Room's bathroom, bursting at the seams in her red outfit. She's laughing.

Banks: I'm too fat!

Barbara and Kristina stand to get a better look. Kristina says, " I've only seen outfits like that in Vogue." Rolenda returns to the bathroom. Soon she reappears, this time wearing jeans and a white shirt.

Banks: I can hug you now. I love you guys.

She waves both hands in the air.

Dep. Shaw: You go girl!
Dr. Bull: This is something. It's great. Nice moment.

Deputies and trusty inmates witness Rolenda's release.

Banks: I'm not going to screw up.

The deputy comes for Kristina. Her last words to us this day are, "My psych eval was good. I showed no signs of violence, and I showed remorse."

2/3/96   Saturday morning
         Phone call

Two days after Rolenda's release, Ellen Conner calls.

This is a surprise. How are you?
Conner: Rolenda's gone. She split from Kiva! I was there
Thursday night. She was helping with the dishes, and
seemed happy. Saturday she was out of there. She refused
to take her meds and walked. She's escaped again!

215. Sergeant San Filippo

2/5/96 Monday Maximum security

We enter the jail, and no one mentions Rolenda's latest escapade. I ask the lieutenant if we can meet more inmates in B housing, maximum security. She says she'll arrange for us to talk to Sgt. San Filippo, the sergeant in charge of the unit. We're sent back to B housing.

As we move in and out of the different levels of criminal sophistication, it becomes more and more clear to me that Karl Menninger was correct in saying, "The inescapable conclusion is that society secretly wants crime, needs crime, and gains definite satisfactions from the present mishandling of it." [36]

9:00 a.m.   B Housing

We sit on the inmate bench as Dep. Price removes an inmate from B1 for disciplinary reasons. The inmate, with a bedroll tucked under one arm, drags a clear plastic bag of belongings to the outside of B2, just ten feet from B1. Dep. Price issues one last warning to the inmate before she opens the door to B2.

Dep.Price: I always tell them, "As long as you follow the rules and regulations, you won't have a problem with me." Excuse me for a moment while I talk to this inmate. He-She, what you up to in there today? You think you don't have enough to worry about without getting on my nerves?
He-She: I ain't gonna cause no trouble no more.

He-She weighs about 85 pounds, wears a cute and perky smile. She's called He-She for her sexual behavior in the unit.

Dep. Price is firm with the inmates. She releases the mechanical lock, and He-She leaves B Control area and enters B2 obediently. Inside the unit, inmates move around, unaffected. I spot Kristina through the wired glass, inside B2. Barbara and I look into the two units housing maximum-security inmates, and notice how they are organized. Women in B1 can stand at their wired-glass window and see into the Day Room of B2 and vice versa.

Beds are bolted to the walls, toilets are low, and ceilings are high. Everything's tied down?
Dep. Price: That's right. It's mainly so they won't hurt themselves. Women start banging their heads. Palmer was a real mental case, beating her head on the door 'til she had black eyes. Let's go up front. I need to check on the inmates in the holding tanks that are coming back to B3 for their classification, another job we do in B.
You've seen us talking to Rolenda. We know she spent time in the restraining chair.
Dep. Price: You want to see the restraining chair? Let's go.

We pass the new Captain, a cold rigid man. At the front of the jail, next to Release, Price opens the Equipment Room door. The restraining chair is hard to miss. It's a steel throne. Dep. Price grabs a dummy leaning next to a wall, and places it in the chair to demonstrate how

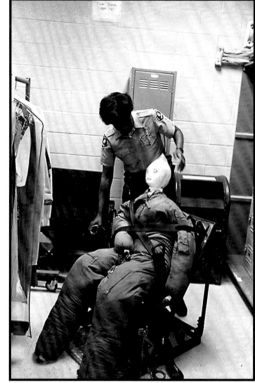

217

deputies practice the procedure of securing an inmate in the chair. She also shows us the shields deputies use during riots in the jail. We notice rows of inmates' personal belongings hanging on racks in clear plastic bags.

Dep. Price: Rolenda spits blood. Spit on me one time. I got it good. She's so bad that we have to put a towel around her head and pull it off after we're clear from her aim. She fights it all the way. I tell her, "I'll get the restraining chair." She answers, "I don't care." This is the riot gear in case we have problems. Hey, you don't have your flash.

I don't use a flash or strobe.

We leave the room. At the Intake-Receiving area where inmates are brought into the jail through the Intake sally port, Holding Tanks and protocol stations receive new detainees. Price is called to check out new arrivals who will be taken to B housing.
Twenty inmates in the Holding Tank make faces at us and act out. Another woman wearing tight jeans, halter-top, and jewelry is passed out in a separate Holding Tank.

Why's she dressed in street clothes?
Dep. Price: We're waiting for her to sober up.

Price checks in with Dep. Chisholm, the deputy on duty, at the Holding Tanks.

Dep. Price: All these women go to CIW tonight?
Dep. Chisholm: Yeah. They're from the Vista Jail. We just give them a bedroll. No sweatshirts.
Dep. Phelps: Dep. Price, could you please move so she could take my picture? Oh man, I ate about two pounds of stuffing and three slabs of turkey.
Dep. Price: By the way, I just heard that Rolenda has escaped again. This time it's from Kiva.

The three of us head back to the unit before the 20 prison-bound women arrive in B housing. Price explains the women headed for B housing will not go to B3 for pre-arraignment, as they have already been to trial and sentenced to prison. Therefore, they will go out on the bus tonight, yet they have a bunk to sleep on for the rest of the day.
Price points out the Safety Cell.

Rolenda spent time in here.
Dep. Price: Oh, yes. Plus we use this cell if someone comes in on PCP and she's going to hurt herself. She's got to be put in a Safety Cell, a cell just for people who're going to kill themselves. If someone's violent, we put her in the chair and watch her.
We were told trusty workers clean up the Safety Cell with spray bottles. We know an inmate who made a serious mess in the Safety Cell. Are trusty workers expected to clean that?
Dep. Price: Yes, but they hook up a hose.

216. B housing unit; 217. Deputy Price with dummy in restraining chair; 218-220. Safety Cell

218-220

Dep. Price stops to talk to Carmen about food services inside B housing deputy office.

Back at B housing, the new inmates line-up in front of the Control counter for bunk assignment.

Dep. Price: You guys are all in B1. You're 274 medium, you, 274 top.

The electronic lock is released with a loud clank, the door to B1 is opened, and all 20 women enter, dressed-out in blues and carrying a cotton blanket roll. The women inside are wild with excitement. An inmate from B2 is standing at the counter with a deputy escort. About to be moved to B1 as well, she bursts out, "Oh baby, it's on now!"

Dep. Price: They all know each other. Oh. They're gonna get the treatment.

Groans and wails, lunch trays clanking, deputies' voices. Price talks to an inmate who's waiting for instructions at the counter.

Dep. Price: That's Boy-Girl. She thinks she's a boy.
Boy-Girl: No I don't.
Price: Yes, you do.

Boy-Girl is not He-She. They both, however, have the same behavioral stigma attached to their identity. The deputies place them in separate B units.

How old are you?
Boy-Girl: Twenty-five. I'm in for violation of probation.
Dep. Price: Selling drugs. OK, trusties. Wrap it up with the lunch carts now.

The trusties, listless, lumber along. They push the heavy metal carts toward the exit.

Dep. Price: We lock down the units until 1:00 p.m. for our lunch.

Price receives a message from Control.

Dep. Price: It's confirmed. Rolenda's walked from Kiva, you guys.
Dep. Gage: Wait a minute! Where's Rolenda?

12:30 p.m.

We head over to the staff kitchen with Price. Dr. Bull joins us, as well as a psychiatrist. I recognize him from early morning arrivals. He rides a Harley and he likes to read the newspaper in his office when he first gets in. His name is Dr. Rand. After the staff lunch line we share a table on the patio.

Dep. Price: Rolenda has a terrible time with authority. She's never been taught to respect much of anything.
Dr. Bull: She's been very deprived.
Dr. Rand: Jim, you don't have the guts to call her what she is.

This psychiatrist, Dr. Rand, is opinionated. Bull is polite. Dr. Rand eats his turkey and snaps at us.

Dep. Price: Inmates legally have three hours a week to go outside on the B housing patio but, we may have a Lockdown, or be short of staff, and can't let them go to the patio. Everyone can be locked down in the cells for a contraband inspection or for action out of line.

Dep. Price stands at the door to B1.

1:00 p.m. Back in B Housing

Dep. Price: We want women who have already been to prison to step forward. Henderson, get Edwards. These ladies are going to conduct some interviews.
Henderson: I don't know who Edwards is.
Dep. Price: That's not true. Besides, I don't care. Go in there and ask her, "Would you just please come out?" What's the matter with you? You trying to give me a hard time today? You get up on the wrong side of the bed? I thought we were buds.

She turns to us and explains:

That inmate is Pam Henderson. She plays this game. Some of these girls are very intelligent, but they don't have common sense. The reason for Lockdown is they don't follow directions. We don't tolerate that. If we ask them to do something as a group, and they don't do it, then we punish them as a group. For example, when I have to say, "You have five seconds," three times, and they don't respond, I write them up. Then they're in Lockdown for four days. I tell them, "As long as you follow the rules and regulations, you don't have a problem with me." They know I'll kid around and joke with them, but they know when I mean business. Seldom do I have problems with inmates.
Dep. Wolf: Inmates don't get to make the choices. They can call us on the box. Like right now, they can call on the intercom box for emergencies only. "Can we have a towel?" isn't an emergency. We get the individuals who commit the serious crimes that go to prison. In maximum we have trusties, not like D. You don't trust these inmates, but you give them responsibilities. They have a little more freedom. They have the door open most of the time. They get to set up, and get the meals. In turn, they get extra food.
Dep. Gage: I can't believe you have those cameras in here.
Dep. Wolf: Don't worry, she doesn't want a picture of you.
Dep. Gage: Society's oddballs. Most of them shouldn't be here. They should be in a mental hospital, or they should be productive. Like Gomez. She's released, and the next night she comes in with her hair matted and no clothes on. When it's cold out, she'll get drunk and vandalize some place to come here. She likes it here. They get medical.

COMMISSARY STORES
ORDER SLIP

QTS	HAIR CARE	QTS	WOMEN,S ITEMS	QTS	SOUPS & DRINKS	QTS	CANDY
___	ACTIVATOR	___	BLUSH	___	ORANGE BRKFST DNK, 12OZ	___	BABY RUTH
___	AFRO PICK	___	CROCHET HOOKS (H,I)	___	COCOA MIX INST 10 OZ	___	BUTTER FINGER
___	BERGAMOT	___	LADIES DEODORANT	___	COFFEE, INST,DECAF 3 OZ	___	COWS TOFEES
___	COMB	___	EYEBROW PNCL (BL/BR)	___	LEMONADE (NEW)	___	JOLLY RANCHER
___	CONDITIONER, BALSAM	___	EYE SHADOW	___	PEACH PUNCH DRINK	___	KIT KAT
___	CONDITIONER, OIL	___	FACE MAKE-UP	___	TROPICAL FRUIT PUNCH	___	MILKY WAY
___	COND. REVITALIZING	___	HAIR BRUSH	___	TEA INSTANT/LEMON/SUGAR	___	M&M PEANUTS
___	MOISTURIZER, HAIR	___	LIPSTICK	___	RAMEN SOUP, CHILI	___	NESTLE CRUNCH
___	SHAMPOO, DANDRUFF	___	MASCARA (BR/BL)	___	RAMEN SOUP, CHICKEN	___	REESE PNUT BTTRCUP
___	SHAMPOO, BALSAM	___	RELAXER	___	RAMEN SOUP, BEEF FLAVOR	___	SNICKER
___	SHAMPOO PROTEIN	___	ROLLERS (M/L)	___	RAMEN SOUP, SHRIMP	___	STARLIGHT MINTS
___	SHAMPOO JOJOBA	___	TAMPAX (RG,SUP)	___	SUGAR 50P/PKG(LIMIT 1)		
___	SHAMPOO REVITALIZING	___	YARN			QTS	SNACKS
		___	PERM				
QTS	SKIN CARE	___	STYLING GEL	QTS	CHIPS & DIPS	___	APPLE PIE
		___	END WRAPS(PAPER)			___	BANANA CHIPS
___	AFTER SHAVE	___	PERM RODS	___	BBQ POTATO CHIP	___	BEANS, REFRIED (NEW)
___	BODY POWDER	___	LARGE LONG	___	CHEETOS	___	BROWNIE CHOC FUDGE
___	CHAPSTICK	___	LARGE SHORT	___	DORITOS TORTL CHPS	___	COCKTAIL PEP STICK
___	CREME, COCO BUTTER	___	MEDIUM LONG	___	FRITOS CHIPS	___	CORNNUTS CHILI HOT
___	BODY LOTION/MOISTURIZER	___	MEDIUM SHORT	___	HOT FRIES	___	CRACKERS, CHEDDAR(NE
___	SHAVING CREAM,BSHLSS	___	SMALL LONG	___	HOT SAUCE, JALAPENO	___	HOT SAUSAGE TJ MAMA
___	SHAVING CREAM,RZLSS	___	SMALL SHORT	___	NACHO CHEESE DIP	___	OATMEAL, INSTANT
___	SOAP, COMPLEXION			___	POTATO CHIPS, RUFFLES	___	MOON PIE
___	SOAP, DEODORANT					___	PEANUT BTR JAR CRNCH
___	SUN BLOCK LTN SPF30+					___	PEANUTS SALTED (NEW)
						___	PEPPER STICK &
QTS	SUNDRIES	QTS	STATIONERY/POSTAGE	QTS	COOKIES		JALEPENO CHEESE
						___	POPCORN CHEESE
___	MENS' DEODORANT	___	ART COLORED PENCIL	___	CHOCOLATE CHIP	___	POPCORN CHS/JALEPENO
___	SOAP BOX	___	DRAWING (ART) PAD	___	COOKIES, BUTTER	___	PORK SKINS HOT&SPCY
___	TOOTH BRUSH	___	ENVELOPE, MANILA	___	COOKIES, SUGAR	___	RITZ CRACKERS
___	TOOTH BRUSH, CAP	___	ENVELOPE, STAMPED	___	CREAM FILLED DUPLEX	___	SWISS ROLL (NEW)
___	TOOTHPASTE	___	POSTAGE STAMPS .32C	___	DUNKIN STICKS NEW	___	TOASTER PASTRIES
___	WASH CLOTH	___	3 CENT STAMPS	___	PEANUT BUTTER COOKIES		SUNFLOWER SEEDS
		___	ERASER/PENCIL	___	OATMEAL COOKIES	___	HOT N' SPICY
		___	PINOCHLE CARDS			___	HONEY ROAST
		___	POKER CARDS			___	TORTILLA FLOUR (NEW)
		___	WRITING TABLET				

QTS	VENDING	QTS	GREETING CARDS	QTS	LLAME A MEXICO DIRECTO	QT	MISCELLANEOUS
___	SODA/SNACKS CARD	___	ADULT BIRTHDAY	___	NOVATEL CARD	___	BASEBALL CAP
		___	CHILD BIRTHDAY			___	MUG/LID, HOT/COLD
		___	FRIENDSHIP			___	WATCH CAP
		___	HOLIDAY			___	TENNIS SHOES
							MEN'S SZ:7,8,9,10,11
							12,13,14,15
							WOMEN'S SZ:5,6,7,8,9
							10

QTS *MEDICATION LIMIT 1 PKG.

___ ACNE/PIMPLE MEDICATION (BENZOYL PROXIDE LOTION)
___ ATHLETE FOOT (MICONAZOLE NITRATE)
___ COLD MEDICINE (COLD CAPS)
___ HEADACHE MEDICATION (NON-ASPIRIN ACETAMINOPHEN)
___ MAALOX (UPSET STOMACH)
___ PAIN RELIVER (IBUPROFEN CAPLETS)
___ TOOTHACHE MEDICATION (HURRICANE GEL)
___ VICKS COUGH DROPS

221. Deputy Castillo

Commissary arrives. Dep. Castillo delivers commissary weekly, and tells us that inmates have a $50 limit per week to order from the commissary stores.

Dep. Price explains we'll enter B1 as soon as the deputy lunch Lockdown ends. First she has to conduct a classification interview for a woman to be placed in a housing unit. The inmate arrives for classification.

Dep. Price: When was the last time you were in jail?
Inmate: Up here in San Diego?
Dep. Price: You still on probation?
Inmate: Yeah.
Dep. Price: Have you ever been in prison?
Inmate: No.
Dep. Price: Any gang affiliations?
Inmate: No.
Dep. Price: Homosexual/bisexual?
Inmate: No.
Dep. Price: Medications?
Inmate: No.
Dep. Price: Tried to kill yourself?
Inmate: No.
Dep. Price: Allergic to bee stings?
Inmate: No.
Dep. Price: Psychological problems?
Inmate: No.
Dep. Price: Drugs.
Inmate: Heroin, cocaine.
Dep. Price: How long you been using?
Inmate: Seven years.
Dep. Price: The last time you injected?
Inmate: Ten days.
Dep. Price: You're in jail for under the influence of controlled substance, prostitution, and offensive words and petty theft.
Inmate: Petty theft?
Dep. Price: Yeah, and you're sentenced to 180 days. You have any questions?
Inmate: I asked you before. Do I do half-time?
Dep. Price: I don't know yet.
Inmate: OK.
Dep. Price: OK, you're going out to F housing for 75 to 100 days.

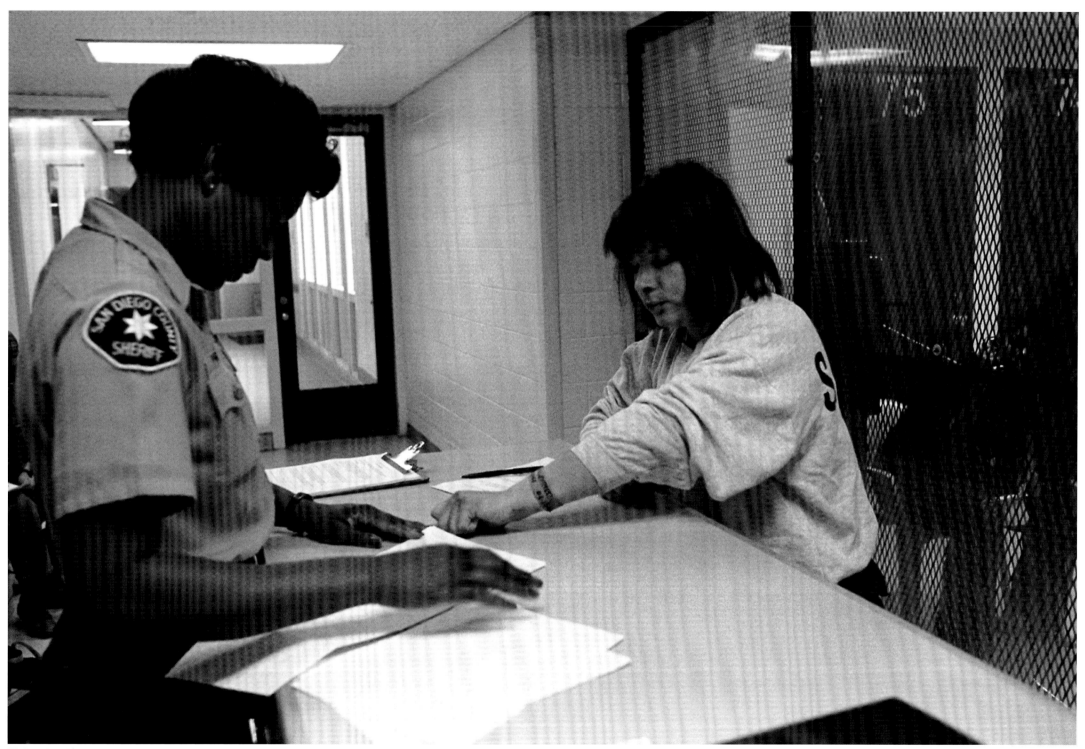

222. Deputy Price with Inmate

Women meander around in the B1 open space; wired glass separates them from the narrow corridor.

Dep. Price: I worked in the private sector prior to working here, in an extremely professional atmosphere. It's just a little different here.

She says deputies sometimes act out on inmates, and it's upsetting to her. She's able to understand the personalities of the jailed and the jailers.

What'll happen when Rolenda returns to jail?
Dep. Price: We dread it. Rolenda's automatically dressed in greens, and she'll go to A housing. We know her history of violence. She has some serious psych problems. When you physically hurt yourself, something's got to be wrong. Sometimes she's fine, other times we have to spray her, and it's the chair.

Dep. Price calls all inmates over the loudspeaker and introduces us. Cell doors are electronically unlatched. Lockdown ends. We enter B2. Inmates gather cautiously in groups of two or three, away from us. We set up the recorder. Inmates hold back and wait until Pam Henderson takes a seat and tension eases. Kristina Edwards pops out of her cell. Price warns, "Shape up. These women want to talk to you. You have to sign a waiver." Shouting breaks out from all directions. Doors are banging. Deputies leave us with inmates and exit the unit.

224

Henderson talks first.

Have drugs played a role in your incarceration history?

I don't use drugs now. I just drink beer. Before, cocaine, I did freebasing. They didn't call it crack then. I did four years in prison and went back out again. But the drug still progresses in you even if you stop. Do it again, it's just like you've been using all those years.

What aspirations do you have?

I'm facing Three Strikes. When you face something like that, it's like there's no future. The attitude the younger people have right now is they don't care. Three Strikes isn't gonna do any good in this society. Society's problem is a problem of love, attention, all of that. A lot of people I've seen, mother and child, are in prison together. Young people just grow up; nobody raises them. They develop the way their surroundings are, and if you live in a drug-infested area where the crime is, that's how you grow up. Locking them up isn't the answer, so sending people to prison for petty theft, society is looking for a quick fix and Three Strikes will fail. If a person's facing 25-to-life, they're gonna say, "Well I don't have anything to lose." It could backfire. It's gonna hurt the kids, and teens are gonna pay.

What happens to these women that leads them to accept a life in confinement?

It's not that you don't think you're gonna be caught. It's that you don't think you're gonna be caught this time.

Is that what you thought?

I figure if I don't get caught by these people, I'll get caught by God. So it's a no-win situation. Nobody made my choices but me. I wish I'd have went past 11th grade and on to college on a sports scholarship.

Did you study in prison?

Black history.

Have you read any of Maya Angelou's writings?

Who?

You're a student of the incarcerated society.

When you have dysfunctional families, somebody always wanders; family splits up. There's no love, no togetherness. They find love and attention on the streets. I don't think anybody makes any impression on kids right now 'cause there wouldn't be all of these kids in with 15-to-life. When I went to CIW, I was put into overflow where they keep the crazy people. I saw many young people in there. It hurt to see one 19-year-old, sitting in a cell with no

clothes on, in a ball, wrapped in the corner. Where are her parents?

You've seen us talk to Kristina and Rolenda, right? I heard you say that you don't know Edwards, yet I sense you know that Rolenda and Kristina are headed to prison.

Rolenda's just a kid, too young for prison. She shouldn't be locked up, not getting help. It's like the one I told you about, the ones that get to me. They lock them up and forget them. Kristina doesn't have a clue what she's headed for. I was saying to my roommate, "I hope Kristina wakes up quick." But I don't see it. She needs to make some adjustments before she gets to prison. She's very susceptible.

Why will it be hard for Edwards to adjust?

She's young. She'll be in with the murderers and serial killers. I've met a lot of them. They don't care. When they get up to those prison cells by themselves, they find somebody to latch onto. Or they're following somebody who is bad for them.

How's prison different from jail?

You never seen the inside of prison before? You read the newspapers? At CIW you can paint your own room. You wear your own clothes. At Madeira Prison you've even got a rose-colored desk, real nice. There're eight people to a big room. You have your own nice bathroom and your own nice shower.

What message do you want to send to young people?

They need to know about the physical nature of prison and the emotional side that they don't want to know about. Kids, like Kristina Edwards, who're immature, think it's not that bad. Some of the kids think once they've done it, they're heroes. Take a 16-year-old kid who's never been a part of a crime and put him next to the 15-year-old who killed five members of his family. That's dynamic. How's that kid going to be able to relate?

Interview with Inmate Sidney

I sense Henderson is the tank captain for B1. Inside the unit with 40 maximum-security inmates, and no deputies, Barbara's uncomfortable. Another inmate approaches us.

Your name is Sidney?
Sid: They call me Sid. This time I'm in on a possession charge for a controlled substance, methamphetamine. I'm an IV drug user. I went to a jury trial because of my priors. I'm looking at four years state time.

What were your priors?
Possession for sales. I'm really stressed. I have two little boys. I really need to be with them.

How old are your children?
Donnie turned five on Friday and JJ turned four on April 29. No, I'm sorry. He turns three. They have me on antidepressants 'cause I'm really stressed. But my habit, the drug I used, was like a big head-rush at first. Mostly people who slam speed do it for the rush. It goes straight to the brain and lasts 20 minutes to an hour.

Then what happens?
You're full of energy. I've stayed up five-to-six days at one time.

How do you parent two little boys staying up five-to-six days at a time?
That's what I didn't do.

What's the magic with the drug?
I had low self-esteem until I used dope. It gives you a burst of confidence.

Your priors?
All drug uses. Some weapons, too.

Education?
High school graduate. I grew up here and Fresno. I held down some jobs. I was a medical-dental claims examiner in Fresno, same at Lane Bruce Trust Fund here in San Diego. Good-paying job.

How did you get started on drugs?
I had a very bad marriage and started drinking. Then I started doing crank. It gave me a lot of confidence when my husband put me down. I was hospitalized for a psychotic episode 'cause of the way my husband treated me. He was in Okinawa, in the Marines. He left me with the house payment and wouldn't send no money. I was around 24. I'm 35 today.

Where are the children?
With my sister. My husband just got out of prison last Wednesday. I love him very much. This time we're going to be friends to the grave. I had my last baby here at Las Colinas and they transported me to prison. I got into the Mother-Infant Program because I was in under six years. I did my time doing chores and taking care of our kids. It was a little bit unfair to the children, but I didn't lose my bond.

Sid introduces us to her roommate, Sandy. Suddenly an alarm goes off. Two deputies enter, shouting at the inmates. We're removed from B1 and sent to a bench outside B Control. Once activity resumes, we're restricted to this area for interviews, unclear what happened inside B1.

225

226

2:00 p.m.   B Housing outside Control

Inmate Sandy, Sid's roommate, arrives for an interview.

Sandy: I'm here from CIW for court. They took me to CIW to dry out for 30 days.

What drug?
Heroin. And cocaine.

How do you feel?
Better than two weeks ago. My PO took me to Grossmont Hospital and they shot me up with Narcon. I got violently ill. I just don't sleep, and my joints are real bad. I need to kill my drugs. I need treatment. Prison doesn't do me any good. I've been going to CIW for 20 years. I'm 42.

All for heroin and cocaine?
Yeah. Ever hear of reverse tolerance? You think you can use the same amount that you used before, and you can't. It's a progressive disease.

Did you support your habit by prostituting?
No. I'm a journeyman electrician, and my husband's a journeyman plumber. We made enough money to support real good habits. He's been clean for over a year and doing real well. The kids are in foster care. One's doing well and getting good grades. The 13-year-old is rebelling and wants to come home to mom. She puts things in my face like, "Mom, I tried crystal." It killed me. She's getting into gangs. She's not a bad kid. She's angry and wants her mom.

How old were the kids when you were busted?
Eight months to eleven years.

How old is your youngest?
Six. There was a five-year span when we were completely clean. We moved to Houston. I was building schools, and he was working for a plumbing company, and we came back to San Diego when it snowballed.

The relationship with him got you into this?
Yes.

Would you go back to him?
No. I need help with my thinking because I harbor so much grief inside for things I've done that I don't want to think about. If I use heroin, I don't have to think about it.

Your veins look like you've taken a beating.
I've been a drug addict since I was 15 years old.

How'd you get started?
My boyfriend. I didn't even know what heroin was.

That was the first drug you took?
Yeah. He offered it to me and I didn't want to look like the little kid that was afraid. They were all doing it. I didn't want to be the one that looked like a silly little kid.

Were you hanging out with a crowd?
Yeah, in Chula Vista. I was a cheerleader and straight A student. I ruined my life.

And your kids, how are they?
They're full of anger, and my oldest doesn't even want to talk to me. My mom's dead. I have nobody in the family who can take my kids. My dad is 80 years old. When I was 17, the day after my mother died, he tried to attack me in his bedroom, drunk. I left the house. I tried to find another life and started shooting up heroin. At least the kids are pretty good kids.

227

225. Inmate Sid; 226. Inmate Sandy;
227. Inmates Sandy and Sid

Interview with Inmate Gomez

Inmate Tecinda Gomez is anxious to speak next.

What do you fear the most?
I dread going out, being cold, and getting rained on. That's a sad thing to say, that I'd rather be in here. I'm 43. I've been getting into trouble since I was 21.

What started it off?
Somebody started me off on heroin.

You were brought in here the last time on heroin?
Yes. I have no family. My mom and dad are deceased, and my little brother drowned in Virginia in a flash flood at 12 years old.

Where will you end up?
I have no idea. I was with somebody for 15 years. I just left him. He's the one who introduced me to heroin.

You used drugs and ended up in maximum-security?
Yeah. But I sold, mostly. When I get out I want something I can go to right away, 'cause the boredom makes me start hustling. I don't have no ID. I can't go to no woman's YWCA with no ID. When I came in this time, I had a pinched nerve in my back, abscesses from fixing, and a temperature. They gave me massive doses of antibiotics, and pain pills. Deep down inside, I have a death wish. I have no family, no job to live for. No place to go except the street.

How long were you at CIW?
Three years.

Were you clean at CIW?
No. My visitor was bringing in drugs for all the girls. At CIW even the correctional officers bring in the dope. When I was there, a black officer had coke and heroin taped all over his body. He was bringing it in for these girls to sell for him. The inmates ratted on him and he got kicked out. I mean, it's corrupt up there.

More freedom?
Oh, yeah. It's a good old city within a city. Half-day work, half-day school. Then go to NA meetings at night, art classes, and the gym. They got everything.
Sounds like you liked it.
Yes, I did. I got a lot of certificates there.

Why are you dressed in greens?
I left the hospital almost a year ago. So every time I come here, even if it's for a ticket, I'll be in greens like people who're really violent. We have to be handcuffed for chapel.

I dread going out there, being cold, and getting rained on. I mean, that's a sad thing to say, that I'd rather be in here. Deep down inside, it's like I have a death wish; there's nothing. Nobody to live for . . . no family . . . no job . . .

Inmate Gomez

Interview with Inmate Regina

An inmate steps forward for an interview. Her name is Regina.

You're 20. What did you come in here for?
Regina: Mayhem.

What's mayhem?
The disfigurement of a facial body part.

Disfigurement?
Yeah. This girl's ear, her lip, and across her face.

Like with a knife?
Yeah. Or something.

Your sentence?
I was lookin' at life, but I'm not no more. One of my crimes had aggravated mayhem attached, and it carries 25-to-life. They had me plead guilty to mayhem, and the judge sentenced me to eight years in prison. Judge Mudd wants me to go home on probation 'cause I have three kids: four years old, two years old, and eight months.

What happened?
This girl, we was fighting. She had a glass and put it down. She got down on the ground tussling, and she broke the glass and was going to cut me. I didn't want her to cut me. So I cut her first.

Have you seen her since then?
Yeah, Preliminary Hearing. She didn't look too good. Ha, ha. I was mad 'cause she was going to cut me up.

What were you fighting over?
She liked my baby's dad. I told her, "Don't mess with him no more." He was my man, but she didn't know it was my baby's father. She was telling her friend, "Oh, I want to get with so-and-so." In the end my baby's dad ratted on me.

And now when you get out what're you going to do?
I met another guy who wants to get married.

How far did you go with your education?
I went to the tenth grade. I'm gonna graduate and take up a trade in college.

How are you handling incarceration?
The hardest thing to handle is everybody's attitudes and stress. At first, I was scared to death. But now, the inmates kinda grow on me. Like Henderson, I thought she was so mean. I was little, 140 pounds. Now I'm about 170.

229

Interview with Inmate Sanders

230

Another inmate, Dawn Sanders, arrives and sits on the bench. Dep. Price tells us to go to the Pro Visit Room.

How old are you?

Sanders: Twenty-two. I been here since January 11. It's a long story. I was out on my own recognizance because of my father. I was in the hospital when they arrested me. I flew back and forth here for court. I don't live here.

You say that you are still in shock?

This could happen to anybody. Just get in a car and ruin your whole life. I looked over at the other car, and I saw blood all over the windshield. All I could see were the little boy's eyes looking at me from inside the other car. Then this woman screamed at me, "I hope you're happy. He's dead!" Then I passed out. I'm in here for involuntary manslaughter. Drinking and driving. I killed the father. Three counts of felonies.

This place is the closest thing to hell. These women are animals. They're sick. It's really woken me up. There's so much homosecting in my room. I pray. I killed somebody. I didn't mean to do it at all. But if one person touches me, I'll go down fighting to the end. I started a Bible study in my room.

What was your childhood like?

I was raised very strict, religiously. I come from a very good family. I found out my mom was dating some other guy and I just . . . you can do two things with a bad situation. I have nightmares every night. I've always been a serious child. My sister went with my mother. I went with my father. I took care of him for three years. Then I met a Navy Seal and we liked each other. I came down to see him. Me and my friend went to a club and met two other Navy Seals. We decided to go to Tijuana and had two margaritas at dinner and everyone else had shots of tequila. My father had just bought a brand new car for me. On the way back, I was going 70 on the freeway. I had to go to the bathroom. I went on the off-ramp at 50. I slammed on my brakes and my brake pads locked up. I T-boned the other car. If only I could change this.

If I had gone five miles slower or faster, this would not have happened. Before this happened, a year ago, I never would have thought that I'd be able to live in a place like this. The hardest thing I ever did was going to court to get sentenced and seeing that little boy again and seeing his mom. I thought it was going to kill me. (Crying) I see his face every day. I set up a trust fund for him so when he's 18, if he goes to college, he'll get the money. If he doesn't go to college he won't get it.

How is the little boy?

Physically, he's OK. He goes to therapy all the time. I mean, I pray for him all the time. I hope he can overcome this.

The mother?

It was hard because the mother and others were good to me. They knew my background. I had people who wrote in to help me. I'm hoping I can get involved in MADD and volunteer my services. It's my responsibility to stop somebody else from making the same mistake I did. It just doesn't seem like reality. It just doesn't seem like it happened to me. It happened to this other person. I don't have fear in here. At first I did. I don't start trouble with somebody. I go to my room and calm down, talk to one of my friends in there, call my mom, or my dad, and I'm fine. I got a lawyer and my dad's best friend is a Congressman so he got me off. I'm very lucky. It's a miracle. I'm doing a year, and that means six-and-a-half months. Get in a car and ruin your whole life. I was going to school to be a nurse. It's all gone right now. I can never be a nurse with a felony. I've never been in trouble, never had a traffic accident or a ticket.

231. Polly Doll

PART FOUR   STUCK IN THE SYSTEM

But what if the caretaker cannot take care? The caretaker will become overwhelmed by the demands of the child. The caretaker will be unable to provide consistent shelter, food, clothing, emotional security, physical safety, or any of the other required needs for a healthy development of a child. Worse still, the caretaker will hit, burn, torture, molest, turn on to drugs, push into prostitution. In these situations the little girl will see herself through the eyes of a bad caretaker. She will grow up thinking of herself as incapable, burdensome, unlovable. She will perceive the world as a hostile place, full of people who are out to exploit her. The little girl who came into this world full of potentials will be damaged and turned into a destructive person. She will grow up to become a hateful, enraged person who will hurt herself and others. And indeed the world will treat her badly.

And when she becomes a caretaker, the cycle will continue.[37]

Maryam Razavi Newman. Ph.D.

The criminal justice system is designed
to set people up to fail, not to
overcome mistakes.

Counselor Dar

3/3/96 6:45 p.m.   Phone call
                      Kristina Edwards

Edwards: I been in the hospital for two days. Day before yesterday I got beat up. It was a girl in the Mexican Mafia. She took a padlock to my face, said next time they'll use a knife. They're out to get me.

Why did it happen?
She said I told their business.

Did you?
Yeah, but it wasn't nothing bad. Now I'm in the Infirmary 'cause the deputies are afraid of what they'll do to me back in B housing. Her cousin's in there [prison] now. The whole family's in here or up at the pen. They're just waiting for me to get to prison. Alex's gonna be real mad. The jury can't see me like this. I might as well not dress-out 'cause I'm gonna look like shit. My eye's all swollen shut. Hey, Banks' back. I saw her in the Holding Tank, all strung out, high on drugs.

3/4/96 8:45 a.m.   Courthouse
                      Continuance Hearing

Alex admits Kristina looks pretty bad. He wants her trial date moved.
  Grant Bellows' family is present. The mother, dressed in a '50s-style red dress, again is handing out carnations to her daughters and their friends. Kristina enters. She's dressed in jailhouse blues, and her eye is as black as an eight-ball.
  Alex and McKenzie tell the judge they are ready. Rick Clabby, the prosecutor, isn't present, so the judge delays the case until tomorrow at 8:45 a.m. Bellows looks back and sees his mother's face redden with the news. All of those carnations for nothing.

3:00 p.m.   Jail, B Housing Pro Visit

Kristina's returned on the early bus. She arrives at the Pro Visit booth looking dirty. Her hair is greasy. She's wearing white socks with her jail thongs. Barbara pulls out more clothes for Kristina to try on for court. Kristina complains, "They look too big." She wants us to purchase makeup to cover her eye so she doesn't have to use the morgue makeup the jail supplies. Kristina's feeling pressure. "They'll put a jacket on me as a snitch when I go to prison. Alex had to change my trial date. He said it will look like I acted out and got into trouble. It's bad back there now."
  Dr. Bull steps inside the Pro Visit Room as Kristina exits.

Dr. Bull: Rolenda's not good. She was very indignant and angry. She couldn't stand Kiva. I'm getting conflicting reports. She was pounding so hard I could hear it all the way in my office. Sgt. Miller and the deputies put her in the chair in front of her cell. There's a lot of unnecessary hostility. Rolenda said the assault charge was for swatting a guy with a stick after he patted her on the butt at a 7-Eleven. She needs to be in a locked treatment facility. She needs to build up some trust in someone or something.

232. Inmate Banks;
233. Inmate Edwards

82960-5

3/5/96   9:15 a.m.   Courthouse

After rain early this morning, it takes an hour to get downtown. I park the car close to the courthouse and run to Superior Court, Department 9. Court's already in session. Alex and McKenzie have approached the bench. I can hardly hear Alex. By the expression on Judge Weber's face, it appears Alex is talking about a continuance. Clabby, the DA, says the People are ready.

Kristina is brought into the courtroom by the marshal. She isn't dressed-out again. Her oversized jail sweatshirt emphasizes her short, overweight body. At least her hair has been washed and crimped, and she worked on the black eye with makeup.

McKenzie tells the judge that he's moving to Alaska and he's ready to go with the trial.

Judge Weber lifts her broken arm and gestures with her cast to the court, "Oh, my God, we have a real problem."

Alex mentions a federal case he has with Judge Gonzales in two weeks. The judge grows impatient. She'll postpone the case for two weeks to allow time for Kristina's eye to heal, but she can't wait for the federal case.

"A case this big can't be treated lightly," she emphasizes.

Alex talks to Kristina for a few moments. When he exits and joins us, I notice his eyes are tearing and bloodshot from a cold. He wants us to understand that the DA could move from torture, a 7-to-life sentence, back to first-degree because "the deal didn't come down. If you don't take the deal one week, and then later go back, it's like buying a car; they'll say, 'Well you didn't take it before, and now it'll cost you $200 more.' That's how it works. It's a package. We were ready to go, remember? That was our objective. The DA kept us from going to trial. Now we can't, due to her injury. They want to keep Bellows and Kristina testifying against each other. It's my job to see that doesn't happen. They want the deal the way they want it. These two can't testify against Ryan or Price [Ryan has pled guilty and Price, the juvenile codefendant, has already been found guilty of second-degree murder]. So it's up to what Bellows and Kristina say about each other. It's strategy."

6:30 p.m.   Phone call, Rolenda

I hear the phone as I enter the house.

Banks: I didn't do anything. They beat me in the face with a gun. Kristina saw it and gave me your phone number.

Next day at the jail

Ellen Conner stops in the Pro Visit area.

Conner: B housing has been put in Lockdown. I think it's because of Kristina's incident. There's a lot of Mexican Mafia in there. She's really learning the hard way. She's gonna be like them. She's gonna fight back. You don't disrespect people in there. You really have to watch yourself in B housing, where a lot of them are going to prison for life. To these people, Kristina's life means nothing. You heard that Rolenda's in for assault with a deadly weapon plus escape? She's in A Isolation. She was singing nursery rhymes and yelling about wanting a TV. She's not on meds.

In dealing with young people who get killed or who kill someone, we have found three markers that predict in some measure the decline of these youths. These are truancy, multiple suspensions, and bullying. These represent important items that need to be addressed early instead of allowing the problems to accumulate over a period of time with no relief and with a deterioration in the life and the activities of the child. It is clear that when we try to deal with youths who are in trouble and try to protect them from further trouble, the intensity of the intervention is, in my opinion, the single most important issue to be addressed in the programmatic efforts. There are thousands and thousands of programs throughout the United States trying to help with secondary or tertiary prevention of young people who are already on the decline. In a program here in Philadelphia called the Youth Violence Reduction Project we have been able to save these children from being murdered by intensely involving them in a program in which they are seen five times a week and in which they are monitored regularly and often by probation, by street workers, by the police, and by others involved in the program.[38]

Paul Jay Fink, M.D.

3/11/96 Pro Visit, Dr. Bull

Dr. Bull: Rolenda's feisty, angry, disgruntled. She's unrealistically optimistic. She had written a six-page grievance to the lieutenant. She handed it to me to read. It's full of complaints against the deputies. She's amplifying her importance, acting out very impressively, yet not mentally disordered. She's very much alive. The angry little girl in her is pouting less, but has more anger and entitlement. She's made herself out to be a special case. She couldn't take Kiva. I find myself getting very bored with it.

I don't blame Bull for his attitude. He's spent more time with Rolenda than any other inmate. She must make a change, or she'll end up institutionalized for years, if not for her entire life.

Phone call, Rolenda Banks' probation officer

PO: The court continued (postponed) Rolenda. She beat somebody with a baseball bat. She has four active cases now. She's never going to get off probation. For sure she's going to prison. She's gone.

Rolenda called me yesterday.
PO: She did? She's gonna blame you for whatever. It's everybody else's fault. I recommend you don't see her.

Last week, when she called, she said she had a new case.
PO: I have to fill out a report and I'm not sure what to do. She's like a six-year-old at times. Other times, she's like an animal. I'm in a quandary. All I can do at this point is explain alternatives: have her do the balance of time in local custody and leave the probation to the court, or she can go to prison. There's no way to let her go to places like Kiva because there's not enough supervision. She won't stay in a group.

She's eligible for CYA (California Youth Authority). How's that different from prison?
PO: It is prison. She'll just get worse. She'll learn more than she already knows. She's a borderline personality.

She seems to have potential. She could be in some place supervised and on meds.
PO: There is no such place.

What about Patton?
PO: Patton State Mental Hospital? I guess I could do a [Penal Code] 1203, but my advice to you is to step back. Rolenda's already angry. You'll see the real Rolenda come out if she wants something from you. It's very scary. Be leery about getting too attached or involved. She's self-centered and impulsive. The

only skill she's learned is take, take, take. Rolenda will stay in prison. The inmates will get numb to her ways, and the staff will get bored. In our society, there's a general refusal to believe there's a problem due to upbringing, yet many of these kids end up truant, on the street, and into criminal activity. Those with redeeming qualities who choose not to redeem themselves, like to manipulate. They're the dangerous ones, the antisocial ones. They become very institutionalized. "I don't care, nobody's going to help me." Rolenda stages everything. She's a very good actress. I'd stay away from court. She'll take it out on anyone who isn't doing something for her. It's gonna be, "Susan, you have to help me."

3/18/96 10:00 a.m. Courthouse

Kristina's eye looks better, but she is despondent and sullen. She's not dressed-out again and hasn't even combed her hair. Why isn't she dressing out? The court's quiet as we wait for Alex to arrive from the federal courts. By the time he gets here, the judge has held the case over until 1:30 p.m.

Alex later tells us that he told Kristina she didn't have to dress-out this time. Barbara had driven all over to deliver clothes and nylons for Kristina to look like that? "She looked like a convict," I tell him.

Surprised, and expecting a qualifying statement, he says "She doesn't want to do this. No one does. It's not going to be pretty for anyone sitting in there when they talk about the autopsy. This isn't easy. What you can do is keep her up, talk to her, and get her mind off of the trial. Be there."

3/26/96 9:30 a.m. B Housing, Pro Visit

Banks: I don't wanna do time here. I wanna go to prison 'cause they been messin' with me. They take the dinner cart and slam it up against my door and yell, "Hey Banks!" Just so they can look at my face. I keep my blanket over my head. I got my mattress on the floor now. They shake my food and hand me my coffee with their fingers in it. I'm in Lockdown, a room by myself with a mattress.

You do have a history with the staff.
Banks: Last time I was here, yeah, I got in trouble. But this time, they gave me raw food. It was a pink meatball thing, about five inches long. The deputy yelled at me to eat it, and I said, "Fuck you." They took me to Lockdown. I hate this place. I want to get out of here and go to the hospital. I got other problems. I don't know what they are, but I have them. I have flashbacks of me in a foster home.

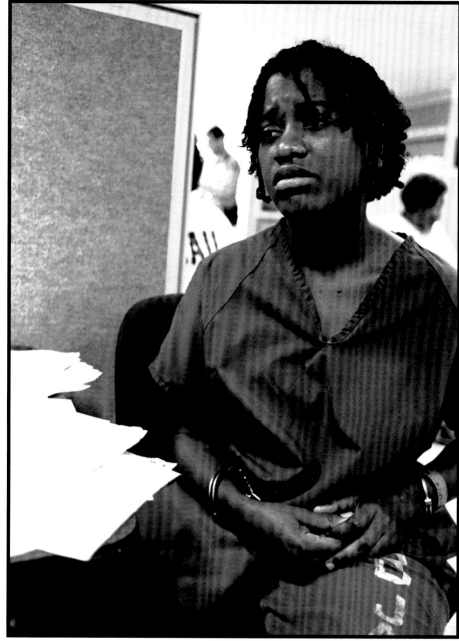

234. Inmate Banks

She tries to quiet herself, pulling at the frayed edge of her green uniform. Barbara tells her to buckle down, tolerate authority, and move on. But Rolenda continues to struggle with authority. Will anything happen to break the pattern between Rolenda and staff? She seethes with deep-seated anger and fear.

Her new attorney, Mike Begovitch, requests that we attend Rolenda's next court date. He tells me, "I've prepared a case, yet this is tough. Her psych evaluations have been done. Everything earmarks that she go to Patton State Mental Hospital, but the judge probably won't recommend Patton. Rolenda's torn a steel bed from the concrete wall of her cell. She's broken the safety-glass window to the outside with her head." We go to court. It's a long wait, and then the judge appears and orders a continuance.

3/27/96   9:30 a.m.   B Housing

Dep. Price approaches us, saying, "You missed it yesterday when Ms. Banks was put in this chair." Things are deteriorating. Tension is building. Five women stare at us from the B2 window. Kristina Edwards is released from the unit to see us in the Pro Visit Room.

The unit's pretty excited. What happened yesterday?
Edwards: All hell broke loose. You heard about Rolenda. It was bad. I saw everything. They beat her, stepped on her face, and pepper-sprayed her. She passed out. They dragged her and put her in the chair.

Then more bad happened. I talked to my mom. She said she had the neighbor take care of my baby, and I lost it. I screamed at her. Then she said, "She's not yours, Kristina. You're in jail. You don't have the right to say anything about her." I got off the phone and scared everyone in here. I was banging my head against the wall. I went crazy. Deputies had to sit on me. They put me in Isolation to cool down. Then Dep. Logan, he's a nice guy, wanted to call my mom and tell her off. He couldn't understand how anyone could be so cruel. Why does she do things like that? She wants to hurt me more. Hasn't she hurt me enough? What if they're bashing Pamela's head in the wall? I don't know what my mother's up to. She's crazy. My mother won't bring Pamela down here, and she won't come to my trial. She won't send me pictures. I'm in this horrible place, and I can't do anything about my child.

Kristina and Rolenda are both experiencing mounting fears. Abandoned by their mothers at an early age, they have no basis for trust. They struggle and often become desperate. Kristina is dejected. Jail lifestyle grinds away at her in tandem with courtroom realities.

We haven't seen you for three weeks.
Yeah. I know. After the incident with my eye, I stayed in my room pretty much. I got to where I was ready to go sign the deal. When I went to court and I was in the dungeon, Ryan was across from me. He was laughing 'cause we were in there together. Then Jack, the bailiff, came for me. I walked in the courtroom and Alex said, "Ryan pled guilty three weeks ago to murder and conspiracy. Do you wanna change your plea and take your deal?" I said, "All right." So he filled out the paperwork. Jack took me back to the holding cell. I asked Ryan, "You pled guilty? I'm surprised." He goes, "Because of the DA, Kristina." If Ryan went to trial and lost, he woulda got two 25-to-life sentences. They

were threatening him with the death penalty, too.

We still have the death penalty if we're convicted of murder and conspiracy in the first-degree. That's what special circumstances are. He said, "We all know what happened out there, Kristina. We all got what's coming to us. I just can't believe Nate." He said that 'cause this was all Nate's idea. I said, "Well, I just pleaded guilty to torture. I'll have a chance in seven years." He goes, "God helped you in that one." I said, "Why?" He said, "Because you can try parole in seven years." And then he says, "I ain't never said nothing bad about you, Kristina. I just said, 'Yeah, the loose tongue.'"

You're able to talk with each other in the Holding Tanks?
This marshal is a nice guy. He said, "Don't you guys talk any louder or the judges will hear you, and I'll move you." So I was quiet. Then Ryan goes, "Let me have a peek." I go, "A peek?" He goes, "Lift your shirt up." I said, "I don't think so." He started laughing. He goes, "Go ahead and go to sleep. I'll wake you up before I go." Then, about 3:00 p.m., I heard them call out, "Ryan!" They took him out. When he came back. I go, "Ryan, are you all right?" He goes, "No. I knew what I was gonna get, but when they tell you, Kristina, it's a different story. I just can't believe I'm goin' away for 25-to-life."

6:45 p.m.   Phone call, Kristina Edwards

Edwards: Alex came to see me, and the DA don't want my deal. A deal is better than taking it to trial or getting life without parole. Why do they want me to go to trial? So I'll lose? Alex said the DA got what they wanted, first-degree murder and conspiracy. Alex was depressed, just like me. I cried and cried. My jurors are picked Monday. I need nylons 'cause I got black stuff on them, and I got mustard on my skirt. I had to go to the hospital 'cause I got red bumps all over. The doctor said it was my hormones. You remember the nice-looking older marshal in Department 8? He died. A heart attack in the courthouse.

The DA determines the deals. I understood that at one point the supervisor wanted one first-degree and possibly a second for Bellows, and a second or voluntary manslaughter for Kristina. The deals aren't openly discussed in courtroom corridors. Alex presents a Motion to Sever the two codefendants into two separate trials to prevent Bellows from testifying against Kristina.

3/28/96 9:00 a.m. Pro Visit

We arrive at the jail and discover Rolenda attempted suicide. Dr. Bull stops us in the corridor.

Is it true? She attempted suicide?
Dr. Bull: Yes, she did. It was more of a gesture than an attempt, however. At one point she said, "You know I really don't have anything to look forward to anymore, plus they've taken all my kids." The deputies told her as long as she's in jail, she'll have to stay in Lockdown. She said, "I'm gonna go to prison; what's the point? I have nothing to live for."

Last week, the staff had a conference and developed a reward schedule for her. After one day in Lockdown she gets a magazine; after two days, she gets books; and after three days, she gets a shower without waist chains. This schedule began a week ago, after she spent hours in the restraining chair. It was hard to get the plan jump-started with the night shift likely to sabotage and undermine the plan.

Day three, I walked by Rolenda's cell, and she held up three fingers. She smiled, "Hey, tomorrow's day four," and I go, "Yeah, go for it!" And from that point, she went right on through to day eight. She moved out of Lockdown and into A2 with a TV and normal setup. Even the staff commented, "Wow, she's just doing great." Yet I talked to her yesterday and she said, "Well, now that I'm here there's really nothing more to work for." After all of that, doing well was sort of a let down.

I heard there may be a new med that could work for Rolenda. Her PO said maybe, but Rolenda won't take it regularly.
That PO sounds quite jaded and cynical. That's unfortunate. Rolenda said she could've made it in Kiva, but not on the meds [she was on]. They made her drowsy. She kept nodding off during their activities.

The deputy says Rolenda called Control, reporting a nosebleed. Bull checks on her, finds that she made up the story because she wanted to get her visit with us. Rolenda arrives, takes a seat, and after she sings a rap song she wrote, she tells us that she doesn't belong in a facility with abusive treatment.

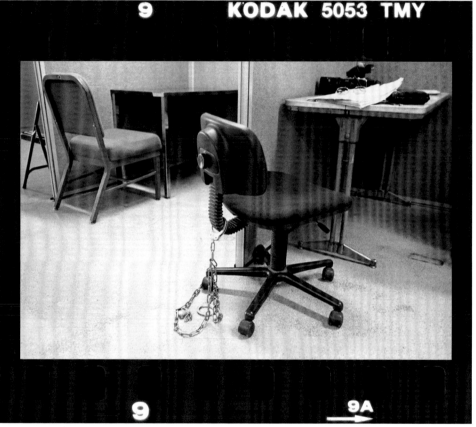

235. Pro Visit area

4/8/96 9:00 a.m. Motions In Limine*
begin for Bellows and Edwards

Someone shouts, "You Susie? I'm Lish."

It's Boy-Girl from the jail. She follows us to the courtroom and sits on the district attorney's side so Kristina Edwards can see her when she looks over her shoulder. Kristina is brought to the side of the courtroom where the prisoners and the judge enter. Her chains are removed, and she enters the courtroom dressed-out in the green outfit Barbara purchased. She neglected to wear the blouse Barbara selected, under the lightweight sweater. Barbara leans over, upset. "Why didn't she wear the blouse? You can see everything."

At 10:00 a.m. the judge enters the courtroom. Everyone's seated. Kristina giggles when she sees Lish.

"What's Kristina trying to do to herself?" Barbara says, "This'll ruin her. Did you see the half cigarette tucked behind that girl's ear? Kristina acts like she's at a party! Her life is on the line!"

Her attorney has told us that the Motions to Sever, the Miranda issue, the Suppression of Statements, and certain photos will be discussed at this hearing. Jury selection will follow.

Now that Ryan has pled guilty, Alex and McKenzie fear DA Rick Clabby will direct questions to Detective Collier that will be prejudicial for a jury to hear. It is the time to determine what testimony will be permitted as evidence.

Outside the courtroom, McKenzie tells us that he was Shelby Roland's attorney before he handed her case over to Daniel Callaway. "Roland was supposedly set up by a doctor to be a call girl. No surprise to any of us, she stole the doctor's credit card and used it, too."

2:30 p.m. Court resumes

Detective Collier takes the stand. District Attorney Rick Clabby begins the direct examination.

DA: What was your intent when you met [Ms. Edwards]?

Det. Collier: To interview her in reference to her knowledge of the murder.

DA: At the close of that interview did you arrest [Ms. Edwards]?

Det. Collier: No. She was a witness. I had no indication she was involved.

He goes on to say that he asked her to come to San Diego, but she couldn't identify the location upon arrival. Later, after a nap, she was taken by helicopter on another search.

DA: And did she tell you where the murder took place?

Det. Collier: She told me it took place in Poway but she did not know where.

DA: Between that contact and the next contact with [Ms. Edwards], did anything significant happen with respect to the death of [Mr. Klotz]?

Det. Collier: I received a voice mail message from [Ms. Edwards] stating she had lied about some of the things she told us in the original interview.

DA: Before you received that voice mail had you found the body of [Mr. Klotz]?

Det. Collier: Yes.

DA: Had an autopsy already been performed on him?

Det. Collier: Yes.

DA: What was the next action you took with respect to her?

Det. Collier: We went back up to San Bernardino for multiple reasons. One, to ask [Ms. Edwards] to come back down to Poway. Two, we were going to take her back up to where we had located the body to see if she recognized it.

DA: Let me digress just a moment. What was the nature of the lie that she told you she had said?

Det. Collier: She told us that she had been kept captive Thursday and Friday at the [Donner] house until she finally escaped. She admitted that was a lie. She stayed willingly at the [Donner] house and drove the suspect vehicle back to San Bernardino and returned it to [Mr. Bidwell].

DA: You made contact with her. Did you also bring [Mr. Bidwell] down to San Diego?

Det. Collier: Yes. We had his car, which we had processed. We needed to get his prints to eliminate him from prints we found in the car. We took her to a plateau above Jacinto Way above 67. We knew that was the area where the murder had been committed, or at least where the body had been left, and we wanted [Ms. Edwards] to confirm that, but we didn't tell her we had found the body.

DA: Why did you want her to confirm that?

Det. Collier: Several things about what she was telling us started to sound like she was making stories up. It was partly to gauge her truthfulness.

DA: Once you were on the plateau did you ask her point blank, "Does this area look familiar to you?"

Det. Collier: Yes. She said, "No." We told her we had found the body. Then she started pointing out places that she indicated the pallets had come from. [Ms. Edwards] indicated that the pallets were used to cover up the body after it was dumped over the ravine.

DA: Now, once you had had the discussion about the pallets, did the topic of fingerprints come up?

Det. Collier: Yes. I told [Ms. Edwards] I wanted to take her prints to see if they matched any prints found on the rocks that we had recovered from the scene. We took her and [Mr. Bidwell] to homicide. I told them I needed major case prints and I told [Ms. Edwards] that she lied to us. Her prints were found on the rocks.

DA: What was her reaction?

Det. Collier: She started to say something and I turned on the tape recorder, and she made a brief statement. Then I said, "Wait a minute. Wait a minute. Hang on." And then I read her her rights.

DA: Were there any prints on the rocks?

Det. Collier: No.

DA: You knew you were lying to her.

Det. Collier: It's a ploy. An innocent person would have said, "I didn't touch the rock. Go ahead, check my fingerprints."

During cross-examination, Alex Landon points out that Collier and another detective went to San Bernardino to investigate a homicide. He asks if the detective had known about this homicide prior to the call from San Bernardino police [and, in fact, he had heard "rumors"] and did he have names of people supposedly involved. He went to San Bernardino with this knowledge. Through cross-examination, Kristina's attorney shows the court that the detective took Kristina Edwards to the plateau, put her in a motel room for three hours to nap, and then flew her in a helicopter over Poway hills to locate the area.

Collier admits to the ploy. Landon says his client wasn't given Miranda (read her rights). He and District Attorney Clabby argue what will be allowed as evidence. Alex tells the judge that the defense's position is that the San Diego Sheriff's Department believed Kristina Edwards was a suspect, and they set up a situation where

Edwards should have been given Miranda beforehand. They also lied to her about the fingerprints. Alex moves that the court suppress comments following the ploy. "The statements that occurred post-Miranda come from the poisoned tree, or the improper obtaining of that statement which preceded the Miranda."

Clabby points out that Kristina Edwards was never in custody and walked in, "volunteered to come down with them." He defends the detective's story and says that they had nothing on Kristina until she volunteered it. Her attorney counters that due to the manner in which she was interrogated, she was actually in custody, but not informed of that fact.

The judge rules that Kristina initiated the two contacts. First, she walked into the police station and second, she left a voice mail message. "Psychological coercion" is denied as a defense for Kristina. The judge denies "the motion to suppress the statements under Miranda." The next issue after a recess will be whether or not Edwards will be severed from Bellows.

We sit outside during court recess. Ryan's attorney is unmoved by events. His client copped a plea of 25-to-life with parole. However, McKenzie shares with us that a second-degree deal for Bellows fell apart. He complains about the DA's actions, saying, "We had a second. The negotiation was for a second if Ryan took a first."

Court resumes to hear severance arguments.

The judge hears from Landon and McKenzie about a conflict of interest that has developed within the public defender's office. The judge doesn't support severance.

236. Courthouse hallway

* Motion In Limine—A motion made at the start of a trial requesting that the judge rule that certain evidence may not be introduced in trial. This is most common in criminal trials where evidence is subject to constitutional limitations, such as statements made without the Miranda warnings (reading the suspect his/her rights).

Connie Taylor's testimony is reviewed. She's a witness who didn't testify at the Preliminary Hearing, yet had "conspiracy evidence" on the part of the four codefendants. The court listens to Alex's requests to eliminate statements from witness testimony. Then the judge listens to McKenzie's reactions and the district attorney's comments and says, "I can see a thousand sidebars as the cross-examinations begin. Think of the splicing we're going to attempt and the analyzing under the two theories of whether it's a statement of a defendant or whether it's a statement of a co-conspirator." The motion is made to sever. Clabby agrees. Edwards' trial will follow Bellows' trial with no break. Clabby now has two trials, instead of one.

Large color shots of body parts are put on the rail. The X rays show fractures to the skull. The cause of death was a blow or blows to the head or possibly cutting off the head. Five panel boards are mounted with a total of 29 horrific photos of Klotz's remains. Alex examines the photographs. They are close-ups of parts of Klotz's body, and it's difficult to discern any location or proximity to surrounding areas mentioned previously.

Judge: I don't know if there is going to be an objection–the location where this particular skull was found. Now, this is a difficult crime scene to describe. I need to see these closer. Animals did apparently get to the body and affected its position and condition.

Clabby: I have in my possession Motion Exhibit Number 2, which purports to be the skull of [Mr. Klotz].

Alex is concerned that the purpose of some of the photos is to inflame and prejudice the jury. He asks that the court keep several of the photos out of the exhibits during trial. McKenzie says they're "gruesome" and agrees with Alex.

Clabby: Now, what's relevant about this is the location where the body is found. [Mr. Bellows], in his statement, admits going in the car, going up, stoning [Mr. Klotz] and handing a knife to [Mr. Ryan], which [Mr. Bellows] described as [Mr. Ryan] slitting his throat. This is probative on the fact. Later on, the head is found severed from the rest of the body. Now, whether animals contributed or not, I don't think anybody is ever going to know. There was carnivore activity.

Clabby asks the court to have a photo admitted, whether a smaller photo would be admissible. The judge tells him that the image does prove that the "head was severed. You can tell it was a skull, but it's not bloody. It looks like a piece of black tar with some eye holes."

Clabby continues with the cadaver photos. [Photo–A watch is worn on the arm bone].

Clabby: His best friend gave him the watch.

The DA wants the photos of the body showing the watch on Klotz's arm as evidence.

The head is clearly detached from the body in the photos. The photos are graphic, yet fortunately, they are not well constructed.

The judge holds up the foam core sheet, #3, delicately with her long, melon nails. She squints, lifting her eye glasses close to her brow.

Judge: These have maggots in them and they don't show the–it's offensive, but–and it

doesn't show actual fractures. It shows the . . .
Clabby: Indentations.
Judge: Hair, yeah.

Kristina cries. A female marshal hands her a recycled paper towel.
There are discussions about how the photos could influence a jury.

Judge: To me, these four pictures are really horrible because the body has obviously been torn apart and eaten. And if the only reason is to show the position, it doesn't because it's so close up to the dirt.

The People will supply a photo from a greater distance to show location. The X Rays are permitted, to prove fractures to the face. Several witnesses are reviewed, and because of the graphic details, this day is overwhelming. Why doesn't an experienced DA have wide-angle photos to show the scene?

"It's unfortunate that we didn't get this severed earlier," Alex tells me. From a strategic standpoint it helps Kristina's case not to have Bellows in the courtroom. He explains that this judge was a DA who was appointed to the municipal court bench and then elevated a couple years later to superior court. If he had challenged her, they might have sent the case to another judge, one more pro-prosecution or less experienced, and all of the photos might have been accepted. The judge kept out three boards which were the most grotesque. "She played a good role in getting the severance," Alex adds. "Anyway, I'm not totally disappointed."

The case is severed from Bellows at the end of the second day of Motions In Limine, April 9.

9:00 p.m.   Phone call, Kristina Edwards

Edwards: I broke down. It was awful seeing those pictures. They hit me pretty hard. You didn't see them, did you? I couldn't stop crying.

Lots of jail noise. Phone cuts out. She calls back.

Hello. Did you see Bellows? What's your reaction that we got severed?

She starts to talk about how she remembers the event.

Kristina you're on the phone . . . besides . . .
Grant's going to get off. Collier lied on the stand.

Does anyone hear you talking inside the jail?
No. They're all watching this good movie, *The Good Son.* You see that? It's about a little kid who's evil and kills his aunt. I don't know what's happening to me now. I feel all of a sudden changed. To see the results, it kills. Seeing his body like that. I can't believe we left him there for the animals to do that. Those pictures keep slapping me upside my face. The skull with the eyeballs smashed, with the head of hair, that Clabby had to put in my face. I didn't sleep at all last night. I picture myself the last day. That guy went through so much. I feel for his family. I wish I coulda stopped that. I'm gonna hyperventilate. I can't help myself at times. That's why I'm a snitch.

4/12/96 Bellows' trial is scheduled before
        Edwards'

I attend Bellows' trial to hear testimony from others who were at the Donner house when Klotz was initially beaten. Donner's daughter, a girl involved with Bellows and Ryan, is rumored to have been sent to Mexico to avoid being called to testify. The trial begins. Connie Taylor, witness for the People, a regular at the Donner house, talks about drugs at the Donner residence as though it's natural for teens to hang out for days at a time getting high. Twilla Donner, Bellows, Ryan, and Price are her friends.

The DA carries a box of rocks to the judge for viewing.

Nate Bellows' taped interview is played. The detective did Mirandize him prior to taping. It's been established during hearings that drugs were commonplace at the Donner residence. Some of these people rented rooms there. The night of the incident, it's estimated that 15 youths were present for the beating. Crystal, alcohol, and pot are the drug diet at the house. Bellows talks about who was punching Klotz, kicking him, and putting him in the trunk and closing it with Klotz's arm hanging out. The testimony indicates that Ryan, Kristina, Price, and Bellows got in the car and drove to a plateau where Ryan pulled Klotz out with a dog chain he wore on his wallet. He tells how the three males kicked and hit Klotz further. When asked if Kristina participated, Bellows answers, "Not really."

Price, the juvenile, threw rocks. Bellows kicked Klotz. Ryan hit him.

The judge reads the transcript as the tape is played.

Bellows tells the detective that Kristina said, "Finish this off. It's taking too long." Ryan hit Klotz again and again, probably more than ten times to the front of his head. Klotz moved around and turned on his side.

"He's gonna die," Ryan shouted, stabbing him.

Later Ryan ordered everyone to bring Klotz's clothes and their own clothes to the Donner Ranch. He burned them in the fireplace.

Mrs. Bellows twists a purple carnation and sniffs it. Mr. Bellows' head is down the entire time the tape is played. The trial continues for a solid week.

4/16/96 Bellows' trial continues

Another long day. Outside the courtroom, two jurors read Dean Koontz's book, From the Corner of His Eye. Mrs. Bellows sits alone wearing her red dress. No carnations today. McKenzie tells me he's ready to leave California. Once the jury returns a verdict, the court has 28 days to sentence Bellows.

Bellows is quickly found guilty of first-degree murder and kidnapping.

4/17/96 10:30 a.m. Jail, outside Control

Dep. Harper's back on day shift and stops to talk about what she sees in this jail.

Dep. Harper: See, a lot of them die. I myself witnessed one die, and it was just horrible. I never want to see another inmate like that. I got her to a hospital before she died, but there wasn't much left of her. She came in with balloons of drugs in her and drank orange juice that morning and ate spaghetti at 4:30 in the evening. By 5:30 p.m., the acids ate the balloons. Never did find out what the drugs were, but she started violently throwing up in the hospital. I told them it was probably the spaghetti she ate, and the doctor came out mashing a lump of something in his hand and said, "No, ma'am, this is her stomach lining. Whatever she ate, whatever she swallowed is eating her up from the inside out, and we can't stop it. You need to call the next of kin." I had the dredging job of calling her mom and saying, "You have to get up, get dressed, call a priest, and come down here." It's about ten at night. The inmate was only 25, and had a three-year-old daughter. It bothered me to watch her die and have to explain to her mother on the phone.

Who are the toughest inmates?
The ones who abuse their kids and then sit there and write letters to the judge, saying they've got to get out of here. They've got to get home to their babies when they never gave a rat's rear end about their babies in the first place! That makes me bitter. What are these people doing having babies in the first place?

You're talking about A housing.
They're in A 'cause B people will kill them.

You're not talking about the chronic addicts who take drugs and leave their children with CPS?
That's part of it, too. Eventually they're gonna kill this kid. Eventually this kid is going to end up being exactly like mommy because that's what this kid has as a role model. You are what you produce. They produce wimps and criminals. They reproduce images of themselves and then they wonder why these kids are 15 and 16 and can't control themselves. Have you interviewed Sheryl Dale? She got sentenced.

Maxwell says she was Sheryl Dale's cellmate.
We call her Lizzie Borden. She did it [killed] to a woman who was pregnant.

Your advice to the inmates when they're released is what?
Pack up your crap and leave. Get out of the state. If you go back to your old neighborhood, you're gonna see your pals doing drugs because they haven't been caught yet. You wanna change your life and make your kid your priority? You're not going to do that hanging around the same place. You can't do it in the city. Go out in the country, rent a little house, and start making a little money. But until they hit that brick wall none of these women will change. They'll keep coming back because it's easier. It's easier to slam a few beers and not think about your problem than it is to say, "I've really got to fix this. How am I going to get my next rent payment?"

The kids are the ones who suffer. Even if these women don't hurt or neglect their children, just by getting on drugs, they're telling their children, "My drugs are my priority and you're second, third, or fourth on the totem pole." A lot of people are habitual drug offenders because their role models, their mothers, lived in here most of their lives. All you're gonna do is breed like a rabbit. And welfare gives you enough money to pay a little rent and buy a little food. The rest goes to dope and alcohol. Why should you work?

How can they leave here and be granted welfare?
Why do we allow these people to stay on welfare while they're in here? I had a rough time 12 years ago with a divorce. I have three kids. I was by myself, and I needed money. Welfare told me, "Well, you're white." I ended up living on the streets in my truck behind the restaurant where I worked. I had joint custody of my kids. I was flipping burgers with pneumonia. These people whine and cry, "I'm all by myself!" So was I! I try and tell them, "Heck, if I can do it when I didn't have any family, no money, nothin' in the middle of the winter, taking showers in the restaurant I worked in, you can, too." Twelve years later, my oldest is 15. I have my house, and I'm stoked. There's help out there if people want it, for battered women and for drug abuse. You just have to want to change.

237

2:00 p.m. B Housing, Pro Visit Room

Rolenda acts out again. Pepper spray was used on her multiple times. There were fights in B1, "a lot of shit was going on." Now Rolenda's in Lockdown once again. Two weeks this time. Dr. Bull is brought in for consult. Rolenda enters the B housing Pro Visit Room in a stupor.

Dep. Harper's willing to pull Rolenda Banks out of Lockdown, if only to have us finally realize how hopeless the inmate is inside this system. Rolenda appears, dissident and drugged.

What happened?
Banks: I don't know. I got starved for three days.

You were placed on a discipline diet?
Banks: Yeah, I didn't eat it. It's everything they serve in a day put in a blender and baked as a loaf.

Are you still on meds?
Yes, Loxatane. It's a tranquilizer for a horse. This whole place had to be Kwelled yesterday for lice. One person had lice and everybody in the room had to be done. Then the sewer worms leap. They're black worms. They are in the drain. Then they got the fruit flies in the shower.

That's Melody, in the window. She cut her hair off, turned dyke. Some people pick on Kristina. They mess with her and talk bad to her.

You feel better on Loxatane than on the Tegretol?
As soon as I take this, I go to sleep. When I feel the drug coming on, I lay down. It ain't no mild tranquilizer. It ain't no mild Zoloft or Klonipin.

Bull enters.

Dr. Bull: Rolenda's on [Penal Code] 1368. This is a legal competency proceeding to see if she's able to cooperate with her attorney in the preparation for defense. The judge had doubts and asked for a hearing. To establish competency, they asked her questions like, "What's the role of the judge?" "What's the role of the DA?" and "What's the role of the jury?" She knew the answers to the questions. Of course she was found competent, and that allows her to get on with the criminal legal process.

What happens now?
Banks: Nothing.
Dr. Bull: You'll have to start the program again, and there's a lot of deputies who just want to kick ass. They don't want to see you succeed because they want to retaliate and get nasty, when they have a chance.
Banks: Why can't I go to my regular Lockdown?
Dr. Bull: I don't know. I have to talk to the Captain about that.
Banks: They gonna give me that discipline diet. They know that I'm not going to eat it, and they want to drag me around.
Dr. Bull: You have to have better self-control than they have.
Banks: I don't have control. I just wish that I could get it over with and go to prison.
Dr. Bull: I agree with you. You have to wait until June 25th, right?
Banks: The 25th is the Prelim and the sentencing is July 9th.
Dr. Bull: Remember before you came back to B housing, I told you there are a lot of deputies back here against you.
Banks: It was hard. There were like seven fights within the first week.
Dr. Bull: I don't know what kind of life you have waiting for you, but I think you probably have much more of a life than anybody knows. Up to now, the only thing you've found is being momma. You're worried about your parental rights.
Banks: I want to change my medication.
Dr. Bull: I'll make a note that you want to change from Loxatane. Even a small amount is way too much.

238

239

237. Deputy Harper; 238. Dr. Bull;
239. Inmate Banks

4/22/96 9:00 a.m. Kristina Edwards' trial begins

Kristina's seated next to her attorney in the courthouse. Alex is wearing a dark brown striped suit and soft-soled shoes. A strip of rawhide is tied around his ponytail. He's focused and ready for action. The bailiff, the court recorder, and the court clerk are present. The judge enters and puts her robe on over a slim gray skirt and white blouse.

There is discussion of possible convictions for the jury to consider regarding Kristina.

Shortly before noon the bailiff informs everyone he's locking up for lunch. Outside, Alex talks to us. He says Kristina could do ten years with good behavior on a plea of 15-to-life. She'll still probably get second-degree murder.

Barbara and I have lunch on the Emerald Plaza patio. In front of us we see Teena, the young inmate we interviewed in Step Study, standing next to a grungy-looking guy and accepting his cash. They get into a cab and make a U-turn, heading up Broadway.

Back at the courthouse, the court secretary opens the door and calls out the numbers for jurors.

Alex questions prospective jurors: "Would someone object to my appearance?" One man says he doesn't like Alex's hair, but he'd judge him "on what you say or how you act."

A widow and former teacher says she was on a hung jury once, and that didn't bother her, but the photos of this trial might make her squeamish. The judge asks, "Even if they are not bloody, but cleaned up, you couldn't force yourself? Ever see any of the *Terminator* movies? I'm inclined to excuse this juror."

4/25/96 10:00 a.m. Courthouse

When I arrive, Barbara's sitting between Marian L. Pasas, private investigator, and Dick Bidwell, the man Kristina lived with and the owner of the car Kristina drove the night of the murder. Dick gets up and comes over to me. He whispers, "I think the DA wants to mention me and some sex thing with Kristina." He's scared. Then he asks me, "I'm still her mommie, ain't I?"

The courtroom is unusually full. The private investigator tells us it's Daughter's Day at work. Rows of teenage girls have information sheets on Kristina Edwards' trial.

The People call Richard Bidwell.

Dick Bidwell, rubbing his hands together, repeats his name, glances at the jury, then sheepishly looks at Kristina. He hadn't worn his ill-fitting dentures at Bellows' trial; it's obvious he wants to look his best for Kristina because he's her only witness.

The car photo board is placed on the rail behind Bidwell. He identifies his car. Members of the jury watch Kristina as Bidwell explains how he found Kristina, age 14, in Crestline behind the Red Lounge bar, sleeping in what they called the surfboard. He didn't have a residence, so he took her into his car. Dick's a sad-looking man. His reddened face and out-of-shape physique tells me getting to the courthouse from Big Bear Mountain and facing a courtroom is more than he can handle.

Later he tells the court he thought Kristina was taking his car to the store, but she didn't return for four days. There's silence in the courtroom.

Andrew Edinger, a pudgy guy in his 20s, takes the stand. He's Kristina's friend, yet he's a witness for the People. He reads to the court his rendition of what Kristina had told him happened to Klotz.

Edinger looks at Kristina several times while he's on the stand. His testimony is the first major information for the jury. They are captive.

Kristina cries out in the courtroom, "I never meant Marcus any harm."

Ray Lang enters and takes the stand. He could play the part of Lennie in *Of Mice and Men*. He says his name is Ray Edward Wrang Lang. The judge, laughing, has to ask him to spell his name. Sitting erect, Lang nervously checks on Kristina as Clabby questions him on his prior record for felony robbery that sent him to prison. He attended the barbeque with Kristina and Klotz the night before the murder. As he tells it, three weeks later Kristina called him from her dad's house and said she was afraid of the Hell's Angels and Skinheads. Klotz was dead because of them. Kristina says she told them to put Klotz in the trunk of the car so he wouldn't get blood on the backseat. His ribs were broken and bleeding. After they were finished throwing knives into Klotz's back, the men decided to drop rocks on his head. Klotz screamed, "Hell's Angels are going to get you!" Kristina couldn't stand it anymore. She went over and picked up a good-sized rock and dropped it on his head. Klotz was moaning when one of the guys picked up a rock and dropped it, smashing Klotz's face.

Alex cross-examines Ray Lang. He leaves no room for speculations; Lang didn't tape record Kristina's story nor did he take notes. Alex asks if Lang's memory is perfect.

Lang replies, "It depends on what the subject is." Alex establishes that Lang and Kristina used drugs together. He points out Lang's prison history. Lang admits knowing Kristina had another boyfriend.

None of the witnesses are credible. They have histories of truancy, drugs, and prison.

At the end of the day, Alex stays back to talk to Edwards. It's late. From the Preliminary Hearing through the Suppression Hearings and from Bellows' trial to Kristina's trial, the stories differ. Transcripts have Bellows telling one story. Since Ryan pled guilty, his story was never told. Kristina's supposed friends, Edinger and Lang, give different versions of the same events. Lang's interest in Kristina isn't congruent with his embellished record of her story.

We see Pasas, the private investigator. I ask if the elderly man and woman are Klotz's parents. She says they're courtroom chasers who always sit on the prosecution's side. Another elderly woman with dyed pink hair, wearing tennis shoes and white tights, carries a Calvin Klein shopping bag full of groceries. She asks me if I'm a law student. She's another courtroom chaser. No one else attends this trial except occasional news reporters.

8:00 p.m.   Phone call, Kristina Edwards

Kristina's upset.

Edwards: I have to be examined by Dr. Bennet. Nothing's going right. And what's with that Connie Taylor testifying she saw me? Where did she come from? I didn't see her at the house. She's lying. Edinger was trying to help me. He looked over at me all the time. I was up most of the night because a girl here was convicted, and she had my judge. Then I dreamed I was slamming dope again. I'll let you know as soon as it's over tomorrow.

4/28/96   Phone call, Kristina Edwards

It's a beautiful day. Court is not in session. I finish reading Thursday's typed transcript and am heading outside with my daughter to wash the dogs when there's a phone call from Kristina.

What's wrong?
Edwards: Didn't go so good with that psychiatrist the court ordered. Alex stayed the whole time. It was OK until I got to the part about the plateau and the rock, and stuff. I just had trouble talking about it. I told him that I didn't recall. Since he had heard the tape with the detective, he said it sounded like to him that I did the act. He smirked and said, "You're trying to say that you didn't participate?" (She's crying) I didn't know what I was supposed to say. Then one embarrassing thing, the doctor asked me who was president. I didn't know. I said Pete Wilson.

Can you remember now?
The only president I remember is Ronald Reagan. Then I got mixed up on ages. I said I was 12 or 13. I could see the expression develop on Alex's face. I got upset. I remembered Alex telling me, "No matter what, don't get upset." Alex got more frustrated that I got things twisted around. He told me later that's why he can't put me on the stand because if I can't handle this–this is nothing compared to what the DA will do. That asshole will chip me into pieces. I can't sleep. I hear the jury say those words that have me guilty. When the interview was over, Alex and the doctor walked me out front to the bench. The woman who slugged my eye was on the bench! She looked up and said, "You fucked-up. You're going to prison."

5/2/96   Closing arguments

Clabby, dressed in a fine blue suit and sharp white shirt, looks serious, as he recaps the prosecution's case. He instructs the jury as to the relevance of:
  I.   Torture
  II. Kidnapping
  III. Felony/Murder
  IV. Premeditated and deliberate murder
  V.   Special circumstances alleged
The jury is bored and tired. I wonder if they've made up their minds.

Alex, like Clabby, looks very serious as he steps up to the rails and removes all of the evidence boards from view. There's total silence in the courtroom. He tells the jury they're "allowed to consider mental disorders, voluntary intoxication, fear for her own life." Richard Bidwell, he says, is important to listen to about who Kristina Edwards is. Bidwell knew Kristina had a drug problem and he let her live with him for four years. They moved from one house to another together. She didn't have a mother or father. She was abandoned at 13. Mr. Bidwell took her off the streets.

"And you can't ignore that, because when Dr. DiFrancesca and Dr. Koshkarian evaluated the evidence of this case and looked at her background, those facts play a role. You may not approve of [Kristina Edwards] using methamphetamine or marijuana or alcohol as a minor... but, again, it's important to understand that [Kristina Edwards] was also a victim at a very young age, and those are factors to consider in determining mental state, in determining intoxication and the reason for it, and in understanding why she may have a particular fear. Circumstances in this case; factors to consider; factors to weigh.

"[Mr. Bidwell] did say that [Kristina Edwards] had taken his car and was gone for a period of four days. You heard the statements about how she came back, but omitted, of course, was the fact that when she returned she was frightened. She was paranoid. She wouldn't let [Mr. Bidwell] turn on the lights. She had him block the door. She was incoherent. She was all things that [Mr. Bidwell] told you about [Kristina Edwards] at that time.

"Is that some sophisticated killer? Or some manipulative individual? Or is that a scared individual, a frightened person who has been through horror herself. An individual who had no intention, as she said, for any of this to occur.

"...Yes, she told some lies. Yes, she took drugs...She cried. She also apologized... and she indicated she did not know what these people were going to do. She indicates she never meant any harm to [Marcus], and she felt terrible about what had occurred."

Lunch with Alex Landon

Alex talks about jurors not giving him any eye interaction. He says he didn't know how to reach the elderly female juror number 6. "I looked at them and they gave me nothing."
We return to the court.
The judge instructs on "read back" of Lang's testimony.

5/5/96   Courthouse

The jury was hung on the kidnapping charge and didn't bring down a verdict on special circumstances in Kristina's trial. The judge didn't press the jury for the verdict.

5/14/96 B Housing, Kristina Edwards

We talk to Kristina. She's upset.

Edwards: I told you I wasn't gonna get off. As a kid, I wanted an education. I didn't want to stop school back then. I had no choice. I didn't have no home. I mean, being with Dick wasn't exactly like living in a home. I got teased by the kids 'cause I was a drug addict and they weren't. You've got kids that like to go to the dances; instead we slammed dope. People looked at me bad.

You first slammed drugs with your dad's girlfriend?
Yeah.

But you'd already been around drugs.
I didn't know that my mom was doing speed until I got into one of her drawers by accident, and found the bags of crystal. I come home and find out she wasn't in that rehab. There was someone in her bed. It was my mom. I ditched school and me and my friend went somewhere else 'cause we were gonna go at my house and kick it. And then later that evening, my dad showed up. My mom told me I was going to go stay the weekend with him. I was brainwashed about my dad. I was scared. She told me he used to beat her all the time, and he was no good. She'd come home and he'd be screwing her girlfriends on the floor. He'd tell her to go wait in her room, he wasn't finished yet. Then he'd go beat her up for walking in on him. She has false teeth now because of what he did to her with a baseball bat when I was three years old. I confronted my mom. I said, "Why are you making me go with him? I know about you not being in rehab." Then I was sent up to the mountains on Father's Day weekend. When I come back four days later, she was gone. She'd moved.

Did you tell the psychiatrists about that?
Yeah, but the jury didn't listen to any of the psychiatrists' testimony.

Did your dad ever hurt his mother?
My grandmother used to be with a girl, and they'd make-out in front of me when I was a kid. The rumor has it that my dad killed my grandmother. Him and a friend named Gary. There's still a guy that took all the blame. They either put something in her drink or put something in her IV, but my mom said she was always having dreams that my grandmother died. When my mom went to the casket, she seen bruises all over her that makeup couldn't hide.

Did your father ever molest you?
Just one time. He was just on drugs real bad.

So the moment you first took drugs, what was going on in your mind?
After I slammed it, I got kinda mad. I mean, the dope made me mad. I turned up those powers and let feelings out.

But you actually wanted to try it?
Yeah. I was curious about my father doing it. I was doing it to try it—to break from reality was all. But after that it was just like a really big high. I don't know how to explain it. You can't explain it unless you've done it.

What would you have wanted to tell the jury about the drugs?
I wanted to be able to say a lot of things, like about Klotz being wired. He was spun. I was spun. There were a lot of things.

Was Connie Taylor right about Klotz's appearance?
I don't remember what he looks like. I just remember his tennis shoes.

Even at the barbeque?
Yeah. I can't remember what that guy looked like. I was busy being high and stealing a couple steaks for us to eat. I'm in my own little world the next night. I remember I turned to him and said, "Don't you remember when we were just down here?" He goes, "I've never been down here before in my life." I go, "We just came down here two nights ago." I'm thinking about Joey and Victoria. That's what drugs did to me.

Plus, if Ray Lang can call us intimate, then he's really screwed up. It's like, "Ray, why didn't you tell them about when you lived in that apartment in the back of the Antlers and you stared at me at night through your window like a freak, writing?" He liked to roam in the cemeteries at night. When we drove off to go to the side of that road, I said, "I can't believe this is happening." While he was writing down what he said I told him, he was getting high on my dope! I told him I needed to tell the police, and I didn't want him to hate me for what had happened. "Should I run? Are they gonna arrest me because they think that I may have done something?" That's what we talked about. And he goes, "Well, I don't know what to think anymore," and I go, "Well, fuck you then. Take me back." He was supposed to be on my side, and he's sitting there on the side of a damn freeway saying he don't know what to think anymore. I said, "Just take me the fuck back."

What was his motive for misconstruing the story then?
I think probably because of Klotz's family. His brother, David, was upset that he couldn't find Klotz. Ray's sister tells me that David was getting ready to sock up Ray for lying to him. She came in yelling at me, "What does my brother know?" Then she says, "Well, he's getting ready to beat my brother's ass out there. You better tell me what's going on." I mean, that's what had happened. Then I wanted to go and get the body and take it to San Bernardino? He made that story up. He's the one that was into the cemetery thing, into that devil worship, that Ozzie Osborne stuff. He wouldn't even look at me 'cause he was lying. But see that's what Alex said the jury went by. They asked to hear the tape again and to see the testimony of Ray Lang. That's what they used to convict me. Another thing, I didn't drive all those miles to come and get a bag of marijuana. That frustrates me so damn bad.

When did you actually get to the Donner Ranch?
It wasn't dark outside during the fight like that Ms. Taylor said. By the time they got him in the trunk, it was dark. There was light above the power lines on the plateau. Ryan was over there trying to fuck around with all the keys, trying to find out which one was the trunk key. And he kept on yelling. So I went back and said, "Give me the keys!" And I took the trunk key off and gave it to him. I told him I'm going back to the car 'cause I thought they were just going to leave Klotz on the plateau.

I didn't want Collier to know that I was scared for him to think that those guys had that effect on me. Collier wasn't on my side anymore. He was accusing me of things. When Collier was driving me to the plateau, I told him, "That road don't look familiar." He was just goin' a little faster speed. Then flashbacks started coming back as he was driving up that road. He told the jury that I said that I didn't recognize any of that, and he's a liar! I said, "There's that four-lane highway." When they took me in the helicopter, later, I was looking for the water tower.

You'll have a chance for an appeal.
But see, I'm not even comfortable being with another attorney. I'm not going to be able to tell whoever it is the things that I told Alex. I only told him 'cause I believed in him.

He's a great attorney. Codefendant cases are especially difficult. The black eye incident didn't help the timing of your trial. On appeal, you could get the sentence reduced to a second-degree or voluntary manslaughter.
I could also get special circumstances and the death penalty. The jury forgot to even vote on that. I'd have to go through another trial, and they're harder on women now. I'm just scared.

5/21/96   11:00 a.m.   B Housing, Danielle Lopez

B1 door opens and a pretty inmate, Danielle Lopez, steps out, throws herself on the bench, and flips off her jail thongs. She pulls up her legs and rocks back and forth. Then she cries out until the deputy calls for assistance. A deputy yells out, "Get Lopez some meds!"

Dr. Bromley enters the unit and asks Lopez if she still feels suicidal. He instructs the deputies to move her to A housing. Lopez looks up at me and begins to talk.

Lopez: I'm spinning right now. I'm on Paxil, and they increased my dose. Too much hostility. I hide in my room. One of my roommates is Victoria Gale. She's not all there. She has a lot of problems and talks a lot. I just get very dizzy. I've been sticking to my bed for two days now, and it's been making me a little vicious toward my roommate. I'm afraid I have a short temper.

The deputy tells her to go back to her room and roll up her belongings. Moments later, Lopez drags a trash bag full of personal items. I notice several paperback books inside the clear plastic bag.

Lopez: I'm being moved to A housing. This is all I have in the jail. I love books. I love to read, and they don't have any educational books here. I love Anne Rice. I read each page over and over and savor each word. I want to get the picture of each scene as she sees it. THE EVIL DAMN is my favorite. I'm 20, and the first time I read it I was 18. I love horror. Also I love rap. I make up my own music. I have my own words, put them in my head, write them and hum.

How far did you go in school?
Ninth grade.

What happened?
I didn't have any friends. I was a nerd. I'd hang out in the library and people just made fun of me the way I looked, the way I dressed.

You stayed at home and didn't go to school?
Yes. I kind of educated myself.

You must have conned your mother into letting you stay home.
Yes! I watched "Jeopardy," and studied encyclopedias. The only library we have here is a little bookshelf and I'm reading Conroy's PRINCE OF TIDES.

What brought you to jail?
I got in a fight with somebody. I think there will be a trial.

Dep. Keys arrives to take Lopez to A housing. Lopez laughs, seemingly happy now. The deputy and Lopez leave the housing unit. Dep. Keys returns to B housing and asks if we want to have lunch with her. She talks about her six-year experience as a deputy in the jail. "They say when they walk away from the mirror, 'Oh, I can handle it now,' and they deceive themselves. They go out there and feel all right, yet totally deceived from the beginning. They don't know truth and reality."

Back in B housing unit, an inmate arrives from the hospital with bandages over her left ear. Kristina Edwards comes to Pro Visit and tells us the girl had to go to the hospital and get 100 stitches because someone in the jail bit off her ear.

241

Edwards: I saw you with Lopez. She's in for assault. She was a heroin addict.

Kristina has changed. She now thinks of herself as one of the lifers.

I got my probation sheet orders, so that means I'm gonna leave for the prison after I get sentenced.

An inmate named Angie passes by the door.

Angie's a snitch. She's turned on a lot of girls. She's a compulsive liar. I wrote my mom a nasty letter just to let her know I'm grown up, but I still need her.

Did you think Collier would understand?
I didn't think that he'd believe anything. I was just trying to think up something, trying to get it over with, trying to get out of there. They had me all puffed up there. Then the detectives told me I had to have picked up the rock. I had to have dropped it was what Ray Lang told them!

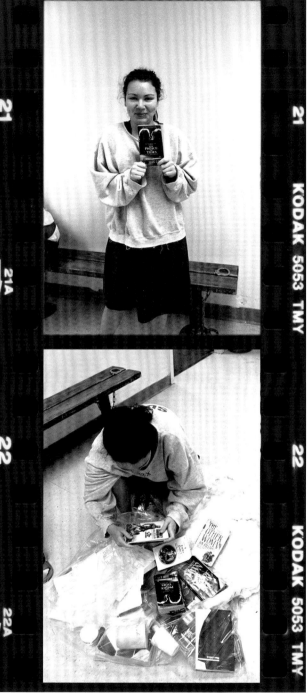

242-243

241-243. Inmate Lopez; 244. Deputy Williams;
245. Inmate Chelsea

245

244

1:00 p.m. F2 Housing

Chelsea's back in jail, 30 days after she was last released. She's sitting at a picnic table on F2 patio. It's an unusually cool Santee day. Dep. Williams is moving Chelsea to D housing.

I'm surprised to see you back so soon.
Donnelly: Nice to see you, too. I get out in 30 days. I didn't get picked up for a new charge. I took a hit, got pissed off, blacked out, and hit an iron plate on the street with the back of my head. Don't look at me like that. I don't have AIDS. I don't even have a jay-walking ticket. It's that same patrol car. All I have to do is walk along the street with governors, senators, republicans and democrats rushing into San Diego. They don't want no riff-raff on the streets.

The cops are looking for prostitutes and druggies?
I'm not a hooker. A hooker goes and sucks dick and takes forever to make $80. I talk people out of their money faster. OK, I'm in here for hooking. Not drugs. Let me tell you, the white boy was fine. He was fine.

But you have a daughter, Chelsea.
You think I don't know that! She's where she belongs, with my grandmother. You met them. They have each other. She's beautiful, and she's smart. You don't get it. You don't come in here, assume a person's in here to take some religious cure, and go out on a new leaf. I have no need to change. I'm not doing anything wrong. It's the way I choose to live.

She laughs angrily as she mingles with the other women in D housing. On the street she had flair. She swished in front of sports cars along downtown San Diego streets like a supermodel, swaying her slender hips, smiling over her shoulder, flipping delicate brown wrists toward handsome men in fine cars. She convinced them that she was worthy of them. She flagged down her victims, wearing a focused, you're-all-mine kind of smile. She got what she wanted, lots of cash to boost her drug purse and feed her ego.

246. *Inmate Angie and Counselor Conner*

You know what's in the street drugs today? Freon that keeps your refrigerator cold. Formaldehyde that preserves you when you're dead. Antifreeze that keeps your radiator nice and cold. Red phosphorus. Rat poison. This is what these people are taking. There's bleach, all sorts of pool acids in the stuff that they're ingesting. Yeah, it's lethal.

Counselor Conner

5/24/96   10:15 a.m.   Ellen Conner, counselor

Conner: All of us who work in the jail are sick. Including myself. Dep. Harper's sicker than a pup. I love her but she's sick. She should be in jail. The amazing thing is that these deputies have to have an impeccable record to be a deputy. How can they be impeccable? They're sick, and they protect each other.

How many women in here practice homosexuality?
A lot of them.

Because of loneliness?
Everybody else is doing it. It's the chameleon thing.

Did you participate in here?
No. But I found out afterwards that I was gay.

So you don't think it affected you while you were in here?
No, it didn't phase me. I stuck to myself. I didn't want anything to do with anybody around here. I've been married three times. I can't tell you my first husband's birthday. I can't tell you my second husband's birthday. How could I know these other people? I didn't know myself.

 Whenever you take that first drug is when you get cut off, emotionally. I took my first drug at six, so when I got clean at thirty years old I was emotionally still six. I didn't just drink to taste it. I drank to pass out. I went for the whole nine yards. When people say, "My kids weren't affected by my drug use," my questions is, "What would their potential be without it?"

How do they practice safe sex in jail?
They don't. They can't. That's what's so scary. Everything is in here. If they want it, they can get it.

 My clean date started the day after I got out because I got loaded everyday I was in jail. Every single day.

 My drug of choice is heroin. I wouldn't do any speed or cocaine in here. Pills, downers, Valium. If it was in here and I liked it, I'd take it. People stuck it inside their vagina. I guess when you work in a jail, nothing is bizarre. I can't blame

the world. It's a joke. Three-to-five-million-dollar budget cuts for treatment in San Diego County, and we lost total programs. We had a prenatal detox for pregnant women and we lost it. Now we have three beds, and they're cutting again. The big people are saying, "Let's incarcerate them." One morning I was teaching AIM (Access for Infants and Mothers), and I saw them bring in a woman they released the night before.

How do you feel being around the inmates?
They could tell you one thing and mean another. Have some boundaries, because they'll take advantage. You have something they want: conversation. You give them undivided attention. It's funny. I can be at the F fence talking to one person, and they all try and break in on that conversation to see if I'll give them the attention over the next person.

Dr. Bob Paxton with CMH said, "It's the damn crystal meth. I'm seeing six out of every seven kids coming in with overdoses on crystal meth. They get totally psychotic and need drugs to calm them down so they don't go and do some destructive thing."
You know what's in the street drugs today? Freon that keeps your refrigerator cold. Formaldehyde that preserves you when you're dead. Antifreeze that keeps your radiator nice and cold. Red phosphorus. Rat poison. This is what these people are taking. There's bleach, all sorts of pool acids in the stuff that they're ingesting. Yeah, it's lethal. **Bob said our society has some very narcissistic people and kids are "wigged out" because they've had no discipline. I asked if we can we retrieve these kids. "A very small percentage of them," he said.**
I agree with that. We work with them. We take them into treatment. We give them the message but beyond that, it's up to them. If they want it, they have to do it on their own.

6/5/96   Kristina Edwards' sentencing

Barbara and I arrive at the courthouse at 3:15 p.m.

The hallway is empty. I take a photo of the jail from the window. A marshal is upset with me for taking the photograph. The court chasers arrive. Landon shows up, wearing a wrinkled tan cotton suit. He looks tired. The bailiff opens the door. Landon and Clabby enter and we follow. The bailiff tells us to sit in the front row.

Kristina looks paralyzed as she sits next to Alex. The judge makes her entrance. Her posture and the tone of her voice add to the tension in the room. She asks Clabby if he has any comments. Then she asks Alex. He stands and makes a motion for retrial and another motion for a reduced sentence. She quickly denies both.

Without a breath, the judge pronounces Kristina's sentence: 25-to-life with the possibility of parole. I'm stunned, and Barbara's shaken. The bailiff hands Barbara the Kleenex box.

Judge's statement:

The court: This is a very sad sentencing, a very sad case. And [Miss Edwards], I want to say a couple of things to you that are apart from the sentencing. Anyone, I think, who listened to this case couldn't help but be moved by the fact that you lost your childhood. And nobody can return that to you or give it back to you or make up for what you lost.

The thought of a girl at the age of 13 being out on the streets is pretty sad, and I am not even sure that you realized what a sad situation it was because it was simply your world and you didn't know any different. But anyone on the outside would look at that and know that you had been a victim in the most serious way that can ever happen to a child in this society. And you went to this ranch of lost children. In the same way that you were lost, this ranch of young adults were lost and they will continue to be lost.

In some respects you may be able to find in incarceration some of the things—some of the security in the surroundings, as bad as they may be--that are better than what you actually had before, and maybe help you to get away from the drugs.

I also hope that you are able to write to your child, at least maintain some kind of contact. Whether or not she is raised by your mother, her being able to have some contact with her birth mother will be important to her. Something you didn't have maybe you will be able to give to her over the years: to establish a relationship in writing. Mentally, for her, that would probably be extremely important and even to you; maybe to break that cycle that's happened.

In looking at your family background one could easily place a lot of blame on your parents, but you can also conclude that they were probably raised with some of the deficits that they couldn't make up for themselves.

Your mother was apparently one of 18 children. She probably got very little special attention. Her mother has apparently forsaken you, which would lead me to believe that she wasn't much of a mother for your mother, and so it goes down the generations.

Your father likewise.

The Sentencing Hearing is over. The bailiff asks if we want to talk to Edwards after her attorney is finished. He is trying to offer her support. Standing next to him, she looks over her shoulder at us, her face twisted like a child's, her eyes bloodshot. We follow Alex outside the courtroom. He manages a kind smile. "What can I say?" he says with the greatest control. I always admire his control. He tells us what he told Kristina. "She needs to stay out of trouble and study when she goes to prison, and she'll have a greater chance at parole."

Alex lays out what happens next.

Landon: We're talking about a year to fully brief her appeal and another 90 days for the appellate court to make its decision. I told [Kristina] the most positive area for the appeal is in the area of jury instructions, as far as the law is concerned. The chances of having the court overturn the verdict are much greater, far more than arguing the sufficiency of the evidence. We have at least three of the four very serious instruction-error issues. The jury hung on the kidnapping charge, and I think the record was very clear that it was not a premeditated and deliberate murder. It means that all of those issues are really crucial. The other thing is that the judge prohibited Dr. Di Francesca and Dr. Koshkarian from revealing some things that [Kristina] said to them. Once again that's something that impacted our ability to present evidence, and that's a constitutional violation under the 6th Amendment to present evidence. I think there's hope.

What about the fact that Kristina was not given Miranda rights at the time of the ploy, and she was under the influence?
The Court of Appeals is going to look at the record as it is now. We made the issue clear about the coerced statement, but the law is not good. That's why I didn't raise it now.

We haven't been to the jail for two weeks. The clerk acts as though she's never seen us. She has to check with the lieutenant. We're locked in the sally port for ten minutes before she returns and releases the grills.

248. Inmate Edwards

We talk to Kristina. She's upset Alex didn't get her a better deal.

Edwards: None of it happened the way Ray Lang said. He called Klotz's family and told them where I was. I said something, but I never said I dropped the rock. It was hard watching 30 girls leave on the bus for prison last night, knowing I'm on the next one. The place is empty. My mom wrote me that my baby gets cereal now. My mom wants to bring the baby and come for a final visit. She can't bring the baby to prison. It'll be too far.

I'm going to Fresno. That's where lifers go, Valley State Prison. It's like a military prison. I heard the school's not very good. Prison is a lot more serious than this place where you jerk around and play your little games. Last night Henderson wanted me to be her girlfriend, but I don't get along with her. She jerked me off my bed. It really smells in here with girls kicking. One girl shit in her bathroom. It came all the way down the hall and everyone was screaming. I don't have any money on my books for supplies, and my scalp is dry. My face is greasy. Oh, hey, remember Gomez?

She's been in and out of here four times since you saw her.

She is afraid to go back to the streets.

She's just a junkie and a prostitute. She should have a lot of places to go.

I've been reading a book about how mothers lie to their children about things and how they are in a state of denial. Talking about the sex part and how they say they love their child, but they send them off to an aunt or grandmother. The child feels neglected. I can't really comprehend it all.

I'm worried about what Little One will do when I get up to prison. Another girl told me that shit wasn't going to follow me up there 'cause they're into the drug scene in prison. They said the lifers will take me under their wings 'cause that's gonna be my home. We're gonna be there longer than anybody.

We tell Kristina that we'll see her Saturday when her mother and baby visit.

Sexuality. Sexuality is one of the most neglected areas in the treatment of addiction, and one of the major causes for relapse. Healthy sexuality is integral to one's sense of self-worth. It represents the integration of the biological, emotional, social, and spiritual aspects of who one is and how one relates to others (Covington, 1991a; Covington, in press; Kaplan, 1981; Schnarch, 1991). Addiction is often defined as a physical, emotional, social, and spiritual disease. Since healthy sexuality is defined as the integration of all these aspects of the self, we can see that addiction can have an impact on every area of sexuality. Therefore, addressing and healing all aspects of the sexual self is critical to a woman's recovery process (Covington, 1991a; Covington, in press).

Creating healthy sexuality is a developmental process that occurs over time. This normal developmental process is often interrupted by addiction. In addition, many women entering the early stages of recovery report the following sexual concerns: sexual dysfunction, shame and guilt, sexual identity, prostitution, sexual abuse, and the fear of sex clean and sober. These issues need to be addressed if we expect women to maintain their recovery (Covington, 1991a; Covington, 1993).

Few women in prisons have a positive view of sex. Some have been prostitutes, many have been abused, and most connect sex with shame and guilt. Even those who have been the most sexually active have little accurate information about sex. Developing programs that can work with this part of a women's recovery can help to create a positive sense of self and a healthier image of relationship.

Spirituality. The root of the word psychology is "psyche," which means "the knowledge and the understanding of the soul." Although we live in a secular culture where traditional psychology does not focus on the spiritual, helping women to reconnect to their own definition of the spiritual is critical to their recovery process. Religion and spirituality are not the same–they may or may not be connected. Religion is about form, dogma, and structure, and is institutionally based. Spirituality is about transformation, connection, wholeness, meaning, and depth.[39]

Stephanie Covington, Ph.D.

10:30 a.m.   Pro Visit,   Dottie Boyle

We haven't seen Boyle since July in Step Study. She arrives with a deputy. She's no longer in F housing. She's in B, where all inmates headed for prison are housed.

What happened to you? You were doing well, and now you're headed for prison?
Boyle: This all took place when my daughter had run away from my ex. He tried to throw her into Juvenile Hall for use of drugs. She got involved with the wrong people. She was with her dad for one summer. It worries me. She's with my ex now. He's a real slime bucket, real self-centered. He got involved with drugs. I got out of jail and headed back to Ramona to catch up with my daughter. I said, "We're going to have this week to get along and talk. We gotta end this." She said, "Let's go ride around on bikes." That's what we did. We stayed together that whole week. I told her to not go to these places, but she did, and there was a raid.

I told her no more drugs. What happened was crystal and pot. Everything seemed futile. I said, "This is it, I'm not going to jail again, and I'm not doing any crazy stuff no more." I lose my life when I sit in jail for eight months and think what I could be doing.

You were doing so well. You were at Gordy's rehab.
And Gwen was my roommate at Gordy's. I got panicked when Gwen started trouble with Gordy. He started coming on to her, and then people were getting high. I was in sober living! I was testing clean, reporting, and calling probation every day, and I had started doing bookwork again. Everything was going along OK up until my daughter brought some checks to my rehab and said, "Hey Mom." I said, "Oh, no, haven't you learned your lesson yet?" I took two of 'em and burned 'em. And the other one she took and cashed. It took me four days to get enough courage to go up to the substation and meet with the detective. He searched my purse, wrote down my information on my driver's license.

I've had it. I'm not going to be a parent anymore. When I get out of prison this time, I'm going to get out of San Diego. I knew when we were sitting there getting in trouble that I'm going to go down for this stupidity. That's the thing. I was calm. I knew I was going to prison. But Nicole doesn't care about that. She finally admitted it to me. The cop said, "Talk to your daughter." And I said, "What do you want me to talk to her about?" He knew that she did it. I couldn't say, "Arrest my daughter." That's why I'm moving away, so she has to deal with things on her own. She's using crystal. That's why she boosted the stuff; she wanted to go and buy an eight-ball. She's money motivated. She wants to go out and sell it. She stole three CDs and a bottle of cologne and some other stuff when we were shopping for Nintendo and car filters, but I didn't know she had stole stuff. Before this she stole some checks from my ex-girlfriend and cashed them. So I didn't want her to get caught for this, too. She'd really be in trouble. So my ex did the paperwork on her. She's at home with him. If she's convicted, they'll send her to Juvenile Hall. She's going to be 18 in June. She could even end up here! Since I had a record, this was a violation, and I got to go to prison. They gave me two years, but I'm going to do eight months. I leave for prison next Tuesday night. I don't know what's gonna happen to my daughter.

249-251. Inmate Boyle; 252. Inmate Mulloy

249-251

Last time we saw Cindy Mulloy was in Mercy Hospital. She's returned to the jail.

We hear once again from Mulloy how useless she feels and how she doesn't deserve anything in life.

In November you came close to dying in the hospital. What's going on?

Mulloy: The jail let me loose from the hospital in November so they wouldn't have to be responsible for my hospital bill. I got arrested again on the eighth of January. I was out of the hospital and started using right away. This time I think the judge is going to send me to prison. He said, "Nothing's worked so far. Maybe a longer rest in prison will keep you clean." You asked me in the hospital what turning a trick was like for me. Here, I wrote this for you and saved it in case I saw you again.

252

Cindy Mulloy: contribution

I need to go to work and turn a trick or two. I don't really want to, but I have to in order to buy some dope. That's the easiest way, fastest way, I know to make some money. I'm dreading it, but "Hi ho, hi ho, it's off to work I go." The thought of getting into a strange man's car and sucking a stranger's dick is totally disgusting. It's easier to fuck. You just close your eyes and think of England.

One of the advantages of all of this is the power of escape. I don't have to be Cindy. Right now I'm not sick, but I will be soon. So out the door I go. I try to stay close to the track so I don't have far to go. Especially if I roll out the door at three or four in the morning. It doesn't usually take long to catch. But now I'm walking up 43rd street. It's 10:00 p.m. Almost shift change for the cops.

I like to be out then because they are less likely to fuck with me at the end of their shift. Damn, I hope I see someone I know. My thoughts are scattered because I've got so much on my mind.

OK! I'm finally on the boulevard. So many things to look out for: the cops, the weirdos, the guys that hang out waiting for hookers to get out of other cars. God, I hope I see someone I know. How much do I need tonight? Seventy-five, $100. It would easily carry me through to the morning. Let's see how things go. Damn, I hate standing on this corner. It's so fuckin' hot, and I don't hardly look like I'm waiting for the damn bus. Oh shit. There's Kay. I hope she doesn't want to stand on the corner with me. She always thinks everyone's stopping for her. Not this time, pal. I was here first. And I ain't walking nowhere. My feet are too sore. Hey! I know him. Please stop. And he does. Thank God. And he's an easy one. Just some head. He's quick. It's only $20, but it's a start. Now I'll be able to go get a bag before the connection closes.

"Hi Dan! How's it going?"

"Okay, Cindy. Wanna go to my place?"

"Not really. I'm kinda in a hurry. Can we just do it in the car?"

"Sure. Where do you wanna park?"

I direct him to one of my favorite places. Not far from the boulevard. But far enough so that I won't trip on the cops. We park.

He hands me a 20. The whole ordeal is over in about seven minutes. Any longer and I'd probably throw up on the sick son-of-a-bitch.

I have him drop me off near 44th and Orange. My boyfriend is waiting not far away, and the dope house is close by. My boyfriend doesn't shoot dope, but he smokes rock. He'll just have to understand. We're not buying rock right yet. Well, not very much anyhow.

I went and got a bag of dope and a dime of rock. Fixed, smoked a little, and hit the track again. By now it's a little late to be standing at the bus stop.

I get to the donut shop, buy a cup of coffee, and walk back to the boulevard. While I'm lighting a cigarette, I look up 41st, across El Cajon Boulevard. Cops like to sit on that street for some reason, but I don't see any. Thank God.

Once again, I'm looking for regulars or people I recognize. Just as I get to 10,000 Auto Parts I see a car is turning off the boulevard. We make eye contact. I'm pretty sure he's gonna stop. I walk on the right-hand side of the street. Hey, that guy turned the corner. I hope he comes around the block. Shit. He drives by. His loss.

6/8/96 Jail, Visitation Room
Kristina Edwards

We arrive at the jail early Saturday morning for Kristina Edwards' family visitation before she leaves for her long prison term. It is the first time she has seen her baby since the birth. Pamela is seven months old.

Kristina's mother and stepfather are sitting on a blanket under the only shade tree in front of the jail with their two young children and baby Pamela.

They smile for photos, realizing this visit will commemorate the last time they will see Kristina for months or years to come. Kristina's mother stands, picks up Pamela and says to me, "It's time." Anxiously, she clutches the baby close to her chest and walks ahead of me into the jail reception. We sign in.

I mentally review the number of visits I've made into the jail and wonder what it must feel like for this mother to enter for the first time, not to mention under these circumstances. We turn and enter the unfriendly Visitor's Room, a dismal space divided down the center by a wall of glassed-in cubicles. All visitors line up along the solid wall opposite their assigned windows and wait for their inmate to take a cubicle.

Kristina appears, smiles, and takes a hold of her receiver, never taking her eyes off her baby. Happy and sad feelings rush inside me as I observe mother, child, and grandmother try and communicate through a glass shield. It's awkward and tight, frustration is high, yet grandmother remains resolute as she encourages Pamela to talk to her mother. I am touched, and feel a real connection from Kristina's mother toward Kristina.

After 15 minutes pass, it's time for us to leave and let Barbara and the other family members say good-byes to Kristina.

Outside, the temperature has soared to 90 degrees in the time we've been at the jail. Barbara and I have met Kristina's family and witnessed a close and painful event. Kristina is maturing through experiences few mothers anticipate for their daughters.

Kristina will learn to survive the toughest section of California women's prison, away from her mother and daughter. At least she had the bonding on this day to carry her to her next home.

Barbara's quiet in the car on the way back. Discontented with the outcome, I need to find out more about Edwards' history in Crestline and decide to call the detective in Big Bear who knew Kristina well enough to have her help him out on an arrest of a transient, Joey. Joey was the one who escorted Kristina and her girlfriend to the Donner Ranch in Poway the first time.

253. Inmate Edwards talking to her baby

The detective in Big Bear said Kristina hung around with shady characters. Her selection of friends was bad, but basically, Kristina's not a bad person.

She had no parents, and no place to stay. She wasn't in school. What happens to truants?
Detective: Nothing. The situation ends up with kids having rights and they don't go to school.

The detective says Kristina "helped him out" in getting the transient kid, Joey. Joey was Kristina's friend's boyfriend. He took Kristina and the girlfriend to Poway and introduced them to the Donner Ranch gang. After getting some pot, they went back to the mountains where the detective picked up Joey.

I tell him that Kristina went to Ray Lang's following the Joey episode and then after meeting Klotz, decided on making another journey.

"I can see how the situation happened," he says.

I explain that the jury believed that Kristina picked up a vulnerable schizophrenic, lured him to Poway, and helped to kill him. Lang lied to the jury when he said he had not done drugs and was going for a job interview the next day. The prosecution said the motive was Klotz's $600 SSI check and Edwards set Klotz up.

The detective says "She wouldn't premeditate and take anyone for a crime. No way."

6/11/96 9:00 a.m. Jail, B Housing

Dr. Bull sees me from a distance and enters B housing. He has returned from a two-week vacation and says he hasn't touched base with Rolenda. I tell him the courts are considering a 12-year sentence.

Several deputies escort a sluggish Rolenda inside the courtroom. She's in chains, her face down. She's holding the letter I'd written to the court on her behalf. When she sees me, she shouts, "Susan, what you mean saying I'm crazy? Why you say something like that!" Rolenda has misread my comment.

After today, in the jail with Rolenda, and seeing her act out last week, I'm more concerned about her future. "She doesn't know her butt from a hole-in-the-wall," her attorney tells me. She has four assault charges, two for beating a pregnant woman in the stomach and pulling a knife on the woman's husband. Rolenda denies the charges, saying the man poked her in the buttocks and she slapped him.

Outside the room I hear screaming, and I'm told there's a fire. A deputy runs, carrying a gas mask and wearing an oxygen tank on his back. B2 is in total Lockdown. It's dark. No one comes out of the cells. Dr. Bromley moves toward the exit, and the deputies warn him not to open the door. He exits anyway. Minutes later the Lockdown is over. An inmate cries out: she was in the shower when they turned off the water; her eyes are burning with soap. I see Kristina asking to get out of her unit to talk to me.

Edwards enters the Pro Visit Room

Why didn't the detective come down and testify?
Edwards: Because they didn't even bring it up in the trial that I helped out with getting Joey. The judge didn't allow it.

You think you're going to be leaving tonight?
I hope not, but I have a feeling they're gonna say, "Edwards, roll up at midnight." I don't wanna spend the rest of my life in prison. Three of us girls were sitting and talking when all of these little boy-like girls came in and it was like the homeboys just came over 'cause they looked like the guys. They came over to me. This feeling came over me like the guys are coming to visit. I felt so stupid. I've always been a good person when I was off the drugs. I always helped people out. I wasn't really like they said, a bad person. I used to get angry when I was drunk, but nothing like what happened that night.

Prison reality is taking place for Kristina. I leave the jail, carrying her personal property that her mother failed to take on Saturday. Now it's up to me to ship it to her mother or the jail will dispose of it.

6/14/96 Jail, Ellen Conner

Conner: Well, Kristina's gone, and she's on the same bus with Little One. Kristina was a different girl after talking to her mother before she left. She said the weirdest thing when we were talking about the baby. She said, "Ellen, my baby's ugly." Isn't that sad? She doesn't know what the baby's supposed to look like other than TV commercials. And Rolenda? Four assaults? That's hard to understand. She's going to go to some state-provided facility without special studies or meds, get out, act out abusively. How can anyone sentence this girl to a term where she'll get out and kill someone? I mean if she went to a respectable place, four years, did her work and got an education, but no. She's going to some situation not dissimilar from Las Colinas.

6/15/96 Courthouse

We're trying to understand what happens in abusive relationships that causes people to evolve into developmentally-deprived states. Kristina and Rolenda demonstrate the pain.

I talk to Rolenda Banks' attorney, Begovitch. He says that Rolenda's Arraignment Hearing sent down another new charge. He's certain she'll be found competent to stand trial. Dr. Bull's writing a report for him. Begovitch rushes along, saying public defenders are overworked.

Rolenda grows more agitated. The jail experiments with her. The system has changed her attorneys three times in one year.

She calls back, sobbing and unable to get her breath. Word had gotten through to her that she wasn't going to court until June 17th. Her wailing is like that of a small child being abused. She begs for help.

7/9/96 Court for Rolenda Banks

Rolenda's not in the courtroom. The room is empty except for the bailiff and a secretary. We enter and take seats in the center of the large rotunda, a courtroom large enough for a trial twice the size of Edwards'. The DA appears, dressed in a flashy pantsuit. Her loud harsh voice resonates through the courtroom as she welcomes another DA, who asks, "Are you going to perform on the comedy hour?"

The loud DA replies seriously, "I haven't done that in ages." She sits back. "The hecklers are so funny. They think they're bad, but they are the easiest to shut down."

Begovitch enters. Young and tall, he turns to the two of us, "Who are you?"

The courtroom is quiet. The marshal has gone for Rolenda.

The dressed-up attorney appears to have no regard for anyone. Begovitch is physically present, but that's about all. Noise breaks out in the hallway. Two marshals enter. Five others follow clutching a handcuffed and shackled Rolenda. How will any letter to the judge override this drama? Rolenda's face is pressed against a wall, handcuffed. She looks over her shoulder and cries out to the short marshal, "I'm tired of this bitch on me. Bad-bootie bitch! I'm walkin' on chains and she's pullin' on me!"

Begovitch watches from the corner of his eye as his client is reined in. "Rolenda, calm down," he says, his face in his papers.

Barbara grabs the armrest of my seat and moans. Marshals are moving about securing Rolenda in a seat next to the witness stand in the jury box. The "bitch" marshal is behind her.

"Bitch! Get your fuckin' hands off me. Bitch with a flat bootie, flat-bootie bitch!"

The drugs are working against Rolenda. Curses continue to fly in the courtroom. The comedy-act blonde DA has moved up into the gallery, sitting with legs crossed and showing calf, pointing her finger. It has a mini-cast on it. "Broke it in a biking outing this weekend."

Rolenda sees us. Once again we hear, "Bitch, get your fucking hands off me! You don't go pulling anyone in chains and feet shackled up a fucking hallway! You don't have to pull me. I was going. Don't any of you understand?"

"I won't pull you, alright?" the marshal says.

Barbara and I say nothing. Rolenda grows quiet, like a child after an outburst. The judge enters. He's a large, red-faced man with yellowed hair. He settles and reads his paperwork for a few moments. Then he lifts his head long enough to declare, "Miss Banks, I sentence you to four years in state prison."

The marshals pull Rolenda out of her seat to stand before the judge. She reacts as though she knew the outcome.

"Fuck you, old man!" she shouts indignantly. Barbara misses the armrest this time and grabs my thigh. Surprised by the outburst, I'm thinking, what does society expect? As Rolenda is hauled out with shackles and chains, she says to Begovitch, "And you! You didn't get me any deals. You didn't help me any!"

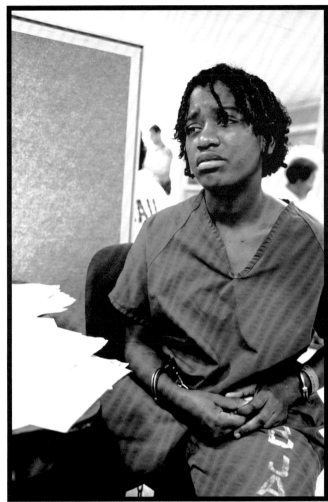

254-255

7/11/96 8:15 a.m. Pro Visit, B Housing

Kristina's gone, and Rolenda's soon to leave. We anticipate the jail wants us to leave as well. The majority of our interviews in the last months have revolved around those two inmates. I decide to call out Danielle Lopez to see how she's holding up inside. We fill out two cards, one for Banks and one for Lopez.

The clerk says, "You going to B?"

I stand in front of Release and Booking. We have the same gear. We're dressed as we normally are in street clothes. But everything around us at the jail seems different. The light is different. The Pro Visit area is more open. The place smells different, too, stuffy, like a nursing home. Barbara pushes me along. "Feels like the last walk," she says. We look inside each door with a glance. A deputy brings along an inmate in a yellow nightie. Deputies shout, "We need backup for a parole visit for Banks." Dep. Lemos escorts us to B housing's Pro Visit and tells me that we'll see Lopez up at the regular Pro Visit after Rolenda. We pass Dr. Bull's group

session. He's in there, listening to someone; the room is full. He doesn't notice us.

The hallway smells nasty. We go into the unit, and the smell intensifies. It's vomit. We sit on the wooden bench in front of B Control. No Rolenda.

Dep. Logan shouts, "I told someone to get this trash picked up."

No one hustles around. No one does anything. After five minutes, the back of my nose burns from the foul odor. I can taste the stomach acid. "What's going on in here, do you think?" Barbara asks.

We wait in the hall. Dep. Lemos says they're getting Banks.

Three deputies escort Rolenda. She has an attitude. She doesn't smile when she sees us.

Banks: "Bitch, I don't have to do anything."

My mouth drops open. We're going to see her with the same attitude she had in the courtroom. They open B and escort her in. She stands in front of us. The three deputies hang around. The cuffs are removed. The deputies leave.

Barbara talks to Rolenda; she maintains her tough persona. I point out my yellow plastic sparkler ring. Rolenda smiles like a child. I show her how it twinkles. She melts down and laughs. Dr. Bull enters and says he heard Rolenda acted out in court. The moment catches us and we all laugh.

You were a bad girl in court.
Banks: I don't care. My attorney lied.

254-255. Inmate Banks;
256-258. Inmate Lopez

256-258

9:00 a.m.   Pro Visit, Lopez

Lopez arrives with an escort from A housing

How are you doing?
Lopez: Better. Balanced. I've been in jail eight months now.

You still like A better than B housing?
Yes I do. I like it better. Except for my roommate. I don't get along with her. She's got a problem. She talks to herself loudly. I can't concentrate. She's scary. I lie in bed with my covers over my head.

What's better about A housing?
I wake up at 6:00 a.m., and I don't have to stand in line for food. I watch the Discovery Channel and educational stuff. A deputy brought me a candy bar, soup, some crackers. I never have any problems with the deputies. I don't want to get yelled at or pushed against the wall or put in the chair. I just want to be good. I like being truthful. I was raised Catholic, and it's the only way I know how to do it. I believe in the way they worship, but I am sick of behaving sometimes. Like the other day, I was just fooling with the deputy—when he opened my cell door and I was covered up. I screamed, and I just went, "Ahh," and he goes, "What is it?" I was playing with myself. I just wanted him to blush.

Last time we saw you, you were reading Anne Rice.
She's a gothic writer. Plus I like educational books, and they don't have any in here. I want autobiographies and history, periods around the 14th century. I want to try Nostradamus. I loved *Wuthering Heights*. That was a good one. My little dictionary is my Holy Bible.

You say that you have special tastes.
Attention. I demanded it. I'm very picky about psychiatrists, ice cream, clothing, and shoes. I was born spoiled, raised spoiled, and will be spoiled. I love it. I like expensive things, like Todd Oldman. I think on my 21st birthday I'm finally going to get a ruby ring.

You're certain that you're going to prison?
I don't understand my case. I did something that was wrong. I had trouble with boyfriends, drugs. I'm looking at maybe 15 years for harming another person. I chased him. I was on medication too much. My parents wouldn't believe me about him because I'd just come out of a mental hospital. Now they believe me. They paid the bill. He had 23 stitches. He has a past of doing the same thing. He'd done it to my cousin. I put something to an end. I had this anger. I let it out that way. The guy's wanting me to do the maximum. I want to go to prison to read more books. I told my

> I'm very picky about
> psychiatrists, ice cream,
> clothing, and shoes.
>
> *Inmate Lopez*

attorney that I want to plead guilty. He said, "No, Danielle, you can't plead guilty or you're going to get 15-to-life!"

Is this the first time you've been locked in a room?
No, when I was 14 my brother beat me, and I had to stay in my room. I didn't have a TV or radio.

Did your mother know you were afraid of your brother?
Yes, but she didn't do anything. My father scolded him, but he wasn't punished. He got away with it. I wanted it stopped. He was seven years older. He was angry at everyone. But that's what got me into books. I was so bored I started reading Jackie Collins. I was glued to it 'cause it was the raw sex and raw material. I daydreamed the highlife. Hollywood. It made me relieved to know human behavior could be that way. I don't consider myself a sex symbol, but I like to go to Mexico, dress up, change everything.

What would you have done if it were your child being beaten?
I would've stopped it.

How?
Better than my parents did.

How did this make you feel, locked in your room as a teen?
It caused a lot of pain. I wanted to kill the pain so I started drinking. It would make me feel better. Then I was doing drugs. I got higher and higher until I graduated to the big one.

Heroin?
Yes.

Did your brother use drugs?
No. It was a tradition, though, on my dad's side.

Were you trying to do Jackie Collins' Hollywood life in Tijuana?
Yes, I was! I was dressing elegant, the best I can and looking the best I can and getting free drinks. That was my goal!

Why do you feel you landed in here?
I had a nervous breakdown. Everything crashes. I cry and I'm sad. Out there I had the best doctor, very smart, highly trained. In here they're play doctors. I'm helpless.

Did you have problems in B housing with the sexuality?
Yes. It was confusing to me. I told my mom on the phone, and she got upset. I see it around, and it just makes me feel like it's right. She said, "No, no, no! I'll throw you out of my house!" I know what my feelings are, but I keep them hidden.

Is there anyone here that you like?
Not really. I was on the patio with this girl, Rolenda. She has no family. She's very unique. I study her and watch her, the way she talks.

Does she make you laugh?
She does. Yes. I know you know her. She wants you to send her 30 pounds of coffee and oysters when she goes to prison. But I see the serious side of her, and we talk serious all the time. She pretty much can tell me most things, I admire her because she's a strong-willed woman and I tell her that. I'm the one who's quiet as a mouse, and I just go with the flow in here. Outside, I'm more stable, I can stand my ground. Inside I don't wanna get pushed against the wall or put in the chair. I watched Rolenda get put in the chair by 12 deputies after she stripped her bed off the wall. She's strong! They video taped her, too. When they put her in the chair, she goes, "You'll remember this day."

259

260

10:00 a.m. A Housing, Rolenda Banks' cell

I put in a blue card for Rolenda. The clerk denies us. I look at her, distressed.

Clerk: Captain's orders.

I call Ben McLaughlin. He tells me that he'll talk to the Captain and it shouldn't be a problem. He does ask, "How much longer are you planning on being at the jail?"

An inmate wearing a mask passes us. She's headed for transport to a jail that has an Isolation Unit for inmates with TB. Dep. Keys sees us and stops to talk. We tell her we've been told we can't see Rolenda. She says, "Follow me," and walks us back to Rolenda's cell. We can briefly talk to her through her door.

261

262

259. Sally port doors, Control; 260. Deputy Keys;
261. Deputy Keys; 262. Inmate Banks

8/5/96 8:30 a.m. Captain's office

Ben arrives. The Captain's not in for us to discuss a final meeting with Rolenda. Ben and his former secretary, Sue, talk about the difficulty in dealing with new captains. Ben admits this Captain's from a different school. Ben also tells me that he's retiring. I quickly make an appointment to interview Nurse Carlos in E housing, the gentleman in charge of the only unit that Ben and Dr. Bull feel offers any hope in the jail.

   Later that day, I call the Captain for permission to see Rolenda before she leaves for prison. He says, "This is in total conflict with everything I ever learned since 1971. What will it take to get you out of here?"

8:00 p.m. Phone call, Ellen Conner

Conner: There's a lot of just really sad cases in here now. It's incredible.

Looks like we're leaving.

Oh, no, you're just getting started!

8/13/96 10:30 a.m. Jail

The clerk leaves Barbara and me in the sally port for 20 minutes. She returns and puts me through a drill. Why do I want to see Rolenda? I somehow convince her that I need to see the inmate one last time. Finally, the door opens. We enter the jail, but it's different.

   Dep. Keys approaches and says, "Come on, I'll take you to her cell." Rolenda's asleep. I take several photos through the window in the door. I feel someone behind me. It's the Captain.

Captain: Don't do anything to wake her up. We want to get her on the bus tonight headed for prison, alive!

He stares at me with a look I imagine he would use on Rolenda.

264. Nurse Carlos

Nurse Carlos

What happens in E housing?

The Habilitative Treatment program. At present, we can only afford 12 inmates in this unit. They have to be voluntary ones. Some are depressed and have a difficult time adjusting to life circumstances. Others have psychiatric disorders. It could be someone who's been using drugs for a long time and hears voices, or someone who hasn't been using drugs and has psychiatric disorders. We deal with a lifetime of behaviors. Even though the group process is rewarding, and they see light, it's comfortable to go back to what's familiar. Criminal thinking, criminal behavior, and antisocial behavior aren't always effectively connected. They may not have the ability to feel somebody else's pain. They may be too distant from their own. In E housing, honesty is paramount. We talk about values. We clarify their values and talk about the conflict of values they grew up with and how behaviors and values were changed by life circumstances.

What happens to a woman who has several children, yet repeatedly comes back to jail?

The family structure promotes this behavior. Everyone should be held accountable for her actions, but you find the majority of the women in jail were abused or neglected, and they produce children when they are still children themselves. It's not only values; the mental structure isn't there. We develop bodies, but we don't develop minds. In many cases they were allowed to make decisions on their own, without parental supervision.

With supervision, mistakes can be caught?

Their families tried to fix the child, but they don't try to fix themselves. In essence, what you see in children acting out are the symptoms of the family. Parents who didn't mature along with their bodies find it difficult to accept that it was something they did that caused this child to act out in the way he or she did. It's not the first time that the child acts out, but maybe it's the first time the father kicks the mother or it's the first time the father comes home drunk. The next morning the mother's telling the children, "Go outside. Father feels sick." These dependencies are established rather subtly within the family. It's not something dramatic. It's day-to-day occurrences.

So the child feels the blame?

No. The child learns the behavior! The mother says, "If I ever catch you smoking, I'm going to kill you." But the mother smokes. Double messages from parents. We try to teach our children to be independent, but the moment they try to do it, we want to hold them back. That's confusing. We have a combination of bad rules that create double messages. When children make mistakes, there's no support to go back to, or they find a support system in a gang. We all grow up to be loyal to our families in one way or another, and encounter situations in here of women sexually molested by a father or uncle and they have developed a history of bad decisions. Now they have children. She's in jail, and her child is with her father. The inmate finds it impossible to say, "My father did it." She'll be perceived as a bad child in the eyes of the family. Underneath is the anger, hurt, and pain. Instead of saying, "Ouch, this hurts," they get angry and leave, not understanding there's hurt and pain that they need to acknowledge. We help them to experience the pain, but they're going to wake up tomorrow alive.

What's behind sarcasm?

It's a defense. It's witty and clever. It prevents them from feeling uncomfortable and motionless. They don't need rewards from outside because they reward themselves. What's interesting is to discover what's being defended. The injured child, unless she acknowledges some of the tragedy and pain, uses humor to keep the family together. They're read as "You're pretty weird," or "Oh, you're smart." When a child uses it as an adult, and people push her away, she's wondering why. It's magical thinking.

As a child, it kept you from difficult situations, like parents fighting and you see problems left and right but eventually they're getting back together. As an adult, with an abusive husband, you say, "Things will get better." These defenses can kill you because we didn't mature emotionally. We have a great percentage of women unable to mature emotionally, who end up breaking the rules and going to jail. If something happens that is dramatic, for instance, sexual abuse, physical abuse, or neglect, we're at a particular time in development that's stunted. You may be 14 years of age, but if the abuse was at age eight, all of the developmental stages have to follow a certain degree of chronological pattern and unless you dealt with it and moved on, you'll remain stuck.

It seems pretty negative, doesn't it?

No, because 25 years ago we didn't have a group of ladies who sat together and talked about sexual abuse. Women didn't talk about their parents. It was taboo. Today, we have more and more people taking less care of their children. We have more extremes. We'll have one breakthrough a week, and if it makes a difference for someone, it'll make a difference for someone else; maybe not during the group period, but maybe in two weeks, two months, or two years they'll say, "That's what we were talking about."

Describe a breakthrough.

The moment the women say, "The past was horrible, but I need to start worrying about myself now. I can only work on the present. I can only change the future." There are people who spend a lifetime as children, developmentally, with magical thinking. They wish their past would get better. The more these ladies wish for a better past, the more they forget the present. We have had young ladies who don't believe that there're men out there who can treat them with respect. They don't believe there're men who don't go drink with their buddies, and then come home to beat the crap out of them. There are family systems in jail, too. These ladies have cousins in one unit, aunts in another, and mothers in prison. Their children come visit mom for a Contact Visit and know when they break the law at 16, this is where they're going to live. There are welfare families. There are jail families.

It seems some children aren't taught the difference between good and bad.

Exactly. Children who are good and act bad at times, we don't take the time to tell them the difference. We have to say, "I love you, but I don't care for what you do." It is the same for adults. We learn we love our parents no matter what they do. In fact, we need to say, "I hate you for what you did, but I still love the image of having a father [or mother]." The more dysfunctional we become, the more vicariously we try to love our children, laying expectations on them of things we couldn't do while in jail. This is a conflict.

But values depend on feelings.

Right. Women from all different cultures in life haven't been allowed to experience feelings. They use drugs because their feelings are getting too intense. I think that some of those ladies don't know how to feel. I'm talking about the feelings that require adaptation on a daily basis. They can't identify feelings they've never touched. They merely know that they hurt, and they want to avoid pain. They teach denial. "I'm hurting," you say. "No, you're not. Go to your room!" your parent shouts. A child learns to fantasize and daydream to not feel the pain. She learns to detach and develop defense mechanisms if she were involved in sexual abuse. Then she takes those defense mechanisms into adult life. Her life becomes a shambles. Eventually her defense mechanisms kill her.

What is the developmental model?

Well, I think that you have the stages of development described by Erik Erickson. They follow a chronological pattern. Every time you experience abuse, unless you deal with it, you get stuck, and as you move on, your emotions don't develop. In here, we're talking about women who are in their 20s, 30s, and 40s, but are still developmentally in puberty or adolescence. Let me ask you a question. How are you going to deal with your own grieving when you leave this jail?

You take me by surprise. I'll miss the conversations. The women led me to believe that my work would in some way ease their sorrow and pain.

We deal with a lifetime of behaviors. Even though the group process is rewarding, and they see light, it's comfortable to go back to what's familiar. Criminal thinking, criminal behavior, and antisocial behavior aren't always effectively connected. They may not have the ability to feel somebody else's pain. They may be too distant from their own.

Everyone should be held accountable for her actions, but you find the majority of the women in jail were abused or neglected, and they produce children when they are still children themselves. It's not only values; the mental structure isn't there. We develop bodies, but we don't develop minds.

In essence, what you see in children acting out are the symptoms of the family. Parents who didn't mature along with their bodies find it difficult to accept that it was something they did that caused this child to act out in the way he or she did.

Nurse Carlos

265. Deputy Williams

On one level our task is to provide better services for the invisible women caught in our criminal justice system. These are women whose lives represent all women's issues— magnified. On a deeper level, we must question whether therapeutic, healing care can be provided in the ultimate system of oppression and domination.

   Our criminal justice system is in desperate need of repair and revision. What changes would make a difference? The Human Kindness Foundation (1995) has suggested "Seven Ways to Fix the Criminal Justice System."[40]

Stephanie Covington, Ph.D.

DOLLS

To this crib I always took my doll . . . It puzzles me now to remember with what absurd sincerity I doted on this little toy, half fancying it alive and capable of sensation. I could not sleep unless it was folded in my night-gown; and when it lay there safe and warm, I was comparatively happy, believing it to be happy likewise.[41]

Jane Eyre (1847)

266. E housing, cell bunks; 267. C housing

PART FIVE   DEEPER LOOK

What can society do? There is prevention, damage control,
and punishment. We can try to prevent immature people from
parenting by doing a lot of public education about the difficulty
of being a good parent. We can open our jails to visitations so
that young people can see the conditions in which adults who
were deprived, abused, abandoned as children live. We can
point out to our young women that babies are cute, cuddly, and
needy, but that they are also little tyrants depriving parents from
their sleep, costing a lot of money, needing constant care. For
damage control, we can assign a good caretaker (social worker)
to every family that needs one. Very expensive, but less than
the cost of juvenile halls, jails, prisons etc. Punishment and
rehabilitation are more complex. None of these women will
become "healthy" through punishment. For some of them it may
be too late for rehabilitation—nothing will mend their broken
souls . . . For others there is some hope, but it will involve long-
term therapeutic involvement on a group or individual basis.

Society cannot raise children. Parents raise children. Society
can only be supportive of the parents.[42]

Maryam Razavi Newman, Ph.D.

How did these women get in this place?

Forbidden wishes, buried trauma, shame and guilt, sadness and despair, obfuscated thoughts, and disorganization. Have they reasonable recognition of their adult lives and/or childhoods?

Inside Las Colinas Detention Facility, inmates talk and act out of diffused states. Irritations, confinement, and fears trigger destructive thoughts and behaviors. Not all inmates operate in disguise. Many of them are straightforward, yet their histories of abuse and pain have not healed.

During a lecture series on child abuse and trauma in Sacramento, Dr. Bruce Perry asks, "How can someone develop the capacity to stalk, torture, murder, and mutilate another human being and feel no remorse—even feel pleasure?" He answers his own question with, "Experience in early life determines core neurobiology. Experience, not genetics, results in the critical neurobiological factors associated with violence.

Talking about a little girl to demonstrate normalcy, Dr. Perry says, "When she is not participating in a scheduled 'externally focused' activity, she will become more internally focused. Her imagination and creativity takes over. She will find and create toys from what is available—sticks become dolls, dolls become royalty, and these members of royalty become actors in the child's play—rocks become blocks, form and maintain healthy emotional relationships. An attachment bond has unique properties. The capacity to create these special relationships begins in early childhood."

269. F housing Inmates

Each year in the United States alone, there are over three million children that are abused or neglected. These destructive experiences impact the developing child, increasing risk for emotional, behavioral, academic, social, and physical problems throughout life.[43]

Bruce D. Perry. M.D., Ph.D., and John Marcellus. M.D.

The profound impact of domestic violence, community violence, physical and sexual abuse, and other forms of predatory or impulsive assault cannot be overestimated. Violence impacts the victims, the witnesses—and, ultimately, us all. Understanding and modifying our violent nature will determine, in large part, the degree to which we will successfully 'adapt' to the challenges of the future—the degree to which future generations of human beings can actually experience humanity.[44]

Bruce Perry. M.D., Ph.D.

TRAUMATIC EXPERIENCES THEORY AND DEVELOPMENT

With optimal experiences, the brain develops healthy, flexible, and diverse capabilities. When there is disruption of the timing, intensity, quality, or quantity of normal developmental experiences, however, there may be a devastating impact on neurodevelopment — and, thereby, function. For millions of abused and neglected children, the nature of their experiences adversely influences the development of their brains. During the traumatic experience, these children's brains are in a state of fear-related activation. This activation of key neural systems in the brain leads to adaptive changes in emotional, behavioral, and cognitive functioning to promote survival. Yet, persisting or chronic activation of this adaptive fear response can result in the maladaptive persistence of a fear state. This activation causes hypervigilance, increased muscle tone, a focus on threat-related cues (typically non-verbal), anxiety, behavioral impulsivity—all of which are adaptive during a threatening event, yet become maladaptive when the immediate threat has passed.[45]

Bruce D. Perry, M.D., Ph.D.

"In the United States alone, at least five to physical abuse, domestic

During a lecture series on child abuse and trauma in Sacramento, Perry asks, "How can someone develop the capacity to stalk, torture, murder, and mutilate another human being and feel no remorse—even feel pleasure?"[46] He answers his own question with, "Experience in early life determines core neurobiology. Experience, not genetics, results in the critical neurobiological factors associated with violence."

Quotations are excerpts from a lecture series with Dr. Bruce Perry, M.D., Ph.D.

The Brain

The human brain is an amazing and complex organ. It allows us to think, act, feel, laugh, speak, create, and love. The brain mediates all of the qualities of humanity, good and bad. Yet the core "mission" of the brain is to sense, perceive, process, store, and act on information from the external and internal environment to promote survival. In order to do this, the human brain has evolved an efficient and logical organization structure.

Brain Development

At birth, the human brain is undeveloped. Not all of the brain's areas are organized and fully functional. It is during childhood that the brain matures and the whole set of brain-related capabilities develop in a sequential fashion. We crawl before we walk, we babble before we talk.

The development of the brain during infancy and childhood follows the bottom-up structure. The most regulatory, bottom regions of the brain develop first, followed, in sequence, by adjacent but higher, more complex regions.

The process of sequential development of the brain and, of course, the sequential development of function, is guided by experience. The brain develops and modifies itself in response to experience. Neurons and neuronal connections (synapses) change in an activity-dependent fashion. This "use-dependent" development is the key to understanding the impact of neglect and trauma on children.

These areas organize during development and change in the mature brain in a "use-dependent" fashion. The more a certain neural system is activated, the more it will "build-in" this neural state; what occurs in this process is the creation of an "internal representation" of the experience corresponding to the neural activation. This "use-dependent" capacity to make an "internal representation" of the external or internal world is the basis for learning and memory. The simple and unavoidable result of this sequential neurodevelopment is that the organizing, "sensitive" brain of an infant or young child is more malleable to experience than a mature brain. While experience may alter and change the functioning of an adult, experience literally provides the organizing framework for an infant and child.

The brain is most plastic (receptive to environmental input) in early childhood. The consequence of sequential development is that as different regions are organizing, they require specific kinds of experience targeting the region's specific function (e.g., visual input while the visual system is organizing) in order to develop normally. These times during development are called critical or sensitive periods.[47]

The brain has a bottom-up organization. The bottom regions (i.e., brainstem and midbrain) control the most simple functions such as respiration, heart rate, and blood pressure regulation, while the top areas (i.e., limbic and cortex) control more complex functions such as thinking and regulating emotions.[48]

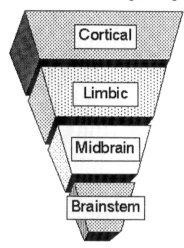

Abstract Thought
Concrete Thought
Affiliation
Attachment
Sexual Behavior
Emotional Reactivity
Motor Regulation
Arousal
Appetite/Satiety
Sleep
Blood Pressure
Heart Rate
Body Temperature

Discussion

These findings strongly suggest that when early life neglect is characterized by decreased sensory input (e.g., relative poverty of words, touch and social interactions) it will have a similar effect on humans as it does in other mammalian species. Sensory deprivation has been demonstrated to alter the physical growth and organization of the brain in animals.

The present studies suggest that the same is true for children globally neglected in the first three years of life. It is important to emphasize the timing of the neglect. The brain is undergoing explosive growth in the first years of life, and, thereby, is relatively more vulnerable to lack of organizing experiences during these periods. These unfortunate globally neglected children (some literally were raised in cages in dark rooms for the first years of their lives) appear to have altered brain growth.

There are likely many factors contributing to this observation. Nutrition is one key aspect. Based upon the relative impact on the brain as opposed to other growth, a total nutritional explanation is inadequate. It is likely that the actual lack of experiences (sound, smell, touch) associated with global neglect in these children plays a major role.

Volumetric studies of key areas are indicated, as are MRI studies to examine the functional impact of neglect, global or chaotic.[49]

million children are either victims of or witnesses violence, or community violence."

Dr. Bruce Perry, M.D., Ph.D.

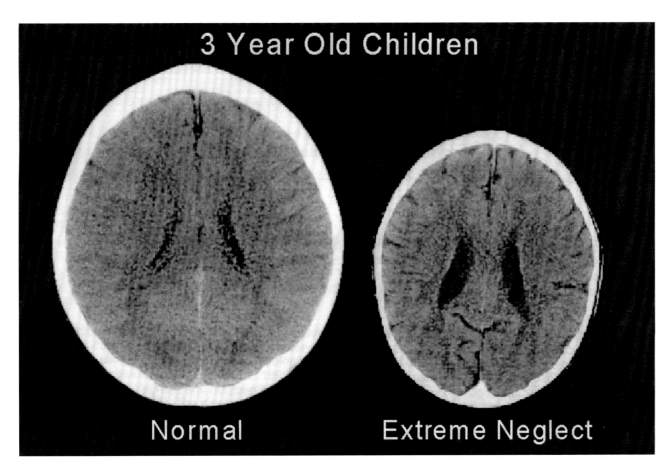

3 Year Old Children

Normal   Extreme Neglect

These images illustrate the negative impact of neglect on the developing brain. In the CT scan on the left is an image from a healthy three-year-old with an average head size. The image on the right is from a three-year-old child suffering from severe sensory-deprivation neglect. This child's brain is significantly smaller than average and has abnormal development of cortex.[50]

The impact of experiences on shaping the organization and functioning of the brain . . . we have learned a lot and have much more to study . . . but what we do know is that traumatic experiences can alter the actual physiological functioning and functional organization of the brain . . . and these changes appear to be related to, or even responsible for, a host of neuropsychiatric problems—including anxiety, dissociation, impulsivity, depression, poor self- esteem.[51]

In the United States alone, at least five million children are either victims of or witnesses to physical abuse, domestic violence, or community violence—all while they are bathed in the powerful images of television which over-represent violent acts and over-value the power of violence as a solution to conflict. (Perry, 1994a; Prothrow-Stith, 1991; Dodge et al., 1991; Osofsky, 1995)

The profound impact of domestic violence, community violence, physical and sexual abuse, and other forms of predatory or impulsive violence cannot be overestimated. Violence impacts the victims, the witnesses—and, ultimately, us all. Understanding and modifying our violent nature will determine, in large part, the degree to which we will successfully "adapt" to the challenges of the future—the degree to which future generations of human beings can experience humanity.[52]

It is not the finger pulling the trigger that kills; it is not the penis that rapes–it is the brain. In order to understand violence we need to understand the organization and functioning of the brain.

In many ways, the brain is what creates you . . . it creates internal representations of what happens in the outside world. Girls often have a different response to stress that doesn't include hyperactivity. They tend to withdraw into an internal world or become numb to their feelings. Since they don't act out, they may be overlooked by teachers or mental-health professionals.[53]

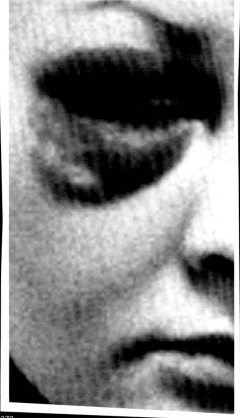
270

In my case I was one of those
disfunctional children as well as
a drug user, By the age of 13 While
a normal 13 year who be out with
parents whopping for clothes for
their last year of Junior High
school. I was learned how to umix
(methenrphetamie?) Speed in a Spoon,
register (draw it in a syringe(needle)
and inject it in my arm. Oh, and
what a high, the ringing in your
ears, the sinsation of the rush,
I never felt anything like it. To
ume I found the solution to every
thing. See, all my life I searched
and searched for something to stop
the pain, the hurt and emptiness I
felt inside of ume since I was a
child.

Psychiatrist Judith Herman (1992) writes that there are three stages in the process of healing from trauma: safety, remembrance and mourning, and reconnection. "Survivors feel unsafe in their bodies. Their emotions and their thinking feel out of control. They also feel unsafe in relation to other people" (Herman, 1992, p. 160). Stage One (safety) addresses the woman's safety concerns in all of these domains. In the second stage of recovery (remembrance and mourning) the survivor tells the story of the trauma and mourns the old self that the trauma destroyed. In Stage Three (reconnection) the survivor faces the task of creating a future; now she develops a new self. As we have seen above, the difficulty is that many women are not safe in our criminal justice system where they are vulnerable to abuse and harassment from correctional staff.[54]

Stephanie Covington, Ph.D.

None of these women will become healthy through punishment. For some of them, it may be too late for rehabilitation—nothing will mend their broken souls.[55]

Maryam Razavi Newman, Ph. D.

270. Black eye
271- 291. (from left to right) 271. Inmate Edwards; 272. Inmate Lorinda; 273. Inmate Rolenda; 274. Inmate Sanders; 275. Inmate Teena;
276. Inmate Rolenda; 277. Inmate Jennifer; 278. Inmate Edwards; 279. Inmate Teena; 280. Inmate Julia; 281. Inmate Ameerah; 282.
Inmate Mindy; 283. Inmate Sanders; 284. Inmate Angie; 285. Inmate Sandy; 286. Inmate Lane; 287. Inmate Arlynn; 288. Inmate Tiffany;
289. Inmate Eloise; 290. Inmate DeeDee; 291. Inmate Ameerah

Inmate's Name: *Nombre del Encarcelado:*	Booking No.: *Número:*	Facility: *Cárcel:*	Housing Unit: *Tanque:*
Life Story.			19/1/98

Tonight and today as another day I'm going to remember on this Journey. You know in the beginning I would of never thought that coming back to Las Colinas would have had such miracles for me, But the truth of it is it has. Its brought me two things that once upon a Time I thought I lost and that is Life and Hope. Up until a few months ago, I lived day to day believing that these cement walls and Bobwire fences were the walls of my home. I never found myself imaging life on the outside or sitting at a table eating with my family. I didn't have that before I was incarcerated. Actually I lived one of the most disfunctional lives a Child and most imagine. I dont think anyone could ever fully understand, for the simple fact each and every individual goes through their own individual emotional and physical experiences, But my intentions are just in hopes to maybe find and help anyone who can relate. Who may feel somewhat of my words and will hold on. I dont know exactly where I'm going with all of this, Right now I'm just using this time to breathe and let out whats on my mind.

292. Inmate Edwards

In time I hope to help someone whether it be a young girl, Boy, maybe even a parent(s). I'd like to tell my story and I would really like to ask if you'll take your time to Listen. There might be something here that you can relate too, that you might be feeling or maybe later in life left to deal with. It might save your life, even your self being. And it can happen to you. Everybody, every teen, every inmate is subject to the games of life. No mention the consequences, that your left with, most of the time you don't even know its coming, till its to late, and either your dying dead in ditch, strung out on your friends toilet, because your out of dope, or even sitting in a courtroom shackled around your waist and ankles waiting for a jury to come in with a verdict. Believe it or not I've suffered all this situations and I may add that there is more. And as I sit and write today I am sitting in an 8 by 5 cell at LCDF awaiting a possibly retrial. Yes, once I was convicted, I automatically was entitled to an appeal and somehow someway my Judgement was reversed. (By the Lord) But you know something? It didn't make me as happy as you yourself would think it would. I had got so lost in the fantasy world inside those fences, that I actually believed that was my life. No stress, didn't exist. Why should it? You have your drugs (maybe not always the Drug of your choice) But its something that gets you high (So you think) and it numbs the pain for the time being till the doors are unlocked and you can trade something else out of you possessions, that your parents

family/friends have sent you. Or maybe you charge it 20/40 rotten monthly. Then you have your sexual pleasure which of course is the choice out of 4,000 women, or maybe you'll be a fortunant one to be on your knees in central Kitchen or bent over in the counselors office with a nice Looking Correctional officer, with his promises to take care of you and maybe bring you a bottle of perfume or something else you can profit from. Of course its worth all your self respect. Then of course your room and board. Furnished with personal clothing, televisions, radios and if your lucky, your lover and companion lives above you. What more could you possibly ask for? Especially when you have more there than ever did outside. And to be honest, I myself never felt more secure. And as far as I was concerned I could've lived the rest of my. side. Doing time.

In my case I was one of those disfunctional children as well as a drug user. By the age of 13 While a normal 13 year who be out with parents shopping for clothes for their last year of Junior High School. I was learned how to mix methenrphetamine? Speed in a spoon, register (draw it in a syringe/needle) and inject it in my arm. Oh, and what a high, the ringing in your ears, the sensation of the rush, I never felt anything like it. To me I found the solution to every thing. See, all my life I searched and searched for something to stop the pain, the hurt and emptiness I felt inside of me since I was a child. I could never pinpoint to

when it all started, But I knew when I started to Realize it. Some of you probably wonder where were the loving people that you yourselves call parents. I couldn't say that before or at least I was to ashamed to admit it. I had a mother and at one time a father, But the life behind the doors wasn't your average "leave it to Beaver." My father had a fetish for beating women. Strip them naked and deprive them of respect as so ego of man increased. My mother was very young when they met and I'll never know until I can bring myself to ask. Personally its something she doesn't prefer to talk about and now that I've witnessed I understand why. That woman went through hell. And what she was able to escape I lived for her. I remember witnessing my father hitting my mother in the mouth with a baseball bat, I believe it was behind her interrupting his sexual intercourse with a friend of hers returning home from work. There were times he would inject the north drugs to the point she'd be so incoherent she couldn't focus on me. Left me with a babysitter or maybe in a playpen at my grandmothers to witness homosexual conflict with a black male partner. Whatever happen to 'green eggs and ham. I guess I was a fortunant one. Eventually my parents seperated. I'm not exactly sure to the day I don't care I'm just glad we both made it alive.

OVER / VEA AL REVERSO

J-56 Side One (Rev. 4/98)

Kristina is back at Las Colinas on appeal of her 25-to-life murder sentencing. I ask Kristina to send me a journal of her thoughts and feelings as she experiences them while back in the jail. Kath Anderson responds to the journal as a former inmate at Las Colinas and a former prisoner at CIW, and writes back to Kristina.

Kristina's Journal

11/11/98

K.E.: This morning I woke up in a very good and pleasant mood. No negative attitudes or vibes. And dreams have stopped. I remember thinking I wished I would have had the paper and pencil near for all those thoughts I was having, but I do remember one and it was the uncomfortable feeling of thinking about the sheriffs reading my story that went out previously. But it's my only alternative, plus I'm not holding anything back, anymore. Those parts of my life are gone. I washed them away as I wrote them. I'll keep the good memories and use the bad ones as learning tools. You benefit from both.

K.A.: It took me a long time to make new memories that were strong enough, both bad and good, to overshadow the memories I kept so closely wound around me for the first half of my life. They served their purpose, then, as K. says. Now I need different ones to draw from.

K.E.: It's a gloomy day outside. One of those days you lie around in bed in flannel pajamas, snuggled under your comforter, watching movies and drinking hot chocolate. Just writing that, I thought about being snuggled up in bed while Mom was in the other room cooking turkey. The scent coming and filling the whole house. The holidays are coming up. I'm not quite sure if I'll be here or back up in Chowchilla. But wherever I am, I hope–know–I'll hold together and make the best of it

I wrote my Mom today. I want to make sure that I help her see positive in everything and that defeat doesn't mean loss. I love her so much and I miss her so. It's still hard. I'm still going through this painful process of healing and changing and letting go. It gets easier the more I realize I'm able to approach things correctly. Just because there's no instant response doesn't mean I'm not progressing or accomplishing. I'm not a bad person! Now, my subconscious mind switches on so often. I think before acting. If I continue to do something I know is wrong, the guilt is automatically felt. I feel that is exactly what happened. I made a commitment to God that I took very seriously and when I felt that evil reappearing, I felt so guilty. Even if it's just a minute thing. Patience is a tool.

My mood has changed a little. I'm still a little down. But I think part of it's weight gain and my monthly time. I haven't really thought about the situation itself. But about how fast the 17th came up. Yes. I wonder where I'll be a week from now. To be honest, I really don't feel ready to go back to prison and I wouldn't mind staying here a little longer. This trip has really had its offerings and brought me to realize a lot. I'm going to remember this for a very long time–actually, for the rest of my life. Sometimes, when I think about it, I can't believe all of this is still happening. How did I get here? I mean, I know how I got here, but how did I survive it all? Was it the numbness all of my life? I'm very surprised I didn't go crazy. But, I did almost lose it. Then, everything started to fall into place and make sense. Here and there little pieces would form a solution in my mind. I'd put them all together and allow myself to see a way out, instead of continuing to torture myself.

Through the trials, through the falls and while I still continue to stumble. I deeply believe God won't leave me. I feel He's right there behind me. Every move I make, I think first. It's a guidance I've always longed for. I've always looked in the wrong places, either with a lover or maybe with a mother figure. I never tried looking above, or in a mirror. Nobody knows what's gone inside of me all these years. The battles between me and I. The suffering, self-inflicted when it wasn't really ever my fault. I think of all those times when my aunt called me a whore because I didn't stop my uncle from touching me. My father, accusing me of not loving him because I wouldn't sleep with him. Being verbally abused and rejected. All the times I beat myself up for others' mistakes and neglect, of life's real pleasures because I could never be happy. Looking at all of that, I see life so full ahead of me now, so much to live for. Twenty-two years and it feels like ages. Amazing.

Desiree and I were no longer an item, but we were on and off with seeing each other. and then I had Jeanette, too. But it wasn't the same. It was a mess, but it was drama and kept me busy. I don't only drive them crazy–myself too. What I think I liked most about being with Desiree was her sternness, her discipline. The chance to love someone special. I could make her feel. With Jeanette, it was a close friendship. The closeness and bonding I never really had. I never had a friend that I didn't end up sleeping with. We had secrets, the staying up late, talking about the future and things we'd done. Then, like in every other friendship I'd had, it led to sex. I saw it as a way to escape my own weaknesses and fears. So intimacy later turned into misery. Once again I'm left without a friend. Now, it's down the tubes. I can't go on like this. I've gotten lost down memory lane.

I cleaned up and tried to have a better attitude with my roommate. I guess it all started last night. She thought I was jealous of her going home. Really I was discouraged because of my visit, and other personal things that had to do with memories.

11/15/98

K.E.: Well, last night's medication kicked my butt and I was out for the count. Got up this morning and felt fabulous.

11/18/98

K.E.: Well, I'm not exactly sure where I left off. I just know that these last two days have been hell on my insides. We went to court yesterday. Got up at 2:30 a.m., got dressed, tied the curls up. I had brand new socks and almost felt as if it were the first day at school. After getting ready, I read some passages in my Bible and prayed. I felt so much better. The girl next door was going to court too, and we would be the only yellow-banders, besides this Cuban. The only English word she knew was the "F" word and she spoke it a lot. Talk about a good day to go to court. After being patted down we were lined up and had to wait for all the general population. Five of the ten girls were involved with the girl I'm in PC with. I just smiled at all of them.

K.A.: The only yellow-banders. Forgive me please, K., for all the times I was hateful to yellow-banders. I never even bothered to find out why they wore the yellow band. I just acted like they weren't even there. Worse, when I was very young, I threw things in their hair and stole their lunches. It never occurred to me that the stigma of the yellow band stayed with them. The band was prevalent in mental preparation for court day. I'm sorry, K., that you had to feel those things.

K.E.: I was in such a good mood. We rode on the bus. I expected to hear them shout obscenities. I even saw the most beautiful scenery I'd seen in the longest time. We were on the freeway. It was still hazy. It was only 6:30 a.m. Through one cloud, there was like a tear and through the middle came a beam of light. It shone down on just one piece of earth and it was beautiful.

K.A.: Riding on the court bus used to remind me of days when I was very small and didn't know how bad my voice sucked. When I'd sit in the back of my daddy's car and sing the songs I heard on the radio. Oldies, anyhow, the court bus was like the back seat. A place I could sing along with everyone else and not care how bad I sounded.

K.E.: We got to the courthouse and waited for the marshals to come so we could be escorted off the bus and into what we call the dungeon.

K.A.: Dark, with yellowed, low-watt bulbs caged naked on the high ceiling, the dungeon is three cold, damp rooms with benches along only two of the walls. The heavy old doors remind me of the old psychiatric ward that's hidden deep in the bowels of the UCSD Hospital, among the broken gurneys and dusty wheelchairs. The dungeon has a stale, hopeless smell of its own. The toilets have no doors and seldom any toilet paper. Pieces of bologna or salami from the court lunches are stuck randomly on the walls. The idea is to wish yourself through your court ordeal as quickly as possible so you can catch the noon bus back to LC. Don't get stuck in the dungeon until evening.

K.E.: Then, there he was. Brandon Smith. He's a marshal. Our eyes locked and held until I got completely off of the bus. He had to give those eyes and that smile . . . about 15 minutes later, I was escorted up to the Third Floor by another marshal who three years ago promised to take me to dinner if I won my case. He didn't remember at first, but when he did, we reminisced a little while. He was flattered and I was glad he cared.

11/23/98

K.E.: I've just been trying to deal with me. Gosh, I wish I could climb in my mother's arms. I feel so let down. I feel so hurt. And there's really no reason to. It's only Satan, Kristina. I think I'm going to lay down for a little while. I'm kind of sleepy. I don't know what's wrong with me.

K.A.: I was 40 years old. My mother had been dead for three years. Still, I wanted nothing more than to curl up on her lap like a fat, warm cat. I wanted that all along the way. The thing was, my mother was never one whose arms I could have climbed into. It just goes to show how the basic instincts remain as do the illusions, when the situation is breaking the heart of a woman.

11/25/98

K.E.: ...still no kite from Margaret. But then, the deputy we have isn't the easiest to get anything past.

K.A.: Kiting needs to be ingenious. Years ago the halls used to share a dust mop. At the end of the clean-up trustees from each hall would gather in the store room to sort out the dust-mop-mail.

K.E.: We served lunch. After lunch we took the lunch cart out and some girl ran up the grass and called me a snitch bitch but I kept my smile. Inside, my beautiful mood was fading. It didn't turn to anger or childishness. It turned to sadness and disappointment. Only because the girl didn't look like someone from the streets. She looked like someone from prison. I never stopped to realize what was going on back in prison. Or the words being said. That just triggered it.

K.A.: Now, here's something that's a lot more serious than the gut-wrenching a girlfriend gives you, or what a racket your roommates make. K., this is serious shit that you're gonna have to confront on a daily basis for years to come. It won't go away. You've tasted it already, I'm sure. This jacket will come back to haunt you every morning you open your eyes in prison for the rest of the years you're there. It makes no damn difference if it's true or not. You can only hope there's someone on the yard that believes you and chooses to befriend you and champion your innocence. And here's the hard part. It can't involve sex or you'll be a snitch and a laughing-stock. It has to just be that someone believes you and chooses to say so.

K.E.: Here it is, time to go back again. Stuff has to have some shape or form. I don't want to deal with all of that again. But I know I will have to. I just hope this will be the end. For some reason, parts of me feel it's the beginning. I miss my mom a lot. Tomorrow is Thanksgiving and I wish I could see my mom with a smile. No matter how much we all deny it, we were all expecting I'd be home for the holidays. I try to ask myself over and over, "What happened to me?" I'm still not the same person who left on the 17th for court. I feel the numbness coming slowly. I feel the walls go back up as I prepare to go back to Chowchilla. It scares me for I don't know how far I'm going to climb back in again. What happened to that little girl who was willing to stand on her own two feet and take whatever was handed to her? My sentence, 25-to-life. What happened? Why don't I feel like justice was served? The honest truth? I don't belong here anymore. Maybe I should have gone to trial. Maybe that's why I feel defeated now.

K.A.: I guarantee you–they are up there telling everyone that you're on your way back and that they know for a fact you're a rat, and it involved people that are somebody, rakka-rakka-rakka. They're setting you up cold.. Holy shit, this speaks volumes. K., you're doing what any animal would do. You're gearing up for Winter, so to speak. You know how horrendously cold it's gonna get, and you're dropping your spiritual temperature to match. You're protecting yourself from the cold, cold time ahead of you. Now that I see you doing it, not much of what follows should surprise me.

11/28/98

K.E.: Where was my will? I'm a fighter, not a quitter.

K.A.: Where was the faith in God that you claim to have found, K? It's not something you can choose to use or lose. You have to keep it around you like a warm coat 'cause you never know when it's gonna get real, real cold.

K.E.: Today, after I got my hair rolled for my visit, I came in the room and gave Rae a massage. She's a really sweet Chinese lady. She reminds me a lot of my friend, Edna Wong, up in Chowchilla. Rae was my roommate for awhile in A housing. It's amazing to see the difference in her now, from when she first came. I remember the first night they put her in my room. I hadn't had a roommate for a long time. She was crying and upset. When she saw me look up from my bed, with all these tattoos—I think that scared her more. She had just been arrested for a 187.

K.A.: California Penal Code 187—murder.

K.E.: The deputy had pulled me out and asked me to watch over her. It was very obvious she was suffering from extreme trauma. I stayed up with her for two and a half nights, rubbing her head, reading her passages from the Bible . . . she was the closest thing I had to a friend and I didn't have sex with her . . . . anyhow, we're roommates now again and I like being around the positiveness and intelligence. She said she didn't know why I didn't fight, I had nothing to lose in the first place.

I can't just sit around waiting for God to perform a miracle. I have to rely on my faith and hope I can change my plea. I hope there is still time. I should have used my brains.

Last week I couldn't look my mom in the eyes because I couldn't bear to see her pain.

K.A.: There used to be this girl that always went to court with me. nobody ever ate the bologna sandwiches they gave us so she'd go around and gather up the packets of salad dressing that came in the sacks and she'd spend the day in the dungeon rubbing it into every inch of skin on her body. She'd massage it into her scalp and work it gently all the way to the tips of her hair which by then stood up from the top of her head in a sharp peak. She reeked. We laughed. But the girl had the most beautiful skin I've ever seen.

12/1/98

K.E.: Today is the first of the month and almost the end of the year. I didn't end up staying awake like I thought I would, lost in this emotional turmoil.

Growing up, I never really experienced physical abuse. Not to where I could remember. I experienced more mental and emotional neglect. Fear of not being loved or wanted, etc. The only thing physical that ever happened to me involving my parents was my father right before I got arrested for this crime. When he hit me in the face. And threw me into a corner. I got up immediately, screaming, crying.

My father had a sexual attraction to me. He kept it to himself unless we were alone, or a male paid attention to me. Then he got drunk and later on he'd come around and tell me how much he loved me. It was sick. It feels weird, living through those memories again. But then again, it only feels like yesterday. I still never heard anything from him. I often wonder how he is and what he's up to. I wonder if he thinks about me or misses me at all. I thought that being away from him, that Life would do me harm, that I would have a hard time functioning. But I had no choice but to grow up on my own.

Did I ever tell you about the time I slept behind the liquor store on what my friend Whiskey Bob called a surfboard? I didn't have any place to stay and it was cold, but the liquor store had a dirt path that led past some cabins to a higher level, sort of a hidden short cut. A wino was there every night, drunk, panhandling. I used to talk to him and help ask for money. He slept with a piece of plywood called a surfboard. One night I slept on the bottom half. My first experience sleeping on the streets, having to pee in the dirt. When I got up the next morning, I didn't have any shoes, only socks and Whiskey Bob was already drinking vodka. Taxi Dick, later I called Mommy, came to do his bar checks and took me on his cab runs. Dick didn't have a house then. He stayed at Howard Johnson's. It got so that every night he'd check on me and if I were around he'd pick up a steak and my 40 ounce and we'd be on our way.

K.A.: My first time sleeping on the streets happened to be in the courtyard of a church that I'd seen my entire life. It never occurred to me that one day I might be shivering under a piece of cardboard in that very spot. When I woke up the next morning there was a dirty guy with a shopping cart standing over me. he said I was in his spot but he hadn't wanted to wake me up in the middle of the night. Oh my God, how sad that makes me, now.

Then he'd get me a hot bath ready and when I got in, he'd bathe me. He never really tried anything. If he did, it would only be little touches here and there, and I let him because he always did so much for me. We never had intercourse and no kind of oral sex, not from me.

K.A.: Do you really have that mindset, K? Do you really feel that someone has the right to touch your body in ways that are uncomfortable or offensive to you, just because he's done a lot for you?

Twice he did it to me and I could feel his soggy penis, wet by my feet. I remember just staring up at the ceiling, thinking, Ew! Just hurry up and get it over with!

Sometimes I would just act like I climaxed so he'd leave me alone. The next day it wasn't discussed or even remembered. After he found a house up on the hill, I met Jamie and I slept in my own bed. A lot more like father and daughter. I used to love cleaning the house. Every morning I'd get up—sometimes not until noon—go make a bowl of cereal and wait for Dick to leave. Then I'd turn on the stereo and start on the living room, then kitchen, bathroom and bedroom. I was always rearranging and I kept the place clean. I loved to cook. I used to make a fancy meal every night. Every Tuesday night we'd go to the church and pick up boxes of food. Dick liked to stock up. We had plenty. He took such good care of me and for nothing. I loved him like a mother —and a father. No one could understand why he put up with so much and the others thought I was giving it up for booze.

K.A.: I can't help but point out a glaring contradiction, K. You once began an autobiography in which you told of sexual abuse, not only by your father, but by your uncle as well.

K.E.: Tomorrow, if Alex comes, I'm going to ask to be put back in general population. I've got to get out of PC. Can't go back to prison like this. I'm going to have enough trouble. It's time I face the music and see how much I can really handle. I'm still very impatient.

Well, I really did it this time. It all started on the 4th of December when they woke me up at four in the morning to tell me I have to go to court. I got angry when, even after telling them it wasn't possible, they still persisted in telling me it was. Didn't even bother to fix my hair or put on make-up. I just threw my hair up in a bun and was on my way to a dry run. It was nice, though, to get away and enjoy a sense of freedom. I was still grouchy when 10:30 came and I was still sitting in the dungeon. All of a sudden, the door opened and there was Alex. He had just come from Las Colinas, to find out I was at the courthouse. First we giggled about it and then we got to the more serious issues, mainly my change of decision about the deal and the trial. He gave me the assurance I needed and with that, it made it closer. From the look in his eyes, I could tell he was being sincere, paid or not, and Alex would have done it out of goodness of his heart. I know down deep beneath that hard surface is a loving and caring man who looks at life in reality, unlike a lot of these idiots trying to function in society. So the trip wasn't all that bad and I even caught the early bus home. Alex was also going to call and have me removed from PC.

K.A.: I have to smile, K., at your reference to "the idiots trying to function in society." I used to think of it all in terms of "them." "They" were doing it all wrong. "They" didn't know how to act. "They" were all idiots.

When I got back they told me I was still being reviewed for general population. To make a long story short, I got into a fight and ended up in Lockdown. This time it was really my fault and I felt really stupid. I could have risked everything I've come so far on. Could have even gotten my third strike.

12/11/98

Kristina appears in Dept. 8, Judge Michael Wellington's courtroom for a Change of Plea Hearing. The judge says, "Do you understand that if you plead guilty you're giving up your right to a jury trial, your right to confront and cross-examine the witnesses against you, your right to remain silent, your right to present your own evidence at the trial, and your right to use subpoenas to order your witnesses to come into court and testify?"

Kristina says, "Yes, I do, sir."

The judge announces the amended information has been filed and it charges her with voluntary manslaughter and aggravated mayhem. Kristina pleads guilty to Penal Code 192(A), voluntary manslaughter, and to Penal Code 205, aggravated mayhem. The formal sentencing of 13 years to life will be given 12/17.

K.E.: I wish I could talk to Susan. I'm just so damn tired. Especially this switching attitudes with myself. I didn't get any dinner. Just two Styrofoam cups of water and two slices of bread. I'm gonna lay down. I don't want to walk the path of evil. I know I've got talent and I want to use it. They can starve me or do whatever. I'm gonna lay back down. Last night they came and moved me back to B3. I'm still in Lockdown though. I got to see Toni. I was glad. She finished reading me the Daily Bread through the vent. It's our telephone. You can hear everything. I now know I'm gonna make it. I need to focus. My sentencing is right around the corner, and considering that I'm going to CIW first, I may leave soon. I'm gonna leave right before Christmas probably. I'm actually looking forward to it. It's cold in here. I get scared to take my pants down and sit on the cold metal toilet.

1/5/99

K.E.: I feel so much better. I finally made it back to Chowchilla and I must admit, it's a relief. Everyone made me feel really welcomed, considering the stress I had at CIW. I was worried what things would be like seeing as I departed Las Colinas from PC status. When I got to CIW, while waiting in the cage outside, a holding area outside the main building that's surrounded by fencing, I seen a lady and realized it was my aunt. I called her several times and she continued to act as if she didn't know me. After getting processed, I ate, and was taken to SPHU. That's where they house the Close custody, problem inmates, or receiving overflow. It's two to a room. Close is mostly Lifers, and the rooms are nicely decorated to one's own satisfaction . . .

K.A.: Being housed with a Lifer or a Long-termer makes it especially nice if you don't have material things. It's nice to walk into a house that already feels homey. By the same token, that homey feeling is what people protect so fiercely. It's a cause for resentments to fester.

K.E.: After they called me for transport, I just sat there looking out the window telling myself, this is it. The time is finally here. It is time to begin. I'm thankful for the time at CIW. I released some of the energy from being locked up in Las Colinas. Who knows what would have happened if I had just come straight to Chowchilla. I probably would have ended up running wild and screwing around. This way I'm here with a slow pace, preparing to become very busy. I'm looking forward to becoming a brand new Kristina and furthering my education.

BACK IN PRISON

1/8/99

K.E.: I wanted to write about the feelings going through me, dealing with all the emotions in my life with this woman situation. The last few days the time spent with Desiree has been the most beautiful time I've ever had with her. Tomorrow we're going to check into GED classes and NA classes.

I'm going on with life and moving on.

1/14/99

K.E.: I'm finally going to Classification today. Hopefully I'll find out my new and recent points and can move into some classes. My head has been going like a treadmill, mainly having to do with my mother and then these two women who have somehow made it into my life. Desiree and I have had discussions the last two nights about Jeanette that turned into arguments. Immediately I'd gotten my defense guards up.

God is not happy with me at all.

I wrote my dearly beloved mother last night and tried to reassure her that everything is all right and I need her to stand strong. I also told her she needs to get herself together.

K.A.: And so we come to my main issue. As I read and type your journal K., I have the luxury of inserting my own comments. Some of the gist of what I say depends on how tolerant I feel on any given day. Not much is going to happen inside you if you don't get honest about your feelings. You haven't done that in this journal. You describe situations quite well, but you skim over the most painful things in your present, if you don't skip them completely. Being seen with your feelings on your sleeve makes you an ideal conversation piece. You then retreat to protect yourself from having to see things that cause you unbelievable pain. You don't want to see Jeanette or Desiree going about their lives without you. You can't stay in your room, K. you'll have to come out.

2/1/99

K.E.: You know I often wonder what the heck is wrong with me . . . Being back hasn't been as easy as I thought. The struggle has been hard, tough and to the point where I about threw in the towel. Things didn't go as planned nor did I get anything together and have one damn thing to show for. Still don't even own a pair of shoes.

2/5/99

K.E.: I got totally sidetracked and haven't been paying attention to anything. It just seems as though my head is clogged, no air coming in, no air going out. I don't know what to do with myself.

K.A.: Have you completely lost sight of the dread you felt when you considered having to go back to Chowchilla? Have you forgotten all the gearing up you did in anticipation of facing the very difficult things?

I spent my whole addiction, my whole
life, running from who I was, who I am.
I've stopped running. I'm becoming
comfortable in my own skin. I believe
that's what it is all about.

[Cindy Mulloy]

Who Am I?

By [Cindy Mulloy]
May 18. 2005

The first and most important thing about me is that
I am an addict. I don't consider that a bad thing.
In fact, it's quite good. I mean, if even one second
were different in my life I wouldn't be who I am.
Sure there are things that I am ashamed of and things
I wish hadn't happened, but those things have shaped
my world, my reality. My world today, my life is far
greater than anything I had dreamed of for a very
long time.

I am a woman who is conflicted with confidence and low
self-esteem. I know what potential I have yet I feel
like I am not worthy. It just seems so crazy to me. I
hate making mistakes and think that my mistakes make
me a loser. Other people tell me that's not so, but I
don't believe them. I am a lost little girl.

In the very next instant, I am that super-confident
woman that can overcome anything. I will probably
have issues with self-esteem, perfectionism, and
self-doubt for the rest of my life. It's just part
of who I am. I figure I am on this path of self-
discovery, self-acceptance. And part of that path
is becoming comfortable with the aspects of me that
don't go along with my ideal of perfection.

I spent my whole addiction, my whole life, running
from who I was, who I am. I've stopped running. I'm
becoming comfortable in my own skin. I believe that's
what it is all about.

As of May 2007, Cindy Mulloy has completed eight years of sober living. During this time she has maintained a career as a counselor and advocate for others seeking recovery and rehabilitation. Presently, she is enrolled in a local college pursuing a Bachelor of Science degree.

This is a segment of an interview with Chelsea Donnelly on the streets of San Diego, 1992.

Chelsea: Last night I was watching this special about this little boy who had been abused. He had been left alone in this building. He had been tied up. Beaten. Burned. His nose was broken. The lady who found him was overly sensitive. And the love that these people gave to him, well, he'll always remember it. I don't think you guys know what you have gotten yourself into.

I was telling the guy I am staying with, I was telling him last night, there was this little girl whose mother died. She was two or three years old. And after her mother died, her grandparents used to beat her. And they beat her until she would stagger around in a daze. This child who was two or three years old. Now there is nothing that a child that young can do to make somebody abuse them like that. And he looked at me. And I said, "Yeah that child was me." And I looked at him and said, "Why am I not insane?"

How do you feel with your daughter living with your grandparents?

Chelsea: Oh, I love it.

But are these the same grandparents who beat you?

Chelsea: No, the people who raised me have passed away.

So, is that your mother's parents then? Or your father's parents?

Chelsea: My dad's parents.

The federal marshal's parents?

Chelsea: Yeah.

How did your mom die?

Chelsea: Leukemia.

Drug and Substance Abuse: Signs, Effects, and Treatment of Addiction.

Help Guide[56]

295

296

297

What is a drug?

A drug is any chemical that produces a therapeutic or non-therapeutic effect in the body. Many prescription drugs that produce therapeutic effects may also cause non-therapeutic effects if taken in excess and/or without a specific prescription.

294

Drugs are categorized into seven different types:

1. Cannabinoids (hashish and marijuana)
2. Depressants (such as Nembutol, Xanax, and Qualudes)
3. Dissociative Anesthetics (such as PCP)
4. Hallucinogens (such as LSD and mescaline)
5. Stimulants (such as amphetamines and cocaine)
6. Other compounds (such as steroids and inhalants)
7. Opioids and Morphine derivatives (such as heroin, opium, and some prescription drugs, including Vicodin)

298

There are literally hundreds of commonly abused drugs readily available to users. The National Institute on Drug Abuse has compiled an extensive table identifying about 50 commonly abused drugs with useful information that includes:

Category
Examples of commercial and street names
How administered (orally or by needle)
Intoxication effects
Potential health consequences

Did you know?

Top 20 Most Abused Drugs

1. Cocaine
2. Marijuana
3. Heroin
4. Unspecified benzodiazepine
5. Alprazolam (Xanax)
6. Clonazeam (Klonopin)
7. Hydrocodone (Vicodin)
8. Amphetamine
9. Diazepam (Valium)
10. Lorazepam (Ativan)
11. Methamphetamine (Speed)
12. Trazodone (Desyrel)
13. Fluoxetine (Prozac)
14. Carisoprodol (Soma)
15. Oxycodone (Oxycontin, Percodan, Percocet 5)
16. Valproic acid (Depakote)
17. d-Propoxyphene (Darvon)
18. Amitriptyline
19. Methadone
20. LSD

299

300

The table is by no means all-inclusive of currently available narcotics and otherwise illicit drugs, and experts warn that additional ones become available every day.

293-300. Chelsea on the streets of San Diego

22 MILLION AMERICANS ARE DRUG-ALCOHOL DEPENDENT

An estimated 22 million Americans abused or were dependent on drugs, alcohol, or both, in 2002, according to the latest report from the Substance Abuse and Mental Health Services Administration (SAMHSA). Some 19.5 million Americans—8.3 percent of the total population ages 12 and up—currently use illicit drugs, 54 million take part in binge drinking, and 15.9 million are heavy drinkers.

While 7.7 million people needed treatment for their drug problem and 18.6 million needed treatment for a serious alcohol problem, the report shows that only 1.4 million received drug abuse treatment and 1.5 million were treated for their alcohol problem. Over 94 percent of people with substance abuse disorders who did not receive treatment said they did not believe they needed treatment.

SAMHSA estimates that 88,000 out of 362,000 people who realized they needed treatment for drug abuse, tried but were unable to get treatment in 2002. Another 266,000 tried, but were unable to get treatment for alcohol abuse.[57]

www.About.com from Robert Longley

THE BRAIN AND INFORMATION

The first time someone uses a drug of abuse, he or she experiences unnaturally intense feelings of pleasure. The limbic system is flooded with dopamine. Of course, drugs have other effects, too; a first-time smoker may also cough and feel nauseous from toxic chemicals in a tobacco or marijuana cigarette.

But the brain starts changing right away as a result of the unnatural flood of neurotransmitters. Because they sense more than enough dopamine, for example, neurons begin to reduce the number of dopamine receptors. Neurons may also make less dopamine. The result is less dopamine in the brain: this is called down regulation. Because some drugs are toxic, some neurons may also die.

A person's genetic makeup probably plays a role. But after enough doses, an addicted teen's limbic system craves the drug as it craves food, water, or friends. Drug craving is made worse because of down regulation.

Without a dose of the drug, dopamine levels in the drug abuser's brain are low. The abuser feels flat, lifeless, depressed. Without drugs, an abuser's life seems joyless. Now the abuser needs drugs just to bring dopamine levels up to normal levels. Larger amounts of the drug are needed to create a dopamine flood or high, an effect known as tolerance.[58]

National Institute on Drug Abuse

Oxytocin

A hormone called oxytocin, commonly referred to as the bonding hormone, is released in women during sensitive times such as nursing, sexual relationships, and even during female gatherings.

UCLA studies have been conducted that suggest oxytocin expands a woman's ability to react at times of stress beyond fight-or-flight, the standard reaction for males. Women release oxytocin at times of stress, creating a self-protecting shock absorber that calms.

When women bond together, they may release oxytocin, giving off a sense of safety and acceptance. On the minimum-security yard, women give each other massages, rally together against the guards, hug, sing, shout. The moments are brief before a change in emotional energy takes place. But whatever time of closeness, the ups and downs of being caged, there appears to be enough togetherness among the women to maintain a status quo day-to-day. Yesterday, Mindy was mad and depressed, today Becky is upbeat. The wave changes with bad news, court hearings, disappointments. Oxytocin may ease the distresses and make jail time more tolerable. Do the women miss this bonding when they leave the jail and return to the sick environments of drugs, abuse, and other negative conditioning? Does this encourage recidivism?

301

301. Inmate Ameerah; 302. Inmate Ameerah
and Inmate Becky

THE IMPORTANCE OF TOUCH

Touch is often referred to as the "mother of all senses" as it is the first sense to develop in the embryo (Montagu, 1971), and all other senses—sight, sound, taste, and smell—are derived from it. Within three weeks of conception, we have developed a primitive nervous system which links skin cells to our rudimentary brain.[59]

O. Zur, Ph.D.
Zur Institute

302

I love to touch them, massage them, rub their heads, and make them feel good.
It brings them pleasure. It brings me pleasure. . . .

Ten million voted for the Three Strikes Law and they didn't have a clue what they did. I have been in this business for a long time and something has to change. We can't keep putting people in jail. Whatever happens in the family unit determines what's going to happen in society. What happens with the way we pass laws and structure our legal system determines how many people are going to be put in jail. The State of California is at 180 percent capacity in their jails and prisons. We don't book misdemeanor crimes except drunk driving, spousal abuse, and DUI of a drug.

Assistant Sheriff Ben McLaughlin

303

On any given day, it is estimated that about 70,000 inmates in U.S. prisons are psychotic. Anywhere from 200,000 to 300,000 male and female prison inmates suffer from mental disorders such as schizophrenia, bipolar disorder and major depression. Prisons hold three times more people with mental illness than do psychiatric hospitals, and U.S. prisoners have rates of mental illness that are up to four times greater than rates for the general population.

The majority of people with mental illness in the criminal justice system are there for misdemeanors and crimes of survival, according to Osher. He said, "There's a whole host of folks who land in the criminal justice system because of their behavioral disorders." The problem primarily affects people on the margins of society. They are often minorities, almost always impoverished, and disabled by their illness.

The federal government's war on drugs has swept up people with mental illness at higher rates than those for the general population because more people with mental illness use and abuse drugs, Osher said. He added, "I think we want to watch the policy around punishment versus treatment, and we want to be advocates for treatment first."

Mentally ill prisoners locked in segregation with no treatment at all; confined in filthy and beastly hot cells; left for days covered in feces they have smeared over their bodies; taunted, abused, or ignored by prison staff; given so little water during summer heat waves that they drink from their toilet bowls. . . . Suicidal prisoners are left naked and unattended for days on end in barren, cold observation cells. Poorly trained correctional officers have accidentally asphyxiated mentally ill prisoners whom they were trying to restrain.

The jails themselves represent a public health opportunity, according to Osher. Given estimates that about 15 percent to 17 percent of people coming into jails have a serious mental illness and that there are 11 million arrests a year, "that's a huge number of folks who are mostly not connected with systems of care." Screening programs could help identify those people so that they can get connected with appropriate treatment programs.[60]

Psychiatric Times
January 2004, Vol. XXI, Issue I

11   KODAK 5063 TX

304

303. Control, Pro Visit; 304. Trusty inmates

Eric Boos, Ph. D.
Journal of Criminal Justice and Popular Culture, 5(1) (1997) 1-20

Human ideas can be wrong, weak, or misinformed. What is needed for true knowledge is consistent, accurate impressions of objects or ideas which in turn form well-developed categories (ideas).

Since the strong ideas a person has are formed from strong impressions, and these cannot be erased, then it stands to reason that criminal justice must concern itself with providing criminals with a whole new set of (positive) impressions. That is, with impressions which will help develop strong, positive ideas consistent with behaviors understood to be socially appropriate. This is another way of saying, that if you want to change a person's behavior, you have to change his/her thinking. The problem in the United States is that few agencies, including educational institutions, are doing much to change people's thinking. What does change people's thinking in America is the media.

Crime and criminal justice constitute the bulk of television's programming. From the 1960s to the 1990s, 25 percent of all shows focused on crime and criminal justice (Surette, 1992). Of this programming, murder and violent crime has been an all too common theme (Lichter & Lichter, 1983). The problem is that television's portrayal of crime is simply not accurate. (Garofalo, 1981)

Crime is often glamorized as activity that empowers. Rather, young minds, especially those who have pent-up anxiety and frustration stemming from dysfunctional family experiences, which experts say includes about 70percent of all young people, tend to focus on how crime empowers and gives voice.

The criminal justice system itself perpetuates myths about crime and has institutionalized a higher immorality (Blumberg, Kappeger & Potter, 1993). The "institutional immorality" is part-and-parcel of a very narrowly defined notion of criminal justice which does little more than punish the act, but nothing towards rehabilitating, or properly "habituating,"

the criminal. Elaborating on this notion of the "immorality" of the system, Gwynn Nettler says, "In prisons, criminals learn that the world is a jungle and that one should deceive outsiders. This is inmates' justice. In prison, 'bad action' becomes 'preferred action,' and the worst actors rule (Nettler, 1982). But this is nothing new. As Weston and Wells concluded long ago, "prison life and criminal attitudes learned while in prison often ruin reform and rehabilitation despite every attempt to help the offender." (Weston & Wells, 1967)

As we have seen, there is very little difference in the reasoning behind criminal action and the reasoning most people use everyday. That is another way of saying, we are all criminals at heart—only most of us don't get caught.

"Catching, convicting and imprisoning criminals will not reduce crime rates so long as our prisons fail to reform those imprisoned." (Latham, 1972)

The public would much rather spend money on incarceration and punishment.

This is reflective of the high level of abandonment during childhood. Acceptance is the primary human need, and when this is not met, the human spirit will take drastic measures to gain any attention.

With the number of adolescents living in single parent homes reaching nearly 70 percent, we can only expect that the anger levels will rise. These angry young people resent adults, the adult world, and society in general, for depriving them of the attention so desperately needed in their formative years. Peer pressure, if not balanced by familial, cultural or communal pressures, will undoubtedly manifest in inappropriate behavior. When punishment ensues, individuals guilty of inappropriate behavior feel further victimized and alienated.

What such "at-risk" children need is dedication and a committed stance on the part of adults to model correct behavior. In short, what is needed for children to combat the violent tendencies rooted in the victim-

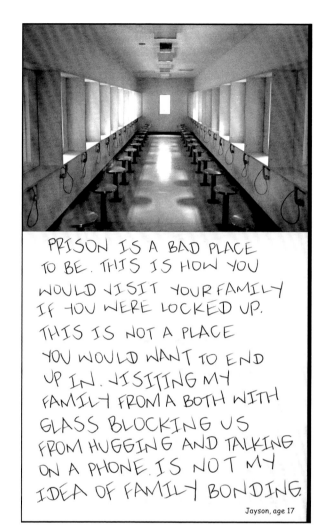

PRISON IS A BAD PLACE TO BE. THIS IS HOW YOU WOULD VISIT YOUR FAMILY IF YOU WERE LOCKED UP. THIS IS NOT A PLACE YOU WOULD WANT TO END UP IN. VISITING MY FAMILY FROM A BOTH WITH GLASS BLOCKING US FROM HUGGING AND TALKING ON A PHONE. IS NOT MY IDEA OF FAMILY BONDING

Jayson, age 17

Juvenile Hall, 1997

stance attitude, which arises from the socio-economic conditions prevalent in our culture, is an exposure to an ethical framework which is consistent and constant. Prothrow-Stith makes a similar claim when she says that such "forgotten topics" as empathy, listening skills, compassion, cooperation/negotiation skills, and most of all forgiveness, must be taught if we are to help break the cycle of violence (Milwaukee Journal/Sentinel, January 17, 1997). Basically, we need a return to virtues.

"Criminals share similar thought patterns. The only way to combat crime is to change these patterns," concludes Winter.

According to Winter, "We need to help criminals realize that they are not the victims, they are the producers of victims." This very task must be approached constructively, not destructively.

But incarceration will only further alienate individuals and thus habituate criminal thinking even more.[61]

Eastern NY Correctional Facility: "Uncaptive Minds"

February 24, 2005

By IAN BURUMA

Education programs used to be widely available in prisons in the United States. . . . Then, in 1994, Congress effectively abolished all federally financed college education for prison inmates when it voted to eliminate Pell Grants for federal and state prisons, despite strong resistance from the Department of Education.

Even though crime rates were actually dropping in the '90s, many argued that judges were letting felons off too lightly and that the "rights" of victims needed to be taken into account. Thus, beginning in the early '90s, prison regimes were tightened, even as mandatory minimum sentences and three-strikes laws meant more and more people came into the system and stayed. In this climate few politicians were ready to stand up for higher-education programs for prisoners. Before 1995 there were some 350 college-degree programs for prisoners in the United States. Today there are about a dozen, four of them in New York State.

It is a tricky situation. Education widens the gap between students and corrections officers and can easily increase hostility. Many of the officers have not been to college themselves and probably don't expect their children to either. But higher-education programs should also make life easier for the C.O.'s, since the prisoners who benefit from them are more inclined to behave themselves. Indeed, a C.O. once told a colleague of mine that life at Eastern was a trifle dull. At the previous institution where he'd worked there were shakedowns, stabbings on the galleries, mayhem in the solitary-housing unit. At Eastern, a guard was liable to fall asleep.

It was obvious to me, as a teacher, how precious education was to the students, not only because they could practically recite every sentence of the books and articles I gave them to read but also because of the way they behaved to one another. Prisons breed cynicism. Trust is frequently betrayed and friendships severed when a prisoner is transferred without warning to another facility. The classroom was an exception.

I knew my students for only a few months. Yet I, too, found it hard to say goodbye. It is difficult to know what they really think of the teachers. We were not C.O.'s, to be sure, but still people on the outside. I do know what they think of Max Kenner, who threw them a lifeline when the government refused them an education. He is a hero to men who had little confidence left in humanity, including their own. It isn't much—a few dozen men out of a thousand who can study for a Bard College degree, but to those men it is everything. It costs the state about $32,000 a year to keep a person in jail. It costs the Bard Prison Initiative only $2,000 to provide a student with a year of college education.[62]

Ian Buruma, a teacher at Bard, last wrote for the magazine about Iraq.

When I teach deputies, one of the first things I tell them is when you work in the jail, or before you work in the jail, it's imperative that you understand what your hot buttons are, what turns you on or gets you upset, gets you mad, or can be used to manipulate you. Do you know what those are? Most people don't. So, you need to learn those if you don't know what they are, then pay attention because the inmates will push them for you and you can learn them real quick, because they will pick up on them so fast you won't have a chance, and they'll be manipulating you all over the system until you finally wise up and go, "Wait a minute, I'm not going to be manipulated anymore now I know what my buttons are." I try to get across to them that they have to learn that.

Assistant Sheriff Ben McLaughlin

We now spend [approximately] 40 billion a year on locking people up . . . .

To take just one example, the rapid increase in the numbers of women behind bars—most of them mothers, many of them imprisoned on relatively minor drug charges or for property crimes related to their addiction—has left us with a growing problem of parentless children.

Incarcerating more women, coupled with their unique health demands, will be a costly crime control policy.

Other hidden costs will be generated by the rapid increase in the proportion of older inmates, which has resulted in part from the growing number of "lifers" under mandatory-sentencing schemes like Three Strikes [law] in California.[63]

. . . Given what we've learned about crime prevention in recent years, four priorities seem especially critical: preventing child abuse and neglect, enhancing children's intellectual and social development, providing support and guidance to vulnerable adolescents, and working intensively with juvenile offenders.[64]

Elliott Currie

Women are the fastest growing and least violent segment of prison and jail populations. 85.1 percent of female jail inmates are behind bars for nonviolent offenses.[65]

Drug War Facts

In 1998, there were an estimated 3,170,520 arrests of women, of which 272,073 were for drug offenses—18 percent of the total drug arrests in that year.[66]

Women's Organization for National Prohibition Reform

LETTERS FROM THE INMATES

Dear Suzy   6-14-97

I've just received The Merrian Webster Dictionary x :)
I wanted to thank you very much, that meant alot to me, and it was
so generous and kind of you! :) By having, this dictionary
it will help me out on my spelling. :) Right now, I've
been stuck on my writings. I'm so unhappy on how much time
I got, and I get out in 10-18-1999 sometime around
there. The one part is the lonesomeness, is hard to deal
with, and it's killing me slowly. I'm just lost, and
miserable since I got caught up messed up system in the
very beginning, it's been a whole nightmare and totally a big
impact on my life, to take all this pain, that I suffer
in my heart.

   I know all these women, are going through it and I
feel for every each one, to me their survivals, the
way I look at it, and I find some of them interesting.
I have to say I learn off these woman in many kinds
of ways, and I'm grateful about it, to find out
some of these woman are strong in spirit and really
good at heart.

My mind is filled with dreams and I always, tell myself
there's a big world out there and maybe one day, they will
come true. I have to, keep reminding myself "Life
will get better, once I'm Free." Right now I got to
stay strong and don't give up, on my goals. I have
my day's, when I feel like I'm deteriorating and
crawl in my shell.   Turn over →

It's very easy, to describe this place I can give
you two words for it (It Suck's!)
Why did you ever want to do a book, about jail and
juvenile Hall? That's what I wonder ?

By one action, I ended up here, a punishment on
my life being miserable. I guess, that's what
the government think's that's what's fair in life, I
have to very much disagree about the whole entire system,
it's stupid of me writing this, who am I to say anything,
I'm just a misfortune prison inmate. Well I'm here and
I have to do 2 year's total, and nothing can change that,
I will have to make the best out of it :) So far, I'm
still working on putting back, the pieces of my shatter
tragic life, back together. I try never to think about
the outside world, it only brings me down, so I block
it out of my mind, I can't keep dwelling on it,
I'll go crazy driving myself Mad, and I don't
need to be more miserable and suffer, it's not
even worth it.

   I'll close for now, please take care and
God Bless you. I hope I hear from you
soon, I promise to send more of my short stories.

                    Love
                         [Danielle]

24 May 97
Saturday

Dear Susie,

Hi! Well, it's Saturday evening & I just caught the end of Sunset thru the window across the hall. I really miss watching them. That's God's little present to me. smile

Today started out not so good. I was just in the frame of mind where I didn't want to be here. I didn't want to deal w/any of the females here. But, one of my roommates & I went to dinner w/a friend of hers and I came back in a totally different space. Thank God. I mean, I started to write this letter* & had to set it down.

On Saturday's we get a hot lunch & today, these kids from juvenile hall were here again for the U-Turn program. A lot of people think it's mean, cruel, the way these kids get treated here. But, I think like it just might keep one of them from going thru what I'm going thru - give it to 'em good & hard. I know they've got to be scared coming up in here & having all these women yelling at 'em, calling them punks. Even young men are in the little group & I know it's hard for them to stand there & take being called a punk.

It's Sunday evening & I've had a really good day today. I went on the main yard & saw a few friends. I got to talk to my old roommate from the receiving yard... Her mother was a drug addict also. She (the mom) got clean - but she'd been to prison, they used together. It's a sad situation. Her mother's dead now.

*Before dinner

She & I are planning on staying in touch with other when I leave. I hope it's not another one of these things where you make all these great p & then leave jail & never hear from each other - un until you end up back in jail.

I also think she likes me. There's no way I do anything sexual w/someone here. Too many games, too many risks (AIDS, etc) & it would detract my program, my recovery. That is my number one priority today.

I heard that the HIV infection rate is really here. And I learned something new - the virus lives ink - as in tattoos - so I'm not gonna go there Damn, all the good things in life - sex, drugs & tatt And there are a lot of tattoo's here. A lot of are fully sleeved.

Always,

[Cindy]

Dear, Susan

I'm still in lock-down, I'll try to write as much as, I, can Okay, it's Hard Back Here, I'm going out to court soon I'll let you know when I get where I'm going Okay, I Have wrote you two Letter, Have you Recieved them yet? Have you Recieve Anything From F. griffith if please, let me know Okay, Susan I Turned 21 july 17, Chantia turned 4 years old, Lorezo turned 2, I Hate this Life, I'm Living, you just don't How Hard it is to walk in these Shoe's of mine if you Felt what I Felt on the inside you'd Be Screaming Right Now, me Aginst the world Stuck in misery I Still tee to be Strong but I feel as if there's No way out, I won't be Release until the End Of 99 Now, I don't Know How I'll make it, Starin At these four walls I'm Havin Visions of Leavin Here in a Hersy, I Need to get Away from all The pressure An pain, I'm exposed to Everee-Day, please me An let know how you Are you the only one who write's to me, [Rolenda]

merry x-mas

December 24 1997

Hey

I have been in prison since, I was 14 years old, I've just spent my 21st, B-day in This Tiny cell, no bigger, then a bathroom an will not be not released until the year 2000, four years down the drain, The outcome of a simple night of drinking an 2-wrong Discision, change my life, an turned it into a nightmare

It's a proven Fact that, once you, enter Adult correctional facilty, the odd's of you never returning, are very, slim,

[Rolenda]

It's not the criminal justice
system that's the problem.
It's our society.

Alex Landon, Attorney-at-Law

FROM THE COURTHOUSE

Alex Landon: I read that San Diego ranks 53rd out of 58 counties for resources for mental health. We're the third-largest county. Everybody agrees that at least ten percent of the population is seriously mentally ill. Take a look at our jails and prisons.

It's chaos. We're incarcerating the mentally ill due to a lack of mental health support?

Say that ten percent of them are seriously mentally ill. We will spend $34,000 a year keeping them in prison, even more in jail, but we won't spend $5,000 to $6,000 a year to provide for outpatient care in the community and support systems in the community, which are more effective, as well as better for society and the individual. That is obscene. If society were a private corporation, then it would have gone bankrupt. It is not producing the product it is supposed to.

Once a woman enters the criminal justice system, it's difficult for her to get out?

Not just with women. Take an individual and look at the background. Which ones come in young, from broken families or families that don't exist, or from our system of foster care? They become institutionalized at that level, and then they come back into the adult system where we further institutionalize them. So, prison or jail is supposed to be a deterrent? What happens instead is that they actually feel more comfortable in that setting. The free world is real scary to these individuals, and they feel weird and awkward, and ostracized from the free community. They actually feel more comfortable in the institutional environment. They continue to return in spite of public perceptions that jail is a horrible place and that the individual should consider it a deterrent.

Incarceration is big bucks. What is society's incentive to not have people go to jail?

You're a taxpayer. For these people to go to jail, it takes your dollars. The money we're spending on all of this is much more than is needed to keep a person out of jail and in a program. It's out of whack. I'm not saying that there are not some people who need to be locked up. What I'm saying is that it's so out of whack now and, politically, it's so unpopular to do some of the other things, that we take a very narrow and short-sighted approach. If we had a more broad-based approach, we would be a better society, and it would cost us less. We'd have more money to spend on the front end, for pre-natal care, nutrition, pre-school, and after-school programs, and it would be better for everyone concerned. Instead, we ran out of space and now are putting people up in jails owned by the private sector. Go through the courthouse and take the judges who are sentencing people to prison and ask them if they've ever been to a prison. Or a prosecutor. Don't you think those people ought to see where they're sending a person before they are in a position to do so? Ask defense lawyers; but how many have seen the inside of a prison?

We pass laws that encourage more incarceration. Is it fear?

Exactly. It's frustrating to me to see what we've done on the Three Strikes Law, where we warehouse people for years and years for petty theft or drug possession. You say, "Well, these people are repeat offenders and they haven't learned their lesson." There's a reason for that. If you really are concerned about them not repeating offenses, there's a way, and we're not doing it. For those of us who work in the criminal justice system, it's very frustrating.

What do you suggest?

We need to confront the politicians and say, "You're not going to get my vote with this cheap rhetoric anymore. I want a responsible approach. You're not going to get away with these inexcusable political statements that are not backed with fact. I want my tax dollars to be used responsibly."

Who cares about rehabilitation? They'll take care of their own.

And that's another factor. Take a look at who's in the institutions. They tend to be everything I've already said, and they tend to be poor. The individuals who have resources and the families who back them up are able to either avoid the system completely because they have private treatment, or other support networks, if they do happen to get caught. They have the resources to get them out. There are plenty of drug treatment programs, if you can afford them.

Once the people who have money or their family gets involved in the criminal justice system, then they're all concerned about their constitutional rights. How did Prop 21* get passed? It's a fear campaign, but it's not based on reality.

It's too complicated, and we have people voting who can't read English.

Nobody I've spoken to has read all of Prop 21. My copy was 48 pages long, and there are parts I still don't understand. There are all kinds of things tucked into it on gangs, Three Strikes, taking away the discretion of judges on juveniles.

That's what irritates me about Prop 21. Juvenile crime had been going down for nine years. So why did we need this thing?

They hear "gang violence" and "juvenile justice initiative," and how can you vote against something like that? Andy Williams** would have been treated as an adult anyway. In order to get kept in the juvenile system for the crime of murder, you have a burden of five factors, and one of the burdens is the nature of the crime. No judge is going to keep Williams in a juvenile system with that kind of crime. He was handled as an adult, and what will happen to him? Are you going to throw him away or try to find out why he did what he did?

---

*   Californians approved Proposition 21, the Gang Violence and Juvenile Crime Prevention Act of 1998, in the March 2000 election. The proposition allows 14-year-olds convicted of felonies to be locked up in adult prisons.

**   Charles "Andy" Williams, 15, opened fire at Santana High School in Santee, California, March 5, 2001, killing 2 students and injuring 13 others.

WHITE-COLLAR CRIME

Criminology

White-collar crime was defined by Edwin Sutherland ". . . as a crime committed by a person of respectability and high social status in the course of his occupation." Sutherland was a proponent of Symbolic Interactionism which examines the construction of personal identity through individual and group interactions. In defining the Differential Association Theory, he believed that criminal behaviour was learned from interpersonal interaction with others. White-collar crime therefore overlaps with corporate crime because the opportunity for fraud, bribery, insider trading, embezzlement, computer crime, and forgery is more available to white-collar employees.[67]

Wikipedia

White-collar crime costs the United States as much as $400 billion annually. That is more than ten times the annual budget of the state of Michigan. According to the Sourcebook of Criminal Justice, 10,700 persons were charged with embezzlement in the United States in 2002. A review of the literature reveals that more is known about offenders convicted of burglary, larceny, and motor vehicle theft than white-collar offenders, even though the latter may have a much greater economic impact on society.[68]

American Academy of Psychiarty and the Law

Interior designer gets prison term

UNION-TRIBUNE

February 11, 2005

VISTA – A Carlsbad woman convicted of illegally operating an interior design business and other crimes was sentenced to nine years in prison yesterday.

A Superior Court judge ordered [Shelby Roland], 45, to pay more than $48,600 to her victims, including former customers and the owner of a Carlsbad boutique where she bought items using a stolen credit card number.

[Roland], also known as [Shelby Roland-Wilson], pleaded guilty in September to 10 felony charges including theft by false pretenses and diversion of construction funds but later changed her mind and tried to withdraw the plea.

Judge Runston G. Maino denied her request yesterday.

Prosecutors argued that [Roland] and her former business partner, [Diana Milan], entered into interior design contracts with clients under the company name Designing Divas, then either performed shoddy work or didn't finish the work at all. Prosecutors said [Roland] and [Milan] essentially acted as contractors even though they weren't licensed, a violation of state law.

[Milan] pleaded guilty in June to a felony count of obtaining property under false pretenses and a misdemeanor count of contracting without a license. She was placed on probation.[69]

308. Inmate Roland

The most compelling
lesson I learned
in prison is how
connected we all are.
The problems of one
of us are the problems
of all of us.

Violence starts in
childhood, in the
home . . . Crime
begins in the crib.[70]

Jean Harris

November 3, 1994: Vol26n9: Crime begins in the crib, Harris tells UB audience

By STEVE COX
Reporter Staff

Jean Harris' life is a tale of two starkly contrasting realities.

Before 1980, her Saturday evenings likely included posh social gatherings with some of this country's highest social elite. After 1980, her Saturday evenings were usually spent playing Bingo on the psychiatric unit of Bedford Hills Correctional Facility.

Her rapid social descent and reemergence has led to her current calling: becoming one of the country's leading advocates for the rights of infants born to incarcerated mothers. Harris spoke about her cause and her celebrated imprisonment during an appearance at UB's Slee Hall Oct. 25.

An inmate at Bedford Hills from the spring of 1980 until Gov. Cuomo granted her clemency in December, 1992, Harris says, "The most compelling lesson I learned in prison is how connected we all are. The problems of one of us are the problems of all of us."

Very low self-esteem is characteristic of women in prison, says Harris. Hopelessness, ignorance and ill health are also rampant among women in prison. "Generally, they are poor, they are angry and they are sick. In Bedford, one in five is HIV positive," she said.

Many are "mentally damaged," a result of years of being beaten about the head, according to Harris, but few receive treatment. "For 11 years, I played Bingo on Saturday nights with ladies from the mental ward," Harris said, "and some of them came in nightgowns that were so filthy you wouldn't use them to wash your car.

"Here is something that just blew my mind," said Harris, pleading for a change in society's attitudes: "up to 76 percent of women who commit felonies are first arrested for prostitution. What do we do? We incarcerate them, fine them and throw them back out on the street." Meaningful intervention after prostitution arrests could prevent many of the felonies, Harris believes.

The separation of a mother and her young children due to imprisonment concerns Harris greatly. She believes that many of these children will be problem children later in life. "As Irving Harris (a sociologist) said, 'Infancy is not a rehearsal, it's the main show,'" said Harris. "When you see a child who learns to laugh when he has killed someone; that is a tragedy."

Harris, a teacher by trade, taught parenting classes to other inmates throughout her internment. Many of her inmate-students lacked the most basic understanding of how to be a parent, she said. Some had more than a dozen children, others began having babies when they were only 12 years old.

"Not hitting your child in the head is something we talked about constantly in the parenting classes," said Harris, "because a 'good smack in the head' is the discipline of choice among most of these people.

"When I arrived, there were five pregnant inmates," she said."On the day I left, there were 64. I've written to the Sourcebook of Criminal Justice Statistics for 12 years asking why there is no mention of babies in prisons anywhere in their book. I haven't gotten a response." Best estimates, Harris indicated, are that more than 9,000 babies are born in prisons each year.

A teacher for 30 years, with a master's degree in education, Harris was headmistress of the exclusive Madeira School in McLean, Virginia. In 1980, her 15-year love affair with Dr. Herman Tarnower, author of the "Scarsdale Diet," ended. She confronted him in his Westchester County home, allegedly to commit suicide there. When the evening was over, Tarnower was dead and Harris was charged with his killing.

The judge "had tears streaming down his face when he sentenced me to 15 years," Harris recalled, in the only reference to her crime during the hour-long speech to more than 350 people. She took the opportunity to decry mandatory sentencing laws, saying "It is just cookie-cutter justice. Why have judges if they can't judge?"

In December, 1992, Cuomo granted Harris clemency, in recognition of her work with inmates and their children through her parenting classes, and because of a heart condition. At 71, Harris shows no sign of slowing down on her crusade. She has authored three books about prison life and prison babies. "Babies," explained Harris, "don't have a lobby in Congress." So she has picked up their mantle.

Shortly after her release, Harris and her former warden testified before a congressional committee considering the federal crime bill, on the needs of children born in prison and the children of incarcerated mothers. Ultimately, the $40 million program they sought was removed from the bill by Rep. Charles Schumer of New York, who requested "hard proof that this would work" before he would support it.

"I thought that was a strange position to take, considering that it was an experimental program," said Harris.

"Violence starts in childhood, in the home," she said. "Crime begins in the crib. It is America's greatest failure. For young children born to the violence and hopelessness of poverty, crime becomes a rational occupational choice." Harris noted that 10 percent of all violent crimes are committed by children between 10 and 17. "Over one million teenagers are raped, robbed, assaulted, shot, stabbed, beaten or killed by their peers."

Harris says building more prisons and incarcerating more women and mothers than ever before, is not the answer. Pre- and post-natal care, and public policies that support keeping mothers and children together, even in prison, are needed, she says. For women already in prison, Harris has three suggestions to improve their lot: program the inmates to get to work on time, take part in group parenting classes, and make federal and state legislators take part in parenting classes as well.[71]

309. San Diego Men's Detention Facility

The links between extreme deprivation, delinquency, and violence then, are strong, consistent, and compelling. There is little question that growing up in extreme poverty exerts powerful pressures toward crime. The fact that those pressures are overcome by some individuals is testimony to human strength and resiliency, but does not diminish the importance of the link between social exclusion and violence. The effects are compounded by the absence of public supports to buffer economic insecurity and deprivation, and they are even more potent when racial subordination is added to the mix. And this—rather than "prosperity"—helps us begin to understand why the United States suffers more serious violent crime than other industrial democracies, and why violence has remained stubbornly high in the face of our unprecedented efforts at repressive control.[72]

Elliott Currie
Crime and Punishment in America

Steps In Criminal Process

1. Arrest
-In order to make an arrest, an officer must have probable cause to believe the suspect has committed a crime
-An arrest can be made with or without a warrant (most are made without).

2. Custody
-A suspect is considered to be in police custody when an arrest has occurred.

3. Booking
-The officer transports the suspect to the police station for booking. The suspect's name, offense, and other information are entered into a police blotter.
-The suspect is usually photographed and fingerprinted, etc.

4. Filing complaint
-A prosecutor reviews the facts and decides whether charges should be brought, based mostly on sufficiency of the evidence.
-If the suspect is to be charged, the prosecutor prepares a complaint.

5. First appearance
-After the complaint has been filed, the suspect (now called "defendant") is brought before a magistrate judge; this appearance must occur without unnecessary delay (usually within a few hours of arrest, or on next business day if arrest is at night or on weekend).
-In this proceeding, the magistrate informs the defendant of the charges; notifies him/her of the right to counsel (and starts appointment process if the defendant is indigent); and sets bail (where police station house bail has not already occurred).

6. Preliminary Hearing
-The next proceeding in felony cases is the Preliminary Hearing, which takes place before a magistrate.
-The magistrate makes a neutral determination of whether there is probable cause to believe the defendant committed the crime charged. Typically, live witnesses are presented and both the prosecution and the defendant are represented by counsel.
-If the magistrate finds probable cause, he/she will send the case to the grand jury if an indictment is required, or send it directly to the trial court if an indictment is not needed.

7. Filing of indictment or information
-The U.S. Constitution does not require states to proceed by means of a grand jury indictment. Thus, states determine which felony prosecutions require an indictment.
-A grand jury proceeding is a closed proceeding at which the grand jurors decide, by majority vote, whether to issue an indictment.
-For crimes where the state does not require an indictment, an information issued by the prosecutor is used. The information cites the charges and is filed with the trial court.

8. Arraignment
-Once an indictment or information has been filed, the defendant is arraigned on the information or indictment.
-In the arraignment, the defendant is brought before the trial court, informed of the charges against him/her and asked whether he/she pleads innocent or guilty.

9. Readiness Hearing
-(see definitions section below for description of Readiness Hearing)

10. Pretrial motions
-Defense counsel has the opportunity to make various pretrial motions. Most common are motions to (a) obtain discovery of prosecution's evidence; and (b) have some of the prosecution's evidence suppressed (such as having a confession ruled inadmissible because Miranda procedures were not followed).

11. Trial
-For felony crimes (and some misdemeanors), all states give the defendant the right to have the case tried before a jury.

12. Sentencing
-If the defendant pleads guilty or is found guilty during the trial, he/she is then sentenced.
-Sentencing is usually done by the judge, not the jury.

13. Appeals
-All convicted defendants are constitutionally entitled to an appeal.
-The most commonly successful ground for appeal is that the evidence admitted against the defendant at trial was the result of an unconstitutional search.

14. Post-conviction remedies
-Even after the defendant has exhausted all direct appeals, certain post-conviction remedies are available; most importantly, both state and federal prisoners may challenge their convictions through federal court habeas corpus procedures.
-In a habeas corpus proceeding, the defendant asserts that his conviction is illegal, such as a conviction based on a confession obtained in violation of the Miranda warning [reading the suspect his/her rights before conducting an interrogation].

Definitions/Explanations of Terms

Miranda Warnings: The Miranda warnings, ordered by the U.S. Supreme Court in *Miranda v. Arizona*, are designed to ensure that a person is aware of his/her constitutional rights when being questioned by police. The Miranda warning must be given to individuals if they are arrested or are in police custody (i.e. deprived of their freedom of action in any significant way) before any pertinent questioning takes place (it is permissible to find out basic details such as name, address, etc.). The exact wording was not specified by the Supreme Court, but it must consist of some version of the following:

1. You have the right to remain silent. Anything you say can and will be used against you in a court of law.
2. You have the right to have an attorney present before you answer any questions, now or in the future. If you cannot afford an attorney, one will be provided to you at no cost to you.

Extended versions of this warning may be given to ensure that the suspect clearly understands what is being said to them.

Once a person has been given the Miranda warnings, they are said to have been "Mirandized." It is not necessary to Mirandize a person when he/she is arrested, only before questioning if the answers are to be used in a court of law. (However, if a person spontaneously confesses, even if he/she is not in police custody, this is admissible in trial).

"Fruit of the poisonous tree" rule: If a detainee has not been Mirandized, any evidence obtained from custodial questioning is not admissible in court, because it is considered to be "fruit of the poisonous tree."

Readiness Hearing: The purpose of trial Readiness Conference/Hearings is to consider the negotiated resolution of pending cases, to confirm trials, to designate trial judges, and to determine the priority of scheduled trials. The court may also discuss other matters that might expedite the trial.

Severance: A defendant should generally move for severance before trial. The judge has a continuing duty to grant a severance (even if the motion is made during trial) if prejudice appears. Generally, two types of prejudice may occur at a joint trial: (i) one defendant may be denied his/her right to confrontation because the hearsay statement of a non-testifying codefendant is admitted [Note: "hearsay" is a statement made out of court, offered in evidence to prove the truth of the matter asserted by such statement. Hearsay is generally not admissible, but is admissible in certain situations]; and (ii) the defenses may be so antagonistic that the trial becomes more of a contest between the defendants than between the People and the defendants.

Motion In Limine: A motion made at the start of a trial requesting that the judge rule that certain evidence may not be introduced in trial. This is most common in criminal trials where evidence is subject to constitutional limitations, such as statements made without the Miranda warnings.

Character evidence: The rules regarding use of character evidence are affected by three major concerns: (i) the purpose for which evidence of character is offered; (ii) the method to be used to prove character; and (iii) the kind of case—civil or criminal.

Purposes for offering character evidence: (i) to prove character when character itself is the ultimate issue in case; (ii) to serve as circumstantial evidence of how a person probably acted; and (iii) to impeach credibility of a witness.

Character evidence in criminal cases: The general rule is that the prosecution cannot initiate evidence of the defendant's bad character merely to show that he/she is more likely to have committed the crime of which he/she is accused.

However, the accused may introduce evidence of his/her good character to show his/her innocence of the alleged crime.The rationale is that even though the evidence may be of some relevance, the prosecution should not be permitted to show that the defendant is a bad person, since the jury might then decide to convict him/her regardless of his/her guilt of the crime charged. But since the life or liberty of the defendant is at stake, he/she should be allowed to introduce evidence of his/her good character, since it may have a tendency to show that he/she did not commit the crime charged.

How a defendant proves character: (i) Reputation and personal opinion testimony:

A defendant puts his/her character at issue by calling a qualified witness to testify to the defendant's good reputation for the trait involved in the case. The witness may also give his/her personal opinion concerning that trait of the defendant. However, the witness may not testify to specific acts of conduct of the defendant to prove the trait at issue.

(ii) Testifying places the defendant's credibility (not character) at issue. A defendant does not put his/her character at issue merely be taking the stand and giving testimony on the facts of the controversy. However, if the defendant takes the stand, she puts his/her credibility at issue and is subject to impeachment.

How the prosecution rebuts a defendant's character evidence: If the defendant puts his/her character at issue by having a character witness testify as to his/her opinion of the defendant or the defendant's reputation, the prosecution may rebut in the following manner: (i) cross-examination of the witness regarding the basis for his/her opinion or knowledge of the defendant's reputation; or (ii) testimony of other witnesses as to defendant's bad reputation.

Degrees of Homicide

First-Degree Murder is essentially murder that is "willful, deliberate, and premeditated," or which is committed in conjunction with a felony, such as during a burglary.

To prove the killing was "deliberate and premeditated," it is not necessary to prove the defendant maturely and meaningfully reflected upon the gravity of his or her act. [Note: in California, premeditation can occur in a split second prior to the killing; it does not require significant planning].

Second-Degree Murder is any murder that surpasses manslaughter, but does not meet the definition of first-degree murder. Second-degree murder may best be viewed as the middle ground between first-degree murder and voluntary manslaughter.

Second-degree murder may involve an unintentional killing, but with an extreme disregard for the value of human life, such as severing someone's arms to dismember them, but causing their death as a result.

Manslaughter can be defined as the taking of a human life in situations considered by law to be less serious than murder. It is usually divided into three categories: voluntary, involuntary, and vehicular manslaughter.

- Voluntary manslaughter occurs when the defendant intended to cause death or serious injury, but the legal culpability is mitigated by circumstances or the defendant's state of mind; for example, killing another person in the "heat of passion."
- Involuntary manslaughter occurs where there is no intention to kill or cause serious injury, but death results from grossly negligent or reckless conduct, or in conjunction with the commission of an unlawful act that is less than a felony.
- Vehicular manslaughter is an unintentional killing that occurs during the commission of an unlawful act while driving a motor vehicle.

[see CA penal code section 187-199 for full definitions of degrees of murder, and their penalties]

Theory of Trauma

The last element we need in order to create a model for treatment is a theory of trauma. A vast majority of chemically dependent women have been physically, sexually, and emotionally abused for much of their lives, and these numbers are even greater within the criminal justice population. Traditional addiction treatment often does not deal with abuse issues in early recovery, even though they are a primary trigger for relapse among women (Covington & Surrey, 1997). Therefore, we need a theory of trauma that is appropriate for women in early recovery.

If we are trying to create treatment for women to help them to change, grow, and heal from addictions, it is critical that we place them in programs and environments where relationship and mutuality are core elements. The system needs to provide a setting where women can experience healthy relationships with their counselors and each other. Unfortunately, the criminal justice system is designed to discourage women from coming together, trusting, speaking about personal issues, or forming bonds of relationship. Women who leave prison are often discouraged from associating with other women who have been incarcerated.

If women are to be successfully reintegrated back into the community after serving their sentences, there must be a continuum of care that can connect them in a community after they've been released. Ideally, these community programs should have a relational basis.[73]

Stephanie Covington, Ph.D.

311. Fencing

ENDNOTES

PART ONE

1. Perry, Bruce D., "Self-Regulation: The Second Core Strength." www.childtrauma.org/ctamaterials/Caregivers.asp

2. Perry, Bruce D., et al., "Childhood Trauma, the Neurobiology of Adaptation and Use-Dependent Development of the Brain: How States Become Traits," *Infant Mental Health* Journal Vol. 16 (1995): 271-291. www.childtrauma.org/ctamaterials/states_traits.asp

3. Perry, Bruce D., "Aggression and Violence: The Neurobiology of Experience," *The AACAP Developmentor* (Spring, 1996). http://www.childtrauma.org/CTAMATERIALS/aggression.asp

4. U.S. Department of Justice - Office of Justice Programs. Bureau of Justice Statistics. Jail Statistics. http://www.ojp.usdoj.gov/bjs/jails.htm

5. U.S. Department of Justice - Office of Justice Programs. Bureau of Justice Statistics. Prison and Jail Inmates at Midyear 2004. http://www.ojp.usdoj.gov/bjs/abstract/pjim04.htm

6. Brandt, Dr. Scott

7. Perry, Bruce D., "The Neurodevelopmental Impact of Violence in Childhood." In Schetky D & Benedek, E. (Eds.) *Textbook of Child and Adolescent Forensic Psychiatry* (Washington, D.C.: American Psychiatric Press, Inc., 2001b), pp. 221-238). http://www.childtrauma.org/ctamaterials/vio_child.asp

8. Perry, Bruce D. and Marcellus, J.E. (1997) "The Impact of Abuse and Neglect on the Developing Brain." Colleagues for Children. 7: 1-4, Missouri Chapter of the National Committee to Prevent Child Abuse. www.childtrauma.org/ctamaterials/AbuseBrain.asp

9. van der Kolk, B., "The Compulsion to Repeat the Trauma: Re-enactment, Revictimization, and Masochism," *Psychiatr Clin North Am* Vol. 12, No. 2 (1989): 389-411. http://www.cirp.org/library/psych/vanderkolk/

10. Perry, Bruce D., et al., "Child Neglect." In *Encyclopedia of Crime and Punishment* Vol 1 (David Levinson, Ed.) (Thousand Oaks, CA: Sage Publications, 2002), pp. 192-196.

11. Drug Prevention Network of the Americas. http://www.dpna.org/resources/druginfo/meth.htm

12. Johnson, Dirk, "Influx of New Drug Brings Crime and Violence to Midwest," 22 February 1996. http://www.umsl.edu/Arkeel/180/nytimes/meth-cri.html

13. Goffman, Erving. *Asylums: Essays on the Social Situation of Mental Patients and Other Inmates* (Garden City, New York: First Anchor Books, 1961), p. 70.

14. NOW PBS. http://www.pbs.org/now/society/womenprisoners.html

15. Covington, Stephanie, S., "Women in Prison: Approaches in the Treatment of Our Most Invisible Population," *Women and Therapy Journal* Vol. 21, No. 1 (1998): 141-155. *Breaking the Rules: Women in Prison and Feminist Therapy* (Judy Harden & Marcia Hill, Eds.) (New York: Haworth Press, 1998). http://stephaniecovington.com/html/womeninprison.html

16. Newman, Maryam Razavi

17. Prendergast, Michael L., et al., "Assessment of and Services for Substance-Abusing Women Offenders in Community and Correctional Settings," *The Prison Journal* Vol. 75, No. 2 (1995): 240-256.

PART TWO

18. Newman, Maryam Razavi

19. MacInnes, Helen, "Apple Seeds," Teachers.Net Gazette. http://teachers.net/gazette/AUG03/seeds.html

20. Levister, Chris, "Inside Jobs - Convict Rehab or Corporate Slavery," 7 August 2006. http://news.newamericamedia.org/news/view_article.html?article_id=22f7bb08424eb621764333f9e6c211d8

21. Covington, Stephanie, S., "Women in Prison: Approaches in the Treatment of Our Most Invisible Population," *Women and Therapy Journal* Vol. 21, No. 1 (1998): 141-155. *Breaking the Rules: Women in Prison and Feminist Therapy* (Judy Harden & Marcia Hill, Eds.) (New York: Haworth Press, 1998). http://stephaniecovington.com/html/womeninprison.html

22. Ibid.

23. Newman, Maryam Razavi

24. California Department of Justice. *Penal Code* (St. Paul, Minn.: West Publishing Co., 1996).

25. National Institute on Drug Abuse, "The Brain. Understanding Neurobiology Through the Study of Addiction," NIH Pub. No. 00-4871. http://science-education.nih.gov/Customers.nsf/highschool.htm

26. Fukuyama, Francis. *The Great Disruption: Humane Nature and the Reconstitution of Social Order* (New York: The Free Press, 1999), p. 84.

27. Perry, Bruce D., "Incubated in Terror: Neurodevelopmental Factors in the 'Cycle of Violence.'" In *Children, Youth and Violence: The Search for Solutions* (J. Osofsky, Ed.) (New York: Guilford Press, 1997), pp. 124-148. www.childtrauma.org/CTAMATERIALS/incubated.asp

PART THREE

28. Newman, Maryam Razavi

29. Perry, Bruce D., et al., "Bonding and Attachment in Maltreated Children: How Abuse and Neglect in Childhood Impact Social and Emotional Development." In *Maltreated Children: Experience, Brain Development and the Next Generation.* Vol. 1 (New York: W.W. Norton & Company, 1998). www.childtrauma.org/ctamaterials/bonding.asp

30. Lord, Elaine, "A Prison Superintendent's Perspective on Women in Prison," *The Prison Journal* Vol. 75, No. 2 (1995): 257-269.

31. Prendergast, Michael L., et al., "Assessment of and Services for Substance-Abusing Women Offenders in Community and Correctional Settings," *The Prison Journal* Vol. 75, No. 2 (1995): 240-256.

32. Perry, Bruce D., "Attachment: The First Core Strength." www.childtrauma.org/ctamaterials/Caregivers.asp

33. Perry, Bruce D., et al., "Bonding and Attachment in Maltreated Children: How Abuse and Neglect in Childhood Impact Social and Emotional Development."

34. Ibid.

35. Rubin, Paula N. and Susan W. McCampbell, "Needle Exchange Program: The Bottom Line for Jails," *American Jails,* May/June 2000. www.cipp.org/needle/jail.html

36. Menninger, Karl. *The Crime of Punishment* (New York: The Viking Press, 1966), p. 153.

PART FOUR

37. Newman, Maryam Razavi

38. Fink, Paul Jay, M.D., Past President, American Psychiatric Association.

39. Covington, Stephanie, S., "Women in Prison: Approaches in the Treatment of Our Most Invisible Population," *Women and Therapy Journal* Vol. 21, No. 1 (1998): 141-155. *Breaking the Rules: Women in Prison and Feminist Therapy* (Judy Harden & Marcia Hill, Eds.) (New York: Haworth Press, 1998). http://stephaniecovington.com/html/womeninprison.html

40. Ibid.

41. Bronte, Charlotte. *Jane Eyre.* 1996 ed. (Harmondsworth, Middlesex, England: Penguin Books, 1847), p. 37.

PART FIVE

42. Newman, Maryam Razavi

43. Perry, Bruce D., and John Marcellus, "The Impact of Abuse and Neglect on the Developing Brain." www.childtrauma.org/ctamaterials/Caregivers.asp

44. Perry, Bruce D., "Incubated in Terror: Neurodevelopmental Factors in the 'Cycle of Violence.'" In *Children, Youth and Violence: The Search for Solutions* (J. Osofsky, Ed.) (New York: Guilford Press, 1997), pp. 124-148. www.childtrauma.org/CTAMATERIALS/incubated.asp

45. Perry, Bruce D., and John Marcellus. "The Impact of Abuse and Neglect on the Developing Brain." www.childtrauma.org/ctamaterials/Caregivers.asp

46. Perry, Bruce D., "Incubated in Terror: Neurodevelopmental Factors in the 'Cycle of Violence.'"

47. Perry, Bruce D., and John Marcellus. "The Impact of Abuse and Neglect on the Developing Brain."

48. Ibid.

49. Perry, Bruce D., and D. Pollard, "Altered Brain Development Following Global Neglect in Early Childhood." Society for Neuroscience Annual Meeting, New Orleans, 1997. www.childtrauma.org/CTAMATERIALS/neurosA1.asp

50. Ibid.

51. Ibid.

52. Perry, Bruce D., "Incubated in Terror: Neurodevelopmental Factors in the 'Cycle of Violence.'"

53. "Doctor evaluates the effects of trauma, abuse," *Houston Chronicle,* 14 May 1998. www.chron.com/cgi-bin/auth/story.mpl/content/chronicle/health/special/child/braindoctor.html

54. Bloom, Barbara, and S. S. Covington, comps., "Gender-Specific Programming for Female Offenders: What Is It and Why Is It Important?" 50th Annual Meeting of the American Society of Criminology, 11 November 1998. www.nicic.org/pubs/1998/015127.pdf

55. Newman, Maryam Razavi

56. Drug and Substance Abuse: Signs, Effects and Treatment of Addiction. www.usnodrugs.com/addictive-drug-information.htm

57. Longley, Robert, "22 Million Americans Are Drug-Alcohol Dependant." 2006. http://usgovinfo.about.com/cs/healthmedical/a/drugabuse.htm

58. National Institute on Drug Abuse, "The Brain and Information." http://teens.drugabuse.gov/facts/facts_brain2.asp

59. Zur, O., and N. Nordmarken, "To Touch or Not to Touch: Rethinking the Prohibition on Touch in Psychotherary and Counseling: Clinical, Ethical & Legal Considerations." www.drzur.com/touchintherapy.html

60. Kanapaux, William, "Guilty of Mental Illness," *Psychiatric Times* XXI (2004). www.psychiatrictimes.com/p040101a.html

61. Boos, Eric J., "Moving in the Direction of Justice: College Minds–Criminal Mentalities," *Journal of Criminal Justice and Popular Culture* Vol. 5, No. 1 (1997): 1-20. www.albany.edu/scj/jcjpc/vol5is1/boos.html

62. Buruma, Ian, "Eastern NY Correctional Facility: Uncaptive Minds," *The New York Times,* 24 February 2005.

63. Currie, Elliott, "Prison Myths." In *Crime and Punishment in America: Why Solutions to America's Most Stubborn Social Crisis Have Not Worked–and What Will.* www.thirdworldtraveler.com/Prison_System/Prison_Myths_CAPIA.html

64. Currie, "Alternatives I: Prevention." In *Crime and Punishment in America: Why Solutions to America's Most Stubborn Social Crisis Have Not Worked–and What Will.* www.thirdworldtraveler.com/Prison_System/Prevention_CAPIA.html

65. Irwin, John, et al. *America's One Million Nonviolent Prisoners* (Washington, D.C.: Justice Policy Institute, March 1999), pp. 6-7. www.drugwarfacts.org/women.htm

66. Greenfield, Lawrence A., and Tracy L. Snell. *Bureau of Justice Statistics, Women Offenders* (Washington, DC: US Department of Justice, December 1999), p. 5, table 10. www.wonpr.org/prohibitionfacts.htm

67. "White-Collar Crime," Wikipedia. http://en.wikipedia.org/wiki/White-collar_crime

68. Poortinga, Ernest, et al., "A Case Control Study: White-Collar Defendants Compared with Defendants Charged with Other Nonviolent Theft," *J Am Acad Psychiatry Law* Vol. 34 (2006): 82-89. www.jaapl.org/cgi/content/full/34/1/82

69. "Interior Designer Gets Prison Term," *San Diego Union-Tribune,* 11 February 2005.

70. Cox, Steve, "Crime Begins in the Crib, Harris Tells UB Audience," 3 November 1994. www.buffalo.edu/reporter/vol26/vol26n9/14.txt

71. Ibid.

72. Currie, "Alternatives II: Social Action." In *Crime and Punishment in America: Why Solutions to America's Most Stubborn Social Crisis Have Not Worked–and What Will.* www.thirdworldtraveler.com/Prison_System/Social_Action_CAPIA.html

73. Covington, Stephanie, S., "Women in Prison: Approaches in the Treatment of Our Most Invisible Population," *Women and Therapy Journal* Vol. 21, No. 1 (1998): 141-155. *Breaking the Rules: Women in Prison and Feminist Therapy* (Judy Harden & Marcia Hill, Eds.) (New York: Haworth Press, 1998). http://stephaniecovington.com/html/womeninprison.html

BIBLIOGRAPHY

Blum, Deborah. *Love at Goon Park*. United States of America: Perseus Publishing, 2002.

Bronte, Charlotte. *Jane Eyre*. (1996 ed.) Harmondsworth, Middlesex, England: Penguin Books, 1847.

Currie, Elliott. *Crime and Punishment in America: Why Solutions to America's Most Stubborn Social Crisis Have Not Worked–and What Will*, 1998.

Diagnostic Criteria from DSM-IV. Washington, DC: American Psychiatric Association, 1994.

Dubovsky, L. Steven. *Mind Body Deceptions: The Psychosomatics of Everyday Life*. New York: W. W. Norton & Company, 1997.

Fukuyama, Francis. *The Great Disruption: Human Nature and the Reconstitution of Social Order*. New York: The Free Press, 1999.

Goffman, Erving. *Asylums: Essays on the Social Situation of Mental Patients and Other Inmates*. Garden City, New York: First Anchor Books, 1961.

Gregory, L. Richard. *The Oxford Companion to the Mind*. New York: Oxford University Press, 1998.

Horney, Karen. *Feminine Pychology*. New York: W. W. Norton & Company, 1967.

Law Reference Manual. Drug Identification & Symptom Manual. California: National Consumer Publications, Inc., 1994.

Lewis, Thomas, Fari Amini, and Richard Lannon. *A General Theory of Love*. New York: Vintage Books, 2000.

Maggio, Rosalie. *The New Beacon Book of Quotations by Women*. Boston: Beacon Press, 1996.

Menninger, Karl. *The Crime of Punishment*. New York: The Viking Press, 1966.

Peck, M. Scott. *People of the Lie: The Hope for Healing Human Evil*. New York: Simon & Schuster, Inc., 1983.

Pollack, William. *Real Boys: Rescuing our Sons from the Myths of Boyhood*. New York: Henry Holt and Company, 1998.

Rhodes, Richard. *Why They Kill: The Discoveries of a Maverick Criminologist*. New York: Alfred A. Knopf, 1999.

Schetky D & Benedek, E. (Eds.). *Textbook of Child and Adolescent Forensic Psychiatry*. Washington, D.C.: American Psychiatric Press, Inc., 2001.

Sheehy, Gail. *Passages: Predictable Crises of Adult Life*. New York: E. P. Dutton & Co., Inc., 1974.

Singer, June. *Boundaries of the Soul: The Practice of Jung's Psychology*. New York: Anchor Books Doubleday, 1972.

Skinner, B. F. *Science and Human Behavior*. New York: The Free Press, 1953.

Watterson, Kathryn. *Women in Prison: Inside the Concrete Womb*. Boston: Northeastern University Press, 1996.

Wright, Robert. *The Moral Animal: Why We Are the Way We Are: The New Science of Evolutionary Psychology*. New York: Vintage Books, 1994.

Susan Madden Lankford, photographer and author of MAGGOTS IN MY SWEET POTATOES: Women Doing Time, is as much a study in contrasts as her striking black-and-white photography.

The purchase of a second-hand Hasselblad and post-graduate studies in photography replaced the mindset of medical school. Soon, she was accepted to attend Ansel Adams' prestigious workshops in Yosemite and Carmel, followed by studies under a number of photography legends, including Roy DeCarava, Paul Caponigro, Richard Misrach and Ruth Bernhard.

She took her lenses to wildlife habitats in the Artic and Yukon Territory, Montana, Colorado, and California. At the same time she operated a thriving business shooting non-traditional portraits of children and families that divulged individual quirks and dynamics.

A business trip to New York provided the impetus for Lankford to first experience many of the recalcitrant homeless, warming their hands around fires of trash, asking questions about her cameras, lurking and growling, yet unlikely to seek shelter. Her curiosity was peaked.

Moved by the thought of both animal and human incarceration, she started at the Humane Society, where some 36,000 abandoned dogs were euthanized each year. Next, she rented an abandoned San Diego Jail to do photo studies.

With time, the suspicions and skepticism of the street people in the area turned to trust and open conversations. As the unlikely companions wandered, they told Lankford their stories, from disrupted childhoods to coming of age behind bars.

She found the women's detention center the most compelling and began shooting inside the walls. Soon her open, inquisitive manner and ability to listen without judgment helped her gain trust among many inmates.

Lankford's insider photojournalistic journey produced the book in your hands, the first in a trilogy. It will be followed by DOWNTOWN U.S.A. which probes the life of the homeless in a major metropolitan city. The third volume, BORN, NOT RAISED: Kids at Risk, will chronicle the plight of youngsters going through the juvenile justice system on their way, mostly, to a life of problems with the law.

Lankford grew up in the Midwest and holds a BS degree from the University of Nebraska. She and her husband raised three daughters and live in San Diego.

Jacket photograph: Susan Madden Lankford
Jacket design: HUMANE EXPOSURES
Author photograph: Polly Lankford Smith

For more information, please visit: www.HumanExposures.com